Cross-Cultural Management in Work Organisations

3rd edition

Ray French

The Chartered Institute of Personnel and Development is the leading publisher of books and reports for personnel and training professionals, students, and all those concerned with the effective management and development of people at work. For details of all our titles, please contact the publishing department:

tel: 020 8612 6204

email: publishing@cipd.co.uk

The catalogue of all CIPD titles can be viewed on the CIPD website:

www.cipd.co.uk/bookstore

An e-book version is also available for purchase from:

ebooks.cipd.co.uk

Cross-Cultural Management in Work Organisations

3rd edition

Ray French

Chartered Institute of Personnel and Development

Published by the Chartered Institute of Personnel and Development
151 The Broadway, London SW19 1JQ

This edition first published 2015

Designed and typeset by Exeter Premedia Services, India
Printed in Great Britain by Ashford Colour Press

British Library Cataloguing in Publication Data
A catalogue of this publication is available from the British Library

ISBN 9781843983675

e-book ISBN 9781843984030

Chartered Institute of Personnel and Development
151 The Broadway, London SW19 1JQ
Tel: 020 8612 6200
Email: cipd@cipd.co.uk
Website: www.cipd.co.uk
Incorporated by Royal Charter. Registered Charity No. 1079797

Contents

List of figures and tables

Acknowledgements and credits

Acknowledgements

First edition:

I would like to thank Colin Knapp for his important role in the development of this book project and for his insightful comments on selected chapters, which in all cases enhanced the content. I have also benefited from particularly positive and constructive feedback from anonymous reviewers of the draft book. At the University of Portsmouth I am grateful to Birgit Schyns and Penny Dossor for their comments on parts of the manuscript, and thanks are also due to Derek Adam-Smith for his support as Head of Department of Human Resource and Marketing Management. I am grateful to Ruth Lake at CIPD Publishing who first encouraged the book proposal and then deftly managed its progress.

On a more personal level, I am grateful for the love and support of my wife Caroline French, and this book is dedicated to her.

Second edition:

I have been delighted to receive so many positive comments on the first edition of the book and hope that taking on some of the suggestions made will help make this edition not only bigger but better. For the second time I have benefited from particularly constructive feedback from the reviewers of this book, so thanks are due to them.

There have been significant developments in business over the past three years, including the financial crisis which has affected so much of the world. This shows again the importance of recognising the potential for rapid change in all business subject areas, and this certainly applies to cross-cultural management, which is developing at pace both for academics and those involved in managing diverse workforces. I hope that this edition of the book accurately reflects recent changes while remaining focused on core principles and enduring scholarship.

This second edition has of course built closely on the first, so the acknowledgements made three years ago hold true. However, I would like to thank the new team at CIPD Publishing for all their help, particularly Ruth Anderson and Kirsty Smy.

Once again Caroline has exhibited considerable patience throughout the writing of the book and has cheerfully foregone much of the free time anticipated when she married an academic. This second edition is again dedicated to her.

Third edition:

It is now approaching ten years since the idea for this book was first conceived. Its progression to a third edition reflects the topical and relevant nature of cross-cultural management, which develops at pace, both for academics and those involved in managing diverse workforces. It is certainly never difficult to come up with new examples to illustrate concepts and models! I hope that this new edition of the book once more accurately reflects recent changes while remaining focused on core principles and enduring scholarship.

I have been delighted to receive so many positive comments on the first two editions and hope that taking on some of the suggestions made will further enhance content, style and learning features. It has been particularly gratifying to get enthusiastic feedback from students in different countries and to be invited to link to their social media sites. This in itself reflects how much more inter-connected we have all become. I have benefited from particularly constructive feedback from some reviewers of this book, so thanks are also due to the people concerned.

At the University of Portsmouth I am grateful to Charlotte Rayner and Gary Rees for their support as Heads of our Subject Group across the period when I worked on this latest edition.

The working relationship with the team at CIPD Publishing has once again been exemplary and I would like to express particular thanks to Alex Krause for his encouragement and to Pauline Allsop for her work in the production phase.

On a personal level thanks are again due to Caroline French for all her love and support. For the third time this book is dedicated to her.

Credits

The author and the publishers would like to acknowledge and thank the following for their permissions to reproduce text extracts, tables and figures in this book.

Pearson Education Ltd, publishers of *International management: a cross-cultural approach*, edited by TAYEB, M. (2003) FT: Prentice Hall (Figure 2.2 Major cultural layers)

Elsevier, publishers of the *Journal of World Business*, Vol 37 No 1, in respect of the table of cultural clusters in the article by GUPTA, V., HANGES, P. J., and DORFMAN, P. (2002) on pp11–15 [as reproduced by permission] (Table 3.1 and Table 7.1)

Sage Publications, Inc., publishers of *Handbook of organizational culture and climate* edited by ASKENASY, N., PETERSON, M. and WILDEROM, C., which included the chart by SAGIV, L. and SCHWARTZ, S. H. (2002) [reproduced by permission of Sage Publications, Inc.] (Figure 3.1)

The publishers of *People Management*, in respect of the article 'Phillips pushes the equality agenda', 27 July 2006 (quoted in Group Activity 4.1)

Nicholas Brealey Publishing, publishers of TROMPENAARS, F. and HAMPDEN-TURNER, C. (1997) *Riding the waves of culture.* 2nd ed. in respect of the figures in that edition numbered 6.3 and 11.5 (Figure 5.1 and Figure 6.1)

The publishers of *People Management*, in respect of the article 'Image-conscious' by Karen Higginbottom, 6 February 2003 (quoted at length in Case Study 6.2); grateful acknowledgement is also made to AXA Insurance for the sample pictograms ('AXAgrams') within that article

Elsevier, publishers of *Organizational Dynamics*, Vol 29 No.4 (2001) in respect of the statement quoted from the article 'Cultural acumen for the global manager: lessons learned from Project GLOBE' by HOUSE, R. J. and JAVIDAN, M. on p297 [as reproduced by permission] (Chapter 7 quotation)

The publishers of *People Management*, in respect of the article 'Pay-for-performance advances in Asia and Latin America', 11 January 2006, taken largely from a Towers Perrin press release, for which grateful acknowledgement is also made to Towers Perrin (quoted at length in Case Study 8.2)

Walkthrough of textbook features and online resources

LEARNING OBJECTIVES

After reading this chapter you should be able to:

- assess the importance and scope of cross-cultural management
- appreciate the interplay of cultural and non-cultural factors within the subject areas of people management and workplace behaviour
- recognise the need for topicality in research, models and theories in the field of cross-cultural management
- understand the structure and main features of this book.

LEARNING OBJECTIVES

At the beginning of each chapter a bulleted set of learning objectives summarises what you can expect to learn from the chapter, helping you to track your progress.

INDIVIDUAL ACTIVITY 7.1

Refer to the findings on Asian leadership set out above and relate these to both Hall's and Trompenaars' models of culture summarised in Chapter 3.

How well do you feel these models explain differences in implicit leadership styles worldwide? To what extent do you think the concept of 'culture shift' could lead to changes in implicit views of culture? Give reasons for your conclusions.

INDIVIDUAL ACTIVITIES AND GROUP ACTIVITIES

In each chapter, a number of questions and activities will get you to reflect on what you are reading and encourage you to explore important concepts and issues in greater depth, either by yourself or via group discussion.

APPLYING THEORY TO PRACTICE 2.1

The Global Gender Gap Report of 2013 identified Sweden as a world leader in gender equality.[2] Parents were entitled to take up to 480 days' parental leave and, in contrast to other countries surveyed, there was a specific provision for fathers to take paternity leave, with 60 days of the overall leave reserved for each parent; it is not possible for this allocation to be transferred between parents. An earlier report noted that this had led to the common sight of 'seeing daddies pushing strollers on the street, giving babies bottles in crowded cafes or meeting up for playtime in the park with their toddlers'.[3] In as much as paternity leave fosters gender equality, freeing mothers up to return to work earlier than might be possible in other countries, Sweden can be seen to be in the forefront of such a social trend. One might expect this to be the case. In Chapter 3 we look closely at the work of Hofstede, who classified Sweden as a society high on the dimension of femininity (one of the few in the world). So we have a cultural explanation for the phenomena. And yet, not all eligible Swedish citizens take advantage of this opportunity. In 2012 fathers took only 24% of the available paternity leave offered, and in most cases it was mothers who applied for the joint parental leave periods. The research institute Statistics Sweden identified an over-representation of women in low-income jobs, meaning that it was economically more advantageous for fathers to waive their paternity leave entitlement if, as was likely, they were the higher earner in the partnership. This last point is strictly non-cultural in nature and we see the interplay of cultural and non-cultural forces in dynamic motion when we analyse this topic.

CASE STUDIES AND APPLYING THEORY TO PRACTICE

Both of these features provide a range of case studies from different countries to illustrate how key ideas and theories are operating in practice around the globe. The case studies come with accompanying questions or activities to make you think about the situation further.

CASE STUDY 5.1

A NEW DIRECTION FOR THE VATICAN

The election of a new Pope brings opportunities for fresh and different styles of leadership and renewed focus on the Catholic Church's mission and priorities. In 2013 the new Pope Francis had an additional mandate: to overhaul an antiquated and dysfunctional Vatican administration. That administration, spirit', asking senior cardinals for their input during meetings which themselves have changed in tone, even down to new seating plans. Cardinal Wuerl concludes that Pope Francis wants the cardinals to be 'speaking with him so that the end of the day he can say this was truly the fruit of the work of the Spirit'.[2]

REVIEW QUESTIONS

1   How useful is it to view culture in Hofstede's terms as 'the collective programming of the mind'? Use examples to illustrate your answer.

2   With the use of examples, show both the positive and negative aspects of using stereotypes to predict and explain an individual's behaviour.

3   In what ways are the terms organisational culture and national culture linked?

REVIEW QUESTIONS

At the end of each chapter a number of review questions will make you think back on what you have just read, helping you to reinforce what you have just learnt.

FURTHER READING

HOFSTEDE, G. (2001) *Culture's consequences*. 2nd ed. Thousand Oaks, CA: Sage. There is no substitute for the original! Read what is widely acknowledged as the seminal work on the subject.

KOEN, C. (2005) *Comparative international management*. Maidenhead: McGraw Hill. In Chapter 2 the author provides a scholarly analysis of major models of culture which includes an in-depth discussion of methodological issues.

MINKOV, M. (2007) *What makes us different and similar: a new interpretation of the World Values Survey and other cross-cultural data*. Sofia: Bulgaria: Klasika i Stil Publishing House. This book will be useful as further reading covering Chapters 2, 3 and 4 of this textbook as it provides both a new model of cultural similarity and difference and an alternative review of previous research in this area.

FURTHER READING

A list of suggested titles for further reading will direct you to other sources of information such as books, journals and useful websites, encouraging you to delve further into areas of particular interest.

ONLINE RESOURCES FOR STUDENTS

● A document containing self-assessment quizzes, a glossary and links to online journals and other articles is available for each chapter.

ONLINE RESOURCES FOR TUTORS

● PowerPoint slides – design your programme around these ready-made lectures.
● Lecturer's guide – provides some responses to the in-text learning features.

To access the online resources for this textbook, visit www.cipd.co.uk/olr

SETTING THE SCENE

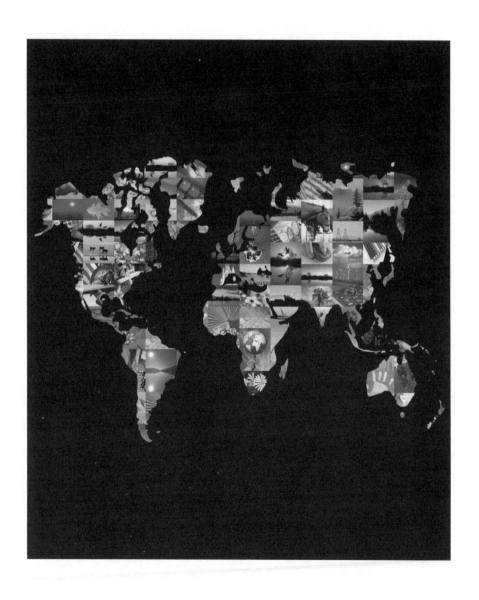

Introduction

1.1 CROSS-CULTURAL MANAGEMENT AS AN EVERYDAY ACTIVITY

Culture matters. Culture is topical and culture is interesting. Formerly located firmly within the domain of anthropology, the period between 1980 and 2015 has seen the study of culture move centre stage into the area of business and management. Cross-cultural management has come to the fore as an important indicator of organisational success (Aycan et al 2014; Hajro and Pudelko 2010). The increasing volume of writing in the field is no coincidence, and enhanced levels of interest – both from academics and practising managers – can be attributed to identifiable trends within business; in particular, globalisation (McFarlin and Sweeney 2013).

Globalisation comprises a number of different strands, not all of which are, at first sight, compatible within a single concept. It is associated with the fragmentation of pre-existing boundaries, including those as fundamental as time, space and nation states. The term also encompasses complex processes such as global flows of finance, knowledge and people. The facet of globalisation which is most relevant for our purposes in this book is its sense of accelerating interconnectedness between nations and people, leading to an increased prevalence and intensity of cross-cultural interactions. Cross-cultural encounters might, for example, occur when companies decide to outsource work to new countries, or when organisations enter into new forms of networked relationships with overseas partners or, finally, as a result of increased migration of labour. As a result, organisational decision-makers and students of business and management have increasingly sought to comprehend the ways in which culture intervenes at workplace level (Patel 2014).

A concern with the effective management of people from different cultural groups is not new. Brewster et al (2011), for example, cite research in the field of international human resource management dating from the 1990s. However, these authors record a significant expansion – 'almost exponentially' (p3) – in new trends, events and research publications in the twenty-first century. What is noticeable in the period since the mid-1990s is the way in which cross-cultural management has affected the working lives of more and more people. It is no longer the case that it is mainly expatriate managers who need to be aware of cultural differences; for example, in people's attitudes towards authority and independent working. Many managers find that cultural differences affect them even if they work in their home country.

In a report on UK migration in the period between 1991 and 2012, Rowthorn (2014) identified significant churn in the UK population, with 7 million people leaving the country and 10.1 million incomers. The net migration figure of 3.1 million involved a changed balance in the population, with a net increase of 4.6 million in the foreign-born group (the number of UK-born people leaving the UK was double that of returnees). In the capital city, a report published by the Greater London Authority in 2008 concluded that one of the main components of London's population growth in recent years had been high levels of international migration. In 2006 the report recorded 170,000 incoming migrants to London, equivalent to 2.25% of its total population, or the population of just one borough, Hammersmith and Fulham. As these were officially recorded statistics, the informal invisible economy was, by definition, invisible and unrecorded, so it is very likely that the true figures were far higher. These labour flows were in part explained by London's status as a major global centre for international business and finance in the years leading up to the 'credit crunch' of 2008, which has accelerated in the recovery years of 2013 and 2014. It can be argued that London became a 'magnet for talent' in that period. However, what Clegg et al (2011) termed 'grunge jobs' – involving both workers in the lower parts of the supply chain (who are easily substitutable) and workers in illegal sectors – were also a factor in explaining London's increasingly diverse workforce.[1]

The multicultural nature of London's workforce, and population more generally, was brought home to many by the city's hosting of the 2012 Olympic Games. In reflecting on the widely perceived success of the Games, ex-Prime Minister Tony Blair claimed that they 'portrayed a modern multicultural Britain proud of both its heritage and traditions and its diverse culture'.[2] Blair was plausibly entitled to stress the multicultural dimension as he had emphasised London's diversity when bidding for the Games in Singapore in 2005. The *China Daily* was among many commentators who concluded that London's multicultural make-up was a major reason for it getting the Games, stressing both Blair's address and an uplifting multicultural video at the Singapore event. The same source speculated that ex-French President Jacques Chirac's comments about British food around the same time (he reportedly claimed it was the second-worst in the world; Finland's was, he said, the worst), displayed a more parochial approach and may have anatagonised the Finnish IOC delgation ahead of the crucial vote, in which London narrowly defeated Paris.[3]

To reasssure readers who may be concerned that this book will take a UK-, or even London-centric approach, the existence of culturally diverse workforces is by no means limited to the UK or, more specifically, to its capital city. For many of us it is now an everyday event to deal with employees from many different cultural backgrounds in a single workplace, and it is no longer necessary to leave one's country of origin – or to be employed in an explicitly international role – to be touched by cross-cultural (or intercultural) concerns. However, we should also recognise that social trends are, by their very nature, fluctuating. It is quite possible that the current trend for global flows of workers may decrease in importance, or even be reversed in future. Throughout this book we will attempt to identify the deep-rooted and long-term changes which affect cross-cultural management, as opposed to those which are surface level and transitory. We should therefore take a measured view of global labour flows. Cohen (2009) found that in England, the majority of the population lived approximately five miles from where they were born, and that there was a strong attachment among the population to locality, with a deeply held community ethos underpinning national values. Notwithstanding this important caveat, there is evidence that workforces in many countries are indeed becoming culturally more diverse. As we will see, the management of diverse workforces throws up particular challenges.

As indicated by its title, the focus of this book is on aspects of cross-cultural management *within* work organisations. Although its content may be of particular interest to existing or future expatriate managers, it is now possible to present a strong case that all managers must possess cross-cultural awareness and sensitivity at the level of managing people at work. Even if it is felt that incomers should wholly adapt to the ways of the host culture, meaningful differences will continue to exist if we believe that an individual's core values are formed at an early age, are deeply held and portable. Many organisations are in any case concerned to secure and foster diversity within their workforce, in order to enhance employee performance and secure competitive advantage, so managers have little choice but to understand culturally based values and behaviour in order to carry out their own roles effectively.

What is very clear is that cross-cultural management is not an abstract body of knowledge; rather, its practical impact can increasingly be seen close to home – wherever that may be.

1.2 BENEFITS OF SUCCESSFUL CROSS-CULTURAL MANAGEMENT

There are clear performance advantages arising from effective cross-cultural management. The concept of diversity is an important concept in this regard. The 'diversity model' suggests that exploiting the potential of a diverse group of workers will help secure competitive advantage (CIPD 2011). French et al (2011) conclude that working groups offer the potential for synergy, which occurs when a group develops to the extent that the whole is greater than the sum of its parts. Multicultural groups offer a particularly fertile setting for synergy, given the very different attitudes and competencies embodied in its members. The bigger and more diverse a group is, the more potential ideas it can generate. One can argue that the economic success of areas such as Silicon Valley in the USA can be partly explained by the talented employees who have been attracted there from different parts of the world.

Diverse groups of people, if they experience success, are more likely to further coalesce into networks which share knowledge, thereby reinforcing high performance. Interconnected networks communicate freely and optimise the complementary abilities of their members. There is a flip side of networks; namely the people who are left out. In our terms, a monocultural group, which does not enjoy the benefits of diversity, is likely to become increasingly isolated and inward-looking. An isolated group of this sort can ultimately develop a mindset in which members no longer want to innovate and where isolation is valued for its own sake.

Surowiecki (2004) popularised the notion of group diversity in his term 'the wisdom of crowds'. An aggregate of people would for him typically outperform the same individuals acting alone. If one wanted to guess the weight of a cat, the average of the crowd's guesses would give the best estimate. The more diverse the crowd, the more accurate it would be. Diversity is linked to success. However, Surowiecki recognised that crowds could also be dysfunctional. Members are less likely to query their peer group if, on the basis of prior success, they believe they are invincible. An unreal sense of euphoria may take over the group. If we come full circle with our London example, it is possible to view the economic collapse of 2008 as an example of the inverted wisdom of crowds. Issuing mortgages to people who are highly likely to default may now appear an obvious mistake. But many employees in the financial services sector, buoyed by a long run of success, came to feel that their talented group was incapable of making errors. The double-edged nature of cohesive groups (in a case such as the City of London, this cohesiveness was deepened by member diversity) is a classical social-psychological construct and is reminiscent of the term 'groupthink'. Groupthink has been defined as the tendency of a group to be propelled towards bad decisions due to in-group pressures (Mullins 2013). It is an important concept within the area of people management.

In conclusion, cross-cultural groups or teams offer great potential for success, but need to be carefully managed. One recurring theme of this book is the finding that cross-cultural teams either perform much better than a monocultural team or much worse (Schneider and Barsoux 2003). So for a cross-cultural manager there is everything to play for.

1.3 THE CENTRALITY OF ETHICS

There should be no doubt that cross-cultural management is centrally bound up with ethical considerations. There is firstly the sense that cross-cultural awareness is itself inherently morally desirable in that it can lead to mutual understanding. In the words of the American spiritual teacher Sally Kempton, 'It is hard to fight an enemy who has outposts in your head.'

Such a view, suggesting that understanding is a necessary prelude to harmonious relationships, has a long track record. The nineteenth-century Scottish writer Thomas Carlyle stated that 'No person was ever rightly understood until they had first been regarded with a certain feeling not of tolerance but of sympathy.' And yet the moral debates regarding mutual sympathy and comprehension have a particular resonance in the often multicultural organisations of the twenty-first century. In 2006 the Uphall Primary School in Ilford, East London included pupils who spoke 52 different home languages. In the light of a very positive government inspectors' report the school can be regarded as a good working example of a diverse organisational environment. Furthermore, the seemingly successful mix of children from different cultural backgrounds can be regarded as positive in its own right. The school's headmaster expressed this view as follows: 'It's like a micro-world. We have got children from all corners of the globe. Our success story is how children who have witnessed really traumatic events – people being blown up and shot in the street – how they have assimilated in school. I think sometimes when you see foreign dignitaries thrashing out a peace deal they would benefit from spending a day here. In 20 years' time, if some of these children were world leaders, the world would be a better place.'[4]

The somewhat idealistic tone of the preceding quotes should not obscure the fact that cross-cultural awareness may not in itself result in positive outcomes. As we have already seen, when people from different cultural backgrounds work together, the likelihood is that they will either achieve high levels of success or significantly underperform. Polarised results in cross-cultural work situations can partly be attributed to clashes of values, themselves linked to ethical considerations. This is a difficult area in which hard choices may be required. In Chapter 9 there is a full discussion of some ethical dilemmas arising from exposure to cultural values which conflict with individuals' own deeply held principles. The ways in which a person reacts to such dilemmas depend on whether he or she adopts a deontological stance in which the inherent goodness – or badness – of an act is the prime concern. Such a view holds that ethical behaviour is evaluated on universal criteria which are not therefore open to varying cultural interpretation.

An opposing stance is that of cultural relativism – not the same as moral relativism – which involves the interpretation of other people's behaviour from the perspective of their cultural background. The question of how to deal with non-negotiable moral issues (for example, relating to the rigid application of rules, perceived nepotism or complicity in sweatshop working practices (all of these are of course culturally laden terms)) raises profound issues and is explored more fully in Chapter 9.

Overall, one important theme within this book is that cross-cultural management is inextricably linked to the field of ethics, and that this interrelationship should be flagged and its practical consequences addressed in order to strengthen the subject area, both in terms of academic rigour and in its potential to inform practice.

1.4 A MULTILAYERED SUBJECT AREA

The view put forward in this book is that an awareness of the impact of culture on people in work organisations can both enhance an understanding of the realities of day-to-day life in an increasing number of work settings, and contribute to effective management of employees, in terms of meeting goals set to measure organisational success. In short, the underlying premise is that culture matters. However, it is important to recognise that culture itself is a complex multi-layered concept. Olofsson, in an interview reported in the CNN news website (2005),[5] notes that her experience as an author detailing cultural aspects of business behaviour suggested that in many cases people's awareness of superficial cultural difference has been increasing, in part due to the impact of diversity awareness programmes. She likens culture to an iceberg in which visible and tangible elements form only a small part of its true nature. Olofsson counsels against the danger of assuming that one is a cultural expert based on an awareness of surface aspects which fail to bring out the deeper levels, comprising people's core norms, values and assumptions.

The 1994 film *Pulp Fiction* memorably illustrated the power of superficial awareness of cultural difference in a scene in which one character – a mobster recently returned to the USA after three years living in Amsterdam – was asked for a summary of the 'little differences' deemed to be all-important, since he claimed that the two societies were essentially the same (these were not the precise words used!). The subsequent monologue included details about the patterns of drugs usage and the dressings put on burgers in fast-food restaurants. Although these details might be important in terms of being streetwise, few people would claim that in any meaningful way they capture the essence of Dutch culture.

Returning to the field of cross-cultural management, this subject area is pre-eminently one in which the adage that 'a little knowledge is a dangerous thing' is highly relevant. In Part 1 of this book the concept of culture as it takes effect within work organisations is analysed in greater depth, together with some models purporting to explain cultural differences. The subject area is an emerging one – we would expect no less, given the dramatically changing relevant business context – and it is important to recognise the existence of different and sometimes competing approaches. Throughout the book the question of which level or layer of culture is under consideration will be highlighted in order to enhance meaning and point to relevant workplace applications. Ultimately, the levels of culture are interconnecting and must be viewed as such.

To return to the *Pulp Fiction* vignette, patterns of drug usage in the Netherlands in the 1990s both reflected and reinforced *institutional* arrangements – in this case the legal system – and were also an expression of more deeply held *cultural values* – for example, on the importance of an individual's taking responsibility for his or her lifestyle.

The study of culture and cultural difference also necessitates a focus on institutional macro-level features of society – including educational, legislative and political systems. In Chapter 10 we will see that worldwide differences in human resource management strategies, policies and practices can helpfully be explained in terms of the particular variety of capitalism prevalent in a specified society or region (for example, the Anglo-Saxon, Rhineland or Asian versions). It has been argued (Hofstede 2001) that the values and institutional approaches to understanding differences between societies are interlinked (values shape institutions which in turn reinforce norms), or are in any case reconcilable within organisational theory (Koen 2005). In later chapters we will see that Giddens' (1990) concept of structuration offers scope for explaining the multilayered nature of culture and the linkages between levels. In any case, both aspects – individual or group values and institutional macro-social features – form a necessary part of cross-cultural business studies, and both are addressed in subsequent chapters.

1.5 AN EMERGING AREA

There are a number of textbooks, published within the last ten years, that deal either directly or tangentially with people management aspects of cross-cultural business activity, including: Adler and Gundersen (2008), Aycan et al (2014), Branine (2011), Broeways and Price (2011), Francesco and Gold (2005), Guirdham (2011), Koen (2005), Magala (2005), Mead and Andrews (2009), Moran et al (2014) and Patel (2014). Important source material textbooks from writers who have devised influential models of culture include Hofstede (2001) and Trompenaars and Hampden-Turner (1997). Other textbooks focus specifically on the adjacent subject area of comparative or international human resource management, and these are referred to where appropriate throughout this book, particularly in Chapter 10.

All of the above-mentioned works have made significant contributions to the subject area. They have also informed material contained in this book and I hope that I have acknowledged them sufficiently. A great deal of existing writing on this topic sets out academic models of cultural difference in order to understand its nature and impact with a view to enhancing managers' knowledge and interpersonal competencies. The newer contributions listed above – see also Holden (2002) – have moved away from merely identifying cultural difference, however, and categorise cross-cultural management in the late twentieth century as being primarily concerned with managing cultural differences, recommending that it should in future focus more on ways of fostering synergy and organisational learning; see also Jackson (2011), Witte (2012), Lu (2012) and Dupuis (2014).

The field of cross-cultural management is a rapidly developing one with an increasing focus on the management of workforce diversity as a means of obtaining a competitive edge. This book aims to take the subject forward in the following ways.

One aim is to provide an evaluative summary of existing models of culture and cultural difference, rather than simply reproducing their main points without further comment. This, it is hoped, will enhance awareness of what is a complex subject area. A brief perusal of some of the main academic perspectives can only ever result in the 'dangerous little knowledge' referred to earlier. Very importantly, surface-level summaries or uncritical synopses of existing models of culture cannot effectively inform the experiences of managers operating in the cross-cultural field. It is more meaningful to survey a range of contributions to the field, keeping in mind the overall context of the subject area and the ways in which individual writers' work interrelate.

One of the writers whose work forms the bedrock of cross-cultural management is Geert Hofstede (2001). Hofstede identified up to five universal dimensions along which individual societies can be compared. One such dimension enables us to assess the extent to which a society is individualist or collectivist in terms of its values (this distinction appears frequently within the cross-cultural business literature). In the vernacular of cross-cultural management, Hofstede's approach is characteristic of an etic perspective – namely, one which identifies a society's features with reference to external measures. Data presented in this book reveal that Hofstede's work continues to provide a source of rich insights into the nature of cultural differences and the ways that these play out in the work setting.

However, it is also necessary to recognise the existence of alternative emic approaches to the topic which, contrastingly, focus on characteristics of individual societies and explain them on their own terms, ie without recourse to wider classification schemes. In later chapters we see how China can be understood within etic frameworks – including Hofstede and Bond's (1988) classification of China as a society high in 'long-term orientation', based in part on the identification of ten fundamental Chinese values. This conclusion follows the construction of another universal dimension – time orientation – and resultant comparison with 'short-term-oriented' societies such as those of the UK and USA. But Chinese culture can also be understood with reference to the emic research of Fan (2000), who identified 71 core values that could be expressed by Chinese people wherever they live. This work concentrated on intrinsic characteristics of Chinese culture, and no comparison with other countries was deemed to be necessary. In seeking to understand Chinese society, both etic and emic approaches have their merits, and a shrewd observer should be aware of both traditions.

The combination of alternative explanations of culture forms a core theme within this book and will, it is hoped, help to deepen knowledge of the individual topics examined.

The evaluative approach taken also leads to some questioning of findings from earlier studies. It is noticeable, for example, that a high proportion of existing research data on cultural values, norms and behaviour was drawn from international managers, so we can legitimately question its applicability across a whole population, as international managers form an atypical group in several respects.

Cross-cultural management is also a rapidly developing field so one can expect new and sometimes radically different insights to emerge, and it is crucially important to be alert to them; there is a clear need for topicality. To take one example, in Chapter 9 readers will note a commonly held view that people who arrive in a new culture – for example, international managers or students – as sojourners experience feelings of culture shock. The process of culture shock is widely believed to comprise key stages – from initial elation through despondency to eventual readjustment (which in itself can take several forms). This model of culture shock is enshrined in the core literature. However, Selmer (2005), on the basis of research, has queried the validity of the processual view of culture shock and, indeed, the concept more generally. Although it might be precipitate to reject established views on the basis of one study, this example highlights the need to include newly published data in any analysis of cross-cultural management – a heightened concern, given the rapidly changing international business environment.

The difficult task – recognised if not actually achieved in this book – is to appreciate what is changing and what is enduring within the subject area. Hofstede (2001, p36) makes a clear statement on the validity of his cultural dimensions and their implications, claiming that: 'Culture change basic enough to invalidate the country dimension index scores will need either a much longer period – say, 50 to 100 years – or extremely dramatic outside events. Differences between national cultures at the end of the last century were already recognisable in the years 1900, 1800 and 1700, if not earlier. There is no reason they should not remain recognisable until at least 2100.' We cannot ultimately know how this prediction will play out but we can locate trends which give early indications and also keep abreast of new directions in academic work in the field (Soderberg and Holden 2002; Tsui et al 2007; Tung 2008; Fang 2012).

1.6 NON-CULTURAL EXPLANATIONS

It is understandable that academic work focusing on cross-cultural management should stress the importance of culture as an explanatory factor: one would not reasonably expect to find a textbook in this area taking a 'non-cultural' perspective on the subject. Nonetheless, a true appreciation of culture's influence on business can only be gained via a realistic appraisal of its relative role. In this book the question of how much culture does in practice intervene in organisational processes will underpin material contained in subsequent chapters; specific reference is made to the relative importance of culture in Chapter 2.

The cultural or non-cultural debate takes place on several levels. It is important to record firstly that even those theorists who stress the centrality of culture as an explanatory tool conclude that it is only one variable affecting human behaviour. Hofstede

(2001), the cultural theorist *par excellence*, makes it clear that individual differences – for example, in personality – account for significant variations: we are all to an important extent truly unique. At the same time Hofstede recognised universal mental programming comprising 'expressive behaviours' such as manifestations of aggression. These behaviours are shared by all people.

The second way in which the extent of cultural influence is called into question arises out of the debate regarding the convergence of cultures within globalisation. Does the spread of global brands like Nike, Starbucks or Chelsea Football Club result in a narrowing of cultural difference between societies – and if so, to what extent and at what level? Youmee (2011)[6] provides an interesting scenario whereby in South Korea respect for older people, deeply entrenched in Confucian culture, could 'lose ground'. Youmee records an increasing number of 'old people being sent to nursing homes, rising abuse cases and fewer parents being supported by their children'. The article in the Singapore *Straits Times* suggests that South Koreans in their 60s and 70s ('in-betweeners') would be the last to assume responsibility for both their parents and their children. Cha Heung Bong, a professor of social welfare, is quoted as saying; 'we believed that the family as an institution would continue and that we were different from the West – but we have become like them'. In this case, we have a suggestion that convergence of cultures may go deeper than surface-level artefacts into the realm of values and beliefs. The convergence versus divergence debate will be considered in this book, together with a new perspective on the topic: crossvergence (Tung 2008), whereby people discard some cultural values in the face of homogenised globalisation, but retain others.

Finally, work organisations can be seen to operate within universal principles. For example, in Chapter 5 we encounter the argument that certain contingent factors affect the ways in which organisations are structured. Within this logic, larger organisations will be more bureaucratic than their smaller counterparts in *all* societies, thus minimising cultural variation. Allied to this pressure for convergence is the possible conscious adoption of one country's working practices by another after observing their prior operation. For example, Dore (1973) noted how Japan as a 'latecomer' industrial nation was able to blend existing Western procedures with culturally specific practices.

All in all, cultural and non-cultural factors combine in complex multiple interlinked ways as they impact on work organisations. In this book reference is made to these linkages when referring to individual topic areas and, as an underlying theme, highlighted again in the concluding chapter.

One recent example of blurring in cultural and non-cultural explanations of working life relates to the 'offshoring' or migration of call-centre jobs to new locations – for example, the Indian subcontinent. Caulkin (2005) in an article in the *Observer* newspaper relates the negative experiences of Indian call-centre workers, many of whom were at the time leaving their jobs following verbal abuse from customers. Caulkin notes the difficulty in disentangling the causes of the problem, which he held to be only partly due to the location of the workers. While some abuse was of an unforgivably racist nature, in other respects it was no different from that experienced by UK-based call-centre employees and could be traced back to unintended consequences of call-centre operation *per se*. As Caulkin notes, 'It was Albert Einstein who defined madness as doing the same thing over and over again and expecting a different result. Tragically, but predictably, this is what is happening in India and elsewhere as supposedly advanced countries export toxic Western management techniques to countries that can be excused for imagining that there is no alternative to what they are told is "best practice".' Readers can possibly input their own examples of the interplay between culture and other factors in reality.

1.7 A CHANGING WORLD

One further theme of this book is the need to reassess the value of 'classical' tenets of cross-cultural management within a rapidly changing business context. In particular, since the focus of this book is on management within work organisations, it is necessary to keep abreast of developments both in thinking on organisational forms (rhetoric) and documented examples of new modes of organisation (reality). Clegg et al (2011) provide a summary of new organisational forms, all retrospectively dated by these authors from 1980 onwards. This includes 'adhocracy', 'virtual organisations', 'network organisation' and 'postmodern organisation'. All of these are differentiated from the bureaucratic or 'Fordist' paradigm assumed to be dominant before 1980 (although this dominance is to some extent questionable).

Given that Hofstede's groundbreaking work on culture was based on research conducted in the IBM Corporation between 1967 and 1973 – albeit supplemented by additions and amendments made prior to his 2001 revision – can we say that his findings (together with those of others referred to in Chapters 2 and 3) are current, ie applicable in a changed organisational context? Some attempt is made to address the issue of topicality within this book. In Chapter 6, for example, we note the importance of an understanding of non-verbal communication (primarily body language) within effective intercultural communication. However, in virtual organisations, or even while using remote communication media such as email within a more traditional organisation, it may be difficult, if not impossible, to see the person with whom one is communicating. Registering nuances of culturally influenced reactions (for example, through eye contact) will very likely not be feasible, so the cross-cultural manager will have to ensure that he or she has guarded against misinterpretation (or outright offence) in other ways. Although this may previously have been relevant to some degree – telephone conversations across national boundaries are not a new phenomenon – the increasing prevalence of new organisational forms and rapidly developing communications media bring such concerns to centre stage to a greater extent than ever before.

1.7.1 WHEN CHINA RULES THE WORLD

An article in the British newspaper *The Guardian,* published in 2009,[7] included an interview with Martin Jacques, author of the book *When China Rules the World.* Jacques points to some very profound changes, anticipated as China rises as an economic power. Jacques believes that the emergence of China cannot be explained in Western terms. He notes that, 'Hitherto, the Chinese story has been overwhelmingly presented in the West as an economic story. This is a mistake because the rise of China will have cultural and other consequences, the ramifications of which will be at least as important as the economic. But no one talks about them because people in the West still believe China will end up in some way like us – it will be democratic like us, it'll have rule of law like us, it will become a Western-style society. This is profoundly wrong. China is fundamentally different in its historical evolution and culture and we need to understand China as a very different phenomenon from Western society.'

Jacques predicts that the emergence of countries currently modernising will be difficult for Western societies, such as the USA and the major European economic powers, to comprehend as 'their [Chinese] modernities will not simply be reducible to Western modernity'. He states that the rise of China, India, Brazil, Mexico and Indonesia will involve the USA and Western Europe 'giving way'. Although this will be a traumatic experience, Jacques sees hope in the form of the current US administration: 'we're blessed to have Obama: there's a humility about him and because he's black it introduces an entirely different sensibility. But this is a long process and Obama will last for only four years or eight years. What happens next?'

This article points to the importance of understanding the culture of a rapidly developing new economic power in the early twenty-first century. It highlights several key areas which are important in this regard and hints at some of the possible barriers which could inhibit that understanding. While acknowledging the major geo-political implications of the 'new modernity', we can also – on a smaller stage – anticipate the potentially profound nature of such changes for the business and management area. Readers can also track the accuracy of the predictions outlined in the article over the early years of the period in question. Similar predictions have been made regarding the emergence of Argentina, Russia and Vietnam into the global business arena. However, all predictions in this area are just that, and previous events alert us to the potential intervention of the law of unintended consequences, upsetting 'sure bets' for change.

Paul (2006), writing in the Singapore-based *Straits Times*, documents the fluctuating history of the Toyota Corporation, recalling how a proposed tie-up with the Ford company was rejected due to the breakout of the Korean War on the day it was first discussed. This appeared at the time to be a major blow to Toyota's fortunes. Subsequently, however, Toyota received large orders from the US Defense Department to supply trucks for use in that same war, described as Toyota's 'salvation' at that time. In early 2006, Ford announced plans to dismiss up to 30,000 workers and close 14 North American plants, this announcement following a few days after Toyota declared record production levels in America. In Paul's words, 'The wheel had come full circle'.

Predicting the future in international and cross-cultural business and management has always been, and is likely to continue to be, extremely challenging. While it is important to retain a topical focus, one should not be seduced by persuasive arguments proposing or even implying a logic of cultural determinism. There are no inevitabilities. That is one of the reasons why the subject area is so exciting.

1.8 THE ORGANISATION OF THIS BOOK

Throughout this book the intention is to approach the subject area from a global perspective. In other words, I have sought to avoid, or at least minimise, ethnocentric assumptions. This ultimately is a futile endeavour since my own (mixed) cultural background – not to mention current location in the UK – must inevitably have insidiously influenced the ways I have approached writing the book. On a prosaic level, many of the examples used relate to the UK, either directly or via comparison, although I have tried to broaden out the material to encompass other societies. Recognising my own cultural values and being explicit about their impact on my approach to the subject is at least the first step to guarding against excessive narrowness in this regard, and it is hoped that this book will be of value to readers located outside the UK. That is, most certainly, the sincere intention.

Part 2: Culture – Uses and Limitations focuses on the concept of culture and the ways in which it has been, and continues to be, interpreted, providing a base for the discussion of topics presented in subsequent chapters. In Chapter 2, *The Meaning(s) of Culture*, the concept is explored through an examination of a number of definitions and perspectives. Culture is a contested concept and it is important to appreciate its multifaceted nature, together with some of the difficulties inherent in pinpointing cultural difference (and similarity), before assessing its importance within people management and an understanding of workplace attitudes and behaviour. Chapter 3, *Models of Culture: Traditional Approaches*, looks at existing popular models of culture and cultural difference, identifying common threads in the literature. An evaluative approach is taken, in order to assess the validity and potential usefulness of some of the most popular models of culture. Chapter 4, *Models of Culture: Developments and Debates*, explores limitations in existing frameworks of culture in terms of both theoretical underpinning and the typical methods used in research within this area. Several newer alternative models are put forward for consideration. At this point the relative role of cultural convergence and divergence as applied to defined areas of business is reviewed and the interplay between these forces is discussed.

Part 3: Cross-Cultural Social Relations in the Workplace considers the impact of culture on a series of topic areas: organisation structure (Chapter 5), intercultural communication and negotiation (Chapter 6), leadership and multicultural teams (Chapter 7) and motivation and exchange (Chapter 8). In all cases, chapters include consideration of whether, and to what extent, traditional models and perspectives within these topic areas can be viewed as universally applicable. The alternative view – that culture can be seen as a contingent factor affecting workers' attitudes and behaviour in these topic areas – also forms part of the discussion. In each case the consideration of culture leads to a reassessment of the original topic, and so has wider currency beyond cross-cultural management. In Chapter 6, communication is also evaluated as a source of cultural difference *per se*.

Part 4: Managing Across or Within Cultures moves the debate on to focus on the competencies needed by cross-cultural managers, and explores the links between culture and one area of management, HRM. Chapter 9, *Intercultural Competencies, Training and Ethics*, reviews existing literature in the field of competencies and puts forward suggestions for additional competencies increasingly required in view of developments in the cross-cultural business environment. The chapter includes a review of the nature of cross-cultural training and its efficacy. The key importance of ethical considerations and the likelihood of ethical dilemmas within the field of study is highlighted at this point. Chapter 10, *Culture and Human Resource Management*, includes a brief summary of how cultural values influence HRM policies and practices, evaluates the extent to which HR interventions can have varying results when applied in different cultural contexts, and identifies how institutional dimensions of culture can affect strategies, policies and practices.

Part 5: Looking to the Future comprises Chapter 11, which concludes the book with an evaluation of frameworks purporting to explain cultural difference in the contemporary context. At this point we also revisit the question of the relative impact of culture as a factor influencing different facets of organisational life. We additionally identify a range of issues that could usefully inform the future study of cross-cultural management.

Subsequent chapters include a number of learning activities. These are short exercises which, it is hoped, will enhance the value of the text for readers. The learning activities in most cases ask for self-reflection and/or consideration of real-life or imagined scenarios. In some cases readers are asked to undertake additional research. Each chapter includes the following features as a minimum: an individual activity, a group activity, a 'linking theory to practice' vignette, and at least one case study.

This third edition again includes online companion material, resources for tutors, **www.cipd.co.uk/tss**, and learning resources for students, **www.cipd.co.uk/olr**.

There are several references to the *People Management* journal, which is a useful source of up-to-date material, particularly in its regular documenting of events, issues and trends affecting cross-cultural management. Summaries of some relevant articles and reports are available via the CIPD website: **www.cipd.co.uk**.

NOTES

1   The focus of this book is on legitimate work organisations, including summaries of existing research studies in the area. There are, of course, more negative aspects of international 'working' associated with globalisation, including the global trafficking of women for prostitution and other forms of illegal labour. While these sometimes come to light in the media – for example, the deaths of the Chinese 'cocklers' in the North of England in 2004 – such practices are by definition difficult to research and so are, regrettably, largely outside the scope of this book.

2   London 2012: Olympics success hailed by politicians (2012). *Guardian*. 13 August.

3   How UK won Olympic bid in the final straight. *China Daily*. Available at: www.chinadaily.com.cn/language_tips/2007–03/23/content_835115.htm [Accessed 27 September 2014].

4   *Independent*, 26 July 2006.

5   Commerce in a cultural context. *CNN.com International*. Available at: http://edition.cnn.com/2005/TRAVEL/07/17/bt.cultural.etiquette [Accessed 16 October 2014].

6   YOUMEE, H. (2011) S. Koreans lament decline in respect for elderly folk. *The Straits Times*. 23 July.

7   MOSS, S. (2009) The love that changed everything. *Guardian*. 18 June.

PART 2

CULTURE – USES AND LIMITATIONS

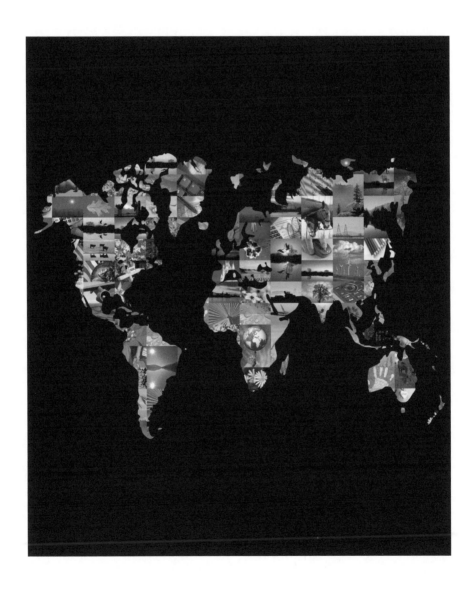

CHAPTER 2

The Meaning(s) of Culture

LEARNING OBJECTIVES

After reading this chapter you should be able to:

- comprehend a range of definitions of the term 'culture'
- list the assumptions underpinning influential models of cultural difference and recognise the contested nature of culture as a concept
- appreciate the difficulties involved in studying culture, including stereotyping
- assess the potential impact of cultural influences and other demographic factors on behaviour
- link the concepts of national and organisational culture.

2.1 INTRODUCTION

In Chapter 1 we noted the topical nature of cross-cultural management as a subject and the potential key importance of an understanding of culture and cultural difference, both for managers in work organisations and students of business. As a consequence, there is a considerable body of knowledge which purports to show how culture impacts on the management of people at work. This includes several influential models suggesting that culture can be explained by reference to dimensions – such as 'individualism' – which enable us to classify a particular country and predict the likely attitudes and behaviour of its citizens. We go on to explore these 'mainstream' academic models, together with more recent contributions to the subject area, in Chapters 3 and 4. This chapter will take a broader focus, however, exploring a range of generic issues endemic to the study of culture. Culture itself should firstly be defined and this is by no means an easy task. Broeways and Price (2011, p9) summarise the difficulty of defining culture, noting that, 'One can never use the term "culture" without being obliged to give a range of definitions that contradict each other!' Patel (2014, p3) makes the same point. Noting that literature on cultural difference can be traced way back to the second century, she concludes that, 'we are no closer to a conceptual consensus regarding culture than our predecessors'. While it is undoubtedly the case that widely different definitions of culture exist, it will be argued here that it is still possible to regard it as a meaningful concept. Indeed, we have to do this in order to engage with the everyday experience of cross-cultural managers. What is especially important is to recognise the essentially multifaceted nature of culture. In other words, cultures firstly have different layers, ranging from obvious differences in cultural artefacts – such as the colour of post boxes and typical mealtimes – through to deep beliefs and assumptions, for example on the extent to which people can control nature. Culture should also be viewed as a multifaceted concept in that it is manifested both in individual members' attitudes and behaviour and also at a macro-social or institutional level; for example, in a country's legal system.

Having reviewed definitions of culture and their implications, we will also identify some challenges that stem from attempts to capture the essence of culture and locate its impact at workplace level. For example, when classifying whole societies into different cultural types, are we guilty of over-generalisation, or even of stereotyping its individual members? We will show how leading writers in the field have attempted to guard against accusations of stereotyping (also known as the ecological fallacy). Another challenge in cross-cultural management is to draw meaningful conclusions on how people across the world typically think and behave, while keeping abreast of changes within societies. Culture is a dynamic concept. It is partly derived from the term 'cultivate', which has important overtones of growth, development and continual re-birth. So one must be wary of accepting outdated views of societies – particularly in such a fast-changing business world, which some believe is characterised by accelerating convergence between countries. In order to achieve these objectives, brief reference is made to some existing models and theories. As previously indicated, the models themselves are explored in greater detail and depth in subsequent sections of the book, particularly Chapters 3 and 4, so this chapter can be regarded as a 'taster' of content explored in greater detail throughout the book.

Before analysing the impact of culture it is clearly necessary to define the concept itself. However, the search for a single all-encompassing definition of 'culture' has proved to be elusive and we can now select from a number of interpretations of the concept. As Francesco and Gold (2005) note, the lack of an overriding definition may be inherent in the subject – see also the quote already cited from Broeways and Price (2011) – suggesting that no single definition of culture can be sufficient due to the complexity of the concept. Francesco and Gold conclude that defining culture has actually become an area of academic study in its own right. More than 30 years after the publication of Hofstede's seminal work, there is still debate concerning the nature of culture *per se*, with some suggestion that it has yet to be fully clarified within cross-cultural business research and theory. In a recent summary of prior research into cross-national and cross-cultural organisational behaviour, Tsui et al (2007) found that 'to their astonishment', the fundamental concept of culture had not been systematically examined. Magala (2005, p36) went further in contending that all cognitive definitions of culture are limited because they imply a single dominant identity which fails to recognise the propensity for people to have 'multiple or overlapping identities' which are, to add to this fluid picture, also constantly changing. The implication of Magala's premise is that culture may ultimately be too elusive a concept to be effectively pinned down.

However, given that most people acknowledge that culture and cultural differences exist, and not least, because those involved in cross-cultural situations will seek solutions to challenges thrown up in the course of their work, we do need to provide a workable definition of culture, complex concept that it undoubtedly is. In this chapter, we try to make sense of this complexity and highlight significant elements of the culture concept by examining a range of definitions and go on to unravel the assumptions contained within them. The contention put forward here is that existing definitions of culture often focus on partial elements of the concept. A more meaningful viewpoint on culture would see it as emanating from different sources, including values, and also impacting at both the individual and institutional levels.

Throughout this book the aim is to examine, with the aid of examples, how and in what ways culture and cultural differences impact on behaviour and business outcomes. The theories and models referred to here are analysed in greater depth in Chapters 3 and 4 and are held to have a high degree of validity (although they are not beyond criticism). In other cross-cultural writings, however, not only is culture itself inadequately theorised, but the links posited between culture and behaviour are at the level of inference or, worse, assumption and speculation. Readers should therefore be alert to the diverse and unpredictable ways in which macro-level culture can play out in individuals' behaviour and organisational arrangements – a theme that is promoted throughout the book.

Previous contributors to the cross-cultural management literature have sought to identify the precise effect of culture in work organisations; for example, whether it can be seen as a constraint on managers' choices and discretion. Culture can also be regarded as an independent variable in business settings, in which case it has a direct effect on behaviour in work organisations, or a moderating variable whereby culture mediates the effect of other contextual variables; see Tsui et al (2007) and Gerhart (2008b) for a fuller exposition of these debates. We should certainly be concerned with identifying how culture can be used to affect change and improve business performance. However we conceive the exact effect of culture, there is a consensus that culture matters, and there is a plethora of research studies and management texts which purport to explain how and why. In this chapter we will consider some of the linkages between culture, behaviour in work organisations and business outcomes.

As indicated earlier, this chapter will also focus on some of the difficulties involved in studying culture. It is very clear that not all members of a society – or indeed a work organisation – share the same values which then convert to consistent patterns of behaviour. And yet many models of culture, in taking a large group (for example, a country) as their starting point, appear to risk over-generalising their findings and even stereotyping individuals within these groups. The growth of multicultural societies could exacerbate these dangers. It is also necessary to recognise that cultures can change, sometimes quickly and dramatically, so that leading-edge thinking on culture has to be flexible and current, focusing on all age groups within a population. We will explore these potential problems and identify ways of overcoming them in order to maximise the validity and, consequently, the applicability of cross-cultural research in the business setting.

The final part of the chapter contains a dissection of the generic use of the term 'culture' as it can be used to explain similarities and differences between people. In particular, we focus on organisational culture as a focal point for shared values and identities and the complex linkages between organisational, professional and national or regional cultures.

2.2 DEFINING CULTURE: VALUES, ATTITUDES AND BEHAVIOUR

One commonly held view on culture links it to the ideas, meanings and, in particular, the values held by its members. Hofstede (2001, p9) summarised this idea in his classic quote viewing culture as 'the collective programming of the mind that distinguishes the members of one group or category of people from another'. In this view of culture, what is called collective programming takes place through socialisation – the processes by which a society (or group or organisation) transmits values from one generation to another. It should be noted clearly at the outset that Hofstede also recognised both individual programming, allowing for individual personality and abilities, and collective programming, comprising behaviour patterns common to all humans; for example, aggression. This last point is often ignored in summaries of Hofstede's work, but is crucially important. The writer who is perceived as the most influential contributor to the literature on culture and business concluded that culture was only one source of difference between people. However, Hofstede concluded that culture was an important source of difference, and that the vast majority of people did learn cultural values through the agencies of socialisation, for example, a national education system.

The view of culture that stresses the key role of learned values, largely shared by members of a group, underlies much of the research and resultant theories in the field of cross-cultural business and management. Lassere (2012), when examining the impact of culture on global strategic management, locates the key importance of cultural heritage which was underpinned by deeply embedded assumptions held by people on concepts such as power, role and hierarchy. This cultural heritage of norms and values arose from past historical experience. We will see in Chapter 3 that Trompenaars and Hampden-Turner (1997) also gave prominence to shared meanings within a society, arguing that culture comprised not only agreed ways of living but also the ways in which a cultural group attributes meaning to their world, ie how they make sense of it. Proponents of such views typically argue that values of particular (mostly national) groupings and/or the ways in which people attribute meaning to situations can and do find expression in workplace attitudes, behaviour and organisational arrangements. Trompenaars and Hampden-Turner (p6) therefore find culture to be an inherently practical concept, defining it as 'the way in which a group of people solves problems and reconciles dilemmas'.

Another example of the links between values, behaviour and organisational arrangements is provided by Schwartz (1992) (see also Chapter 3), who firstly identified a series of universal values and then located individual countries along bipolar dimensions based on these values, in order to categorise each society. One of Schwartz's bipolar dimensions contrasted hierarchical and egalitarian cultures. In a hierarchical culture, rules and clearly defined roles are seen in a positive light as a way of maintaining security through loyalty; contrastingly, in an egalitarian culture, values such as workplace equality and employee autonomy are viewed as positive features.

It is claimed that work organisations operating in egalitarian cultures may also express a particular concern for the interests of wider society. As is typically the case with a highly respected model of culture, it is not too difficult to find evidence to corroborate this claim. Schwartz's model identifies Finland as an egalitarian society, and research conducted by Panapanaan et al (2003), examining the role of business ethics in Finland, found the notion of corporate social responsibility to be integrated into core corporate values and principles in most Finnish companies. This would appear to provide a good example of the value of conceiving culture as expressed in a series of values, linked to nation states and manifested in organisational policies and practices.

One further example of the link between national-level cultural values and workplace practice can be seen in Hofstede's work. One of Hofstede's dimensions of culture examined the extent to which societies could be characterised as high or low on uncertainty avoidance (UA). Where a society exhibits high UA, it has low tolerance for uncertainty and one would expect a preponderance of unambiguous rules, policies and regulations in work organisations.

One society whose 'scores' (more on this later in the chapter) mark it out as high on UA is South Korea. Koen (2005) summarises previous findings on the role of *chaebol*, which are very large Korean family-owned businesses (one example is the vehicle manufacturer Hyundai), noting that there is data suggesting that the *chaebol* display high levels of centralised decision-making and a top–down decision-making style. Again, we see research findings which indicate that national cultural values can feed through to the day-to-day reality of working life via the culturally derived preferences of managers.

Even if we accept that culture is primarily characterised by values, one should not assume that the linkages between national values, embodied in key actors within organisations and manifested in the everyday life of work organisations, are straightforward. Mead and Andrews (2009), while essentially endorsing the importance of cultural values, counsel against making predictions on future behaviour based on such values. These authors note that in extraordinary and non-routine situations, individuals can respond in unexpected ways; for example, within a culture that normally stresses group collective norms, any individual might choose to act out of self-protection in an extreme situation.

Nonetheless, despite the above-mentioned note of caution, it remains the case that models which stress the centrality of values and shared meanings form a very major part of theories of culture and its effects. These are discussed more fully in Chapter 3. Throughout this book the relevance of such models is held up to scrutiny by considering their value in specific topic areas.

In summary, culture is often conceptualised as being closely linked with attitudes and values which are first learned and subsequently manifested by members of a group. Consider, for example, the significant levels of similarity between the following three statements about, and definitions of, culture put forward in popular organisational behaviour textbooks:

- 'The knowledge, languages, values, customs and material objects that are passed from person to person and from one generation to another in a human group or society' (Bratton et al 2007, p523).
- 'The most deep-rooted element of culture is the set of values and fundamental taken-for-granted assumptions held by a group of people' (Brooks 2009, p285).
- 'The totality of everyday knowledge that people use habitually to make sense of the world around them through patterns of shared meanings and understandings passed down through language, symbols and artifacts' (Clegg et al 2011, p216).

 INDIVIDUAL ACTIVITY 2.1

Understanding core values

In order to understand other people's values, attitudes and behaviour it is necessary to have a clear view of ourselves – what psychologists term a 'self-concept'. In the same way, learning about other cultures involves re-examining the values we take for granted. It is often said that the best way of understanding our own society is to travel abroad because we are then forced to explain differences by reflecting on how things are done back home (and why). Once we have made the comparison we could decide to change our behaviour to adapt to the new culture or decide that this would involve our compromising our own personal values too much.

Before you digest the frameworks for understanding culture set out in this book, make a list of the values you think form part of the culture in which you were raised as a child.

Which, if any, of these values would you be unwilling to compromise on?

2.3 DEFINING CULTURE: CONTEXT AND COMMUNICATION

Another approach to comprehending culture places communication at the heart of the concept. There are several ways in which communication and culture are linked:

- Values underlying culture could be communicated to the group either unconsciously via enculturation or more explicitly through agencies of socialisation such as formal education systems (see Chapter 3 for a fuller discussion).
- The use of language varies across cultures, affecting both what is said and how it is said, thereby both reflecting cultural values and framing meanings and action (see Chapter 4 for a summary of recent work linking culture and language).
- Cultural differences become explicit through communication: for example, some cultures are not comfortable with expressing disagreement, so nodding during a business meeting may not indicate support for the speaker's position but could, rather, denote respect while refraining from active opposition. Such differences and their implications are discovered in the course of intercultural communication.

- Cultures are sustained by communication between members: there is a greater level of communication within cultures than between them. Guirdham (2011) takes this argument to its logical conclusion by suggesting that cultures would in fact vanish if their members communicated as much with people from outside the culture as they do with those within their cultural group.

More generally, some models of culture take *communication styles* as their main point of comparison between different cultures. Hall (1976) used the notion of high- and low-context communication as the basis for understanding cultural difference. In an earlier study which laid the foundations for his later work, Hall (1959, p186) made a fundamental connection between the two concepts, stating that, 'Culture is communication and communication is culture.' This statement is profound – if we accept it – with clear and potentially infinite practical implications within cross-cultural management.

To take one example: in a high-context culture such as Thailand, verbal communication might be perceived as ambiguous, even allegorical, to someone from outside that culture, and non-verbal communication, including facial expression and other forms of body language, thus assumes a particular importance. This communication style for Hall may therefore form the main significant cultural comparison with Australia (characterised contrastingly as a low-context culture), where precise verbal communication is valued and may, indeed, be expected in the domestic business setting.

There are many guides to business etiquette for existing or aspiring international managers which refer to the importance of communication and (sometimes implicitly) to the work of Hall. The following quote from a website offering advice to potential exhibitors at the Dubai Airshow in 2013 provides a typical example: 'In the Middle East, initial meetings are all about relationship-building. Building trust and establishing compatibility are key requisites for doing business in the Middle East. One should engage in conversation and try to get to know the "person" you are doing business with.'[1] This contribution in its practical advice echoes the work of Hall, who noted that relationship-building in high-context cultures was particularly important and should not be rushed. Such a theoretical insight may be of great value in the business world and indicates the potential importance of communication-based models of culture.

The conceptions of culture set out so far in this chapter are referred to by Holden (2002) as 'essentialist', in that culture is seen as internally consistent, relatively enduring (culture change will be addressed in a following section), ie something that exists and which members belong to. Holden's contrasting view of culture envisages it as changing and diffuse, as it is in reality produced and reproduced through the shared meanings of members. The definition of culture which emerges from this philosophical stance (supported by real-life case material) is: 'varieties of common knowledge; infinitely overlapping and perpetually habitats of common knowledge and shared meanings' (p316). This model of culture, together with other emerging and alternative approaches, will be examined in Chapter 4, following a summary of 'mainstream' models within the cross-cultural management canon in Chapter 3.

2.4 LEVELS OF ANALYSIS

If culture is conceived to be either manifested in the minds of individuals and expressed through attitudes and preferred behaviour or, alternatively, made real through communication, it follows that the focus of cross-cultural study should be at the individual or small group level. It will be seen that considerable research into cultural differences as they affect business has indeed been based on questionnaires and surveys completed by individuals. Trompenaars and Hampden-Turner's work, again analysed in Chapter 3, provides a good example of this approach. In identifying the relative extent to which a culture was oriented towards either rules or relationships, these authors compared individuals' responses to hypothetical situations requiring them to consider their underlying norms, values and attitudes.

For example, participants were faced with a dilemma in which a close friend had run over a pedestrian. As a passenger in the car and therefore a witness to this awful event, would they lie about the speed of the car? It was claimed that the individual responses to this dilemma would reflect culturally held norms and values regarding loyalty and strict adherence to rules and laws. Of course, not every individual could be predicted to act in a particular way; nonetheless, there would be general patterns of individual response. For Trompenaars and Hampden-Turner, the cultural differences could be wide. In the car/pedestrian dilemma, for instance, participants from Switzerland – a 'universal' culture placing great store in the importance of rules – nearly all of the respondents said they would not 'assist' their friend by supporting his or her story. By contrast, a majority of Venezuelans in Trompenaars and Hampden-Turner's sample stated that they would feel such an obligation to their friend that they would lend support to the driver's account of events surrounding the accident. Here we see that cultural classifications – Venezuela was categorised as a 'particularist' society in Trompenaars' original work – can emerge from the individual or micro-level of analysis.

Other writers on the topic of culture have addressed their work more at the institutional level of analysis. This more macro-level perspective regards culture as comprising more than the sum of individual members' attitudes. Figure 2.1 depicts a complex multifaceted model of culture with a range of institutional or society-wide factors combining with attitudes to feed into a country's culture.

Figure 2.1 Society-wide factors contributing to a multifaceted model of culture

The notion of culture implicit in Figure 2.1 allows for a reciprocal relationship between values and culture. It is possible here to view elements of a political system as having a profound effect on national culture and in turn influencing the 'collective programming' of the minds of individuals. For example, a centralised command economy and one-party political system – as was found in many Communist societies until the early 1990s – might be expected to be associated with widely held values of collectivism and low risk-taking among their populations. These findings were borne out by, amongst others, Hofstede and Sondergaard (1993). However, Thompson and McHugh (2009, p75) noted that a newly capitalist Russia exhibited 'rampant individualism and uncertainty following the collapse of the old solidaristic norms'. These authors went on to propose that major changes in values had in reality been driven by dramatic developments in the political economy of that country.

It is also entirely plausible to see economic and political institutions as being amalgamations of cultural values and beliefs. To return to the example of the ex-Communist eastern European countries, we can view the change to a multi-party capitalist socio-economic system as having been fuelled by changes in values of their populations partly as a result of their increased awareness of other societies. It is also interesting to record that changes in a country's political economy may lead to altered values and actions on the part of organisational members which are by no means straightforward or predictable. Ralston et al (1999) provide an insightful example of the complexity of current change processes evident in China. Ralston's research suggests that younger Chinese managers, while exhibiting some elements of greater 'individualism', which might be expected in view of changes within the wider society, in other respects have reverted to more traditional Confucian attitudes, this itself the result of less pervasive political control by the ruling party.

One should be wary of becoming too immersed in an inconclusive debate on causation. As we see in Chapter 11, Hofstede (2001) concluded that the institutions or values debate – as presented as contrasting and competing explanations – was a non-issue, akin to the clichéd chicken-or-egg argument. However, the fact is that culture can be viewed both at the individual and at the institutional level. We will find that aspects of culture are typically located at the level of artefacts (for example, food and clothes) which both influence and are influenced by cultural values.

One useful concept which can assist us in understanding the nature of culture and its effects is provided by Giddens (1984) in his theory of structuration. Giddens developed this theory in an attempt to explain the nature of social reality. In particular, he addressed the question of whether individuals are dominated by social systems or can themselves make individual choices via agency. Agency involves action; for Giddens to be human involves being an agent. Giddens' depiction of the interplay between social structure and human agency centred on what he termed the duality of structure. This term implies a reciprocal relationship, whereby all human behaviour takes place within the confines of existing social structures, which constrain the actions of individual agents. However, as agents are aware of the structures in which they operate (expressed, for example, in so-called common frames of meaning) their actions reproduce that structure as their actions are bounded by it. Giddens does not view social structure as static, however, and believed that agency could generate shifts in structures leading to social change. The concept of structuration and, in particular, the notion of duality of structure, can be a fruitful source for considering the nature of culture and how it develops – see also the section on culture change later in this chapter.

In summary, it is necessary to view culture as a concept that is manifested at the level of both individuals and social institutions in order to comprehend its nature and potential effects.

VALUES AND INSTITUTIONS IN PORTUGAL

In Chapter 3 we will examine in depth the work of Geert Hofstede, a leading writer on culture, and its impact in business. Hofstede concluded that societies differed along specific pre-set dimensions, two of which are power distance (PD) and uncertainty avoidance (UA). PD deals with how people feel about inequalities – are they accepted, and to what extent? UA focuses on people's attitudes to change and uncertainty.

When we look at guides on business etiquette in Portugal we typically find that the business traveller is told that Portuguese people are conservative, formal and concerned with status and hierarchy, all of which can be seen as manifestations of Portugal's high score on Hofstede's PD index. When approaching negotiation with Portuguese business people, the visitor is habitually advised to keep the same negotiating team as sustaining trust is particularly important, along with a need to develop relationships more generally. Such guides also point to the probability of deals being delayed in Portugal. Therefore, in both cases we see that culture can be manifested through the preference, attitudes and behaviour of individuals and small groups.

However, dimensions such as PD and UA are also manifested in the institutional structures and arrangements of a country. The 2014 Index of Economic Freedom placed Portugal 32nd out of 43 European countries on its freedom index. This report concluded that Portuguese business was still burdened by political interference and a rigid labour market. While entrepreneurial activity was encouraged, there were also deterrents such as the cost of licensing (four times annual income). Whatever we think about this business environment in political and/or ethical terms, the relative conservatism highlighted in the Portuguese business environment can also be viewed as a reflection of cultural values such as PD and UA.

See: **www.heritage.org/index/country/ Portugal**

Question

Choose any one country, locate it along Hofstede's PD and UA dimensions and show how these dimensions can be manifested both in individual attitudes and behaviour and political and economic structures and institutions in that country.

2.5 NATIONAL CULTURE AND OTHER CULTURAL LAYERS

We have already looked briefly at the work of Hofstede and Trompenaars, and both of these significant contributors to the cross-cultural literature take individual countries as the starting point for their comparisons, although both, importantly, refer to other sources of difference. Tayeb's depiction of the different layers of culture reproduced in Figure 2.2 is useful in drawing our attention to cultural strata which are both above and below the level of nation states. Later in this chapter we explore more fully the notion of organisational culture and how this concept could fit into a model of this type. Tayeb's model additionally identifies several other strata worthy of consideration at this point. Her work indicates both regional and occupational dimensions.

Figure 2.2 Major cultural layers

Global layer	Example: wishing to succeed in life	*Behaviours*
National layer	Example: avoiding loss of 'face' in Japanese culture	*Attitudes*
Regional layer	Example: Bengali culture in West Bengal, India	*Beliefs*
Community layer	Example: helping neighbours in a mining community in Wales, UK	*Values*
Personal layer	Example: caring for wildlife	*Taken-for-granted assumptions*

In the first case, it is undoubtedly true that some nation states contain within them regions that have a strong sense of identity, resulting in significant cultural differences. These differences may, of course, be reflected at the institutional level with federal or semi-autonomous structures in such areas as education. One should be wary of assuming that individual countries are homogeneous to any significant extent, and key researchers in this area have been aware of the regional dimension. Hofstede (2001) compared Belgium and Switzerland, both of which are countries with areas in which two or more languages are spoken. Interestingly, regional differences as they affected Hofstede's dimensions of culture were not uniformly important. In Belgium the two language areas (French and Dutch) were found to share, in essence, the same characteristics. In Switzerland, contrastingly, Hofstede (2001, p63) notes that 'respondents from German-speaking Switzerland were culturally associated with Germany and those from French-speaking Switzerland with France; there was a wide culture gap between the two language groups.' Hofstede goes on to identify intricate historical/developmental factors which could account for the different patterns in these two specific societies.

More generally, the importance of regional cultural variation is in part due to the sometimes arbitrary construction of national boundaries, as can be seen in the case of much of the African continent. An extreme example was provided by the former state of Yugoslavia, which as a country was engulfed by conflict and ultimately disappeared, although not before having been classified as a unified state by cross-cultural management writers. It is clearly necessary to consider the regional dimension when analysing and classifying cultures.

The issue of race and ethnicity should also be considered in this context, and again there is the potential for significant difference within countries, and once more a range of factors may render such differences more or less significant. The current designation by US government agencies of the US population on ethnic grounds (for example, the term 'African-American') provides an interesting case in point, allowing, at least in statistical terms, for intra-societal comparison of groups. In the UK at the time of writing there was considerable debate on the nature of citizenship and integration more generally within a multicultural society. Ed Miliband, the leader of the UK opposition, in a speech delivered on 14 December 2012, stated that 'people living separately is like a country just being a hotel: you are simply a paying guest who can put the do not disturb sign outside the door.' Underlying these comments was a view that diversity in any one country can to an extent result in separate communities, with a clear implication of significant differences amongst subcultures within that country (which again has been treated as a unified whole in much of the cross-cultural management literature).

At this point it is appropriate to introduce gender as another dimension in the debate on the nature of culture and its effects. It is not possible to do anything even approaching justice to such a profound and wide-ranging subject within the context of this book. It has frequently been stated (see, for example, Wilson 2010) – that an individual's identity is profoundly influenced by his or her gender, and there is a very large body of evidence that indicates that males and females may experience their world, and specifically their working lives, in significantly different ways. This raises the possibility of working experience and attitudes and values diverging between male and female citizens *within* a single society. In Chapter 7 we attempt to examine the relationships between culture, gender and leadership styles. There is some evidence (Rosener 1990; Broeways and Price 2011) that men and women have different preferred leadership styles. However, these differences were found to be consistent across all societies. In this sense, gender can be viewed as a non-cultural factor in explaining organisational life, and in particular the experience of work in all societies. van Emmerik et al (2008) conducted research examining associations between gender and cultural clusters and aspects of leader behaviour; namely the relative concerns with accomplishing tasks and consideration for subordinates. Their conclusions were that cultural background of the leader was a greater predictor of a task preoccupation style than their gender. These researchers also found that differences between male and female leaders were in any case less evident than they had anticipated, leading them to conclude that gender stereotypes might be diminishing worldwide. Futhermore, where gender-based variance in the consideration style was evident, this occurred mainly in Western countries. So, actual research points to a complex multi-dimensional relationship between the demographic factors of gender and culture. At a more prosaic level, however, it is undoubtedly the case that the comparative role and status of the two genders differs between societies. We consider examples of this phenomenon throughout this book.

To take one example at this point from the field of cross-cultural management, it is illuminating to record the findings of Forster (1999), whose research revealed a clear under-representation of British women in expatriate postings, in part due to assumptions made concerning their ability to undertake overseas assignments for domestic reasons and their perceived 'acceptability' in other cultural settings; see also Harris (2004) and Linehan (2005).

Finally, it should be recorded that Hofstede's model of culture included as one dimension for classifying societies their place on a 'masculinity' index, one group of societies including Scandinavian countries then being classified as 'feminine'. This interesting and controversial aspect of Hofstede's model is discussed in Chapter 3, where some concerns are expressed regarding the assumptions that underpin this dimension.

Overall, then, it is clear that gender does link with the concept of culture in several ways, and that cross-cultural theory cannot and should not be 'gender-free'. I would, in fact, wish to go beyond this rather neutral statement and propose that the ways in which men and women are regarded and treated within a society or any other social grouping forms a key part of its culture.

APPLYING THEORY TO PRACTICE 2.1

The Global Gender Gap Report of 2013 identified Sweden as a world leader in gender equality.[2] Parents were entitled to take up to 480 days' parental leave and, in contrast to other countries surveyed, there was a specific provision for fathers to take paternity leave, with 60 days of the overall leave reserved for each parent; it is not possible for this allocation to be transferred between parents. An earlier report noted that this had led to the common sight of 'seeing daddies pushing strollers on the street, giving babies bottles in crowded cafes or meeting up for playtime in the park with their toddlers'.[3] In as much as paternity leave fosters gender equality, freeing mothers up to return to work earlier than might be possible in other countries, Sweden can be seen to be in the forefront of such a social trend. One might expect this to be the case. In Chapter 3 we look closely at the work of Hofstede, who classified Sweden as a society high on the dimension of femininity (one of the few in the world). So we have a cultural explanation for the phenomena. And yet, not all eligible Swedish citizens take advantage of this opportunity. In 2012 fathers took only 24% of the available paternity leave offered, and in most cases it was mothers who applied for the joint parental leave periods. The research institute Statistics Sweden identified an over-representation of women in low-income jobs, meaning that it was economically more advantageous for fathers to waive their paternity leave entitlement if, as was likely, they were the higher earner in the partnership. This last point is strictly non-cultural in nature and we see the interplay of cultural and non-cultural forces in dynamic motion when we analyse this topic.

Taking a primary focus on the nation state at the expense of other demographic factors when analysing and comparing cultures must therefore be regarded as problematic to some extent. However, it has already been noted that the most sophisticated models of culture do incorporate intra-country differences into their analysis, and this process of further delineation – via the unravelling of other determining factors such as religion and military history – can be said to have enriched the study of culture. There is also evidence that some recent writers on culture and management have reasserted the potential importance of the nation state as a focus for analysis and comparison. Koen (2005, p69) articulates this view in a cogent way: 'Once in existence, the nation state can exert a strong influence on the culture of its inhabitants, in particular through the institutionalisation of the educational system. As education is one of the two main mechanisms for the transfer and change of culture (the other being the child-rearing practices of parents), it is plausible that if a country has been in existence for long enough, it will have had sufficient influence to enable us to speak of a "national culture".' This notion is addressed at several points in this book and has particular resonance in the area of cross-cultural awareness training (see Chapters 9 and 10).

It has also been suggested that occupational groups may have distinctive norms, values and patterns of job-related behaviour which both define them as a cultural group and differentiate them from other members of their society. This could be evident, for example, in the case of occupations classed as professions where a pan-national code can define their identity and working practices. Many readers might readily consider the medical profession, underpinned by the Hippocratic oath, to be a plausible example of this phenomenon.

The notion of 'orientations' to work developed by Goldthorpe et al in the 1960s is also relevant in this regard. These authors identified a particular set of attitudes to work and the place of work within people's lives, which they termed the solidaristic orientation. Characterised by a strong sense of community identity in the occupational group, such workers bestowed a particular importance on their work, viewing it as a key part of their lives so that individuals often socialised with co-workers, and whole towns or cities were in effect based around the workplace. In the UK the year-long miners' strike in the 1980s can be understood in part as a conflict between an occupational cultural group and the state (one should be aware that class-based analyses are also highly relevant here). While it can be argued that many occupations – and sectors – exhibiting such collective patterns have been in decline in recent decades, the possibility of seeing occupations in cultural terms remains real. Readers might consider what they have in common with people working in the same occupation in other countries. Are the similarities greater, or more meaningful, than those shared with people in different jobs in their home country? The question raises interesting points for discussion.

 ### GROUP ACTIVITY 2.1

Refer to Figure 2.2 and identify ways in which your own values are influenced by factors impinging at the following levels:

- personal
- community
- regional
- community/occupational
- national
- global.

In a group of between three and five people (ideally fellow students), compare and discuss your responses.

1   Discuss how your values have been influenced by the levels of culture listed above.

2   Identify how these levels of culture form part of your identity.

3   Which of the following levels of culture has been most important in shaping your identity?

- national
- regional
- community/occupational.

2.6 DEALING WITH THE ECOLOGICAL FALLACY

The ecological fallacy is more commonly known as stereotyping, which many commentators consider to be a potential problem area when we engage with cross-cultural research and theories. Brewster et al (2011, p48) propose that stereotyping occurs when 'cultural values which are known to be held by a group are projected onto an individual who is a member of the group'. Readers familiar with concepts of interpersonal psychology might recognise the phenomenon of perceptual grouping in this context: put simply, it is difficult to gain an in-depth understanding of an individual's unique attributes and, consequently, easier to perceive people in terms of common features. The oft-quoted statistic that interviewers take a view on a job applicant within a very short time shows how we tend to take short cuts when perceiving others – stereotyping is yet another incidence of this tendency. More generally, the fact that psychologists generally state that our core values (those most difficult to change) are in place by the age of ten, or even earlier, adds to the importance of recognising stereotypes and attempting to overcome them where appropriate, difficult though this may be.

Stereotyping has largely negative connotations and may lead to unhelpful over-generalisations. For example, in the EURO 2004 football tournament, following a disallowed England 'goal', the (Swiss) referee concerned was described in an article in the London *Evening Standard* on 25 June as an 'Emmenthal-eating appeasement monkey'. This is typical stereotyping by which perceived national-level characteristics – in this case relating to food consumption and pacifism – are projected onto an individual citizen and we have little chance of knowing whether they are accurate reflections of his culinary habits and geopolitical views!

There are more serious consequences of stereotyped views. In December 2002 the then German ambassador to the UK, reacting to an assault on two ten-year-old German schoolboys in London following xenophobic verbal abuse, drew attention to what he saw as widespread negative portrayal of Germans in the British media often using World War II analogies. The fact that the ten-year-olds in question had absolutely no personal connection with the war counted little with their attackers in the face of powerfully held stereotypical views.

Academic research intended to inform those involved with cross-cultural aspects of business should clearly not be based on inaccurate, over-generalised or dated work if it is to retain value and credibility. Notwithstanding this point, it is true that much of the work in the area does involve macro-level conclusions based on data collected from individuals. In Chapters 3, 4 and 11 there is further questioning of whether insights gained from research in cross-cultural business and management are significantly flawed by over-generalised conclusions.

At this stage, while assessing the concept of culture in general terms, the following points may be helpful in clarifying the nature of stereotyping related to cross-cultural awareness and the theories underpinning the role of culture in business:

- A stereotype could, in practical terms, be useful in forming a template of how another person may behave. However, the stereotype must be capable of being amended or discarded in the light of experience.
- A stereotype can serve as a statistical statement about a group (for example, a country) rather than as a prediction about individuals. We will see that the work of Hofstede and Trompenaars accords with this notion: both refer to 'central tendencies' within a population, and country scores, with a recognition that individuals may depart from the norm.
- In allowing for central tendencies within cultures and deviation from the norm, stereotypes can be validated through research. In this sense much of the cross-cultural business literature can be seen to contain elements of stereotyping that are objectively arrived at and accurate.
- Cultural differences identified in existing models are presented in a descriptive rather than evaluative way. Although culture is often linked to comparative economic performance, the values underlying culture are not, typically, depicted as better or worse than any others. Even accurate stereotypes should not therefore be associated with cultural superiority.

2.7 CULTURE CHANGE

'The past is a different country; they do things differently there.' This 1953 quote from L.P. Hartley in the novel *The Go-Between* evokes the puzzlement we can feel when looking back at the 'mysterious past' and the extent of change possible within any one society. For our purposes it is essential that any viable view of culture, while acknowledging it to be deep-rooted and enduring, should also recognise its dynamic nature. In the literature on cross-cultural study such change is often referred to as 'culture shift'. There is indeed evidence indicating that cultures can be transformed within a relatively short time period, certainly at the macro institutional level.

Estonia provides a good example. Part of the Soviet bloc of countries until 1991, the country's new government immediately embarked on a radical reform of economic policies, which included a flat rate of income tax and the abolition of tax on non-reinvested corporate income. One aim of these changes has been to engender an entrepreneurial mindset among the population, although it is interesting to record that the implementation of flat-rate taxes was also presented as an appeal to feelings of fairness – a very different, but in this case complementary, value. It may be that the very suddenness of economic and political change in this country has enabled it to embark on a programme intended to change attitudes and values.

Writing in the American magazine *Newsweek* on 21 February 2004, William Underhill stated that, 'Fiscal thinking among the pols [sic] of Western Europe is still coloured by ideas of social justice that radicals in the former socialist East are ready to junk.' There is a suggestion here that cultural change may be more rapid in particular societies. Alternatively, one could claim that the Communist era in Estonia and other eastern European states represented something of a 'blip' and that fundamental underlying values are now re-emerging. The impact of economically driven change on people's attitudes is a topical area of study and is addressed again in the next section on convergence and divergence. Of course it is possible that change of this sort may be regarded as superficial and that underlying cultural values will remain latent and re-emerge in the future. It is clearly the case, however, as evidenced in the case of Estonia, that cross-cultural research findings must be frequently re-evaluated in order to ensure currency and hence value to those, including international managers, who refer to them.

2.8 CONVERGENCE AND DIVERGENCE

No tourist or business traveller can fail to notice some convergence of culture, at least at the 'outer' layer of brands, products and artefacts. In Singapore, the Manchester United store, numerous Western food and drink outlets and musical tastes, at least among part of the younger population, indicate aspects of growing cultural homogeneity. We can also cite the adoption of working practices and technologies of particular cultural origins across the world (see Vaghefi et al (2001) for an insightful analysis of Toyota's worldwide practices in the field of car production). It is interesting to note that apparently 'surface-level' working practices often contain within them culturally derived values and philosophies such as teamwork and employee involvement.

In this context we should consider the extent to which working philosophies and practices emanating from one society can successfully be introduced in another possibly far-flung location. There is evidence to indicate that this cultural transplantation may indeed be possible to a degree. When the car manufacturer Nissan set up a plant in the north-east of England, the local workforce were required to adapt to a new and greatly changed working environment: they worked in teams, were introduced to the notion of *kaizen*, or continuous improvement, and came within single employment conditions. The UK car plant initially acquired a reputation for high quality and productivity, although the latter (always a relative term) has been subsequently undermined by a non-cultural factor, ie currency fluctuations. Although it is open to question whether these British workers truly internalised the new values underlying the working practices, it can be stated that cultural change and a degree of convergence may occur through the consequences of globalisation, in this case manifested through cross-border investment and acquisition.

Another argument for cultural convergence can be seen in the modernisation thesis, in which it is argued that economic evolution follows effectively the same pattern for all societies – they just reach the particular stages at different times. The historical determinism put forward by Karl Marx could be argued to fall within this tradition, and the thesis has a current echo in the oft-heard suggestion that developing countries such as China and India are becoming centres for manufacturing industries, superseding Western societies. Johns (2005, pxi) opines that, 'There is no realistic possibility whatsoever that the UK will ever again become a significant manufacturing resource for the global economy,' implying that this phase of economic development is over in the UK and is now being undertaken by other countries. It is interesting to note that some parts of the service sector are also increasingly associated with new entrants into the sector; for example, the profusion of call centres operating in India.

Much of this book is devoted to exploring an alternative approach; namely, the culture-specific hypothesis, a fundamental tenet of which is that there have been, and continue to be, important cultural differences in the business setting. As a result, cross-cultural awareness becomes critically important.

One important strand of argument within this book is that a significant body of evidence indicates that important cultural differences continue to exist despite an apparent growing homogeneity in the organisational world. Hofstede (1980 and 2001) exemplified the 'culturalist' approach when contrasting attitudes and values of employees from different countries who worked for a single employer – in this case IBM. He found that even in the same company, profound national cultural differences were evident, and that these were manifested by employees. Subsequent chapters will take an essentially culturalist stance, while at the same time moderating this view in the light of theories and actual research studies which emphasise the influence of non-cultural factors on a variety of issues and topics. It should also be recognised that even where there is documented evidence of homogeneity in terms of organisational policies and practices, this similarity – or overriding norm – is itself related to a particular cultural model, whether Anglo-American or Japanese or indeed any other combination. It is eminently possible that another culturally derived form of standardisation may become prevalent in the future.

One interesting attempt to balance the culture-free and culture-specific schools of thought stems from the work of Inglehart (1997) (see also Inglehart and Baker 2000). Inglehart puts forward the thesis that economic developments are likely to result in cultural change at the level of people's values. For example, he finds evidence that when countries industrialise – that is, move away from a mainly agricultural economy – one can perceive significant changes in the values of their population. These are exhibited in a move from concerns with basic needs of survival to a preoccupation with economic and material well-being. At the same time Inglehart identifies a change whereby people become less concerned with social norms such as caring for their extended families or wider community. He proposes that such collective norms are supplanted with others centring on individual achievement and social mobility. It is also noteworthy that in this model of development there is a decline in organised religion, although it is debatable whether this last point applies to any meaningful extent outside the European context.

Inglehart then goes on to examine a further economic phase of development from the industrial or modern to post-industrial or postmodern. This phase is associated with an emerging services-based economy. The cultural values linked with this economic period are said to be based around a concern with the quality of life: there are spiritual and environmental preoccupations and people increasingly turn to individualistic 'new age' beliefs.

In summarising current global economic and cultural models, Inglehart and Baker identify clusters of societies which are more or less traditional or rational and concerned with either survival or self-expression. For example, they depict the Netherlands as, currently, a rational-secular society concerned with self-expression, whereas Russia, although again oriented towards well-being, is characterised by contrastingly traditional values in religion and towards authority. This model is analysed again in Chapter 3. The purpose of referring to it here is to emphasise the complex nature of culture change with the possibility of an emerging revised set of country clusters linked together by a mix of both stages in economic development and cultural attitudes.

The debate on the relative impact of convergence and divergence has been given a new twist with the advent of the notion of crossvergence (see Ralston et al 1997; Witt 2008; Aycan et al 2014). The advocates of crossvergence suggest that individuals are subject to national cultural influences and economic ideology in a synergenistic way, ie the combined influence of these two factors is more than the sum of both added together.

If we then also include the effect of harmonisation of technology across the world, we reach a situation in which people discard some values while consciously retaining others.

The forces of convergence and sustained cultural difference should be seen as evolving in dynamic motion (as with the concept of crossvergence) and continue to play out in the future. It is extremely difficult to predict where they will lead. Some suggestions on how these interrelated forces can be studied in future in order to inform cross-cultural management scholars and practitioners are put forward in Chapter 4.

2.9 INTERPRETING CULTURE PROFILES

One more challenge within the field of cultural analysis concerns the need to apply the findings of cross-cultural theorists with care and, in particular, with due regard to the complexity of subject matter and the interlinked nature of cultural factors. Two examples may serve to illustrate this point.

The USA is characterised within models of cultural difference (Hofstede, Trompenaars and Hampden-Turner) as a strongly individualist society with a well-established ethos of individual achievement, social mobility and acceptance of inequality. There is an apparent anomaly, however, when we look at the cases of several national sporting leagues and competitions in that country, where it can be seen that players' salary caps exist, coupled with the redistribution of pooled income downwards through the competitive leagues. One explanation for this apparently paradoxical finding lies in a desire to maintain competition (another strongly held value) in the relevant sports. If one team or even a small group were to grow richer at the expense of other participants, this could militate against realistic competition – hence the attempts to maintain some degree of equality of opportunity.

A second example can be seen in Hofstede's individualism/collectivism index. Three countries – Germany, Norway and Poland – obtain similar scores on this dimension: they are 'individualist' societies but are not at the extreme end of this scale because they retain elements of collectivism too. It is possible to identify these countries' collectivist features as being manifested in quite different ways: through the systems of employee consultation and industrial democracy in Germany, in a concern with the environment in Norway, and in the strong influence of the Catholic Church in Poland. The overall conclusion here is that the findings of cross-cultural research must be applied within the particular intricate cultural environment of each country. In this regard we are fortunate that most of our analysis is applied to work-based situations, but nonetheless, a broad approach to cultural study is needed.

2.10 IS NATIONAL CULTURE STILL MEANINGFUL?

The previous sections have set out a series of challenges within the study of culture. It is crucial to avoid stereotyping; subcultures may behave quite differently from the general population under study; and no model or finding is fixed – culture is always changing. Faced with this complex picture, some readers may be tempted to abandon the concept of culture altogether, considering it impossible to pin down. After reviewing the evidence, one can counsel against this view (understandable though it is) and conclude that the study of national cultures remains meaningful as a source of important insights within the field of business and management. Ultimately, you should personally consider whether you believe that other cultures have significant beliefs and behaviour patterns which take effect in work situations. Consider another country in which you have either holidayed, studied or been employed. How did it differ from the country in which you were brought up? Were the differences significant, and if so, would you expect them to show up in work organisations in the future?

2.11 ORGANISATIONAL CULTURE

At the start of this chapter it was noted that one reason for the current interest in cross-cultural study has been the impact of a proliferation of books, articles and training and consultancy programmes promoting the importance of organisational or corporate culture. The two terms are not synonymous. French et al (2011, p385) distinguish these two terms in the following way: 'Organizational culture representing values, beliefs and principles of organizational members, which have grown within the context of a particular setting, and corporate culture, the latter term referring to cultures deliberately created by management to achieve specific strategic ends.' The latter concept is associated particularly with the work of Peters and Waterman (1982) and Deal and Kennedy (1982). These writers posited a correlation between company-level culture and success: excellent companies, they argued, have strong cultures which deliver success. This distinction is valuable in explaining the resurgence in interest in the topic area in the 1980s, although with hindsight it would not be implausible to regard the term 'corporate culture' as oxymoronic if it is felt that culture must by definition be seen as organic and not amenable to imposition.

It is, in any case, possible to view the concern with culture at the organisational level as continuous rather than time-framed, centring on an excessive focus on the 'excellence' literature and subsequent critique of this approach. The study of workers' values, beliefs and principles has a longer timeline and can be traced back to the Hawthorne Studies carried out between 1924 and 1932 and the 'human relations' school of management. In recent years, paradoxically, the importance of organisational culture has been revisited when explaining a series of corporate-level scandals. For Clegg et al (2011, p227), 'In some organisations, such as various police services, or firms such as Enron or WorldCom, a dominant culture of corruption has become widespread. Although such cultures are not "officially official", their proliferation suggests that formal tolerance enabled them to flourish and to become established as the local norm.'

Cultural differences, largely but not entirely focused at the national level, are presented in this book as important in terms of helping us to explain aspects of business and management. The long-term focus on organisational culture (from Hawthorne to Enron) suggests that this too is a highly significant area. How can we link these two levels of culture, and to what extent is it valuable to do so?

2.12 NATIONAL AND ORGANISATIONAL CULTURE: SIMILARITIES

Figure 2.3 depicts a view of culture as comprising three levels. This type of model – here comparing layers of culture to those in a visually appealing layer-cake – is not new. Sathe (1985) provides two other ways of conceptualising the importance of the layers by comparing culture to either an iceberg or an onion. In this context Figure 2.3 can be viewed as a generic model of culture – and the layers identified therefore also apply at the national – or regional – or occupational, or any other group level.

As can be seen, the outer or surface level comprises artefacts or readily apparent manifestations of culture. Writers on the topic of organisational culture have laid stress on the importance of this level, emphasising the importance of logos, of office or factory layout and of the role of stories and archetypal heroes or villains in company history. These artefacts can serve as a powerful way of symbolising culture – note the similar role and function of corporate identity and national flags. Values can also be expressed in a variety of ways; for example, the 'dress-down Friday' ritual followed by a number of companies with implicit messages regarding formality and hierarchy. Consider, for example, how Barack Obama used cultural aretfacts to symbolise his message of change when running for US president, even making known what music was on his iPod during the campaign.

Figure 2.3 Culture as a three-level layer-cake

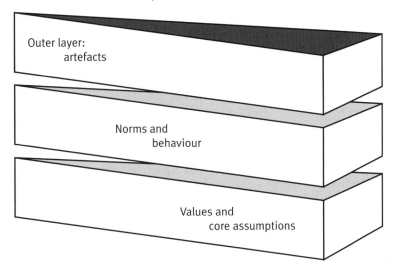

Another way in which the concepts of national and organisational culture are linked can be found in the use of typologies and classification schemes. We look more closely at national classifications in Chapter 3 and have already referred to several, including the work of Hofstede and Trompenaars, both of whom distinguished societies along dimensions such as how 'individualistic' they were. In terms of organisational culture, Deal and Kennedy (1982) distinguish between a variety of cultures, including process cultures, characterised by Mullins (2013, p699) as 'a low-risk/slow-feedback culture where employees find difficulty in measuring what they do'. This type of culture is apparently prevalent in parts of the financial services sector. A work-hard/play-hard culture, contrastingly, requires employees to maintain a clear focus on customer needs and is more common in sales-oriented organisations such as estate agencies. Deal and Kennedy go on to identify several other types of corporate culture. For our purposes it is important to recognise that at both the national and organisational levels it is commonplace to attempt to classify cultures in order to give meaning and reference.

Another common feature shared by cultures at both national and organisational level is the reality of subcultures. It is sometimes thought that work organisations may be less subject to the activities of potentially mischievous subcultures since those who control them can have a large input in appointing organisational members (although the predictive validity of many employee selection methods has often been questioned). Nonetheless, organisational sociologists through the years have not had to look far to unravel 'unofficial' practices running counter to the policies put forward by management. Watson (2006) identifies a number of such outcomes of subcultures including an illuminating conversation with a manager from the airline industry who recalls real-life instances of workers pilfering complementary drinks and 'managing' disliked customers; for example, the rude passenger who had his coffee laced with laxative.

The important role of subcultures at the national level has already been discussed. It may also be that both levels of culture experience countercultures where members actively seek to undermine or destroy the dominant culture. The two layers combine here in the example of the 'Cambridge network' of Soviet spies who were able to rise to senior positions within the British intelligence services with apparently devastating results, both for the intelligence agency itself and the nation more generally.

Finally, and interestingly, it may be that the very preoccupation with organisational culture is itself influenced by developments in the wider society. Grey (2013, p63), in an attempt to put into context the popularity of writers such as Peters and Waterman, suggests that 'There were other strands in American culture which helped to explain the popularity of the culture approach. America had been in the vanguard of the youthful counterculture which emerged, especially on the West coast in the 1960s. Those involved or influenced by it were, by the early 1980s, in their thirties and coming to positions of influence in organisations. The backwash of this movement may well have created a climate in which talk of empowerment and harmony had an appeal which at other times it might have lacked.'

At this point it should also be mentioned that one difference between organisational and national culture lies in its treatment by academics, with a far greater number of studies of individual work organisations carried out on an ethnographic case study basis. For reasons that may be readily apparent, the study of work-related societal difference has relied more on data drawn from population samples. In Chapters 3 and 4 we review the nature of some of this sampling, which has at times focused on well-educated and widely travelled managers, and the implications this may have both on data and current models of culture.

2.13 LINKING THE MACRO AND MICRO LEVELS

There are several ways in which national or societal-level culture can impact at the workplace:

- Classifications of culture which focus on differences in values (for example, 'individualism') and attitudes towards ambiguity and change will be embodied by actors in the workplace, including those in positions of influence, and imported into work organisations in the form of policies and work arrangements. These could include views on autonomy and job satisfaction which can influence both employees' perceptions and managerial strategies.
- Institutional factors (for example, the role of trade unions) and government legislation (for example, on employment protection) will also influence attitudes and practices at the workplace level – and may also account for a company's choosing to operate in one country as opposed to another.
- Other aspects of the 'cultural map' may also take effect in organisations (for example, a litigious culture such as the USA is likely to be associated with protection of individual rights at work and have strong policies on health and safety).
- The economic system and philosophies prevalent at a particular time are also likely to take effect in a variety of ways. For example, in France in the 1990s, concerns regarding the encroachment of 'Anglo-Saxon capitalism' resulted in a reduction in statutory working hours at a time when many other countries were moving in the opposite direction.

Although there is evidence in existing research and academic models to support incidences of societal-level culture impacting on work organisations via all four of the routes listed above, we must guard against making links based on assertion or inference. In Chapters 4 and 11 we argue that there is a need for more detailed work to expand on and refine our understanding of the linkages between societal and organisational culture. In this context one could also envisage instances where organisational and national cultures come into conflict; for example, where an 'international organisation' has a distinctive pan-national or home-country-specific culture which does not sit easily alongside that of the host country. The tie-ups between BMW and Rover and the Daimler/Chrysler merger both experienced varying levels of difficulty that could be attributed partly to this sort of tension.

2.14 NON-CULTURAL EXPLANATIONS

Although the importance of culture within business is stressed throughout this book, it would be misleading and unsatisfactory not to record the potential influence of a range of factors which impinge on business in all cultures and which can themselves have a major impact on employee attitudes, managerial actions and organisational arrangements. Put simply, culture is only *one*, albeit important, variable influencing behaviour in organisations and business outcomes. There follows a very brief summary of other explanatory factors in this regard; please refer to either of the texts listed in the Further Reading section at the end of this chapter for a fuller analysis.

- *Organisational size* – There is evidence, which we go on to analyse in Chapters 3, 4 and 5, that the size of an organisation has an important influence on its structural arrangements. Larger organisations tend to be more formal and bureaucratic in all societies, and the size of an organisation also determines investment in other areas, for example, technological infrastructure.
- *Product/sector* – The 'Aston studies' of the 1970s found that organisations operating in the same sector could be more alike, certainly in terms of structure, across societies than those occupying a different market within an individual country. It is also the case that employees in certain occupations within specific sectors may be required to exhibit similar and increasingly standardised behaviour in organisations worldwide. French et al (2011) cite the example of air cabin crew in different national airlines.
- *Technology* – The work of Woodward (1958) was influential in pointing out the crucial influence of the technology employed by an organisation on both its structure and work arrangements, including job design. Again it is possible to see this logic taking effect in all societies. In the 1990s the 'McDonaldisation' thesis offered the prospect of greater global harmonisation in business through the spread of identical or very similar technologies.
- *Ownership* – This provides an interesting topic for the culture-free versus culture-specific debate. Is it generally more true to say that a foreign-owned organisation can successfully import its own practices into a new country, or is it more likely that it will have to adapt to local (culturally specific) conditions in order to survive and even thrive in the new environment? It may also be, of course, that there are multiple answers to this very broad question.

All of the above points are examples of contingencies (factors which organisational decision-makers are likely to adapt to). As indicated, these are non-cultural in nature. Some authors (for example, Child 2005) question this reactive picture and give greater scope for managerial choice in framing organisational arrangements. Exercise of such choice could be on the basis of culturally derived preferences. The interesting question centres on the relative importance of these culturally specific choices and the universal contingencies identified, together with the interplay between them.

2.15 CONCLUSIONS

While many people have an intuitive belief that culture is a meaningful concept within business studies, and that significant cultural differences exist across the world, the term culture has often been used in too relaxed a way with little detailed attention paid to how, and it what ways, it takes effect within work organisations. A proliferation of sometimes competing definitions of the central term adds to what has at times been a confusing picture. Nonetheless, it is possible to identify some common strands in thinking on culture and business. There is a consensus that culture is linked with people's values and attitudes, learned via socialisation, which are then manifested in preferred courses of action by key players in the workplace. In this sense, culture could be seen as a constraint on managers' action or either an independent or moderating variable affecting their actions. An alternative view of culture regards it as being primarily bound up with language and other forms of communication, and hence sees the major cultural differences between societies essentially as comprising variances in communication styles. As we will see in later chapters, effective communication is also key to successful cross-cultural management. Culture itself comprises levels – from visible artefacts through to deep belief systems – and takes effect not only through embodied values but also at the macro-social level of institutions. Giddens' concept of structuration may provide a useful way forward in terms of understanding how culture interacts with human agency and pre-existing social structures.

While a person's cultural background can be seen to affect their values and behaviour, so too do other demographic factors such as class and gender. These demographic factors can be seen to exist in dynamic interplay when we attempt to explain human behaviour. While it is important not to make over-generalised conclusions and to stereotype people according to cultural background, stereotypes have some degree of usefulness in helping us explain behaviour, particularly if we are aware of them.

Work organisations are also affected by national culture but their structures and processes are influenced by other factors too, such as their size and the sector in which they operate. Organisational cultures are also important and the concept of organisational culture mirrors that of national culture in certain important respects.

Culture is not an easy term to comprehend and the impact of culture on business is complex and multifaceted. However, culture remains a core concept both for students of business and managers in work organisations. In Chapters 3 and 4 we look in more detail at specific frameworks and models which can further elucidate the area of cross-cultural management.

 NO MORE 'STIFF UPPER LIPS'?

CASE STUDY 2.2

The reaction to the death of Diana, Princess of Wales, in 1997 seemed to many to signify a cultural change in the UK. Across the country people spontaneously set up impromptu floral memorials and there were numerous examples of publicly expressed grief. In the days following the Princess's death, many people took to the streets, or at least the parks of London and other cities, to express their sadness collectively. Some observers found these public displays of emotion to be at odds with the typical perception, or stereotype, of the British as a private and emotionally reserved people, viewing the cathartic expressions of grief as evidence of a country more at ease with itself and also reflecting a changing demographic profile. Others took a more judgemental view. A BBC News report dated 23 February 2004 summarised the report of a 'think-tank', Civitas, which was quoted as claiming that 'Britons are feeding their own egos by indulging in "recreational grief for murdered children and dead celebrities they have never met".' The Civitas report went on to claim that 'wearing charity ribbons, holding silences and joining protest marches all indicated the country was in emotional crisis'. Although to many the public displays of grief were a new phenomenon in the UK, it can be noted that they represented an example of cyclical change since there are documented cases of similar outpourings in the past, and the (possibly stereotypical) notion of the British 'stiff upper lip' can itself be emerging from a particular historical time – in this case, the Victorian era.

Questions

1 Identify some possible explanations for culture change in the UK, as manifested in the reaction to the death of Diana, Princess of Wales.

2 Identify one example of culture change in the country in which you were either born or currently reside. Have all or only some members of the population been affected by the change? How would you explain your example of 'culture shift'?

NOTES

1 www.dubaiairshow.aero/exhibit/tips-advice [Accessed 9 May 2014].

2 WORLD ECONOMIC FORUM. Global gender gap. Available at: www.weforum.org/issues/global-gender-gap [Accessed 9 May 2014].

3 Swedish dads steer clear of paternity leave (2008) *The Local: Sweden's News in English.* 12 March 2008. http://www.thelocal.se/10420/20080312/ [Accessed 2 September 2009].

REVIEW QUESTIONS

1 How useful is it to view culture in Hofstede's terms as 'the collective programming of the mind'? Use examples to illustrate your answer.

2 With the use of examples, show both the positive and negative aspects of using stereotypes to predict and explain an individual's behaviour.

3 In what ways are the terms organisational culture and national culture linked?

FURTHER READING

BREWSTER, C., SPARROW, P., VERNON, G. and HOUDSWORTH, E. (2011) *Human resource management in an international context.* 3rd ed. London: CIPD. Chapter 2 of this book includes an alternative summary of some of the issues set out in this chapter, within an overall focus on human resource management and the role of multinational companies.

MULLINS, L.J. (2013) *Management and organisational behaviour.* 10th ed. Harlow: FT/Prentice Hall. This book includes a detailed summary of types of organisational culture within a wider discussion of organisation development.

NEEDLE, D. (2010) *Business in context.* 5th ed. London: Cengage. This text offers a lucid summary of aspects of the business environment as they affect business, including globalisation and cultural convergence and divergence.

Visit this book's companion website (**www.cipd.co.uk/olr**) to find further exercises including self-assessment questions and also weblinks to media and academic journal articles.

CHAPTER 3

Models of Culture: Traditional Approaches

LEARNING OBJECTIVES

After reading this chapter you should be able to:

- identify and understand mainstream models purporting to explain cultural differences in diverse societies
- see how these models go on to explain differences at workplace level
- recognise commonalities between frameworks of culture and the development of thinking in this area
- evaluate the usefulness of mainstream models of cultural difference in explaining aspects of work organisations
- be aware of emerging alternative approaches to understanding culture (discussed in more detail in Chapter 4).

3.1 INTRODUCTION

In Chapter 2 we reviewed the nature of culture as a concept, noting its multifaceted nature and the ways in which its effects could be manifested at different levels. We now go on to look in more detail at some of the more popular and influential models which claim to both define the characteristics of culture and also classify and differentiate individual cultures and cultural groups or 'clusters'.

We have already noted that the field of cross-cultural management emerged relatively recently and one might reasonably conclude that it must, therefore, be in its infancy both in terms of its conceptual frameworks and scope of application to business operations. The non-global nature of most business activity prior to the late twentieth century meant that until that point cross-cultural study was mainly carried out by anthropologists, so the field of business and management studies was largely culture-free. However, in the period from 1980 to 2015, there has been a steep rise in interest in how culture affects processes and behaviour at work. There are, of course, good practical reasons underlying the increasing volume of academic contributions. Gerhart (2008a) posits that culture became a topical area because it is regarded as a constraint on management action. In other words, managers would need to be aware of culture and cultural difference in order to adapt their ideas and practices to local settings. Patel (2014) concludes that a changing role for managers, who were increasingly required to link with many agents within networks, had led to a need for cultural understanding of those agents and the ways in which managers connected with them. More specifically, Holden (2008) highlights growing awareness of a distinctive Japanese model of management as another springboard to a focus on cultural difference, noting that Japanese organisations would themselves stress differences between their own management systems when setting up operations elsewhere in the world. The desire to learn from (currently) successful competitor nations continues to be a spur to greater cross-cultural awareness. Gelfand et al (2007) characterise the cross-cultural study of similarities and differences in organisational behaviour as having a long past but short research history, identifying the 1980s as the key period when both managers and academics began to focus on culture in a rigorous way.

If cross-cultural management theory is in its infancy, it is, nonetheless, possible to identify a dominant paradigm – in other words, a mainstream approach – in cross-cultural management thinking in the period after 1980. This mainstream approach can be located within the etic perspective introduced in Chapter 1. While alternative models of culture have emerged and become increasingly influential (see Chapter 4), new mainstream work continues to be published. In 2014, for example, Minkov and Hofstede produced evidence replicating Hofstede's 1980 cultural dimensions in 25 European countries plus Israel. So in identifying and evaluating the mainstream etic approach we are looking at live as well as historical data.

This etic approach is essentially comparative, involving, firstly, the identification of core dimensions of culture and then plotting (or scoring) countries along these dimensions. A key point is that differences are relative rather than absolute. So the UK is more individualistic than China but one cannot characterise it as individualistic *per se*: it is only individualistic in comparison to China – and indeed many other countries. The majority of writers within this tradition perceive culture as primarily expressed through individuals' values, although there is some focus on the institutional level as well. Other etic models of culture stress the centrality of communication styles when understanding and classifying cultures. Jackson and Aycan (2006, p10), in summarising the development of cross-cultural management thinking, conclude that, 'cross cultural theory has developed strength in comparing nations [as the cultural unit of analysis] in terms of broad value dimensions'. These authors go on to look ahead to newer preoccupations such as cross-cultural interactions at work. We will explore these developing themes in Chapter 4, but at this point will examine in greater detail models within the etic frame of reference, which a number of writers suggest continues to dominate research in the field (Tsui et al 2007; Aycan et al 2014; Patel 2014).

In this chapter we will set out the major theories identified within the etic approach to cross-cultural management which, as indicated, has formed the mainstream view of the topic since 1980. We will not only summarise these models, but will also provide some brief evaluation of individual contributions to the cross-cultural management canon. This is necessary to ensure that these models are more than superficially understood and can also be applied in a thoughtful and feasible way. A deeper understanding can advance the academic debates, and at the same time, provide relevant insights for current or aspiring cross-cultural managers.

At the end of the chapter, we will pose some more general questions concerning the validity of the mainstream models of culture identified. These broader questions will be explored in greater detail in Chapter 4. For example, it is possible to overplay the impact of culture as an explanatory variable and so it is necessary to look at explanations of organisational structure and behaviour which *minimise* the influence of culture as an explanatory factor. While recognising and in many cases stressing the importance of culture as a key influence upon organisational life, the aim here is to balance this perspective by comparing the culture-specific approach with an alternative view emphasising similarities between organisations across the world and, in some cases, pointing to increasing *convergence* between them. The true value of a cross-cultural perspective can only be ascertained if it is held up to critical scrutiny against competing approaches. I contend that *culture matters*, but do not assume that this view should be unchallenged or held to be self-evidently true, as is the case in other writings in this field.

We now go on to examine commonalities in thinking in the cross-cultural management mainstream literature by taking a 'time-tunnel' approach, beginning with a summary of one recent study in the field and, via an examination of its academic roots, travelling back to refocus on some classic models of culture and their potential role in understanding aspects of work organisations.

3.2 PROJECT GLOBE: TRACING THE BLOODLINE

Project GLOBE is a large-scale contemporary research programme which explores the relationship between national (or societal) culture, organisational culture and leadership within organisations (Chokar et al 2013). In one introduction to their study the principal authors (House et al 2001, p492) note that, 'The meta-goal of GLOBE is to develop an empirically based theory to describe, understand and predict the impact of specific cultural variables on leadership and organisational processes and the effectiveness of these processes.' The precise findings and significance of this study are reviewed more fully in Chapter 7. At this stage we examine the theoretical underpinnings of the programme, and in particular the earlier academic influences which frame the approach taken in Project GLOBE. These are explicitly stated by the GLOBE researchers who have sought to apply insights obtained from existing models to a particular area of study – in this case, leadership.

The GLOBE researchers in approaching their study were concerned to identify *dimensions* of culture (in their case, both societal and organisational) in order to identify intra-cultural similarities and inter-cultural differences. We have already recorded in Chapter 2 the need, when engaged in cross-cultural study or management, to identify differences which are meaningful and consistent. In this way one can develop models of culture which focus on the core elements of the concept and do not deal with spurious or insignificant aspects. This preoccupation has been shared by all of the major contributors to this area since the 1950s.

In Project GLOBE the following nine dimensions of culture were identified. These are listed together with a summary of characteristics or, as the GLOBE authors refer to them, culture construct definitions.

- *Power distance* – This refers to the extent to which an identified group expect that power will be distributed relatively equally or unequally. Furthermore, in GLOBE the researchers also examined whether individuals agreed with existing power relations or wished things to be different.
- *Uncertainty avoidance* – In this dimension the focus is on the extent to which group members welcome unusual events and uncertainty as opposed to seeking to avoid such situations and circumstances.
- *Collectivism I* – This dimension differs from the previous two in that here the emphasis is on actual practice rather than the preferences of individuals – specifically, the degree to which a society or work organisation enables and encourages collective rewards and collective action.
- *Collectivism II* – This refers to the extent to which an individual is bonded with, and is loyal to, a sub-societal group – for example, a family or work organisation.
- *Gender egalitarianism* – In this dimension the focus is on how far males and females are treated relatively equally in a society or workplace setting, and whether gender-based role differences are comparatively insignificant.
- *Assertiveness* – Here the researchers sought to identify the prevalence and acceptability of assertive behaviour on the part of individuals within a particular society.

- *Future orientation* – The focus in this category is on the extent to which individuals plan and generally consider future implications of their actions.
- *Performance orientation* – This dimension examines the incidence of cues and outcomes within organisations or the wider society which are intended to encourage ongoing high performance.
- *Humane orientation* – If societies or organisations elicit and reinforce qualities of kindness, generosity and altruism, they score highly on this final dimension.

Readers who have already been introduced to the cross-cultural business literature may recognise a number of these dimensions, and it is interesting to record that this major contemporary research project very evidently has many of its academic roots in earlier work. It is possible, after more than 30 years of work in this area, to discern an emerging consensus on the question of which dimensions of culture are significant in terms of their impact at workplace level. Power distance (PD) and uncertainty avoidance (UA) are taken from the work of Geert Hofstede, and both gender egalitarianism and assertiveness are adaptations of Hofstede's masculinity/femininity dimension, while his individualism/collectivism bipolar scale emerges in the GLOBE study as collectivism I and II. The GLOBE authors also acknowledge another source (House et al 1999, p16) as follows: 'Collectively, the nine dimensions reflect not only the dimensions of Hofstede's theory but also David McClelland's theories of national economic development (McClelland 1961) and human motivation (McClelland 1985). The humanism, PD and performance orientation of cultures, when measured with operant [behavioural] indicators, are conceptually analogous to the affiliative, power and achievement motives in McClelland's implicit motivation theory. We believe that the nine core GLOBE dimensions reflect important aspects of the human condition.'

In summary, the GLOBE study marks the reappearance of pre-existing dimensions of culture, which point to some measure of acceptance in locating those aspects of culture which most significantly affect policies and practices within organisations. The GLOBE research programme also adopts a theoretical framework which partly draws on previous work in the area. Again, we can see how particular themes emerge from pioneer research into the impact of culture on organisations and are then expanded on and/or applied to specific areas of organisational activity.

Selected parts of the conceptual model developed by the GLOBE researchers (see House et al 2001) are set out below. A full listing of the 13 elements which make up the model is provided in Chapter 7.

- Societal cultural values and practices affect what actors (in this case, leaders) do.
- Societal cultural values and practices affect organisational culture and practices.
- Relationships between strategic organisational contingencies and organisational form, culture and practices are moderated by cultural forces.

All of the insights listed here can be viewed within the context of developing knowledge in the cross-cultural field, and again the earlier work of Hofstede can be seen as an important influence. The notion that societal-level cultural norms affect behaviour through individuals' socialisation into their own culture was put forward by Hofstede (1980) in his oft-quoted conception of national culture as the collective programming of the mind, which, he concluded, would characterise the members of one culture and hence differentiate them from others.

With regard to the second point addressing the impact of societal culture at the organisational level, the GLOBE model again follows on from a line of researchers, including Hofstede, who concluded that individuals bring their 'collective programming' into organisations, thereby influencing them. However, it should also be noted that organisations are frequently viewed, within these frameworks, as microcosms of society, so organisational culture – as a mini-version of societal culture – may in turn affect individuals within them.

The third point taken from the GLOBE model deals with the relationship between 'strategic contingencies' and culture as explanatory factors. In claiming that culture will moderate the effect of contingent factors (such as size of organisation, technologies employed and the relative volatility of the market within which the organisation operates) on organisational arrangements, the GLOBE project reinforces earlier findings, namely, that culture can itself be seen as a contingent factor, albeit an important one. We can see this line of reasoning in Hofstede's approach in his choice of one organisation (IBM) as the main focus for his study. Here we have an organisation which should be largely similar across the world in that its technologies and, more generally, its *raison d'être* as expressed by its organisational or corporate culture, were uniform. The important differences uncovered by Hofstede are, it is argued, due to the impact of national or societal culture. This is in effect an earlier manifestation of GLOBE's 'modified contingencies' approach.

It can, finally, be seen that Project GLOBE draws upon a tradition common in cross-cultural studies in this area, of identifying clusters of societies. Gupta et al (2002) identified ten clusters arising from the GLOBE findings, positing that particular societies could be grouped together along particular measures of similarity, which then enabled them to be differentiated from other clusters. The full list of ten country clusters is again detailed in Chapter 7. At this point for illustrative purposes we identify two: the Southern Asian cluster and the Anglo cluster. Countries grouped within these clusters are listed in Table 3.1.

Table 3.1 Societal clusters by country

Southern Asian country cluster	'Anglo' country cluster
India	England
Indonesia	Australia
Philippines	South Africa (white sample)
Malaysia	Canada
Thailand	New Zealand
Iran	Ireland
	USA

One purpose of grouping societies into clusters is to identify policies and practices which align with both cultural preferences and institutional arrangements present in that society. In these cases the Southern Asian cluster is associated with high degrees of loyalty to sub-societal groups such as work organisations and high PD, whereas the Anglo cluster is classed as individualistic (although, interestingly, people in that cluster often express a desire for more in-group collectivism). The GLOBE researchers suggest that participative leadership is, accordingly, likely to be more readily accepted and hence effective in the Anglo cluster of societies.

Clustering societies in this way does not preclude the identification of practices which could work in different clusters. For example, in these two cases charismatic leadership is valued highly in both Southern Asian and Anglo cultures.

INDIVIDUAL ACTIVITY 3.1

Choose any one country from each of the two clusters in Table 3.1 and identify any three ways in which you might expect relationships between managers and subordinates to differ in workplace settings in the two countries. Why would you expect these differences to be present?

● After completing your list, refer to the work of Hofstede (set out later in the chapter; see also **www.geert-hofstede.com** for a quick guide) to see whether your analysis is borne out by the findings of probably the most influential academic in this field.

Project GLOBE provides a good example of the existence of enduring themes underpinning the study of cross-cultural differences at organisational level, namely:

● the classification of societies according to dimensions of culture
● a theoretical framework which stresses individual socialisation as an important factor in maintaining differences between cultures
● the grouping of named societies into clusters which share specific features according to individual models of culture. These are often – but not always – located in a particular geographical region.

3.3 GEERT HOFSTEDE'S PIVOTAL CONTRIBUTION

Hofstede's work has been alluded to both in this and previous chapters, and it is now time to devote a section of this book to an outline and brief evaluation of his work. Hofstede is an absolutely key figure in the whole area of cross-cultural studies applied to work and the business area more generally. Koen (2005, p63) is among many commentators holding this view, claiming that, 'Comparative cross-cultural research at the societal or national level gathered significant impetus through the well-known work of the Dutch scholar Geert Hofstede.' Brooks (2009, p292) notes that, 'In many ways Geert Hofstede is seen as the major writer on cross-cultural analysis because the model he developed has survived the test of time, is relatively easy to use and is comprehensive.' Although not immune from criticism, as we shall see, Hofstede's contribution to the area can undoubtedly be viewed as pivotal.

The genesis of Hofstede's work dates back to the 1960s when he led two major surveys on cross-cultural differences in different centres of the computing company IBM. The surveys were carried out between 1968 and 1973, although Hofstede continues to publish in the twenty-first century. As we shall see, his work was further developed in the mid-1980s when, with Canadian academic Michael Bond, at that time working in Hong Kong, Hofstede identified an additional cultural dimension, Confucian dynamism – subsequently renamed 'long-term orientation' – which expanded the scope of the original work to encompass countries in East Asia. However, the essential approach adopted by Hofstede dates back to his original work in IBM when he devised surveys in which IBM employees were asked to complete questionnaires which required them to indicate the importance of specific items, thereby revealing their own preferences in these areas. The following questions are taken from Hofstede's IBM attitude survey as an illustration of his methodological approach:

● How important is it for you to have considerable freedom to adopt your own approach to the job? (1–5 scale)
● How satisfied are you with the freedom you have to adopt your own approach to the job?

- How often would you say your immediate manager insists that rules and procedures are followed?
- Respond to the statement that, by and large, companies change their policies and practices much too often (strongly agree through to strongly disagree).

Hofstede's very extensive IBM database drawn from his questionnaire responses included 116,000 participants from (eventually) 72 countries. Additional data has been collected from other populations unrelated to IBM.

Hofstede's theories can be grouped into two areas: the notion of collective programming, in which he sought to explain how culture was made up and maintained, and the 4+1 dimensions which sought to conceptualise differences between cultures.

In collective programming, Hofstede posited that individuals held 'portable' mental programmes which were first developed in early childhood via the influence of 'significant others' such as parents or other guardians. These mental programmes were subsequently reinforced in schools or other influential institutions (eg the media), and ultimately acted out through the values held by individuals from the relevant culture. In his own words (2001, p3), 'It is at the middle collective level that most of our mental programming is learned, which is shown by the fact that we share it with people who have gone through the same learning processes but do not have the same genetic makeup. The existence of the American people as a phenomenon is one of the clearest illustrations of the force of learning: With a multitude of genetic variations, it shows a collective mental programming that is striking to the non-American.' Critically, Hofstede's model then sets out a framework for understanding characteristic patterns of workplace behaviour. We have already considered this underlying approach to understanding culture in Chapter 2.

Hofstede initially put forward four dimensions of culture:

- *Power distance* – the degree of inequality that members of a culture both expect and accept (see earlier discussion of Project GLOBE).
- *Uncertainty avoidance* – the extent to which members welcome uncertainty and change as opposed to desiring structured situations (again the earlier discussion of GLOBE refers).
- *Individualism/collectivism* – individualism indicates the extent to which people in a culture learn to act as individuals and stress their own (or their immediate family's) interests; in contrast, a low index score on individualism (now referred to as collectivism) signals interdependence with wider groups and an associated desire to foster and maintain group harmony.
- *Masculinity/femininity* – the degree to which a culture emphasises so-called masculine values such as competitiveness and performance, or assumed feminine values such as relationships and a concern for the quality of life.

Immediately open to accusations of using outdated and stereotypical perceptions of gender-linked behaviour, it appears that this dimension when applied to countries does expose differences in consumer behaviour. For example, it can be argued that masculine cultures put a stress on car engine power whereas feminine cultures have more coffee-filter-makers per capita! Interestingly, the Project GLOBE researchers did not discard this dimension, but rather refined it in two sub-categories: gender egalitarianism and assertiveness.

3.4 THE CHINESE VALUE SURVEY AND THE FIFTH DIMENSION

Hofstede in his later work located some countries along a fifth (long-term orientation, or LTO) dimension, including all the societies listed in Table 3.2. In the previous section we noted the contribution of Bond, who, together with Chinese academics, first compiled the Chinese Value Survey (CVS), building on a list of values suggested by Eastern scholars. The survey was initially carried out with students living in selected countries. As a result, a new dimension emerged, linked to but separate from the previous four, which was related back to aspects of Confucianism. Hofstede added a fifth *time dimension* as a result (see Hofstede and Bond 1988), which has become synonymous with the term 'Confucian dynamism'. Many cultures scoring high on Confucian dynamism and therefore classified as long-term-oriented were at the time enjoying substantial economic growth, so considerable attention was paid to the possible cultural factors leading to their success. We should, of course, also consider whether such factors have played a role in explaining subsequent leaner economic periods; for example, the Asian recession following financial crises in 1997 (see Chen 2004).

Table 3.2 Hofstede's five dimensions of culture in respect of selected countries

	Power distance	Individualism/ collectivism	Masculinity/ femininity	Uncertainty avoidance	Long-term orientation
Australia	36	90	61	51	31
Brazil	69	38	49	76	65
China	80	20	66	30	118
Czech Republic	57	58	57	74	13
Germany	35	67	66	65	31
India	77	48	56	40	61
Singapore	74	20	48	8	48
Sweden	31	71	5	29	33
Thailand	64	20	34	64	56
UK	35	89	66	35	25

Table 3.2 shows Hofstede's five dimensions of culture applied to selected countries. Scores for the full range of countries can be found in Hofstede (2001), Hofstede et al (2010) and at **www.geerthofstede.com**

In some ways it is possible to argue that the fifth (LTO) dimension reflects differences in thinking on issues beyond uncertainty avoidance, PD and the other dimensions identified by Hofstede – and indeed beyond the specific business implications of taking a short- or long-term perspective. Rather, this additional dimension refers to generic differences between the tradition of analytical thinking in Western societies and the more holistic thinking predominant in East Asia. In East Asia, for example, a new supplier might not necessarily be chosen instead of an old supplier even though the new supplier's price is more competitive. The decision could depend on many other factors beyond price and ability to supply the product, such as historical relations with the old company, third-party references for the new company, and personal relations with executives in the new company.

Such considerations are of course not unique to Asian business – the issue of trust is a very important factor in inter-organisational relations in any society. However, the widely divergent scores apparent in Table 3.2 point to a greater preponderance of the combination of factors making up the long-term orientation in particular societies. As an increasingly major player in global business, China's score of 118 along this dimension is especially worthy of note.

3.5 HOFSTEDE'S LATER WORK

In 2010 a new edition of Hofstede's seminal work *Culture's Consequences* was published. Co-authored with his son, Gert-Jan Hofstede, and the Bulgarian academic Minkov, this edition included a new sixth dimension of culture: indulgence versus restraint. As a new contribution to the culture literature I have included this dimension, along with two others developed by Minkov, in Chapter 4; however, I will also summarise the new dimension at this point to round off our overview of Hofstede's work. A country scoring high on indulgence allows 'relatively free gratification of basic and natural human desires related to enjoying life and having fun' (Hofstede 2011, p15). In contrast, high levels of restraint are found in societies with stricter norms. In restrained societies (amongst other things) there are fewer 'very happy' people, one finds proscribed attitudes to sex, there is less importance attached to leisure and one finds a higher number of police officers per head of the population.

This sixth dimension of culture was included from 2010 as it dealt with aspects of culture not previously covered in Hofstede's model and also to reflect a growing 'happiness literature' both in psychology generally and in people management in particular. In common with the other five dimensions, country clusters were 'mapped'. In this case indulgent societies can be found in South and North America, Western Europe (eg the UK) and parts of sub-Saharan Africa. Restraint characterises Eastern Europe, Asia and the Muslim world (Hofstede 2011).

Two further dimensions of culture identified by Minkov (2007), but not added to the Hofstede framework, are set out in Chapter 4.

3.6 UTILISING HOFSTEDE'S MODEL OF CULTURE

When considered with caution, Hofstede and Bond's model (including its later variants) provides the user with an ability to make qualified assumptions about a culture's values. It is certainly the case that researchers continue to apply the models to individual and comparative settings, while training programmes for international managers also frequently utilise the models as a basis for activities.

Todeva (1999) provides just one example of a plethora of continuing academic research, based on what have now become well-established theories. In her research based on a sample of Polish students, Todeva (p621) concluded that, 'According to students' perception of what is typical for Polish culture, it is medium PD, low uncertainty avoidance, high individualism and medium masculinity. The medium PD means that they believe in equality and shared democratic values. The low UA could be interpreted as a strong support for entrepreneurial activities. The belief in high individualism means that people are prepared to take responsibilities themselves, and the medium masculinity response suggests an attitude of balance and harmony between the personal and the societal sphere.'

Although it is interesting to record Todeva's view that respondents can express different values in response to different research tools, suggesting that specific models and their application can predetermine results, she nonetheless provides one of many seemingly successful applications of Hofstede's model. Almost 50 years after the commencement of his work, it is realistic to claim that Hofstede's dimensions of culture and underlying theoretical stance have now entered the everyday vernacular of cross-cultural business studies.

There is no apparent sign of any waning of interest in Hofstede's research. Instead, we find continuing evidence of the durability of his work. Even so, there is a growing body of criticism highlighting the limitation of his paradigm, which ranges from an identification of perceived anomalies in his data to the fundamental questioning of the models' explanatory usefulness and efficacy. Notwithstanding these reservations Hofstede's work continues, as we have seen with the addition of new dimensions. For example, in the run-up to a significant expansion of the European Union, he was involved in a research programme (Kolman et al 2003) which measured his cultural dimensions in four acceding countries: Poland, the Czech Republic, Slovakia and Hungary. Once more the findings of this study were significant, unravelling both consistencies in the values displayed in these Central European countries and differences between them. The Czech Republic, for example, is distinctive in that it emerges from the research as the most individualist of these four countries, whereas Slovakia (with which it was previously conjoined as Czechoslovakia) is shown as the most collectivist. One can only speculate as to the next wave of societal comparisons which will employ Hofstede's classic dimensions. Meanwhile, new work emerges on an ongoing basis, locating cultural differences between countries and explaining behaviour in terms of central tendencies in values. Research data continues to be extracted from factor and correlation analysis from survey data based on constructed dimensions of culture; see Minkov (2007), whose work we will examine in detail in Chapter 4.

GROUP ACTIVITY 3.2

Look at the corporate websites of two companies, one whose ownership places it in a 'high LTO' society and one originating from a country whose score is low in this regard.

1   Is there any appreciable difference in the statements made on the two companies' websites which could be linked to

Hofstede and Bond's theories? Account also for any similarities between the rhetoric employed by the two companies.

2   How useful in practice do you think Hofstede and Bond's model is in explaining such differences?

3.7 CRITICISMS OF HOFSTEDE'S WORK

McSweeney (2002) devotes an entire paper to a critique of Hofstede's work. Including in the title of his critique the phrases 'A triumph of faith – a failure of analysis', McSweeney identifies four main areas of criticism:

- It is questionable whether Hofstede's IBM employee sample is nationally representative – did the IBM average response reflect the national average?
- Has Hofstede demonstrated that societal-level cultural factors affected the mental programming of his respondents to the exclusion of organisational, occupational and other influences?
- Has Hofstede's questionnaire method captured – or even, could it capture – the dominant dimensions of culture, as was claimed?
- In that the data was restricted to the workplace, it is limited in application and by definition excludes the non-employed from the analysis which followed.

Hofstede (2002) responds directly to McSweeney's criticisms of his work. He states that the IBM data was intended to bring out differences between cultures, and that by using well-matched data, ie from a company with a strong corporate culture and which allowed the inclusion of a large number of countries, such comparisons became meaningful. Hofstede concludes that McSweeney's critique of his research methodology essentially missed the point of what he (Hofstede) was attempting to achieve. Furthermore, and importantly, Hofstede claims that his findings have been validated by other studies, noting 400 significant correlations obtained via a variety of methods, not merely surveys. Readers are encouraged to read the exchange between Hofstede (2002) and McSweeney (2002) to assess the validity of arguments on both sides.

Methodological criticisms of Hofstede's work continue. Venaik and Brewer (2013) conclude that both Hofstede's and the GLOBE culture dimensions, scales and scores are unreliable and invalid. As such, Venailk and Brewer propose that methodological flaws inhibit the usefulness of the data for both management theorists and practitioners. Once again the arguments are intricate and best followed up with a detailed reading; for example, on the question of whether items used to intercorrelate culture dimensions are low and even negative at the level of individuals. Clegg et al (2011, p241) also questioned the validity of Hofstede's methodology in that it resulted in average scores taken from national sample data. The results, according to these writers, are 'similar to saying that the average Dutch person is taller than the average Chinese person – the statement accepts that the average is a summary device. The average tells you nothing about what any Dutch or Chinese person's height may be any more than it informs you about the values he or she holds. An average of values, although it is economical, is about as meaningful as an average of height.'

It is undoubtedly the case that Hofstede's comparative focus, which is shared by most of the researchers who relate societal cultural variables to the workplace, results in a large-scale approach thereby including a very wide range of cultures. In using such an approach he does not attempt to take an ethnographic qualitative stance which focuses on the subjective experience of being a member of that culture. For Hofstede, the value of using dimensions of culture lies in systematically differentiating cultures from each other. Similarly, the criticisms relating to his sampling could plausibly be seen as missing the target in that what was important in Hofstede's results was the extent to which groups differed in a meaningful and consistent way from those in other cultures.

We have already indicated that there is danger in the cross-cultural field of basing models on culturally derived assumptions. This in fairness may be unavoidable, but it should be explicitly acknowledged – which, while it may detract from the perceived universal applicability of the approach, would in practice enhance its relevance. This criticism can be laid at Hofstede's door. For example, his interpretation of masculine and feminine attributes could be seen as strictly derived from a particular time and place, despite his recognition (2001, p279) that 'duality of the sexes is a fundamental fact with which different societies cope in different ways'. Linstead et al (2009) also characterise Hofstede's model as being static and conservative. These authors propose that Hofstede's view of socialisation as occurring through family, school and workplace underestimates the extent to which young people have access to more social networks than ever before via new technologies such as the Internet and mobile phones, thereby enabling them to adopt shifting multiple identities.

It is also possible to criticise Hofstede's tendency to oversimplify complex social phenomena in two ways. Firstly, doubts persist over whether responses to values questions provided in surveys do in fact correspond to the operative values of managers, and even if they do, whether the values held are actually converted into behavioural outcomes. Secondly, the bipolarised approach in itself does not cope well with the diversity, complexity and dynamism of different cultures or give credence to the possible impact of other variables such as institutional frameworks, competitive environment, corporate cultures and sector/industry imperatives. Lu (2012) notes, for example, that Hofstede's work does not incorporate ethnicity and multiculturalism (a critique already put forward in more general terms in Chapters 1 and 2). Lu addresses these concerns squarely at Hofstede's work, giving the example of how Chinese culture is conceptualised. Lu indicates that Chinese culture is often viewed as the culture of the Han people, which does not reflect a multicultural society such as the People's Republic of China (PRC). Research findings which do not incorporate ethnicity and multiculturalism could paint an incomplete and inaccurate picture of the society in question.

Ultimately, there is no better way to gauge the value of Hofstede's work than to read his original books and articles with their wealth of data and insights. His research is the most extensive within the field and his model of culture typically takes a very prominent place in analyses of cultural differences as manifested at work. Buelens et al (2006, p606) in fact go further in stating that, 'The tremendous impact his research had on the contemporary thinking is reflected by the fact that Hofstede is currently the world's most cited author in the entire area of the social sciences.'

3.8 AT THE CORE OF CROSS-CULTURAL STUDIES: KLUCKHOHN AND STRODTBECK'S WORK

We have seen that Hofstede's model of culture points to classifications of societies – usually, but not only, countries – along dimensions which ultimately link back to *values* held by members of a group. His work has gained considerable attention, in part due to his concern with work-related values at a time when cross-cultural aspects of business became highly topical. However, our reverse chronological or 'time-tunnel' approach, which began with a look at a very recent contribution, Project GLOBE, and which was then traced back to Hofstede's work, now leads us even further back in time to the pioneering studies of two anthropologists, Florence Kluckhohn and Fred Strodtbeck (1961), who did not focus on the realm of work. These writers were influential in identifying core elements of culture more generally, which they considered arose from responses and, ultimately, solutions to eternal and universal problems faced by all societies.

Brief summaries of their work can be found in a number of cross-cultural management books, including Tayeb (2003). Hills (2002) examines their model in greater detail and takes a perspective grounded in the discipline of psychology. Kluckhohn and Strodtbeck put forward six value orientations based on how societies typically dealt with the following core issues:

- relationship with nature
- attitudes to time
- views of human nature
- activity
- relationships between people
- space.

Kluckhohn and Strodtbeck's model was formulated as a result of research conducted among five cultural groups including Navaho Native American Indians, Mexican-Americans and members of the Church of Jesus Christ of Latter-day Saints (Mormons), all of whom were at that time to be found in the south-west of the USA. The six generic problem areas set out above are of such a profound nature that they are faced by all social groups and consequently form the basis for a group's values. Nonetheless, it should be recognised that the sixth problem – how to relate to space – was not fully incorporated into their findings.

These anthropologists also concluded that the solutions to these problems could be conceptualised within a range of possible choices. For example, the problem of how to relate to time ultimately comes down to a choice of past, present or future orientations. The problem of how to relate to others is resolved according to either a preference for hierarchical relations, by which people will tend to defer to those they perceive to be in authority, or collateral relations in which the emphasis is on consensus among people who are seen as largely equal – although there is finally a third alternative: an individualistic orientation in which the emphasis is on individuals who make decisions independently of others.

The dimension relating to how we regard nature is worthy of particular consideration at this time. Where groups respond to problems of nature by exercising mastery, they go beyond both being submissive in the face of natural and/or supernatural forces and merely existing in harmony with the forces of nature, to attempting to exert control over nature. The attempt to conquer space resulting in the moon landings achieved by US astronauts has often been cited as an example of the assertive attitude to nature displayed in

American culture. The sharp angles of the Bank of China building in Hong Kong were contrastingly said to have violated principles of *feng shui*, and there have been documented fears that the building's shape will attract ill fortune, thus providing an illustration of the need for harmony with nature expressed in Chinese culture.

However, this dimension can also be related to sub-groups within a single society – as was Kluckhohn and Strodtbeck's original intention. Consider, for example, the following extract from an article from the *Boston Globe* newspaper (18 September 2005), commenting on the devastating floods in New Orleans following Hurricane Katrina, and in so doing drawing attention to the 'Southernness' of the disaster: 'You see a distinct sense of fatalism in the resignation both in advance of and after Katrina in terms of seeing these things as more a matter of God's will than anything under man's control. This interacts with a stronger attachment than most other Americans have to a particular place to produce a willingness to risk death and disaster in a familiar setting.'

If Kluckhohn and Strodtbeck's work continues to find echoes in contemporary world events, their legacy is more in the specific area of cross-cultural organisational studies. In a recent historical review Fink et al (2005, p6) state that, 'The fundamental approach of Kluckhohn and Strodtbeck provided the basic principles for all further research in the area of cross-cultural research aiming at quantitative measures of cultural values. Since the effective research was limited by scope and scale, further research based on Kluckhohn/Strodtbeck offers variation by sample, context and the set of values/dimensions used to describe cultures.' Put another way, their work can be seen as the building blocks on which contemporary models of cross-cultural differences at work have been constructed. No overview of cross-cultural aspects of business can be complete without a thorough appreciation of their groundbreaking work.

3.9 FONS TROMPENAARS' 7-D MODEL: PRACTICAL STEPS FOR DOING BUSINESS

Fons Trompenaars' work on culture – part of which was carried out in collaboration with Charles Hampden-Turner – draws on the central premises of Kluckhohn and Strodtbeck's theories, expanding their dimensions of culture to create seven, which we now come on to review. Before considering Trompenaars' contribution to this area it is also important to recognise his background as a business consultant with an expressed aim to provide practical guidance for managers engaged in cross-cultural business activity. His data is drawn from quantitative questionnaires supported with cluster and correlation analysis. As a result, Trompenaars has created an impressive body of evidence to support his theoretical stance. His work spans 30 years, and is ongoing, resulting in a database with over 50,000 participants, that includes over 50 countries, and has been derived from and reinforced by over 1,000 cross-cultural training programmes.

Trompenaars and Hampden-Turner (1997 and 2004) claim that their work can help managers construct a mental picture of culture which identifies the core assumptions or basic foundations of culture. They note (1997, p8) that 'every culture distinguishes itself from others by the specific solutions it chooses to certain problems which reveal themselves as dilemmas. It is convenient to look at these problems under three headings: those which arise from our relationships with other people; those which come from the passage of time; and those which relate to the environment.' These three areas underpin the seven dimensions of culture in their model.

An important aspect of Trompenaars' work is his questioning of managers on 'extreme scenario' situations – ie how people think they would respond if x or y occurred. As we will see, one part of his model examines the extent to which members of cultures adhere to rules which apply in all situations. The other end of this bipolar dimension identifies cultures where relationships are particularly important, even at the expense of rules. In Chapter 2 we confronted one of Trompenaars' extreme scenarios, namely, when a respondent faces an imagined situation in which they are a passenger in a car driven by a close friend which hits a pedestrian. The dilemma faced by the passenger is whether or not to lie about the accident if the friend asked him or her to. In a further complication, the driver was exceeding the speed limit and requests that the passenger make a false statement about the car's speed on impact. Trompenaars is clearly fond of this specific scenario, since it supplies the title of a 2002 work, *Did the Pedestrian Die?* The point of this additional question is to illustrate the strength of the relationship dimension where the propensity to lie – and by so doing support the friend – is positively related to the severity of the pedestrian's condition. It also has the effect of bringing home the importance of relationship cultures to those at the other, rule-bound, end of this spectrum, who may (wrongly) have assumed that the passenger would only lie if the pedestrian had emerged from the accident relatively unscathed!

The use of the extreme scenario method is certainly evocative in its illumination of the practical ways in which cultural differences might manifest themselves, and it also, importantly, brings into focus the *ethical dimension* of the subject matter (see also Chapter 9). It is furthermore inherent to the underpinning view of culture as deriving from group responses to dilemmas: here the core premise of the concept is mirrored within the methodologies employed in the research.

Trompenaars and Hampden-Turner located societies along each of the following seven dimensions:

- *Universalism v particularism* – Deals with the relative perceived importance of rules which would be applied in all cases (universally) as opposed to those where rules are applied more flexibly and where relationships assume particular importance – as illustrated by the 'pedestrian' story. The USA scores highly on universalism in contrast to China, which is classified as particularist.
- *Neutral v affective* – Cultures contrast those where emotion is 'masked' (neutral), with others in which emotion is displayed openly (affective), in particular within business settings. For example, Trompenaars' research revealed differences in the percentage of his national samples who would not be comfortable with expressing a strong emotion such as distress at work. This figure varied considerably: 74% of the Japanese sample indicating that they would not want to express this emotion in that context, whereas only 19% of the Spanish group agreed with the same statement. There are a number of countries where scores effectively divide the individual populations; for example, the percentage who would not show distress at work in the Indian sample was 51, whereas scores for both Australia and Singapore were 48. These findings, although realistic, pose their own dilemmas for managers who deal with nationals from these countries! Trompenaars goes on to refine this dimension by adding another sub-question: should emotion be separated from reasoning? Does the first vitiate the second? Thus according to Trompenaars and Hampden-Turner (1997, p73), 'Americans tend to exhibit emotion yet separate it from "objective" and "rational" decisions. Italians and south European nations in general tend to exhibit and not separate. Dutch and Swedes tend not to exhibit and to separate.'
- *Individualism v communitarianism* – Examines the extent to which individuals act independently as opposed to expressing high degrees of loyalty within tightly bonded groups. People form into groups in all societies; this dimension contrasts the degree to which people hold a strong shared sense of a greater public or group identification. The dimension is very close to that set out by Hofstede, although Trompenaars makes more frequent reference to managerial implications (1997, p52): 'Practices such as promotion for recognised achievements and pay-for-performance, for example, assume that individuals want to be distinguished within the group and that their colleagues approve of this happening. They also rest on the assumption that the contribution of any one individual to a common task is easily distinguishable and that no problems arise from singling him or her out for praise. None of this may, in fact, be true in more

communitarian countries.' We will look again at the implications of Trompenaars' work for the motivation of employees and human resource management more generally in Chapters 8 and 11.

- *Specific v diffuse* – Cultures contrast in that in specific cultures people compartmentalise their lives. For example, managers and subordinates in specific societies such as Finland and Switzerland may be on informal terms outside the workplace. One of the scenario questions posed to draw out this dimension was 'Would you paint your boss's house?' – assuming that the individual concerned is not a painter by trade. In a diffuse society such as China a higher proportion of employees (68%) would at least consider this unusual request, as opposed to only 9% in Sweden. Another key implication from this dimension is the need to prevent workers in diffuse societies from 'losing face': the casual phrase 'It's nothing personal' is meaningless in the diffuse society context, where everything is linked to everything else and an individual cannot easily separate out the personal from the work domain.

- *Achievement v ascription* – Cultures differ in that in the first status (eg Norway) is denoted by achievement whereas in an ascription culture status (eg South Korea) is more ascribed to a person due to inherent factors such as his or her age or education or social connections. Trompenaars, in common with other academics, recognises that cultural differences emanate from a number of aspects of a society's cultural environment. In this case religious traditions are important, as Trompenaars alerts readers to the presence of the Catholic, Buddhist and Hindu faiths in ascriptive societies as contrasted with the more Protestant background of the achievement cultures.

- *Inner- v outer-directed* – Societies also differ; note that in Trompenaars' more recent work this dimension is renamed as 'internal v external control'. The fundamental question in this case is whether people can control their own environment or merely have to work with it. The origins of this dimension lie very clearly in Kluckhohn and Strodtbeck's work. Trompenaars noted that although no country appeared to believe that it was totally worthwhile to control natural forces (Romania had the highest score, with 68%) there were still significant differences as expressed by his respondents (for example, 42% of his Canadian sample as against only 9% of the Egyptian group). There were also differences in the extent to which people felt that what happened to them was of their own making. Selected scores (on whether people agreed with this proposition) were: Israel 88, Ireland 77, Indonesia 70, Germany 66, Kuwait 55, and China 39.

- *Sequential v synchronic* – Cultures deal with time in different ways. A sequential orientation sees time as linear, comprising a series of discrete events, whereas synchronic perceptions of time are circular, seeing interrelationships between the past, present and future. It is therefore possible to identify societies with a greater overall focus on the past, present or future. In a sequential, time-oriented culture, activities are undertaken one at a time, punctuality is valued, there is a stress on rational planning, and time is measurable – a finite resource to be used effectively. Synchronic cultures are perceived as taking an opposing standpoint on each of these categories.

3.10 EVALUATING TROMPENAARS' WORK

The strength of Trompenaars' contribution lies in its applied focus whereby existing or future international managers are presented with a clearly defined framework within which to consider their own actual or anticipated work experiences. The use of the extreme scenario method results in some richly evocative examples which can be modified to fit more mundane and yet important situations. Trompenaars and Hampden-Turner certainly expected that an awareness of their approach would bear fruit in practical terms, believing that they could help managers structure their real-life experiences and give them insight into frequently experienced difficulties that might occur when dealing with people from diverse cultures.

Most importantly, these writers advocate that managers operating across cultural boundaries should *reconcile* the differences they would inevitably encounter. This is a new departure since without this steer such managers might otherwise polarise or, more commonly, compromise their own beliefs and actions, resulting in a diluted indeterminate cross-cultural management style which is largely ineffective and which satisfies none of the parties concerned. Recognising difference, being reconciled to it and retaining one's own cultural style would be more likely to result in success in the cross-cultural field. The strengths of individual societies' values could in fact be a source of competitive advantage.

In academic terms, Trompenaars and Hampden-Turner are realistic about the role of culture in business. Their country or society scores on individual dimensions are frequently 'middling', which may not propel the managers on their training courses along particular courses of action but do reflect the complex reality of their findings. They also express a guarded view on the role of societal culture at the organisational level, believing (1997, p151) that corporate culture 'is shaped not only by technologies and markets, but by the cultural preferences of leaders and employees', therefore acknowledging that societal culture is only one of a range of explanatory factors to be taken into account in understanding organisations.

There is, finally, an attempt to examine the role of gender in cross-cultural research, after which they conclude that there are some differences in scores which can be attributed to gender, although societal-level cultural influences remained paramount. Nonetheless, there are interesting findings. As Trompenaars and Hampden-Turner (1997, p223) note: 'There is some evidence that the French want their women to be different, while Americans want their women to be the same. The American female manager is more individualist than the male, the French female significantly less individualist.' We are aware that there are some assumptions in this statement which may need unpicking; however, the very recognition of a role for gender in this subject area is welcomed.

Criticisms have also been levelled against Trompenaars' work. Fontaine and Richardson (2003), in a preface to their own research carried out in Malaysia, summarise several critical comments made by Hofstede (1996) and (1997), who has claimed that Trompenaars' dimensions are based on literature emanating from the USA in the 1950s. In other words, the charge is that his dimensions are themselves rooted in a particular cultural context, which casts doubt on their applicability in a worldwide model. Hofstede (2011) has also questioned whether the seven dimensions identified by Trompenaars are self-standing or whether, alternatively, they are essentially sub-sets of one dimension (individualism v communitarianism). The final criticism levelled by Hofstede was that, in contrast to his own work, Trompenaars did not establish a correlation between findings at the individual, organisational and country-wide levels.

Broeways and Price (2011, p106) comment on Hofstede's critique of Trompenaars' work. They note that Trompenaars and Hampden-Turner have acknowledged the influence of Hofstede on their model and record the latter authors' view that their own view of culture sees it as, 'dancing from one end of a dimension to another when encountering various dilemmas'. Broeways and Price conclude that Trompenaars' work therefore contrasts with Hofstede's depiction of culture as linear, with individual countries being positioned either high or low or in the middle of dimensions. They claim that Trompeneaars and Hampden-Turner's contribution is 'a model to learn with' (as opposed to what they see as Hofstede's search for a perfect model).

Notwithstanding the validity of Hofstede's reservations, it is apparent that both he and Trompenaars and Hampden-Turner have worked within the same methodological paradigm, so the comments can be viewed as akin to a theological debate within a religion – the basic tenets are not questioned.

Koen (2005), in comparing the work of Trompenaars with both that of Hofstede and Schwartz (whom we consider next), submits the conclusion that the work of the first-named is overall less academically rigorous. The final comment we will make in this context concerns the extent to which Trompenaars' sample is representative. In that it largely comprises international managers – by definition, comparatively well-educated and travelled – one can certainly level an accusation that the data underlying the model was drawn from a narrow segment of society. Ultimately, much as was the case with Hofstede's data, the key point is that Trompenaars was comparing 'like with like' in an attempt to isolate the impact of culture on attitudes and behaviour so that this one variable would not be confounded by other socio-economic factors.

3.11 SHALOM SCHWARTZ'S UNIVERSAL VALUES MODEL

Schwartz's relatively recent contribution to this area – his work was first published in 1992 and continues to be refined and adapted in current studies – is widely regarded as a significant step forward in cross-cultural understanding. His work offers the promise of particular insights into work values and motivation, and as such is analysed further in Chapter 8. Here, we summarise the work of Schwartz and his colleagues, recognising that their strand of thinking on this subject is likely to be developed further in the future. Dahl (2004) provides a cogent summary of Schwartz's theories on values as they affect culture, and his work is recommended as an alternative source of understanding of a model which has not always been clearly elucidated in the cross-cultural management literature.

The first element within Schwartz's conception of values is his notion of *value types*. He defined values as desired goals which we can envisage as akin to a compass which guides the direction of people's lives. Schwartz identified ten value types, as listed below:

- power
- achievement
- hedonism
- stimulation
- self-direction
- universalism
- benevolence
- tradition
- conformity
- security.

It should be noted that discrete values contain a variety of associated 'sub-principles' which coalesce into a wider combination of values. Dahl concludes that self-direction (to take one example) will be linked to a desire for autonomy, creativity and independence. Such value combinations will characterise an individual over a long-term period, since in his original article in 1992 Schwartz proposed that values would typically be enduring. We could take this further by claiming that within this framework values are 'portable' in that we retain them in the course of our daily lives, leading to the possibility that a particular situation will result in the value's being activated. For example, someone about to leave home for a beauty therapy session, thereby attending to hedonistic concerns, might see an underweight hedgehog in their garden. If their underlying value priority was for benevolence, they would feel compelled to abandon their intended journey and instead take the hedgehog to an animal shelter. Although Schwartz saw the value types as generic to all of us, and indeed overlapping, he also indicated that we place the values in order of the importance they have for us, thereby allowing for very diverse ranking of values.

The second element of Schwartz's work, which is highly relevant for our purposes, concerns the relationships between values. In claiming that some values were less compatible with each other (for example, security and stimulation), he then moved on to the issue of value dimensions.

The two core bipolar dimensions initially identified were:

- *Self-transcendence and self-enhancement* – Where there is self-transcendence we accept others on their merits and may express concern for others' well-being. Self-enhancement, contrastingly, involves the pursuit of self-interest and potentially the exercise of dominance over others.
- *Conservatism and openness to change* – These could again be regarded as bipolar dimensions, the first stressing security, conformity and even submissiveness, and the second stimulation, independence and action.

There is clearly scope to expand this analysis to incorporate cross-cultural comparisons. Sagiv and Schwartz (2000) provide a model which locates a large number of countries along what by this stage had become three classification indices. These are set out in Figure 3.1.

- *Hierarchy v egalitarianism* – A culture veering towards hierarchy (eg Zimbabwe) places emphasis on social power and authority, whereas one closer to the egalitarian extreme (eg Spain) exhibits values of social justice and shared responsibility.
- *Embeddedness v autonomy* – In embedded societies, values include group identification and respect for social order. Derived from the conservatism/conservation index, there is here a desire to prevent fragmentation of groups or the established social order. In autonomous societies there is a preoccupation with self-expression, whether in the intellectual (int) sphere or affective (aff) area; for example, the enjoyment of a challenging and varied life outside work.
- *Mastery v harmony* – Mastery represents a greater effort to control and change the natural and social environment. As can be seen, this applies to Japan in this model. The harmony value when manifested in societies represents a desire to understand and protect the environment.

Figure 3.1 Countries located on Sagiv and Schwartz's three cross-cultural dimensions

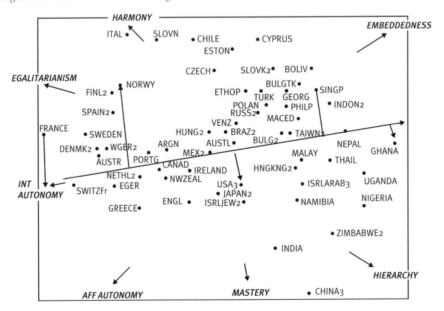

Note: Information in this figure is pre-1990, as, for example, in the references to East and West Germany.

To plot an individual country along any of the bipolar dimensions in Figure 3.1, identify the middle point of the particular line that links the two extreme positions, eg between hierarchy and egalitarianism (see above for further description of the dimensions). The same exercise should be completed for all three dimensions, and a country's position on all three can then be identified.

Having extended the model from the individual to the societal level, it was only a relatively short step to move the analysis back to the national workplace level. Schwartz (1999) has, as a further development of his work, developed data based on the extent of work centrality within a society, postulating that where there is emphasis on mastery and hierarchy, as in Hong Kong and the USA, work itself is more likely to be regarded and experienced as central to life than in those societies plotted towards the relevant opposing dimensions. As indicated earlier, there is scope to apply this finding within the field of managing people. In Chapter 8 we describe the implications of worker motivation.

To take just one example at this point, Fisher and Yuan (1998) report that notions of job enrichment and redesign were perceived to be more important to American workers than to their Chinese counterparts, although it was recognised that this could change with the anticipated economic developments in China.

3.12 A POTENTIALLY VALUABLE DEPARTURE

Although Schwartz's work can be located within a well-established tradition of bipolar constructions of culture based on embedded individual values, his approach is distinctive in several important ways. Respondents were asked to assess 56 values in terms of how they regarded them as deeply held life principles. No scenario or dilemma was indicated as a stimulus for action, so one can anticipate that the respondents were not influenced by the demands of a particular situation. In other words, their values should not have been compromised; save, of course, for the ever-present 'Hawthorne effect' whereby merely being part of a research effort could possibly distort responses. Schwartz also clearly demarcated the individual and cultural levels, by separating out his samples by occupation: chiefly, teacher and student. However, it is possible to argue that the idealised nature of Schwartz's research in itself could have led to unrealistic responses, and we are also – typically in research undertaken on values or attitudes – faced with the difficulty of separating out the cognitive (beliefs), affective (emotional) and behavioural (acting-out) components of the values.

Patel (2014) makes a renewed case for Schwartz's framework as a useful tool for analysing cultures. She concludes that Schwartz's cultural dimensions are linked and integrated so we can conceive of seemingly conflicting values coexisting within any one society. This might accurately reflect the picture of modern diverse societies; more so than the models of other influential writers. Patel also sees potential for explaining behaviour in Schwartz's notion that values are influenced and activated by specific situations and circumstances. This, she suggests, offers scope for understanding how values can play out in action – as opposed to an implicit view of values as pre-determined and therefore unchanging. In summary, Schwartz's work, while offering a classification scheme for understanding cultural difference (a classic etic formulation), also points towards a view of culture, based on values, which is dynamic and open to change.

GROUP ACTIVITY 3.3

It is likely that among your class, or your university/college more generally, there are students of different nationalities. Ask up to six of your fellow students to rank Schwartz's ten value types in terms of their guiding life principles. Include within your sample at least two students from countries different both from you and from each other.

Can you identify any responses which may be influenced by national culture? (Ask your fellow students whether they think this too.) Or are their responses more the result of individual personality differences?

Share your findings with your tutor as part of a discussion of Schwartz's work.

3.13 CULTURAL DIFFERENCES IN COMMUNICATION STYLE

In Chapter 2 we suggested that communication and culture were interlinked in several important respects. Firstly, cultural values are communicated to individual members either implicitly (enculturation) or explicitly. It is also realistic to claim that cultures are sustained through communication between members. Guirdham (2011) took this idea to its logical conclusion by suggesting that cultures would ultimately disappear if the levels of intra-culture communication dropped in inverse relation to frequency of communication with people outside the cultural group.

More generally, whereas the majority of explanations of cultural difference stress the importance of values held by group members – this of course having been one of the main themes of this chapter – an alternative perspective on the topic views cultural difference primarily in terms of differences in the ways people communicate. Particularly relevant in this school of thought is Edward Hall, some of whose work was co-authored with his wife, Mildred.

It is important to recognise at the outset that this approach to the topic raises the possibility of a 'deep' model of culture in which we may not be entirely self-aware of our cultural influences. The role of subconscious forces is integral to the study of, for example, non-verbal communication (NVC). Social psychologists, eg Argyle (1967), hold the view that some NVC (eg gestures or body movements) are in part vestigial examples of early childhood behaviour. For instance, children may hold their hands over their ears when they listen to an unpleasant message. This would be deemed inappropriate behaviour for adults in most social settings. But touching the ear can be understood as a substitute for that childlike response. Importantly, we may not be consciously aware of even making the gesture, let alone appreciating its significance. Hall (1976, p69) applies the same notion to cross-cultural study: 'Frequently we don't even know what we know. We pick expectations and assumptions up in the cradle. We unconsciously learn what to notice and what not to notice, how to divide time and space, how to walk and talk and use our bodies, how to behave as men or women...This applies to all people.'

Hall's entire conceptualisation of culture was as a series of *languages*; for example, the language of time, the language of space and the language of agreements. To pick one part of his framework – the language of time – uncovers some very different assumptions concerning time found across the world. In monochronic cultures such as the USA, UK and Germany, time is regarded as a resource (to be spent); limited and sequential. One practical consequence of adopting this viewpoint on time involves clearing delineated timeslots for particular activities, which is regarded as good business practice within this overall perspective. In contrast, polychronic cultures view time as malleable: it should accommodate events rather than be determined by task achievement, and it is deemed more acceptable to undertake simultaneous tasks. Hall located Latin cultures (both in the European and American continents) as exhibiting polychronic features. Hall also identified differences in attitudes towards time in terms of relative perceived importance of past, present and future. Trompenaars and Hampden-Turner's later work also encompassed time as a dimension of culture, as we have seen.

In respect of a 'language of space', it is widely recognised that cultures vary in terms of acceptable physical distance between people in specific situations (this field is referred to as proxemics). For an American we are told that personal space, when with friends, varies between 18 inches and four feet (45 centimetres and 1.2 metres). Acceptable intimate space is perceived as anything less than 18 inches, while social space (measured against strangers) begins at four feet and extends to 12 feet (3.66 metres). There are two important points arising from this measurement exercise: firstly, that space may be regarded differently across societies (we examine this area again in Chapter 6), and secondly, that such perceptions may not be fully present at the conscious level, thus pointing again to deeper manifestations of cultural difference.

Hall's best-known contribution to the study of culture involved the organisation of his languages of culture into an explanatory model which contrasted high- and low-context societies. We have already referred briefly to this categorisation in Chapter 2. According to Hall (1990, p6), 'Context is the information that surrounds an event; it is inextricably bound up with the meaning of the event. In a high-context society, the context of communication can be equally as important as the content.'

One example of context in communication is the relative power and status of the communicating parties. Guides to business practice in high-context societies often stress the importance of establishing good social relations based on trust and respect. The China ASEAN Business Net in its online business guide to Vietnam outlines a series of steps relating to the exchange of business cards when on a business trip to that country, noting that this behaviour replaces verbal introductions at the start of a first meeting, thus becoming in effect a form of non-verbal communication. The ritual described in this guide – there are clear norms on who to present one's card to first and on the extent to which cards should be read – is clearly intended to establish and reinforce part of the context of the encounter, namely, the communication of status.

Hall characterised high-status societies as having the following features:

- implicit shared understandings among the cultural group
- little coded (ie spoken or written) information transmitted in communication
- indirect communication styles, including great use of non-verbal communication
- relationships regarded as of great importance: an example can be found in the Chinese term *guanxi*, or network of reciprocal relationships.

Additionally, Hall considered that high-context societies regarded time in a distinctive way. There was great emphasis on the importance of the past, and business transactions could take a relatively long time and depend on the build-up of strong relationships.

Low-context societies unsurprisingly contrast on all of these points:

- much information is coded (put into words) in communication
- direct communication style; essentially verbal or written, and including detailed precise information
- low importance attached to the past and an emphasis on concluding business quickly
- significant value placed on performance and expertise.

Although Hall provides a distinctive starting point for his analysis (ie identifying communication as the underlying factor in explaining culture and cultural difference), it is evident that his work has produced some findings similar to those of other writers. For example, the emphasis on relationships and understanding 'the whole person' in his high-context category and the contrasting compartmentalisation of people's lives in the low-context type is similar to Trompenaars' diffuse and specific society model (respectively). Indeed, the underlying issues dealt with in Hall's work could be seen to have their antecedents in Kluckhohn and Strodtbeck's fundamental problems (eg of how to conceptualise time and how to deal with others).

The other commonality which emerges from Hall's contribution lies in his clustering of countries into types, thereby both linking the societies within a group and distinguishing them from those in other categories. It is important to realise, however, that Hall accepted that there are incidences of both high- and low-context communication in *all* societies. For example, within a family or other close social grouping, a great deal of information and emotion can be expressed without the use of words even in a low-context society, while an employment tribunal held in a high-context country will proceed in a low-context fashion, ie by establishing facts.

The following societies are selected from Hall's categories. As is apparent, these can be linked to some extent by geographical region.

- High-context: China, Korea, Japan, African and Latin American countries.
- Medium-context: France, Spain, Greece and Middle Eastern countries.
- Low-context: USA, UK, Germany and Scandinavian countries.

Hall's work provides another reminder for us that because a very high proportion of theory regarding management and business has emanated from one cultural cluster – in this case, the low-context group – and in the light of the fundamental nature of the differences he uncovered, we must question the worldwide applicability of much of the business studies canon.

Many of the generic criticisms of cross-cultural work in this area can be seen to apply to Hall, including the scientific status of his work in terms of obtaining the original data and some measure of over-generalisation in both his findings and consequent clusters: accepted personal space, for example, is different in the UK and USA, which are, however, clustered together in Hall's work.

3.14 REVIEWING HALL'S WORK: RECENT DEVELOPMENTS

There has been renewed interest in Hall's work from 2011, with contrasting views put forward on the value of his specific work and overall approach to understanding culture and cultural difference. Kittler et al (2011) reviewed literature relating to Hall's high- and low-context model. These authors found that research based on Hall's model, identifying societies falling within the high-/low-context classification, was based on weak and unsubstantiated findings. They concluded that there is no comprehensive list of countries within each category. Research based on Hall's original dichotomy had a USA/Asian bias with Arab and African countries 'blind spots' in the data. Kittler et al also identify a number of countries which have been classified as both high- *and* low-context societies, including the USA and India. Other research did, however, support Hall's original classification. Kittler et al (p78) conclude, however, that, 'virtually all studies that utilized HC/LC country classifications are based on less-than-adequate evidence and stem from dated, unsubstantiated claims, which can even be traced back to Hall's own anecdotal-evidence based classification'. A critique of methodology (as we saw when evaluating Hofstede's work) should be taken seriously, although it is possible that even if we accept the critique, Hall's work may contain underlying truths and serve as a useful starting point for ordering our thoughts on culture and how to connect with other people.

Warner-Soderholm (2013) also draws attention to limitations in Hall's work. She identifies ambiguity in Hall's concepts which makes them difficult to apply via quantitative research. A further problem is that Hall offered no ranking to show where individual countries are positioned along the high-/low-context continuum. Warner-Soderholm develops a new scale in order to 'resurrect and quantitatively measure Hall's cross-cultural dimension' (p34). The scale was derived from Likert-type responses; in this case along a seven-point range from 'completely agree' to 'completely disagree'. One statement used for this purpose was, 'In our region we like to say it as it is.' Warner-Soderholm carried out her research in Norway, receiving 714 questionnaires electronically from Norwegian individuals working in Norwegian private sector companies. This contribution is interesting both in its validation of Hall's classification – in this case pointing to difference between regions in Norway – and also the scope it offers for a more quantitative treatment of what hitherto has been a topic studied via subjective methods and even relying on anecdote.

APPLYING THEORY TO PRACTICE 3.1

In 2002 the Hong Kong and Shanghai Banking Corporation (HSBC) introduced a worldwide advertising campaign which defined this banking group as 'the world's local bank'. This highly successful campaign included advertisements run on British television, which showed how cultures differed via a series of cultural misunderstanding scenarios. One such advert depicted a Western businessman in an unspecified Asian location who is taken out for a meal by his hosts. He considers it polite to finish eating the food offered to him, while his hosts interpret him clearing his plate as a sign that he is still hungry. The upshot is that he is presented with more and more unusual dishes which he does not want to eat, but continues to do so.

HSBC wish to portray the world as a rich and diverse place in which local cultures need to be recognised and respected. The advertisements stress the importance of communication in cross-cultural encounters. It is possible to see echoes of Hall's characterisation of high- and low-context cultures in the scenario depicted in the HSBC televison advert. Consider also the relevance of Trompenaars' classification of culture to this situation, for example his distinction between neutral and affective cultures.

3.15 CONCLUSION

The emergence of cross-cultural management as a topic area is a relatively recent development which was given huge impetus with the publication of Hofstede's seminal work, *Culture's Consequences*, in 1980. Hofstede's contribution, together with much subsequent work, can be characterised within an etic perspective, involving the identification of differences between cultures, or more accurately, between clusters of cultures, on the basis of core dimensions – for example a society's degree of individualism as opposed to collectivism. Soderberg and Holden (2002, p107) characterise this notion of culture as, 'a relatively stable, homogenous, internally consistent system of assumptions, values and norms transmitted by socialisation to the next generation'. The etic approach provides a useful framework for managers to consider the nature of culture, cultural difference and the key importance of cross-cultural awareness.

The etic approach to some extent inevitably precludes in-depth analysis of individual cultures, and also neglects the forces accounting for change, while it has been argued that an etic perspective solidifies cultural differences by highlighting them while offering only limited guidance on how to make cross-cultural teams work effectively. All of these points will be addressed more fully in Chapter 4 when we turn to analyse alternative approaches to cross-cultural management that have emerged in the early twenty-first century.

One final interesting point to note when evaluating etic models of culture involves questioning whether there are, paradoxically, ethnocentric assumptions underpinning the models; for instance, concerning the choice of dimensions which form the building-blocks for comparing cultures. It would be interesting, to take one example, if a Chinese professor in the late 1970s had formulated a model based on bipolar dimensions. One could reasonably anticipate that the categories selected would have been fundamentally different from those addressed by the writers considered in this chapter. Furthermore, it is arguable whether such a hypothetical model could have adequately explained Western management and work organisations, based as it would have been on Chinese cultural assumptions.

CASE STUDY 3.1

NORWEGIAN VALUES IN THE AIR AND ON THE GROUND

Norwegian, part of the Norwegian Group, is an airline which in 2014 was the second largest carrier in Scandinavia and the third largest low-cost airline in Europe. Its corporate website (**www.norwegian.com/uk/about-norwegian/our-company**) contained a section on 'Vision', which in turn included a brief summary of some of its core values. The website also had a section on 'Human Worth'. The following paragraphs are extracts from these parts of the company website:

'Norwegian values are simplicity, directness and relevance. Everyone has a joint responsibility to create a good working environment and develop a sound corporate culture marked by openness and tolerance.

'Norwegian supports the international human rights as outlined by The UN Declaration and Conventions. No one shall in any way cause or contribute to the violation or circumvention of human rights. We place great importance on ensuring compliance with employees' basic human rights as outlined by the International Labour Organization's core conventions.

'Equality must be guaranteed between men and women in terms of employment, working conditions and remuneration.'

Read the case study above, and respond to the following questions. In answering keep in mind Norwegian's status as an airline, which grew up and is headquartered in Norway.

Questions

1   Locate Norway within Hofstede's model of culture. Account for the preceding statements from Norwegian's corporate website with reference to Norway's position and scores on Hofstede's dimensions of culture.

2   With reference to material from Chapters 2 and 3, state how accurate you would expect Hofstede's analysis of Norwegian culture to be and identify three criticisms of his work.

3   Identify some non-cultural factors that could have influenced Norwegian's organisational culture, and in particular, the values set out in the above statements.

4   Which of the factors identified in your responses to Questions 1 and 2 do you think are the most significant in shaping Norwegian's expressed values? Give reasons for your answer.

REVIEW QUESTIONS

1   What do you understand by the etic approach to cross-cultural management? Provide two examples from academic sources to illustrate your answer.

2   What are the distinctive features of Hall's model of culture and cultural difference? Show how his model can be applied to work situations.

3   Indicate how people from different cultures may exhibit differences in preferred communication styles. Refer to both academic sources and your own experience when answering.

FURTHER READING

HOFSTEDE, G. (2001) *Culture's consequences.* 2nd ed. Thousand Oaks, CA: Sage. There is no substitute for the original! Read what is widely acknowledged as the seminal work on the subject.

KOEN, C. (2005) *Comparative international management.* Maidenhead: McGraw Hill. In Chapter 2 the author provides a scholarly analysis of major models of culture which includes an in-depth discussion of methodological issues.

MINKOV, M. (2007) *What makes us different and similar: a new interpretation of the World Values Survey and other cross-cultural data.* Sofia: Bulgaria: Klasika i Stil Publishing House. This book will be useful as further reading covering Chapters 2, 3 and 4 of this textbook as it provides both a new model of cultural similarity and difference and an alternative review of previous research in this area.

Visit this book's companion website (**www.cipd.co.uk/olr**) to find further exercises including self-assessment questions and also weblinks to media and academic journal articles.

CHAPTER 4

Models of Culture: Developments and Debates

LEARNING OBJECTIVES

After reading this chapter you should be able to:

- consider the relative impact of national culture on work organisations
- appreciate the trends for cultural convergence and divergence and the growing importance of diversity management within work organisations
- identify limitations of existing frameworks for understanding culture and cultural difference
- understand several emerging alternative approaches to cross-cultural management.

4.1 INTRODUCTION

In Chapters 1 to 3 we highlighted the assumptions which underpin popular models of culture within the field of business and management studies. It is apparent that much of the cross-cultural academic work that has been applied to the business context is predicated on the construction of bipolar dimensions of culture and consequent location of individual nation states along these dimensions; for example, placing countries on comparative scales listing items such as 'uncertainty avoidance' or 'universalism'. Although there is some acknowledgement of the impact of culture shift, the mainstream models of culture set out in Chapter 3 broadly view the concept as relatively stable, consistent and measurable. This conception of culture enables societies to be firstly categorised and then compared with one another. The fundamental focus is therefore on intercultural difference. Cross-cultural management as a subject has, unsurprisingly, taken its bearings from the existing research canon as practising managers are concerned with evidence and 'what works'. The result has been a preoccupation with the twin themes of, firstly, understanding how culture impacts in the business setting, and secondly, the need for cross-cultural sensitivity in interpersonal encounters. In both cases the 'raw data' of the subject has usually been extracted from the picture of cultural differences painted by writers such as Hall, Hofstede and Trompenaars.

The intention in this chapter is to revisit the theoretical assumptions of these mainstream models of culture in greater detail and depth and also to highlight and examine some alternative emerging models of culture. In addition, there will be some further unpicking of the methods employed in research studies which informed some of the most hitherto popular models, which have increasingly been questioned in newer contributions to the subject area.

Many textbooks in this area contain only sparse reference to 'deep' theoretical and methodological assumptions when analysing frameworks purporting to explain cultural difference, instead providing broad summaries encompassing the main features of such models. While this is useful to some extent, a more evaluative approach should foster an appreciation of the inherent validity of the mainstream models and hence their applicability in actual situations. A meaningful critique of the underlying assumptions of existing cross-cultural theory also ties in with an analysis of changing insights which have informed some new work in cross-cultural management in the period from 2000 to 2015. One might expect no less given the massive recent changes in the business environment, including profound emergent forces of globalisation, convergence and divergence. Fang (2003, p364) makes this point vividly: 'Geert Hofstede is a great scholar of our times; he has been inspiring us to catch up and move on. Culture is full of life, energy, complexity, diversity and paradox. Our cross-cultural theories should capture such dynamism.'

Before turning to evaluate the mainstream models of culture in greater depth, I will revisit the core issue of the actual impact of culture, by assessing its role in explaining organisational processes and activities in the light of potentially counterbalancing non-cultural factors. This will be followed by an examination of globalisation and cultural convergence with a suggestion that these forces have led to a new domestic stage for cross-cultural management alongside an accelerating focus on diversity in the workplace.

4.2 NON-CULTURAL EXPLANATIONS

In Chapters 1 and 2 it was suggested that although there is consistently strong evidence to support the view that culture can impact on work organisations in a profound way, it was also necessary to balance this view by examining data which points to a less important role for culture.

Firstly, we can refer to the contingency theories of organisation which posit that policies and practices within organisations are influenced by a range of contingent factors. The key message emanating from this approach is that there is no one best way of organising or managing; rather, it all depends on the external variables impacting on the organisation. Hickson et al (1974) provided evidence to support this idea. In a cross-cultural study they discovered that organisations in different societies but of a similar size and operating in equivalent markets and with the same technologies would in fact look remarkably uniform in terms of their structure: cultural influences would be secondary to the other contingent factors impinging on their operations.

However, their findings were questioned by Child and Kieser (1979) who, in an Anglo–German comparative study, concluded that while organisations' structures may indeed look alike on paper, in reality there were different interpretations of managers' roles and contrasting beliefs on the desirable extent of delegation. In practice, German employees would have greater autonomy than might be denoted by a formal organisation chart, in part because senior managers are content to delegate, and also because of the impact of an institutional feature, namely the national system of industrial democracy evident in Germany, which again may not show up from an examination of a formal organisation structure diagram.

Maurice et al (1980), in undertaking a French–German–British comparison, also found that institutional-level factors were significant in influencing organisational forms. For example, the prevalence of British specialist professional bodies such as the Chartered Institute of Personnel and Development (CIPD; at that time known as IPM), and similar marketing and accounting bodies led to a greater preponderance of specialised managers in UK organisations. We return to these studies and their possible implications in Chapter 5.

This brings us to the second approach which questions the impact of culture as manifested in different values or communication styles. This proposes that system effects – that is, features of the political economic system in a particular country – exert the dominant influence on work organisations in that society. These effects range from the nature of the economic system in place (eg free-market or mixed economy, open or closed) through the political framework (multi-party democracy or one-party hegemony) and further down through the industrial relations system underpinning work relations; for example, the extent of trade unionism and the powers available to unions.

While this institutional approach may locate societal differences at another level – although even the values approach acknowledges the impact of the macro level via formal socialisation – it by no means plays down the extent to which societal differences are found in reality. We have already referred to differences between countries in the European Union in Chapter 2 (for example, legislation reducing working hours in France in contrast to other member states). It would also be difficult to claim that distinctive US, Swedish and Japanese political and economic systems have not resulted in significant variations in workplace policies and practices which have a real impact on the day-to-day experiences of employees.

The next school of thought indicating that cultural differences may be less important, and indeed diminishing, emerges from literature examining the phenomenon of globalisation. 'Globalisation' is a broadly defined term, with significant implications for the subject matter of this book arising from the greater interconnectedness of people within the business setting. However, globalisation can also refer to greater homogenisation of brands, products and services which have the potential to minimise cultural difference, at least in the outer or surface layers. The increasing influence of multinational corporations (MNCs) could also affect culture at the level of organisational practice. It is certainly possible to identify some standardisation of organisational life across the world resulting from the influence of global corporations such as Disney or McDonald's (although even in these cases one can see some adaptation to local cultures). One can nonetheless argue that the effects of globalisation are felt by only a narrow band of any population, and that the phenomenon has by no means spread across the entirety of the globe. Even if we accept that globalisation has resulted in major changes to organisational life, its continued spread is not guaranteed and there are groups mobilising in opposition, as seen for example in the protests at the G20 meeting in Los Cabos, Mexico in June 2012. Finally, it is feasible to regard the effects of globalisation as manifested more at the levels of systems and structure than behaviour. The mantra 'think global, act local' is still prevalent in a great deal of business rhetoric at the time of writing.

If globalisation is more likely to impact at the macro level, we should still recognise the possibility that it can result in changes to people's values and beliefs. This could be liberating or constraining for the individual. Grint (1998, p298) offers two alternative visions of such a scenario: 'At last we are approaching an era where what is common between people transcends that which is different; where we can choose our identity rather than have it thrust upon us by accident of birth.' This is as opposed to a scenario in which 'We are heading for global convergence where national, ethnic and local cultures and identities are swamped by the McDonaldisation and/or Microsoftisation of the world' (p298). Either vision of the future shows that globalisation can be experienced by people 'in their heads'. In Chapter 2 we located the idea of 'crossvergence' (Tung 2008) whereby managers made a choice to adopt some new values when encountering a new culture, while at the same time making the decision to hang on to some of their original values. The notion of crossvergence can provide a useful staging post as we reflect on globalisation's spread and impact.

Finally in this regard, we should keep in mind Inglehart and Baker's thesis (see Chapter 2), which proposes that cultural values follow on from economic developments in all societies. If we accept this, it is possible to view cultural differences in terms of the economic stage reached by an individual society at an identified point in time. The particular values exhibited at that time are then likely to change following further economic development, albeit in subtle and (paradoxically) unpredictable ways.

4.3 CONVERGENCE, DIVERGENCE, GLOBALISATION AND CROSS-CULTURAL MANAGEMENT

It is commonly held that the processes contained within the term 'globalisation' have both increased interactions between members of cultural groups and at the same time led to some degree of homogenisation between cultures. Needle (2010, p12) summarises this widely held view in the following way: 'Globalisation is a process in which the world appears to be converging economically, politically and culturally. Globalisation is seen by many as a fundamental change where national borders become irrelevant, a process accelerated by developments in information and communications technology. It is considered by many to be the dominant force in modern business.'

In Chapter 2 it was suggested that globalisation has clearly led to some harmonisation between societies in the outer or surface layer of culture. For example, in Asian countries one can find ample evidence, particularly among younger people, of the adoption of Western dress and musical taste along with a more general brand awareness, reflecting supra-national patterns of consumer behaviour. However, this level of convergence is not a new phenomenon and in any case allows for concurrent and potentially wide differences in the deeper layers of culture with their associated core values. Reference was also made to the introduction of business philosophies and techniques across cultures; for example, the spread of Japanese concerns with quality assurance and a more 'hands-on' approach to management. At this stage it is deemed necessary to expand the debate on globalisation and possible resultant convergence, unravelling what is still a speculative and often confusing picture of the interplay between convergence and divergence and the implications of globalisation for cross-cultural management. The starting point for this analysis should be a review of how globalisation has itself been conceived.

Globalisation refers to an apparently escalating process of inter-connectedness across parts of the world. This process has been given a huge impetus by advances in electronic communication. Clegg et al (2011, p583) find an important expression of technology-driven global interlinking in the current worldwide financial system, noting that 'The global integration of financial markets collapses time, creating instantaneous financial transactions in loans, securities and other innovative financial instruments, while the deregulation and internationalisation of financial markets creates a new competitive spatial environment. Globally integrated financial markets increase the speed and accuracy of information flows and the rapidity and directness of transactions.'

Such a manifestation of globalisation also leads us to an appreciation of two further realities of the concept. Firstly, there is a sense of interdependence in that events in one part of the world are profoundly affected by actions taking place in far-distant places. Secondly, events influencing economic and business life may increasingly occur supra-nationally in 'real time', with individual country-based actors shown to be relatively powerless in the face of international (or even virtual) knowledge generation and information processing. Events have shown that global financial markets are, at times, more important than nation states. One example was so-called 'Black Wednesday' in 1992 when the British Government was forced to leave the European Exchange Rate Mechanism, membership of which was central to its economic strategy, due to co-ordinated activity on international money markets by speculators selling the Sterling currency. Such co-ordinated activity was, it is claimed, facilitated in part by 24/7 instantaneous trading.

It is crucial to appreciate that globalisation is not merely the latest incarnation of internationalisation. Banerjee and Linstead (2001) are among several commentators who point out that international penetration of foreign markets was greater pro rata in the early years of the twentieth century than at its end. However, the speed and complexity of current global communication, coupled with increased mobility due to enhanced transport links (at least those between countries!) have, it is claimed, resulted in a new phenomenon whereby globalisation (in Giddens' (1990) phrase) has led to intensification of worldwide social relations.

What, then, does the advent and rapid advance of globalisation mean for the study – and practice – of cross-cultural management? It should be clearly stated at the outset that the impact of this phenomenon is by no means consistently felt. Whereas it has always been the case that some organisations, and their workforces, remain largely untouched by the effects of globalisation, at least directly, Sorge (2004, p136) indicates that 'Internationalisation of economic exchange also entails an intensification of the international division of labour. Countries have come to specialise in sectors, industries or their segments, or in product-market combinations. When they do, the implication is that the properties of business systems may become more locally specific, rather than following a more international model.' The paradox here is that the spread of globalisation may in fact *reinforce* local difference. Nor is there any kind of fixed logic by which globalisation is seen to reduce cultural difference or determine managers' actions when dealing with different groups.

The debate on the relative influence of globlisation is complex and continues to evolve with increasingly subtle explanations. In 2014 Bond and O'Byrne identified eight facets of globalisation. Some facets, for example 'McDonldisation' – again characterised as standardisation of practices and processes within a drive for efficiency – did indeed result in convergence. However, others such as 'Balkanisation' (the division of the world into distinct and conflicting blocks) had the opposite effect. Readers with an interest in business strategy are encouraged to read Bond and O'Byrne's work as the authors conclude that the differing facets of globalisation have important implications for the development of business practices.

In earlier chapters we have examined models which claim that the deep-rooted nature of culture means that norms, values and ways of communicating still vary across cultural groups in a relatively consistent way. This point will be supported in subsequent chapters looking at individual topics. It is also the case that globalisation can affect how individual organisations view and experience culture, which can vary enormously. In a paradoxical sense, globalisation can both increase and at the same time decrease culture's importance to an individual organisation. Crowther and Green (2004, p200) elaborate on the reasoning behind this seemingly symbiotic relationship as follows: 'One of the most important factors affected by globalisation is the significance of culture to organisations, making it both more important and less important. It is less important because the dominant culture of any society becomes less significant to an organisation. Similarly, the organisational culture becomes less important because of the way it must necessarily change in an era in which the organisational boundary is less important and more subject to change. It is more important because of the need to recognise different cultures across the world and the way they affect established *mores* of organising.'

We have already considered the concept of crossvergence in earlier chapters and it is useful to refer to it again at this point. Ralston et al's (1997) study of four countries – the USA, Russia, Japan and China – tested their earlier (1993) premise that there was a middle ground between cultural convergence and divergence. We have already identified both ideas. The former proposes diminution of cultural difference due to forces for homogenisation, eg converging technologies. The latter view, exemplified by Hofstede, regards the core of culture as stable and long-lasting. Ralston et al (see also Ralston et al 1999; Egri and Ralston 2004) have conducted a series of studies focusing on different countries showing how economic ideology, political systems and technology all played a part in accelerating and inhibiting convergence. In summary, crossvergence tells us that we discard some cultural values while consciously retaining others.

The foregoing points are not intended to confuse the reader but will hopefully serve to counsel against taking a simplified and deterministic view of the links between globalisation and cross-cultural management, because these are in reality multi-dimensional and unpredictable. Future research in the cross-cultural management area should also build on models of divergence and convergence which envisage these forces as developing in dynamic motion and in a complex interrelated fashion. Students and practitioners will not benefit from one-dimensional thinking on these topics.

4.4 A NEW DOMESTIC STAGE FOR CROSS-CULTURAL MANAGEMENT?

Much of the writing on cross-cultural management has taken as its primary focus either multinational/transnational corporations, particularly when they enter new national markets, or companies involved in international strategic alliances or joint ventures. These important situations are also referred to in this book, particularly in Chapters 6, 10 and 11, because it can be argued that such scenarios continue to provide rich material for cross-cultural comparison. Anyone whose current job involves them in these ventures or who wishes to progress to a career in this aspect of international management should also gain valuable and applicable knowledge from such material.

However, it is proposed that another aspect of globalisation has been relatively neglected in the literature – namely, labour flows across the world, whether of professional 'knowledge workers' or skilled manual employees filling local labour shortages, or even those occupying the secondary labour market, possibly without legal worker status. Although national labour laws can reduce these labour flows, it is normal in many countries to find culturally mixed workforces within 'domestic' single organisations. This trend has resulted (certainly in the UK) in an emerging literature on managing diversity.

4.4.1 DIVERSITY AT WORK

There are different aspects to diversity which encompass differences in educational background and work experience, and also diversity in terms of personality and attitudes. Each of these could be linked to a person's culture. For our purposes in this book, however, the focus is on another dimension of diversity – namely, that centring on social categories, including race, ethnicity and nationality. Diversity management can crucially encompass the management of cultural difference, but also, and more importantly, it emphasises the sharing of knowledge and experience to be gained from a diverse workforce within the aim of securing added value for all parties. It should be acknowledged that this approach is self-evidently restricted to workplaces committed to its implementation – the sweatshops, brothels and houses with 'unofficial' domestic help sadly remain beyond its scope and off the radar of most academic studies.

A CIPD report, *Managing diversity: measuring success* (2006), notes that the concept of diversity embraces both a concern with securing distributive justice for individuals based on their membership of wider categories and a desire to foster a sense of inclusiveness within organisations for such (and indeed, all) individuals. In terms of this second aspect of diversity, the CIPD report (p3) suggests that 'To avoid high turnover rates in a diverse workforce, appropriate culture changes are needed to create a more open and comfortable environment in which everyone fits in, feels valued and can contribute their best. Rigid, traditional workplace cultures tend to exclude non-traditional employees and can undermine business performance.'

Pilbeam and Corbridge (2010) summarise the business case for managing diversity, which includes enhanced customer relations, cost-effective employment relations and enhanced creativity and innovation, while acknowledging (p249) that, 'The business case for diversity is complex and difficult to quantify.' Allard (2002) identifies disadvantages of diversity management programmes, including blocks on decision-making within diverse groups, miscommunication, ambiguity, and actual resistance from members of majority groups. The 2006 CIPD report locates research showing that where diversity programmes are put into effect, white males react more negatively than women or ethnic minorities, and display symptoms of demotivation. Nonetheless, there appears to be a consensus in the business studies literature regarding the overall benefits of recognising and harnessing diversity within workplaces, linked to what are in ethical terms broadly accepted negative consequences should managers ignore the area. Christy and Brown (2009, p80) conclude that, 'Workers who are new to a business where an alternative culture prevails, based for example on ethnic or religious grouping, could find themselves in a hostile work environment where unethical victimisation, harassment, loss of dignity, bullying, ignorance, prejudice, stereotyping and discrimination may arise.'

In view of the impact of increased flows of labour across the world, a major part of cross-cultural management involves effective management of diverse employees. French et al (2011, p31) record examples of increasingly multicultural workforces in many locations noting, for example, that, 'Australia and New Zealand are among the more multicultural countries in the world. Almost one in three members of the workforce in major Australian cities such as Sydney and Melbourne was born outside Australia...managers – whether or not they are directly involved in international business – must be able to manage people from different cultures effectively and make the most of the advantages that a diverse workforce can bring.' Such figures are indeed striking and bring home the scale of this social trend.

Multinational corporations, in particular, have come increasingly to regard workforce diversity as integral to their success. As Allard (2002, p14) points out: 'In international ventures diversity is not an option – it is automatically part of the package, and some sort of diversity management framework is a necessity.' Yet multiculturalism within countries, together with further movement of labour, should now expand the scope of cross-cultural management to the domestic sphere. This preoccupation is by no means limited to business organisations. The *Independent* newspaper edition of 26 July 2006 carried a front-page story describing a primary school in East London (recently the subject of an excellent report by government inspectors) in which pupils speak 52 different home languages. Andrew Morrish, the school's headmaster, is quoted as saying, 'It's like a micro-world – we have got children from all corners of the globe. Our success story is how children who have witnessed really traumatic events, people being blown up and shot in the street, how they have assimilated in school.'

Here we see a real-life test bed for cross-cultural management in a single location – one could argue in the most important type of organisation of all. While much of the teaching and learning activities in this school will undoubtedly involve intercultural communication, there must also be elements of wider cross-cultural management within Holden's conception of this set of activities as needing to provide 'direction and purpose to the cross-cultural activities of people [in order to] facilitate their interactions to achieve organisational goals' (2002, p293). It is recommended that the study of cross-cultural management should increasingly move from an emphasis on the experiences of global expatriate managers to an attempt to understand the everyday reality of life in an ever-growing number of domestically anchored organisations which are influenced by globalisation through the identities of their members.

Much of the most recent writing in the field of cross-cultural management, very possibly responding to the social trends outlined above, has recommended that academics should in future refocus the scope of their studies to reflect this new business reality. Jackson and Aycan (2006, p11) express a hope that contributors to one leading journal will address 'cross-cultural interactions and interfaces at multiple levels including, inter-continental, inter-national, inter-ethnic, inter-group and inter-organizational levels'. Gelfand et al (2007, p499) state that a new research paradigm should involve a shift from 'the study of intracultural comparisons to the study of the dynamics of cultural interfaces in multicultural teams, in negotiations, and in global companies and mergers and acquisitions'. The debate on where cross-cultural management plays out in reality and which arena should now form the location of cross-cultural research points to a sea change in thinking in the new century.

GROUP ACTIVITY 4.1

Phillips pushes the equality agenda

Substantial movements in the labour market means equality is 'more critical than ever'.

Equality is 'more critically significant to our success as a society than ever before' because of substantial movements in the labour market, according to Trevor Phillips, chairman of the Commission for Racial Equality.

'In the UK, half of all migrants arrived in the previous generation and a third in the past decade,' Phillips told delegates at the CIPD's employment law conference. 'This indicates the scale of change. There are about 200 million international migrants across the globe – twice the number there were 25 years ago. There is also huge churn. Figures from the Office for National Statistics for 2004 show that half of all migrants left the UK within five years of arriving – so people are coming and going faster. They are also more diverse.'

As a result, Phillips said, the task of the new Commission for Equality and Human Rights would be to 'ensure that equality and diversity continue to sit together'.

Source: *People Management*, 27 July 2006.

1 List reasons for the 'huge churn' of migrants remarked on by Trevor Phillips. Refer to business and other media sources when compiling your answer. To what extent should this 'churn' be seen as a problem for work organisations?

2 If you were a manager charged with helping to assimilate migrant workers within a work organisation, would you give higher priority to arranging cross-cultural awareness training for indigenous employees or implementing a diversity management programme? Give reasons for your answer.

4.5 EVALUATING BIPOLAR VALUE-BASED MODELS OF CULTURE

The contributions of Kluckhohn and Strodtbeck (1961), Hofstede (1980), including his later collaborative work with Bond (1988) and Hall (1990), Schwartz (1992), Trompenaars (1993) and the GLOBE research dating from 2002, provide the bedrock of cross-cultural management theory. The central messages of each of these important contributions are set out in Chapter 3. It is important to recognise the overarching rationale of these writings, namely, that cultural differences are located in the ways that people think and in their preferred values and preferences for dealing with particular situations. Moreover, all of the aforementioned approaches to culture attempt to capture and gauge cultural differences with reference to *dimensions of culture*. This has resulted in the bipolar categories previously referred to, which it is claimed identify the critical differences between cultures. As noted by Fink et al (2005, p8): 'Researchers on cultural value dimensions imply that their system of value dimensions is explaining a large part of the observable variances across cultures.'

While acknowledging that individuals may respond in unique ways to their own socialisation, these mainstream models of culture conclude that there is sufficient 'collective programming' (to use Hofstede's oft-quoted phrase) within societies for the essential focus to be on comparison, ie a search for differences between cultures. However, this is not the only philosophical and methodological stance that can be taken, and there are a number of writers who question whether the 'comparative value dimensions' school of thought does in reality deliver the richest – and most accurate – analysis of culture.

4.6 UNDERSTANDING CULTURES IN THEIR OWN TERMS

Fang (2003, 2012), in looking back at cross-cultural research in business over decades, questions the validity of previous work analysing culture by locating polarised dimensions. Fang examines Chinese culture using indigenous knowledge and as a result comes to question whether Hofstede's analysis, and in particular Hofstede and Bond's (1988) five dimensions of culture, reflect the richness and complexity of Chinese culture. We noted this possible line of critique when considering Hofstede's work in Chapter 3. Yet Fang goes further through a more general questioning of the comparative perspective on culture, which we have previously referred to as the etic approach. As mentioned earlier, attempts to locate meaningful intercultural comparisons and to identify clusters of similar societies form by far the larger part of the research effort in this area, certainly as applied to business and management. It is important, though, to recognise the existence of an alternative approach stressing the *distinctive essence* of individual cultures. Koen (2005, p55) describes this contrasting view as the emic approach, concluding that this viewpoint 'emphasises the need to understand social systems from the inside and through the definitions of its members. It attempts to analyse the internal coherence of single examples and condemns any attempt at classification across cultures as denying the uniqueness of each culture.'

The emic approach also necessitates the use of particular research methods when conducting actual studies in this subject area. Research within this tradition seeks a way to 'understand culture from the native's point of view' (Lu 2012, p109), so methods used are likely to vary considerably from the survey-based work that underpins the mainstream etic approaches.

Fang (2003) traces the development of Hofstede's fifth dimension of culture (see Chapter 3 for a fuller account of its genesis, including the important contribution of Michael Bond). He claims that the original term 'Confucian dynamism' put forward in Hofstede's 1991 work and which initially appeared to be used interchangeably with the concept of long-term orientation (LTO) had by 2001 evolved into a fully fledged fifth dimension, itself containing another bipolar construct for comparing societies along a long-term v short-term continuum. However, Fang questions whether another bipolar dimension can in any meaningful sense capture the essential features of Chinese culture as they impact on the business sphere. For example, he casts doubt on the assumed prevalence of long-term thinking in Chinese business practice, suggesting (2003, p355) that, 'An inside look at the Chinese business psyche reveals that short-term orientation, such as opportunity-driven behaviours and heavy reliance on cash transactions to expedite business deals, has been a salient Chinese trend throughout history. Running after short-term commercial interests without long-term vision in business ethics is an overriding problem of mainland Chinese business enterprises.'

Fang's reference here to an inside look at the Chinese psyche is interesting because once again the clear inference is that an emic or intra-cultural analysis may result in more meaningful research data. Yet Hofstede had been sensitive to the dangers of imposing culturally bound classification measures when developing his fifth dimension, which had been specifically intended to engender a deep understanding of Chinese culture. Hofstede (2001, p352), in reviewing the genesis of this element of his work and in particular the contribution of Michael Bond, noted that, 'Recognising that the results of surveys designed by Westerners are necessarily biased by the designers' Western minds, Bond decided to introduce a deliberate Eastern bias. He asked four Chinese colleagues from Hong Kong and Taiwan to prepare in Chinese a list of at least ten "fundamental and basic values for Chinese people". So how can it be that such an attempt to locate values of one culture can be criticised both on its own terms and as an underpinning for a wider bipolar comparison with other cultures?'

Fang puts forward the following criticisms of Hofstede and Bond's fifth dimension of culture which resulted in the emergence of the long-term v short-term classification measure.

- Bond's Chinese Values Survey drew excessively on Confucianism, other philosophical traditions such as Taoism and Buddhism being relatively neglected as influences on contemporary values. In this sense Fang is suggesting that an emic or intra-cultural analysis may itself – possibly inevitably – result in an incomplete picture of the essential features of a specific culture.
- Possibly as a result of an over-reliance on Confucianism in terms of explaining Chinese culture, the list of 40 'fundamental values' excludes other core values which can equally well, or even better, explain Chinese business values and behaviour. One such omission for Fang was *guanxi*, a term that is analysed in depth below.
- The data for the Chinese Values Survey was obtained from university students. Fang proposes that even within an emic research study there should be a concern with how representative a survey sample is, and in this case he suggests that the student population may have been, in important ways, less conservative than an alternative more balanced sample population. This point is addressed again later in the chapter in the context of wider methodological issues.

Perhaps the most profound criticism of Hofstede and Bond's work put forward by Fang is that the division of cultural dimensions into divergent poles – in this case long- or short-term orientation – goes against what is for Fang the most fundamental aspect of Chinese culture, the *yin-yang* concept. He expands on this notion (2003, p363): 'The *yin-yang* philosophy suggests that human beings, organisations and cultures, like all other universal phenomena, intrinsically crave variation and harmony for their sheer existence and healthy development. We are "both/and" instead of "either/or". We are both *yin* and *yang*, feminine and masculine, long-term and short-term, individualistic and collectivistic...depending on situations, circumstances and time.'

In 2012, Fang took the concept of *yin-yang* further, proposing that it could serve as a way to understand all cultures. In other words, we are invited to consider a *yin-yang* perspective on cultural dynamics which can allow for people holding 'multiple cultures in their minds and switching between representations of cultures' (Fang 2012, p45). Fang offers a radical shift in cultural theory, which not only explains Chinese culture, which has been an area of intense focus, but also shines a new light on all cultures, if we accept his conclusion that culture *per se* comprises, 'opposing, paradoxical and potentially incompatible cultural values' (p45).

It may be that in this holistic and harmonious concept we see a new way forward for cultural explanation both within and between cultures, and this line of reasoning is explored again in Chapter 11. At this point we can note that Hofstede and Bond's fifth dimension, which began as an attempt to construct an in-depth model of one particular culture, ultimately evolved into a device for comparing cultures and, in the opinion of Fang, led to a 'philosophical flaw', namely, the undermining of a key element of the culture under scrutiny. For in his view any bipolar scale must profoundly misunderstand and misrepresent Chinese culture. Nonetheless, it does not follow that all emic or intra-cultural studies must develop into etic or comparative models, and the emic approach has significant potential in terms of both evaluating individual cultures and providing guidance for people dealing with that culture in a business setting.

Even if we do not yet fully take on board a *yin-yang* model of culture, such an emic approach can inform and enhance our understanding of mainstream models. For example, in Chapter 1 we referred briefly to the work of Yin Fan (2000), who developed 71 core values springing out of Chinese culture and which, interestingly, would find expression by Chinese people wherever they lived and worked, ie not just in predominantly Chinese societies. Fan attempts a tentative comparison with Hofstede's dimensions of culture and finds that while some of the 71 core values can indeed be mapped on to Hofstede's model, many others cannot, suggesting that an analysis of a unique culture (in this case the Chinese) may reveal important aspects which fall outside a comparative typology. We now go on to explore this point in more detail via analysis of one commonly identified feature of Chinese culture.

4.7 AN EXAMPLE OF THE EMIC APPROACH – *GUANXI*

The concept of *guanxi* looms large in many analyses of Chinese culture. In the twenty-first century the emergence of China as a major economic power has led to a renewed preoccupation with this important feature of Chinese life. Although it is interesting to record that the Chinese Values Survey which formed the basis for Hofstede and Bond's summary of Eastern culture did not include *guanxi* among the 40 values listed, this omission can now be seen as exceptional. Chen et al (2013) summarise research on Chinese *guanxi* over the preceding 20 years and locate over 200 journal articles on the subject, attesting to the great curiosity towards what is perceived as a significant part of the way that business is conducted by Chinese people wherever they are located.

Chen et al (2013) distinguish between three distinct streams in *guanxi* research. The first focuses on the interpersonal dimension, including antecedents, outcomes and factors influencing the quality of *guanxi*. The second dimension addresses the organisational level, eg business-to-business (B2B) and firm-to-government *guanxi*. The third – and most recent – stream examines social and moral dilemmas within a focus on the ethical dimensions of this phenomenon. Readers are recommended to look at this article to gain an appreciation of the scope of the phenomenon.

Chen (2004) devotes an entire chapter in her book on Asian management systems to an extended analysis of the interpersonal side of *guanxi* and its effects on business processes. She notes (p4) that, 'Anyone who has had experience in dealing with the Chinese could hardly fail to observe that Chinese people attach great importance to cultivating, maintaining and developing *guanxi* (connection or relationship). Anyone who has associated with the Chinese at even a minimum level would easily notice the Chinese sensitivity to "face" and *renqing* (humanised obligation) in their daily life. These traits are shared by the Chinese living not only in mainland China but also in Taiwan, Hong Kong and other overseas Chinese societies all over the world. Simply put, these three concepts of *guanxi*, face and *renqing* are the keys for understanding Chinese social behavioural patterns and their business dynamics.'

All three of the Chinese cultural characteristics mentioned by Chen are addressed later in this book when discussing specific topic areas; for example, intercultural communication in Chapter 6. At this stage the purpose is to highlight their importance within more general frameworks for understanding culture and cultural difference. The view put forward here is that a concept like *guanxi* is an integral part of one specific culture and cannot readily be moulded to fit superimposed models of culture which originate from another part of the world.

Guanxi is defined as referring both to interpersonal relationships and connections. It therefore denotes both a special relationship between two people and a more widespread network which guides an individual's social world. A *guanxi* relationship is inherently reciprocal in that both parties can trust the other to be committed to their joint interests. This commitment is expressed in practical ways; as Chen (2004, p45) notes: '*Guanxi* binds people through the exchange of favours rather than through expressions of sympathy and friendship. The *guanxi* relationship does not have to involve friends, although this is often preferred. The relationship tends to be more utilitarian than emotional. The moral dimension functioning here is that a person who fails to observe a rule of equity and refuses to return favour loses face and looks untrustworthy.' It is possible to understand the importance of *guanxi* within Chinese culture by reference to comparative etic-style models of culture. Thus the preoccupation with reciprocity in human interaction could be seen as indicative of a relationship culture – to use Trompenaars' term – while the search for mutually beneficial networks could be linked back to the perception of China as a collective culture put forward by a number of writers in the field.

It is proposed here that *guanxi* should, however, also be viewed as indicative of a specific element within a unique culture. Chen (2004) gives an in-depth account of how *guanxi* forms part of the Confucian philosophy which is underscored by the principle of social harmony. This in turn links to the notion of 'face', which underpins interpersonal encounters in Chinese culture. An individual must protect, maintain or even gain face when interacting with other people. *Guanxi* can therefore be an important means for guarding against loss of face. *Guanxi* is in fact so intrinsically bound up with Confucianism that it feels highly inappropriate to interpret its perceived behavioural consequences within a model of culture emanating from Europe. To characterise *guanxi* as evidence of a group-oriented culture underestimates the centrality of social bonds within Chinese society. Chen (2004, p47) provides an evocative illustration of this point: 'The Chinese character *ren* consists of two components, one illustrating a human being and the other depicting the number two. As this implies, *ren* refers to the way people relate to each other. In other words, man cannot exist alone and must be able to interact with others. *Ren* as the highest virtue of Confucianism would be meaningless if not understood in the context of the social interactions among men.'

In conclusion, therefore, an in-depth understanding of *guanxi* – and, of course, of its effects in business encounters – may best be gained by reference to the emic tradition of cultural analysis, involving understanding a culture 'from the inside' and through the interpretations of actors from that culture. Even when we focus on culture at the institutional level, an etic approach contains powerful advantages. As an example, Child (1998) records an absence of commercial laws in China, leading to the possibility of great uncertainty when engaging in inter-organisational alliances in that country. He notes that as a result, high trust between parties is of paramount importance and that implicit and tacit agreements assume a critical role. He claims that this institutional setting both reflects and reinforces a situation where *guanxi* flourishes.

Nothing in the foregoing section is intended to state or imply that comparative etic models of culture are worthless or even seriously flawed: rather, what is proposed is that insights derived from such mainstream models should be combined with, and evaluated against, an alternative perspective which takes as its main focus an in-depth approach focusing on individual cultures both at the level of individuals' meanings and institutional frameworks.

 INDIVIDUAL ACTIVITY 4.2

Contracts or *guanxi*?

Companies from outside China entering the dynamic Chinese market are often faced with a choice of different strategies and tactics for doing business. Luo (2002) describes a proactive strategy centring on networking or *guanxi*, opening up the possibility of an escalating reciprocity of favours. The main alternative highlighted is the defensive strategy of using rigid contracts to minimise uncertainties. The author advocates the use

of a blend of both strategies, claiming that they are in reality complementary and that both have to be used in any case. He notes (p297) that, 'Contracts counter the threats of opportunistic behaviours of local business partners and alleviate the hazards from disturbing competitive environments. These benefits reduce an MNE's transaction costs. *Guanxi*, however, facilitates an MNE's adaptation, localisation and legitimacy. It increases revenues by obtaining institutional support and reciprocal assistance from suppliers and buyers.'

There is some suggestion that *guanxi* is declining in importance as more universal business practices have become widespread since China's entry into the World Trade Organization, and following efforts made at government level to guard against perceptions of impropriety. The current and future importance of *guanxi* is being openly questioned in some quarters.

1   What do you understand by the terms 'opportunistic behaviour' and 'facilitating

adaptation, localisation and legitimacy', as used in Luo's article? Provide one example each of how both phrases might take effect in reality. In what ways could the use of *guanxi* and contracts be complementary?

2   How realistic in your view is it to expect *guanxi* to decline in significance within Chinese business in the period up to 2025? Give reasons for your conclusions, referring to material set out in Chapters 1 to 3 of this book.

4.8 A TIME FOR NEW RESEARCH METHODS?

In Chapters 2 and 3 it was suggested that previous cross-cultural research studies, several of which underpinned influential theoretical models, could be open to some level of criticism on methodological grounds. Hofstede, in an attempt to compare like with like, based his main research on one organisation, from which he derived average country scores. While Hofstede allowed for genuine differences within each country sample, therefore claiming that his methodology resulted in a realistic picture of any society, Clegg et al (2011) question the value of these average scores to an explanation of individual attitudes and behaviour. It is also unclear whether respondents in some research studies were representative in terms of gender and age: the latter point is of potentially critical importance in detecting possible culture change. Schwartz's work is exempt from this critical comment in that his sample comprised teachers and students, mostly differentiated by age. However, this choice of category is itself questionable in that it is restricted to the educational sector. Similarly, Trompenaars' work was drawn from data obtained from management workshops, again bringing the issue of generalisability into play.

All of these criticisms stem from the researchers' attempts to delineate cultures and to highlight significant differences between them – this being the essence of the etic approach to the subject. The etic theoretical stance necessitates the use of a methodological approach in which the primary aim is to identify matched samples in different societies, achieved through holding certain variables constant, eg the type of organisation or employee. The sample data is then compared with that obtained from similar populations in other countries in order to locate significant differences which could be culturally based. But, as previously noted, even the most rigorous attempts to control some variables in order to isolate the impact of culture have been censured for omitting others, while large-scale projects such as those led by Hofstede have been criticised for their very scope, in that important individual variations could be hidden within the researchers' concluding average score data.

The emic approach to culture, contrastingly, suggests that an entirely different methodological stance is more suited to research efforts in this field of study. Long-term observation of a single group has a venerable tradition within anthropology. Ethnographic research within this discipline has frequently involved the researcher's engaging in observation or participant observation (becoming a member of the group under study). This research tradition enables a deep understanding in a natural setting, although one has to place considerable trust in the reliability and objectivity of the researcher. There has been a comparative dearth of studies conducted within this tradition in the area of business and management, although Kluckhohn and Strodtbeck's 1961 work examining five ethnic groups within the USA (see Chapter 3), while not itself dealing with work situations, has played some part in informing thinking in cross-cultural aspects of business in more recent years.

D'Iribarne (1997) questions whether the survey methods typically used within etic studies of culture do in fact provide realistic pictures of cultural differences and the ways in which these operate in practice. He concludes that Hofstede's classification of France as a high power distance (PD) society arises from a juxtaposition of hierarchy and power. D'Iribarne's view is that a steep hierarchy need not result in a concentration of power at its top levels, so actual experienced PD in France may be considerably different from that as deduced from Hofstede's work. D'Iribarne goes on to attribute what he sees as Hofstede's skewed conclusion to the questions posed within Hofstede's research programme. In particular, an expressed preference for democratic styles of management is, according to D'Iribarne, interpreted by Hofstede as a reaction to the experience of autocratic styles.

However, there are alternative interpretations, and D'Iribarne's own research, which looked at single plants within countries – in his case France, the Netherlands and USA – led to quite different conclusions, including the actual isolation of senior French managers due to steep organisational hierarchies which left them dependent on the practical knowledge and expertise of their subordinates. D'Iribarne accordingly calls for a different style of more ethnographic research in the cross-cultural field involving observation, document analysis and open interviews which, he claims, could more accurately reflect the reality of working life in – and consequently the wider categorisation of – particular societies. In later work in 2009, D'Iribarne elaborates on this idea noting that within single countries, life is characterised by a common concern, but that concern is unique. In France he claims that a central concern 'that one should have to bend to somebody's will, by fear or by interest' (2009, p319) will find expression in the words people use when talking about their experiences. A single-country focus can unravel 'a dimension much more local, given concretely to singular situations' (p319).

Yet, as we have seen, the etic approach and its associated methods of study have been and continue to be prevalent. Perhaps, though, it is time for a change in this regard. Just as it is suggested that a resurgence of the emic approach can reinvigorate this subject area at the current time, so its associated research methods could be activated in order to provide a richer, deeper picture of culture and cultural variation than currently exists following several decades of domination by the etic tradition.

Tsui (2004) made a plea for more country-specific studies in a wider range of societies, in order to rebalance the spread of knowledge in cross-cultural management across the world. She records the overwhelming dominance of thinking emanating from Europe and North America in the field. There is undoubtedly scope to develop work based on some parts of the planet hitherto neglected in the literature. In this chapter, for example, it can be seen that many examples cited so far relate to China, reflecting the great interest shown in this (from the Western perspective) fast-growing key economic player. This reflects the often skewed nature of geographical coverage in cross-cultural management. Tsu expresses a wish to see this gap filled by single-country studies from South America and other developing regions. She furthermore sends out encouragement for so-called indigenous research which does not seek merely to test an existing model in a new context, but rather aims to develop new theories in new contexts.

4.9 SENIOR MANAGERS AS THE OBJECT OF STUDY?

Thompson and Phua (2005) applied Hofstede's dimensions of culture, and their consequent impact on attitudes and values, in a study of 'Anglo-Saxon' and Chinese managers operating in the Hong Kong construction industry. In formulating their research, they hypothesised that senior managers might comprise a distinct group exhibiting characteristics which separated them from average employee populations. Furthermore, these researchers speculated that actual decisions made by managers may link as much to task and business imperatives as the managers' cultural background. Following a study which included up to 398 respondents, Thompson and Phua (2005, p65) concluded that there was no evidence of expected cultural norms, but rather that, in contrast, 'Senior Chinese managers exhibit no significant differences from their Anglo-Saxon counterparts in terms of collectivism or cooperation, and even manifest significantly lower in-group identity than Anglo-Saxons. Moreover, Chinese managers, contrary to what Hofstede's categorisations would lead us to expect, are associated negatively with collectivism and intra-firm cooperation.'

There are important conceptual implications which could be drawn from this study and its main findings. It may be, for example, that the Anglo-Saxon managers' values have changed when operating in the new context, which points to the impermanence of such values. Alternatively, Hong Kong may have quickly evolved from a Chinese society (with all that implies) to one which has taken on a wider range of cultural influences. Finally, it is possible to infer that senior managers conform to a separate set of cultural norms, set apart from those previously associated with countries or geographical clusters.

This last point relates most closely to the current discussion on research methods within cultural studies. It is possible to argue that senior managers (with their particular ability to influence corporate policies and practices) should be studied as a separate group if average employees' scores do not, in the event, adequately reflect managers' own values and behaviour. This point can be inverted in that a more exclusive focus on senior managers in some research studies would free up others to look at the everyday work experiences of non-executive workers, possibly using more ethnographic methods. These studies could also be free from possible constraints arising from a managerial perspective. In particular, it is possible to argue that a more realistic picture of work organisations would be obtained – and this in turn should lead to a situation in which managers can make better-informed judgements.

Grey (2013, p7) refers to the paradoxes and ironies of referring to managerialist writings as follows: 'The managerialist-positivist camp, for all their desire to speak effectively to the world of practice, have consistently failed to come up with anything of much use to managers or others, a fact for which they are consistently criticized and over which they themselves persistently agonize. Whereas the constructionist critics at least provide an account which is recognizably about people in organizations, rather than the abstract statistical hypothesis testing of their more mainstream colleagues.' Without entering into a deconstruction of the terms used by Grey, there is very definitely a case for a new focus on ethnographic non-statistical work in the cross-cultural management field, in order to reinvigorate the field in academic terms and to provide more meaningful data for practitioners. In recent years there is some evidence of research studies which have moved away from a focus on top management, and by implication, a view of culture as embodied in key actors through socialisation which then becomes solidified within work organisations through top–down decision-making. Soderberg and Holden (2002, p108), in contrast, suggest that, 'cultural differences are manifesting themselves in new ways: for example, in the working environment of a multicultural project team collaborating across geographical, organizational and occupational boundaries and involving e-mail interactions and video conferences, maybe even with a foreign language as their "lingua franca".'

4.10 SOME EMERGING THEORETICAL APPROACHES

4.10.1 CULTURAL STANDARDS

Fink et al (2005) propose that cross-cultural studies could profitably examine actual norms of behaviour which emerge from value dimensions, noting that whereas values may appear to be the same across cultures, what they call 'available norms of behaviour' can differ. They propose that the notion of 'cultural standards' in which a person in reacting to a specific situation will consider the views and judgements of others and may seek to behave within the parameters set out by specific people and their own culture more generally, would be especially relevant in understanding the reality of cross-cultural encounters. Fink et al suggest that a key part of cross-cultural research involves the identification of critical incidents found to occur in cross-cultural business interactions. However, they cast doubt on the extent to which existing models of culture do capture the reality of these real-life situations, suggesting (2005, p11) that 'general culture concepts with 4 to 11 dimensions from Hofstede (2001) to Schwartz (1992) have limited predictive value for the coping capabilities of individuals with difficulties in cross-cultural encounters'.

In terms of our focus in this chapter on methods of study, Fink et al diverge from many previous researchers in their use of narrative interviews in which they asked respondents to tell short stories detailing real (critical) incidents from their own past experiences. These stories were then given to cultural experts who had lived and worked in either the home or foreign culture. The experts were asked to interpret the events depicted in the respondents' stories. One aim of involving experts in this way was to reduce interpretation biases and to strip out incidents which were the result of non-cultural factors. The reference to cultural standards does take the subject forward in terms of looking at actual behaviour rather than speculative examples of how values could be operationalised in the workplace. The methods used are reminiscent of Trompenaars' discussion of scenarios; however, there is a crucial difference in Fink's exclusive focus on situations that were actually experienced. The cultural standards approach represents an emerging school of thought with the potential to further illuminate the area of cross-cultural business.

4.10.2 CROSS-CULTURAL LEARNING AND KNOWLEDGE-SHARING

Holden (2002) is another contributor to the sphere of cross-cultural management who has sought to redefine the scope of the subject while putting forward a different model of culture. He criticises what he sees as the classical essentialist model of culture which has been predominant within the cross-cultural management literature. This view of culture is characterised as comprising stable and consistent categories, centred on values and norms, which distinguish cultural groups – mainly, as we have already seen, focusing on individual countries. Holden (p28) questions the currency of this traditional approach, recording his view that, 'This essentialist or functionalist view can be valid if we want to understand the characteristics of a particular cultural system, such as a country or company, but when, as in everyday international business practice, cultures clash and fuse with each other in myriad ways, the concept is unhelpful: it is virtually programmed to exaggerate the differences between cultures and to generate criteria to rank them competitively.' Holden declares that mainstream models of culture, exemplified by Hofstede's work, have resulted in an excessive preoccupation with the identification and management of cross-cultural differences.

Holden goes on to reformulate a view of culture that is relational, based on shared meanings and interpretations by members. He goes on to propose that (2002, p56) 'These patterns of meaning are produced, reproduced, and continually changed by the people identifying with them and *negotiating* with them in the course of social interaction.' Culture as exhibited at national, organisational, professional or any other levels is both changing and diffuse in that the boundaries between cultures may frequently dissolve and reappear elsewhere. The task of cross-cultural management for Holden is to manage the many cultures existing both at intra- and inter-organisational levels, with particular reference to knowledge transfer and continuous learning. This for him involves (p285), 'a significant shift from cross-cultural management seen as the management of cultural differences, in which these differences are all too often represented as inescapable vortices of corporate undoing. Part of the shift entailed regarding culture, or rather cultural inputs, as an object of knowledge at the organisational level of analysis.'

Holden's work has particular resonance for us in that his conception of culture points to a critical role for managers' competencies including cultural know-how (we return to this theme in Chapter 10). Furthermore, there is an implication that the terrain of cross-cultural analysis should be at organisational level. Holden casts doubt on whether it is appropriate to refer to cross-cultural management across national cultures at all, which is a clear departure from most previous work in the field. Holden's work takes the subject forward in that while he recognises that cultural values are still important, it may not be possible to be aware of the values held by all people in a diverse multicultural team. Furthermore such knowledge would not, in any case, be sufficient to explain actual events. What is more important for Holden is, to reiterate, the need to provide situations (including structures) which allow cross-cultural learning and knowledge-sharing.

4.10.3 CROSS-CULTURAL COMPETENCE AND LANGAUGE

Magala (2005), in a wide-ranging treatment of cross-cultural management, firstly conceptualises culture as a language in which people express themselves, as a result of which they become aware of meanings. He views cultural learning as analogous to breaking a code, both linguistic and behavioural. In order to function in a society it is necessary to both communicate complex messages and respond to them. In this sense, language can be viewed as a system of signs. If we accept the views of linguists such as de Saussure, language is both signifier and signified – the latter element enabling concepts to be communicated and understood. From this perspective one can go on to link language to culture in that it too transmits meaning and maintains the assumptions held by a particular group of people.

Magala also links language to cultural competence. He notes that expatriates' children develop a dual cultural identity, becoming fluent in two cultures and languages including expert use of non-verbal communication forms such as touch and gestures (see Chapter 6 for more detail in these areas). While children find this process easy – as Magala puts it, they learn tacitly and spontaneously – adults (for example, managers on an overseas secondment) may have to be prepared in a more formal way. However, cultural competence overall is likened to linguistic fluency, within the underlying view of culture as itself constituting a language.

Holden (2008, p242; see also Holden and Tansley 2008) makes a strong case for language to be brought centre stage within cross-cultural management, noting that, 'management cannot be conducted without words: words often with long histories and *always* with moveable meanings in any language and variable meanings among them. This relationship between management and language is waiting to be examined through the systematic comparative study of management terminology in various languages.' Holden (2008) puts forward examples to substantiate his view, recording Japanese managers' use of language to create and sustain an atmosphere that is conducive to harmonious relationships. We could, in this context, locate this finding within the notion of Japan as 'collectivist', a 'relationship culture' and 'high context', terms (from Hofstede, Trompenaars and Hall respectively) that are covered in Chapter 3. Bringing language into view at this point could therefore be seen as akin to shining a torch on a familiar object, but from an alternative viewpoint. A language perspective offers the possibility for ongoing explanation into new situations. Holden highlights recent developments in Russia, suggesting that the Russian language was unable to take on the vernacular of the market economy and that the frequent use of proverbs might result in people easily reverting to past situations. There is therefore a suggestion that Russian business terminology might evolve as a sub-language; what Rathmyr (2004) referred to as 'russgligskii', an odd mix of Russian and English language.

The importance of this notion is reinforced by a suggestion that the adoption of a hybrid language could be critical in political and economic development in creating a melting pot in which attitudes and values could ferment and prosper.

The unique language of German organisational life

The German term *Der Akadmiker* can be translated simply as 'an academic': a person working in academia. This would miss some subtleties, however, as the term has additional layers of meaning with significant behavioural consequences. It denotes a person with university-level education who has considerable prestige. This aspect of the term is specific to German culture and is, in an important sense, untranslatable. An *Akadmiker* may also feel that he or she can behave in a manner reflecting this high status. In German universities the phrase *akasdemicshe Viertel* refers to a period of time (typically 15 minutes) that elapses before an *akadmiker* appears to deliver a class – it is a form of legitimised lateness. Some German students speculate that this lateness is staged: the *akademiker* uses a relaxed attitude of time to convey their superior status.

Here we see how unique language not only conveys a specific feature of organisational life in a particular society, but also in itself both denotes and reinforces distinctive ways of behaving based on an individual's self-awareness of nuances in their own culture.

4.10.4 SOCIAL IDENTITY APPROACH

We have already stated that mainstream models of culture view the concept as underpinned by shared values and norms, which tend to exist over a long period of time as they are passed on from one generation to the next thorough socialisation. While all writers on culture prudently allow for some measure of culture change (or shift), mainstream perspectives hold that culture is something that a society exhibits and which its members belong to. French et al (2011), in analysing organisational culture, draw attention to multiple perspectives on the subject area. While many contributors to the area see organisational culture as comprising shared values and beliefs, French et al identify competing approaches which question the reality of such conformity. Alternative perspectives include the differentiation approach, which proposes that different groups within an organisation might have different values; at least from time to time. This could apply to groups differentiated by function, location, or demographic variation; for example, gender. This raises the possibility of the existence of sub-cultures or even counter-cultures. We have acknowledged the existence and impact of such groups when analysing national cultures in Chapters 1 and 2. French et al also highlight the ambiguity/ fragmentation approach when considering organisational culture. This approach questions the existence of clearly defined patterns of culture. In place of shared meanings we instead see meanings interpreted by individuals in random ambiguous ways. These meanings might be widely shared – but not necessarily – and change is continual and by definition difficult to plan.

Soderberg and Holden (2002, p112) make similar observations with reference to national cultures, stating that these are, 'produced, reproduced, and continually changed by the people identifying with them and negotiating them in the course of social interaction'. Futhermore, one can suggest that people identify with different cultures. A person can have multiple identities; for example, a Polish female, single, Catholic marketing manager. Any one of these identities forms only one part of this woman's life. If we accept the tenets of social identity theory, it clearly poses some important challenges to mainstream treatment of culture and its role in work organisations. It would certainly imply a down-playing of national culture as explanatory variable. Soderberg and Holden propose that the future of cross-cultural management (as set out earlier in the chapter) should lie in the management of multiple cultures rather than highlighting differences based on more static conceptions of culture. These authors also conclude that if individuals have multiple identities then any communication and negotiation is intercultural. So, paradoxically, while the focus of cross-cultural management may need to shift and take place in a new arena, it actually becomes more important and prevalent than ever before.

4.10.5 THE STRESS AND COPING APPROACH

The interlinked concepts of stress and coping are increasingly visible within the study of cross-cultural management. This has come about in two ways. There is, firstly, a connection with intercultural competence and, in particular, the notion of culture shock or acculturative distress. We will examine this concept closely in Chapter 9 within a summary of the personal sphere of cross-cultural management, which has especial resonance in the experience of sojouners (much of the literature dealing with expatriate managers). It has been claimed that the experience of working abroad habitually results in situations in which we experience some measure of psychological distress, possibly resulting in us questioning our values and even conceivably losing our sense of identity. In as much as stress is normally defined as a force emerging from the environment which interacts with an individual producing strain, there is certainly reason to suppose that the experience of cross-cultural managers may well be a potentially stressful one. We will also see in Chapter 9 that success in cross-cultural work has been linked to 'adaptation behaviours'; in other words, coping strategies. In Chapter 1 I suggested that a high proportion of the academic and management literature in cross-cultural management has been devoted to the topic of culture shock. While some of the assumptions in this literature will be questioned in Chapter 9, there is little doubt that stress and coping are important concepts with clear practical implications.

Some writers also conclude that people in different types of cultures have different characteristic coping or control strategies when confronted by stressful events. The roots of such work can be traced back to Triandis (1989), who identified differences in how 'the self' was conceptualised across the world. The self here is identified by Triandis (p506) as consisting of 'all statements made by a person, overtly or covertly that include the words I, me, mine and myself'. The self, following on from this broad definition, is broken down into private, public and collective elements. Triandis found that in collectivist societies the collective self could be identified with more readily; the reverse, of course, being true of individualistic societies. Reasons for these patterns included child-rearing – with parents in collectivist cultures giving greater weight to obedience, reliability and 'proper' behaviour, while parents in individualist contexts are concerned to instil qualities of self-reliance and independence. It is also the case that individualistic cultures tend to have smaller family sizes allowing children more leeway to 'do their own thing' (the one-child policy in collectivist China would be an interesting test bed to see if this holds true). These are relative trends as some degree of obedience, etc is required by parents in individualistic cultures and vice versa. Trinadis's main contribution is to locate the self as a source of behaviour and then extend his analysis to cross-cultural comparison.

Tweed et al (2004) conclude that culture is related to ways of coping with stressful events. Based on research involving students of different descent (namely indigenous Canadian, European Canadian, East Asian Canadian and Japanese exchange students), these authors located important variations in coping strategies. They note that European Canadians and Asian Canadians all incorporate aspects of externally targeted control into their coping strategies but that those from Asian backgrounds are more likely to engage in coping strategies involving internally targeted control. What does this mean in practice? Internally targeted control involves an attempt to control the self when faced with stressful situations whereas externally targeted control, contrastingly, occurs when an individual tries to control or alter the environment. Tweed et al refer to Hofstede's work, citing his view that people from societies where PD is high are more likely to accept situations *per se*. The cultural map of a society also comes back into view here as Tweed et al suggest that Buddhist and Taoist beliefs respectively stress the inevitability of suffering and the need to adapt oneself to the rhythms of nature. It is also possible to hear echoes of Trompenaars' distinction between inner- and outer-directed cultures and Schwartz's mastery v harmony dichotomy in Tweed et al's findings.

We see here that this new focus on stress and coping brings forward practical recommendations when analysing culture shock, while the comparative study of coping mechanisms, more generally, has resulted in a reversion to more traditional etic style models in order to explain a contemporary phenomenon in comparative terms.

4.11 WHAT MAKES US DIFFERENT AND SIMILAR? A NEW INTERPRETATION

We have seen that much of the traditional cross-cultural management literature views culture in terms of cultural values as central tendencies located along continua. An individual country's profile can then be categorised by reference to identified dimensions and then compared to that of other nation states. As we have seen in this chapter, there has been some reaction against this core idea, particularly after 2000. However, the focus on cultural variation has an enduring appeal and new work continues to emerge which is very much within this tradition. Minkov's (2007) recent contribution to the cross-cultural management literature provides an excellent example. Minkov (2007, p18) makes a renewed case for the value of nation-level dimensions, noting that, 'No matter what cooking method you use, the important thing is to be aware of the properties of the dish that you have cooked. Once you have your dimensions and your country indexes on it, you should look for correlations with the results of other studies. Your indexes should correlate convincingly with previous measurements of cultural differences in important social domains, and – most importantly – with real issues; for example in savings rates, crime rates, birth rates, traffic death rates, educational achievement and IQ measurements, religiousness, sexual practices, suicide rates, etc. If your dimension predicts some of these real-life phenomena, it is interesting and useful, no matter how it was discovered.'

Minkov acknowledges the antecedents of his own work, including that of Hofstede, Trompenaars and Hampden-Turner, Schwartz and the GLOBE researchers. In particular, he draws on the contribution of Inglehart and his associates (see Chapter 2), and the World Values Survey (2006) (WVS). Minkov identifies three new cultural dimensions extracted by factor analysis and correlation analysis from the WVS data.

- *Exclusionism versus universalism.* Exclusionism involves treating people in a privileged way on the basis of group affiliation, eg family and friends, while excluding outsiders from this special treatment. Universalism contrastingly involves treating people on the basis of who they are as individuals. There is a strong link here to earlier categorisation of individualism/collectivism. However, enrichment and globalisation have led to 'universal' values taking hold in more affluent Western societies so it is interesting to examine the impact of greater affluence in other countries. Minkov identifies a complex pattern of possible change (reminiscent of Inglehart's model). In Bulgaria, young couples can increasingly afford to move from their extended family, which is (p103) 'the first step to distance, physical as well as emotional between in-group members'. But the experience of Japan and Greece is that a preference for in-groups has not disintegrated as these countries have become richer.

- *Indulgence versus restraint.* The distinction in this category is between allowing relatively free gratification of feelings and desires (indulgence) as opposed to a lesser sense of control of life events, freedom, leisure and happiness (restraint). Anglo societies are among the highest scorers on the indulgency index, with those in Eastern Europe scoring high on restraint. Minkov, reflecting his concern with real issues, notes a positive correlation between indulgence and obesity rates which is indeed marked when one eliminates the role of poverty. Drawing on his conclusion, it is interesting to record that in the UK (an indulgent society) recent government campaigns have linked obesity positively with poverty, thus providing paradoxical confirmation of the value of this dimension.

- *Monumentalism versus flexumility.* In this dimension, monumentalist cultures, which include the Arab world, Northern Latin America, parts of South Asia and the Anglo societies, are characterised by people's consistent and inflexible sense of self, resulting in (amongst other things) high self-regard, interpersonal competition and poor educational performance. Cultures high on flexumility, including those in East Asia, Eastern Europe and part of Western Europe, exhibit opposing characteristics, eg humility and lower self-regard, lack of interpersonal competition and flexible values and beliefs. Using World Health Organization (WHO) data, Minkov records the high suicide rates in high flexumility societies such as Eastern Europe, some Asian countries, Finland and some French and German-speaking countries. He concludes (p174) that, 'it seems that being proud and having good and strong family bonds is more important for suicide prevention than happiness or life satisfaction'.

In a review of Minkov's contribution, Smith (2007) points to Minkov's deep understanding of cultures which have hitherto been relatively neglected by cross-cultural management researchers, including Central and Eastern Europe and Arab cultures. Smith also suggests that by using WVS data, together with the wide range of nations sampled, Minkov is well placed to flag up aspects of cultural difference that might otherwise be missed. We see that the comparative, values-based notion of culture is far from extinct, and new contributions drawing on this tradition continue to inform the cross-cultural management canon in the twenty-first century.

4.12 CONCLUSION

The development of models for understanding cross-cultural management post-2000 has seen some movement away from the etic approach exemplified in the traditional literature by Hofstede. New areas for scrutiny have included: in-depth, one-country, etic-style research; the notion of (changing) social identity; the management of multicultural teams; a renewed examination of the role of language in underpinning cultures; and a concern with stress and coping. Patel (2014, p8) makes a distinction between traditional theories and models which regard culture as essentially stable with more recent contributions which promote a dynamic view: 'the idea that culture is refreshed each morning and concerned primarily with everyday experiences rather than some kind of historically distinctive achievement'. Nonetheless, the work of Tweed et al and Minkov denotes a continuing interest in comparative values-based approaches to the subject area which may point to the enduring appeal, and lurking behind this, the inherent value of these traditional perspectives.

MICHELLE OBAMA VISITS A LONDON SCHOOL

In April 2009 the US First Lady, Michelle Obama, chose to deliver her first speech on a foreign visit at the Elizabeth Garrett Anderson girls' school in London. The students' demographic profile in this inner-city school reflects the multicultural make-up of Britain's capital city. Pupils speak 55 different languages and 20% of them are the daughters of refugees or asylum seekers. Ninety-two per cent are from a black or other minority ethnic background. After listening to a performance by pupils, Ms Obama said, 'When I look at a performance like this, it just reminds me that there are diamonds like this all over the world. All of you are jewels. You are precious and you touch my heart. And it's important for the world to know that there are wonderful girls like you all over the world.' There are powerful reasons why this school might have been singled out for Michelle

Obama's visit. It could, for example, be regarded as a test bed for cross-cultural management and fostering integration given the diverse nature of its pupils. As an example of diversity management it appears to work: the last UK government Ofsted inspection judged the school to be outstanding.

Questions

1   What models of cross-cultural management do you think are most useful in helping staff and pupils at this school to achieve success? Give reasons for your answer.

2   How might the diverse nature of this school's student intake both bring challenges and be integral to its success?

This evaluative review of existing frameworks underpinning cross-cultural management, together with pointers to future developments in the subject area, concludes Part 2 of this book. In Part 3 the focus shifts to an examination of particular topics encapsulating cross-cultural management within work organisations, starting in Chapter 5 with a look at the extent to which formal organisational arrangements such as structure are subject to cultural variation.

REVIEW QUESTIONS

1   What do you understand by the etic approach to cross-cultural management? Provide two examples from academic sources to illustrate your answer.

2   Identify the ways in which language forms part of a person's culture and contributes to cultural understanding.

3   Evaluate the usefulness of any one model of culture which has emerged since 2000.

FURTHER READING

The following three books all focus in depth on different aspects of culture and cultural difference. All are twenty-first-century additions to the literature and can be read to gauge the development of the subject area at this time and to identify contemporary themes and debates.

HOLDEN, N. J. (2002) *Cross-cultural management: a knowledge management perspective*. Harlow: FT Prentice Hall.

MAGALA, S. (2005) *Cross-cultural competence*. Abingdon: Routledge.

PATEL, T. (2014) *Cross-cultural management: a transactional approach*. Abingdon: Routledge.

Visit this book's companion website (**www.cipd.co.uk/olr**) to find further exercises including self-assessment questions and also weblinks to media and academic journal articles.

PART 3

CROSS-CULTURAL SOCIAL RELATIONS IN THE WORKPLACE

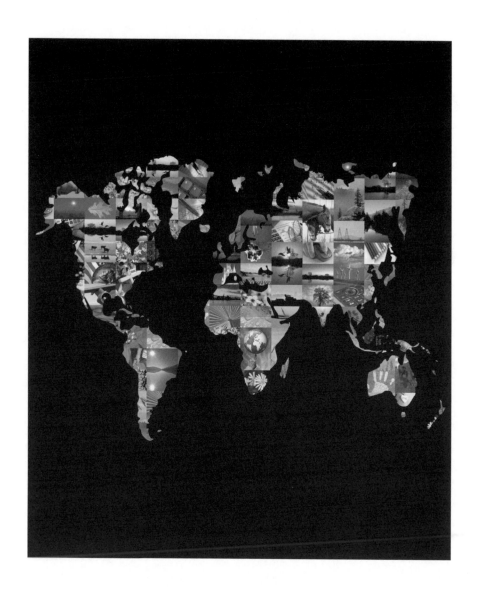

Culture and Organisation Structure

5.1 INTRODUCTION

In previous chapters we have examined the complex multi-layered concept of culture and have pointed to ways in which it can be applied within the field of business studies. We now look more specifically at the possible impact of culture within individual business-related topic areas, beginning with a focus on organisation structure.

Organisation structure is typically conceived as comprising the ways in which organisational actors, most frequently managers, group activities in order to best meet the goals of their organisation. There is an assumption within this statement that structures are designed on the basis of considered choice, although, as we shall see, many commentators have suggested that this choice is at the very least constrained both by the circumstances – or contingent factors – facing the organisation and by the bounded rationality of the actors, whose diagnosis of situations and consequent actions are circumscribed by their own definitions of reality and what is acceptable. The debate concerning the degree to which organisational structures are shaped by a deterministic logic common across cultures, thereby leading to converging outcomes – as against the exercise of individually based diverse choices – will itself give an important pointer to the degree to which organisations can and do vary in different cultural settings.

It is readily apparent that business topics underpinned by interpersonal relationships, eg communication and leadership, are significantly impacted by culture and cultural difference. However, areas such as organisation structure are seemingly more impersonal and so it is less obvious how they would vary across cultures. There is, though, some evidence of cultural divergence. In 2011 Branine pointed to distinctive patterns of 'management and organisation' in selected country clusters. Branine's findings identified some distinctive features of structural arrangements, including:

- In Greece, Italy and Spain most companies are family-owned with decision-making centred on the founder or owner. In such companies there is relatively little delegation and the founder/owner typically acts both as line manager and specialist functional manager, eg HRM.
- In Norway and Sweden autonomous work groups are common, in which team leaders support rather than control their team. Such team leaders have often replaced traditional supervisor figures.
- In Japan and South Korea one finds clear mechanisms for consultation and decision-making coupled with an emphasis on single status between leaders and subordinates.

Branine's findings are interesting as they suggest that businesses that are similar across the world in terms of their size, sector and use of technology may, nonetheless, display distinctive features of organisation. But how and to what extent does culture influence the choice and operation of an organisational feature such as structure?

We now go on to consider this question in more detail by referring both to academic models and the real-life experiences of work organisations. Before we do this it is necessary to define the central concept that underlies the debate.

5.2 WHAT IS ORGANISATION STRUCTURE?

'Organisation structure' as a term has several different components within an overall broad definition. These are set out below:

- *Formalisation* – This relates to the degree to which an organisation stipulates the way work or particular roles should be carried out. We can refer, in this regard, to the extent to which procedural manuals or job descriptions pre-ordain working styles and practices.
- *Specialisation* – This aspect of structure refers both to the extent to which work roles involve a range of specialist activities and to the ways in which workers with similar or related roles and tasks are grouped together. Many organisations have historically operated in a highly specialised manner, typically by setting up discrete functionally based departments.
- *Vertical differentiation* – This sub-set of structure links to power and authority. An organisation could, for example, specify many levels within a hierarchy, each with distinct reporting responsibilities. The concept of span of control in which the ratio of workers reporting to managers is prescribed is also relevant here.
- *Centralisation* – This deals with decision-making, in particular whether responsibility in this regard rests with senior managers, as against where it is cascaded throughout the organisation. Closely associated with this central idea is the degree to which tight control is exercised by a head office or whether, contrastingly, greater autonomy is granted to operating units or divisions. We return to this idea in the discussion of multinational, global and transnational firms outlined later in this chapter.
- *Line and/or staff functions* – In this element of structure there is a distinction between 'line' functions which are intimately connected with the primary purpose of the organisation, and contrasting (although complementary) 'staff' functions which supplement and further the aims of the organisation through the provision of ancillary services. In a large college, for example, the organisation's prime objective will be the education of students – so that lecturers form part of the 'line', while an HRM department may be categorised as a 'staff' function. The relationship between line and staff (and their relative importance) raises issues of horizontal (as opposed to vertical) co-ordination and control.

It can be seen from this categorisation of structure that we are in essence dealing with formalised features of organisations. The classic way to depict an organisation's structure is via scrutiny of a chart or other diagram, in effect taking an impersonal view of what should happen in that organisation. As we noted in this chapter's introduction, our depiction of culture (see Chapters 1 to 4) may lead readers to conclude that its influence may take effect more in the interpersonal sphere of work, such as leadership or motivation, rather than via impersonal structures and systems. Schneider and Barsoux (2003, p85) made a similar suggestion based on practitioners' views: 'While many managers are willing to accept that national culture may influence the way people relate to each other, or the "soft stuff", they are less convinced that it can really affect the nuts and bolts of organisation: structure, systems and processes. The culture-free argument within this topic area holds that structure is determined by organisational features such as size or technology.' In this chapter we will identify evidence which suggests that culture is less important in determining organisation structure than so-called universal imperatives such as the nature of the work involved in producing a product or providing a service. Nonetheless, as already indicated, other writers such as Mead and Andrews (2009) and Branine (2011) identify the case for the existence of sustained culturally based differences in organisational arrangements.

The debate concerning the extent to which organisation structure can be subject to cultural variation is a key theme within this chapter. As stated earlier, while some writers have played down the potential impact of culture on organisations' structural arrangements due to the seemingly impersonal nature of structure, other studies have, contrastingly, pointed to significant differences in this regard. Ouchi (1981), in his tellingly titled work, *How American Business can meet the Japanese Challenge,* identified a 'distinctive Type Z' organisation which he claimed characterised Japanese work organisations at that time. The Type Z organisation was run primarily on the basis of trust, gave higher levels of involvement to workers and, importantly in this context, had a less bureaucratic and hierarchical structure than would typically be found in the USA. While several features of the Type Z organisation have fallen out of favour since 1981 (for example, the promise of long-term, maybe lifetime, employment), we have here an early example of the notion that national cultures can impact on formal work arrangements. For Ouchi, the values of Japanese managers and the institutional arrangements prevalent in that country had led to the emergence of a unique form of organisation, which, for a time, was associated with national competitive advantage. Later in the chapter we will examine Hofstede's (2001) contribution to this subject area, in which his identified dimensions of culture (for example power distance and individualism) find expression in how structures are designed and put into effect in the workplace. Once again the conclusion is that culture matters in this regard.

The links between national culture and organisation structure become clearer when the concept of organisational culture is brought into view. French et al (2011, p339) define organisational culture as, 'a system of shared beliefs and values that guides behaviour'. Organisational cultures are manifested in common assumptions, rituals and symbols such as dress code and office layout. But such cultures are also operationalised in formal arragements. Consider, for example, one of Handy's (1989) types of organisational culture: the so-called role culture. Handy describes this as a culture dominated by set rules, procedures, job descriptions and hierarchies. This sounds very much like the bureaucratic model of organisation structure which we will go on to examine in greater detail later in the chapter. It is indeed normal for role cultures to be reinforced through a bureaucratic structure and the two concepts – culture and structure – are in an important sense akin to two sides of the same coin. If we accept this link then it would be possible for key players in organisations to take a view on preferred organisational culture which is influenced by their upbringing in a national culture, and which then finds expression, via organisation design, in formal arrangements such as structure. We explore this idea in greater detail when examining Trompenaars' contribution to this debate. Before returning to the debate concerning the extent to which structures vary across the world, it is necessary to look both at different types of structure and approaches to understanding their effectiveness.

5.3 CLASSICAL MODELS OF STRUCTURE

The early part of the twentieth century saw a proliferation of academic work which set out both to understand the nature of large-scale work organisation and to provide principles for effective management and administration. Relevant writers include Henri Fayol (1841–1925) and Frederick Taylor (1856–1915). For our purposes the key point is that such writers lived at a time when work organisations in specific societies were undergoing revolutionary change: their rapidly increasing scale had led to a desire for stability, predictability and systems which could deliver these objectives. These authors' work can be viewed within this historical context – namely, a search for rational principles of organisation across the industrialising world, centred at that time on Western Europe and North America. These so-called classic models of organisation were underpinned by an assumption that it was possible to develop scientific thinking as applied to work organisations, and that such organisations could be studied and categorised in an objective way. The principles these authors identified and advocated were therefore perceived as being culture-free in that they could be applied throughout the industrialised world.

We now look in greater detail at a famous academic model emanating from that period, the ideal type of bureaucracy developed by Max Weber (1864–1920):

- tasks allocated according to certified expertise, with resultant specialised (for example, departmental) structure
- jobs defined through clear and often simplified routine tasks
- control exercised through a hierarchical structure, typically with many layers denoting levels of authority
- rules and procedures clearly set out in the form of written documentation
- formal systems of communication via specified channels with hierarchical authority paramount
- employees are appointed and, where appropriate, promoted on the basis of clear criteria often relating to their qualifications
- managers are salaried officials and do not have a financial stake in the organisation
- rules are set and all decisions made rationally in an attempt to eliminate non-rational elements such as emotional involvement or personal preference.

Weber's conception of what bureaucracy would be like in an extreme or pure form saw this type of structure as reflecting a more general stress on rationality in the societies he observed. At that time many societies were becoming increasingly characterised by a search for systematic solutions to the challenges they faced. This concern was manifested in work organisations by a stress on rational decision-making. It was claimed that this distinguished them from the ways in which previous communities' workplaces operated more on the basis of traditional authority. Watson (2006, p38) states that, 'Out of this major cultural shift came bureaucracy. And bureaucracies are what modern organisations are.'

We might expect therefore that bureaucratic structures would emerge across all societies at the point in which they exhibited 'modern' concerns – in particular, a preoccupation with managing large-scale work organisations. In this sense the impersonal nature of bureaucracy, in addressing problems intrinsic to running such organisations, should work well in all societies in which bureaucracy is a prevalent organisational form, and national cultural differences should be submerged within this logic.

One ought to express some measure of caution when restating this fundamental premise. Firstly, Weber himself did not claim that bureaucracy was the perfect type of structure: he recognised that it contained potential in-built inefficiencies. The solutions to problems associated with bureaucracy (for example, over-rigid application of rules and excessive identification with sub-units or departments) could be formulated in culturally specific ways. Secondly, because Weber's model was a highly idealised concept, it is unsurprising that its purest manifestation was in reality only to be found in selected situations. Ackroyd (2002, p57), in examining the highly bureaucratic mass-production operation at the Ford Motor Company plant near Detroit in the USA, suggests that, 'Major British companies did not develop into the highly centralised bureaucracies that appeared in the USA, although the tendency for centralised administrative structures did emerge strongly in the organisations of the state,' and that furthermore, 'Researchers who went out looking for fully-developed bureaucracies in the UK in the 1970s actually had difficulty finding examples.'

This last contribution indicates that the extent of bureaucratisation could vary between societies – and we already know that cross-cultural research models typically locate the UK and USA within the same cultural cluster. Nonetheless, studies of the emergence of the bureaucratic organisation structure tend to posit a universal logic of development whereby powerful determining forces influence the ways in which organisations are shaped in all societies, allowing little scope for the impact of national-level culture.

5.4 THE CHINESE SMALL BUSINESS MODEL

The logic outlined in the previous section, whereby bureaucratic forms of organisation structure are assumed to emerge when societies enter a 'modern' or industrial era, contains an assumption that all such societies contain a significant number of large work organisations. However, there is evidence that there can be departures from this pattern. Montagu-Pollock (1991) identified a series of principles underpinning Chinese business practice which he claimed diverged from prescriptions contained within Western management theory. In the context of this chapter, it is important to record that one element of Chinese business practice related to the optimal size of businesses. Montagu-Pollock summarises the Chinese view as believing that firms function best when they stay small, in contrast to the notion that large businesses benefit from economies of scale, which, he claimed, is a view emanating primarily from Western management theory.

The distinctive nature of Chinese organisations was also noted by Chen (1995) in a comparative study encompassing Japan and South Korea. With reference to Chinese organisational forms, Chen noted the prevalence of Chinese family businesses (CFBs) both in the home and overseas contexts. CFBs are often (but by no means always) small, and kept small, and as such lend themselves to particular structural arrangements. For example, one can anticipate less employee specialisation in a CFB. There is also a relative absence of rules and procedures which facilitates a personalised style of management, specifically centred on patriarchal authority. In both cases these features are in stark contrast to those identified within Weber's ideal type of bureaucracy.

Francesco and Gold (2005) note that mainland family businesses were officially outlawed by the Chinese Government for a long period. That they continued to exist might plausibly be explained in part by recognising that this is a type of organisation with deep cultural roots. The same authors also interestingly claim that CFBs retain their less prescribed structures as they grow. It appears therefore that Weber's theory that bureaucracy is the normal modern form of organisation, presupposing the dominance of large-scale organisations, may be subject to cultural difference after all.

It is also the case that although models of organisation structure reflect the overall concerns of a particular era, the precise detail of models and theories are influenced by the context in which they are framed. At the start of this chapter we located the contributions of Weber, Fayol and Taylor within an epoch which sought to formulate rational principles of organisation in response to challenges thrown up by significant elements of industrialisation. However, as Schneider and Barsoux (2003, p86) suggest, 'theories about how best to organize – Max Weber's bureaucracy, Henri Fayol's administrative model and Frederick Taylor's scientific management – all reflect societal concerns of the times as well as the cultural background of the individuals.' In this sense national cultures (in these cases German, French and US, respectively) have a role in influencing the ways writers frame the reality which forms the basis for their work, which in turn leads to such models becoming more embedded in practice.

    A NEW DIRECTION FOR THE VATICAN

CASE STUDY 5.1

The election of a new Pope brings opportunities for fresh and different styles of leadership and renewed focus on the Catholic Church's mission and priorities. In 2013 the new Pope Francis had an additional mandate: to overhaul an antiquated and dysfunctional Vatican administration. That administration, according to the same commentator, had been revealed, in documents stolen by a previous Pope's butler, to be a 'Machiavellian world of petty turf battles, corruption and political intrigue'. Such dysfunctional processes were seen by the incoming Pope as a barrier to achieving the Church's aims. So while a new simplified control structure was intended to improve internal controls, it would also free resources for deployment on core work; for example, supporting the poor. Cardinal Francesco Coccopalmerio, who in 2014 headed the Vatican department writing Church laws, was reported as being focused on 'breaking down barriers among silos so that information flows around departments rather than from top to bottom'.[1]

Changes to an organisation's structure should be made in association with changes to its culture. Cardinal Donald Wuerl of Washington D.C. reports that Pope Francis advocates a 'collaborative

spirit', asking senior cardinals for their input during meetings which themselves have changed in tone, even down to new seating plans. Cardinal Wuerl concludes that Pope Francis wants the cardinals to be 'speaking with him so that the end of the day he can say this was truly the fruit of the work of the Spirit'.[2]

In organisation theory terms, the Vatican provides an example of external circumstances leading to a change in structure and organisational culture – in this case supporting a strategy of more collaborative working. As the Vatican City is an independent state we also have an example of macro-level culture and culture change in operation.

Questions

1   Identify the assumptions that have underpinned the Vatican's organisation structure and the extent to which these have changed since the election of Pope Francis in 2013.

2   What external circumstances have led to pressure for internal changes to structure and culture in the Vatican?

In summary, there are several ways in which classical models of organisation structure can be influenced by culture – seen most clearly in the example of China, in which pressures towards increasing dominance of large-scale bureaucratic organisations appears, so far, to have been mediated by a culturally derived preference for the small business model. Notwithstanding this and other related findings, readers should also recognise the extent of bureaucratic organisational forms worldwide, both numerically and in terms of influence. The powerful advantages (at least for those who control organisations) of predictability, longevity and depersonalisation have resulted in very widespread adoption of this form of organisation in both business and governmental settings. Many textbooks begin sections on this topic with a reminder of how previous civilisations (for example, those in ancient Greece and Rome) provided early examples of such structures in action, thereby alluding to bureaucracy's enduring character. All the same, this is not to imply that the pure form of bureaucracy is not amenable to some adaptation. Watson (2006, p271) notes that, 'Strategically, managers have the option to shape their organisations in a broad tightly bureaucratic way or broad loosely bureaucratic way. Hence the [previous] comment that we cannot remove or dispense with bureaucracy. We can only modify or "loosen" bureaucratic principles when trying to shape organisational structures and cultures.'

In similar vein, Linstead et al (2009) made a renewed case for the value of the impersonal virtues of bureaucracy as they are based on principles of equality. These authors posit that bureaucratic structures are best placed to regulate markets, in order that markets serve the interests of the many rather than the few. Such arguments gathered pace in the aftermath of the financial crash of 2008, which many commentators attributed to a lack of regulation in parts of the financial services sector. Nonetheless, the period from 1950 to 2000 had seen both academics and managers searching for alternatives to the bureaucratic model. We will now go on to examine such alternative models, and the ways in which culture could affect these, in the next section.

 ## GROUP ACTIVITY 5.1

One distinctive form of business organisation in the Asian context are the *chaebol* operating in South Korea. Search for academic sources which analyse this term (seek guidance from your tutor) and prepare a presentation dealing with the following points:

1   Define the term *chaebol*.

2   Identify three companies which fall within this typology.

3   What are the key distinguishing features of *chaebol*?

4   Provide a brief summary of why this form of business group developed in South Korea; in other words, explain how it is culturally distinctive.

5   With reference to material presented in earlier chapters, assess the extent to which the *chaebol* form of organisation is likely to endure given pressures for convergence of business practices worldwide.

5.5 ALTERNATIVES TO BUREAUCRACY – ADAPTING TO 'CONTINGENCIES'

As previously mentioned, Weber (the supposed advocate of bureaucracy) recognised that bureaucratic organisation structures contained within them certain in-built potential inefficiencies, particularly associated with unintended behaviours displayed by workers operating within such structures, these resulting in turn in undesirable consequences. One example was possible over-rigid interpretation of rules and excessive identification with sub-units (resulting in a loss of focus on the overall goals of the organisation), while other negative aspects were minimal performance levels – when promotion prospects are curtailed by rigid hierarchies – and defensiveness or even strong resistance to change: in effect, the obverse of the advantages engendered by the stability and longevity of bureaucracies.

From the 1950s onwards, a second wave of critical comment emerged centring on a perceived inability of bureaucratic structures to cope well in the face of changing circumstances. The underlying idea that organisation structures are influenced by external factors, to which they must be adapted to ensure high performance, is commonly referred to as the contingency approach. Before examining the factors that have been identified as relevant situational events or contingencies, it is timely to look at some alternative structures which are either extensions of bureaucracy or radical alternatives. Note that other contemporary and emerging organisational forms, such as 'de-layered' and transnational organisations, are covered later in this chapter.

5.5.1 PROJECT TEAM STRUCTURES

Project teams are normally seen as temporary structures set up for a specific purpose where cross-functional expertise is required (see Needle (2010) for further detail). In some sectors (for example, consultancy) such structures could be seen as the norm, groups of employees from different functional areas routinely being assembled to provide an integrated service for a particular client. Another possible scenario in which such a structure would be relevant is where a project group comprising potential users of a new IT system, including representatives from different functional departments, work together to consider the implications of a new system for their own sub-unit. One advantage of such a structure is that it encourages workers to consider their contribution to organisational goals from a variety of perspectives and can therefore facilitate cross-fertilisation of ideas.

5.5.2 THE MATRIX

Matrix structures are by no means recent phenomena, having been identified in significant numbers from the 1970s onwards. The key defining point of a matrix structure is multi-reporting, in that employees are required to consider at least two aspects of their job, typically their functional specialism and the products or services provided as part of their work. We have already referred to the distinction between 'line' and 'staff' functions, which is addressed directly in the matrix form, the notion of facing in different directions being reinforced in the structure of the organisation itself. Many students and academics reading this book will be familiar with the idea of the matrix since it is by no means uncommon in the higher-educational sector (the author can identify examples from a number of different countries). A lecturer may form part of an academic department based on his or her academic subject area but also have to report to senior managers whose remit could be courses (the product), or quality assurance, or international developments, or knowledge transfer. In such a case the individual lecturer could report to five separate managers.

Advantages of matrices are similar to those put forward for project teams in that they allow for easier collaborative working and even synergy. On the other hand, the major criticism of matrix structures has centred on their potential for ambiguity and even outright confusion in reporting. The matrix idea could readily lend itself to transnational or global working; this aspect is pursued more fully later in this chapter. The concept of a matrix is indeed similar to the ideal type of the 'global firm' based on divisional structure.

5.5.3 DIVISIONAL STRUCTURE

The divisional form of structure, also known as the multi-functional model, was originally conceived as an alternative to the functional bureaucracy. In this form, entire divisions are set up to deal with all aspects of a product or service. It can be argued that the focus of such a structure is on *outputs* (that is, the end product) rather than on the inputs (all resources including human skills, knowledge and effort) needed to turn the end product into a tangible entity. General Motors (GM) for many years provided an example of this type of strategic approach to structure. GM's divisions were based on brand names and associated products. Individual divisions were largely self-contained and operated as profit centres. However, headquarters – sometimes known as 'the centre' – co-ordinated overall strategy and centralised other activities. The divisional nature of this multinational company became evident in 2009, when GM, following financial problems caused by global economic turbulence, sold off whole divisions of the company hosted outside the

USA. These events demonstrated that this form of structure can readily be applied to the transnational firm, and we examine it again later within that context.

5.5.4 ORGANIC STRUCTURE

This model was originally put forward by the researchers Burns and Stalker (1961) as an idealised counterpoint to the classic bureaucratic structure. As we shall see in 'Contingency factors' below, Burns and Stalker found that this type of structure, or rather its component features, would be effective when organisations operated in a turbulent environment of rapidly changing technology, fierce competition and uncertain customer demand. The features of this abstract model were:

- network (as opposed to hierarchical) structures of control and communication
- knowledge spread throughout the organisation (rather than located at the top)
- employee commitment to their tasks (compared with loyalty to the organisation)
- knowledge, skills and experience applied to diverse tasks (compared with long-term specialisation)
- communication flowing up, down and across the organisation rather than essentially top–down.

Burns and Stalker's organic structure is overall characterised by informality and flexibility. Originally applied to the fast-changing micro-electronics sector of the 1960s, it has increasingly been advocated in other areas of the private and public sectors because their environments are perceived as more turbulent as a result of economic, political and technological change.

5.6 CONTINGENT FACTORS

There are many potentially distinctive forms of organisational structure: we have only outlined some general principles here. As suggested earlier, the essence of the contingency approach is that particular types of structure should be adopted or chosen in the light of the contingent factors acting on the organisation in question. Although contingencies are by definition framed by unique circumstances, overarching factors usually put forward are listed below.

5.6.1 TECHNOLOGY

The work of Woodward, published in 1965 (but based on research carried out in the mid-1950s), identified a link between technology – here referring to production methods – and the ways in which the companies she studied were organised. Woodward's research sample comprised firms in Essex in England whose production technologies were designated as 'small-batch' (essentially specialised or even customised production on short runs) or 'large-batch' (bigger production runs which could turn into mass-production) or 'process', in which the production system operated on a continuous 24-hour basis.

Woodward's conclusion was that the production systems used by the companies she researched resulted in differences in those companies' structures. To take one type in greater depth: small-batch production was associated with relatively few specialised employees, a short span of control for both supervisors and the chief executive, and few hierarchical levels or rungs in the authority ladder. Reasons for these findings, according to Woodward, were that organisations employing small-batch technology required employees to have more generalist skills (maybe a forerunner of today's flexibility debate) and tended to be smaller, thereby reducing the need for complex hierarchical authority. Large-batch production methods led to higher numbers of specialised staff with wide spans of control because these organisations were larger and their chief concern was efficient administration of production. The large-batch technology was most closely associated with the classical model of bureaucratic structure. Process technologies had a low number of specialists because these were often *de facto* the companies' managers, who were concerned to ensure that demand for the continuous production was met. It follows that in this situation there would be narrow spans of control and that these organisations were overall less bureaucratic.

The purpose of this detailed unpacking of Woodward's work is to give a flavour of the logic that flows through it, namely, that an organisation's technology is a powerful determinant of its structural arrangements. Woodward, in addition to demarcating forms of structure and linking them to technology, also, and very importantly, concluded that there was an optimal situation in which organisations that aligned their structures according to the technologies they used would be the most efficient. In other words, the structure would have to fit with this particular contingent factor. For our purposes such logic appears to be largely culture-free.

Koen (2005, p6), commenting on the contingency approach, suggests that, 'Cultural and societal specifics are perceived as negligible. While these influences are not entirely denied, contingency constraints are argued to override them. The contingency perspective claims that variance in organisational structure is due primarily to the contingencies faced and not to societal or cultural location.'

5.6.2 SIZE OF ORGANISATION

A research team from Aston University in England proposed that an organisation's size would be the most important determining factor in terms of its optimal structure (see Hickson and Pugh (1995) for an account of the research by members of the original group). The Aston researchers examined the extent of specialisation, the degree to which formal policies influenced work in reality, and standardisation in terms of procedures. The Aston academics then identified a number of points for comparison, all deriving from Weber's ideal type of bureaucracy, finally correlating these with statistical data from their own research sample. Within this highly positivist framework their conclusion was that the independent variable which most strongly impacted on the dependent variable of organisational structure was size. The *post hoc* logic which purports to explain these findings was fundamentally that as organisations grow in size there is considerable pressure for them to become more bureaucratic. Once again, this logic appears to be universal in that it should apply in all contexts, including those of different societies. In this case, several of the Aston researchers extended their studies by comparing similar organisations in different countries to ascertain whether the contingency logic – according to which increased size of organisation led to greater bureaucratisation – would inevitably apply across the world, or whether culture could intervene as another causative factor.

Hickson et al (1974) therefore attempted to discover whether relationships between variables such as size of organisation and structure were stable across societies. From their research, which focused on 70 manufacturing units in the USA, Britain and Canada, Hickson and his research team concluded that there was consistency in terms of the relationship between variables of organisation context and structure in all three societies. In particular, there was a clear correlation between an organisation's size and the extent of specialisation and formalisation within its structure. This research project found that the anticipated relationship between technology and structure was not significant, and technology was disregarded as a determining contextual factor.

These research findings did not presuppose that organisations would be similar in different societies even within comparable sectors. Rather, the conclusion was that the relationship between size and structure would be consistent and national culture would not have any significant mediating effect on that relationship. We have already noted that the Chinese experience is different in that there is a greater preponderance of small businesses within that country. This in itself could be related to that country's culture. For those writers adopting the culture-free contingency approach, however, it would be necessary to establish a causal link between China's cultural profile and the prevalence of small firms – otherwise, this characteristic could not be claimed to be the result of cultural distinctiveness.

5.6.3 ORGANISATIONAL ENVIRONMENTS

Earlier in this chapter we referred to the work of Burns and Stalker, who in 1961 proposed their dichotomy of mechanistic and organic structures. The mechanistic category is very similar to Weber's model of bureaucracy, while the diametrically opposite organic form is flexible, is network-based and requires commitment, compliance and loyalty from employees within this structure. The key contingent variable for Burns and Stalker was the particular environment facing the organisation. The more turbulent the environment, in terms of technological advance, competition and customer or client demand, the more organic the organisation should be, if it were to prosper and even survive in such a challenging milieu. Burns and Stalker identified organisations that had failed to adapt via changed structures, thus adding weight to their central proposition.

Clegg et al (2011), returning to Burns and Stalker's fundamental idea, identified contemporary organisations that face constant turbulence and that in turn require perpetual innovation, and go on to suggest that the optimum structure in such cases is adhocracy (a term coined by Mintzberg in 1981). The application of this model to a cross-cultural perspective is potentially interesting. In as much as organisations in particular sectors in all societies face turbulent environments, the logic of this particular contingency approach is culture-free. However, it may be that culturally derived values may themselves lead decision-makers in organisations to redefine the nature of environments and their responses to the challenges these environments bring. Globalisation in itself could also lead to more turbulence in the environments of many organisations. These ideas are explored in greater detail in the following sections.

5.7 CULTURE AND THE CONTINGENCY APPROACH

The research findings of Hickson et al (1974) were originally conceived as strengthening the view that organisations develop in very similar ways across the world, and that a logic in which causal variables such as size determine structure would leave no room for cultural impact in this regard. However, their findings were partly challenged soon after publication by Lammers and Hickson (1979), who, in referring to Hickson et al's 1974 research, highlight those potential causal variables which failed to predict consistency in organisation structures across societies. Thus the 1974 research found a link between size and decentralisation in Britain and the United States but not in Sweden and Japan. With the benefit of hindsight, one could now incorporate the contributions of Hofstede and Trompenaars and propose that the similarities between Britain and the USA might have been expected in that they have subsequently been located within the same cultural cluster.

Other writers have accepted some of the broad principles of contingency theory and have adapted them to make space for the effect of culture. Child and Kieser (1979) undertook research examining 82 British and 51 (West) German companies. Child and Kieser used a 'matched pair' comparative method in which identified variables are held constant. In this case this approach resulted in cross-cultural comparison of companies of similar size and product range and which employed comparable technologies. Their conclusions can perhaps best be illustrated by referring to one particular finding. In analysing the extent of specialisation in their sample firms, the authors found that the size of the firm was a predictor of level of specialisation: as expected the bigger the firm, the more specialisation was found. However, *within* specialised functional departments, operational decisions were consistently made at a higher level in the German sample firms, where departmental managers perceived themselves as having significantly less authority than their British counterparts. Child and Kieser found this to be evident in different functional areas, namely, marketing, production and human resource management (or 'personnel', as it was then more commonly called). Their findings on the impact of culture were that:

- Culture intervened at the level of the realities underlying structural features, ie in role characteristics and actual behaviour.
- Culture is manifested in the preferences and philosophies of those involved in designing organisations, implying that such actors can exercise strategic choice in the face of apparently universal pressure.
- Culture also shows up in the prior orientations of managers and other workers towards concepts like authority, thereby influencing their perception of what is and what is not acceptable.

Tayeb (1987) conducted a study which compared Indian manufacturing companies with a 'matched' sample from the UK. Again, the methodological perspective chosen is interesting in that companies in the two countries were selected for comparison according to their perceived similarity in terms of size and industry so that culture could be isolated as an explanatory factor. Tayeb's findings are similar to those of Child and Kieser. She concluded that matched organisations in both countries exhibited common structural features as could be viewed on an organisation chart. The number of hierarchical levels, and extent of specialisation and centralisation, could be linked back in a consistent way to the contingent factors faced by individual organisations in both cultural settings. At the same time the matched pairs showed differences in the interpretation of procedures and job descriptions, together with diverse patterns of delegation and communication. In the Indian sample, for instance, managers were found to be consistently more autocratic in their decision-making styles.

Needle (2010), in a summary of the different types of organisation structure, noted that divisional structures have been associated with US companies' response to structural imperatives, while in Britain similar concerns have more often resulted in development of a holding company structure. In Japan a particular version of the holding company known as *keiretsu* is evident. Such organisations are depicted as large conglomerates with highly diversified structures. The *keiretsu* are linked to particular banks and aim to set up an integrated supply chain, incorporating all relevant players – most importantly suppliers, distributors and retailers. 'Horizontal' *keiretsu* are headed by banks and include the Mitsui group and Fuyo. This type of *keiretsu* spans a wide range of different industries and sectors. Each member firm within a horizontal *keiretsu* has a minority financial stake in other members of the group. 'Vertical' *keiretsu* are industry-based groups including Toyota, Hitachi and Sony. The implication of this distinctive model's prevalence in Japan is that it originated and survives because of the particular values and preferences of key players within the Japanese business and political domains.

Similar strategic choices regarding governance and structure, based on cultural values, were also revealed in an earlier study by Dyas and Thanheiser (1976). These researchers examined different adaptations to strategy by firms in the USA, France and Germany. In diversifying rapidly into many new product areas, the companies all experienced similar problems of control. For example, the flow of information to and from functionally specialised departments became inadequate for any effective determination of strategy in different product areas. In this study the response to the strategic issues faced by the companies was broadly similar in the adoption in all cases of a multi-divisional form with semi-autonomous units that each managed an identifiable product market. However, once again we can see different patterns of delegation in each country, the most gradual hierarchies being observed in the American sample. In Germany, rather than reporting to a chief executive, divisional managers themselves comprised the executive board, thereby perpetuating an existing preference for collegial management within the parameters of a new form of organisation.

5.8 THE INSTITUTIONAL LEVEL

Maurice et al (1980), responding to the early attempts to reconcile cultural analysis with contingency approaches to organisation, claimed that the variables used as data in comparing organisations were *ipse facto* supranational. These writers suggested that by comparing such variables, which in their inherent generality apply in all societies, one could fail to identify the truly unique features of cultures and their consequent impact in the workplace. Although a focus on the preferences of organisational designers shed some light on the ways in which culture took effect in organisations, these researchers proposed that a more direct link was apparent in the ways in which the educational system of a country not only socialised workers but also supplied its workforce.

In their collected studies in the late 1970s and early 1980s, Maurice et al compared organisations in Britain, France and West Germany. They concluded, through an analysis of matched pairs of companies, that British organisations were the most specialised, which was attributed to more individualised education systems, particularly in the post-18 or further-education sector, and also the key role played by professional bodies in the UK, who in setting curricula and standards via qualifications, both produced and perpetuated a high number of functional management specialists; for example, in marketing and HRM. In France, contrastingly, elite business schools produced a cadre of senior managers who it is suggested embody the centralisation of authority, reflected in hierarchical structures which typify many French organisations. In Germany, finally, the influence of apprenticeships fostered a site orientation rather than an occupational orientation, and a preponderance of managers with technical qualifications led to a concern with performance and *technik* (no direct translation of this German term is possible) as opposed to functional specialisation. Here we have an echo of the point made in Chapter 2: that culture takes effect at different levels, both in the values and beliefs of individuals and also, importantly, at the level of institutions.

5.9 DO CULTURAL VALUES UNDERLIE ORGANISATION STRUCTURE?

So far in this chapter we have examined the views, firstly, that universally applicable pressures or logics effectively rule out significant cultural variations in formal organisational arrangements, and secondly, that culture itself can be seen as one variable within a range of factors which influence structure. The overall message emanating from this second school of thought is that structures are essentially the same in similar or matched organisations across the world, but that there could be (admittedly important) culturally based variations. An alternative perspective views culture as an underlying force which exerts a profound influence on organisational arrangements. We can here return to some of the cross-cultural theorists and practitioners referred to in Chapters 2 and 3.

Fons Trompenaars has devoted part of his analysis of cross-cultural aspects of business to an explanation of how societal-level culture can influence organisational culture and structure. He states (Trompenaars and Hampden-Turner 1997, p157) that, 'When people set up an organisation, they typically borrow from models or ideals that are familiar to them. The organisation is a subjective construct and its employees will give meaning to their environment based on their own cultural programming.'

This statement would imply a very prominent and proactive role for cultural influence far removed from the culture-free or adapted contingency approaches reviewed earlier. In part it points to the suggestion that an organisation's formal structure, while important, is only one part of the realities of life within that organisation. We have seen that formal structures which on the surface, or in diagrammatic form, look very similar may conceal a wealth of actual difference in terms of delegation and authority. Trompenaars' PhD thesis examined the way culture affects how people perceive organisational structures. His early work focusing on how organisations are given meaning by their members gave prominence to the notion of organisational culture. The model he has subsequently developed links societal culture to organisational culture, and views structure in turn as a manifestation of an organisation's culture.

Trompenaars and Hampden-Turner (1997) identify four types of 'corporate image' which represent organisational culture:

- 'family' or power-oriented culture
- 'Eiffel Tower' or rule-oriented culture
- 'incubator' or fulfilment-oriented culture
- 'guided missile' or project-oriented culture.

Each of these types can be located along two dimensions: hierarchical v egalitarian and person v task. Taken in turn, each type may be described as follows:

- *family* – highly personalised and hierarchical
- *Eiffel Tower* – highly task-oriented and hierarchical
- *incubator* – highly personalised and egalitarian
- *guided missile* – highly task-oriented and egalitarian.

Trompenaars and Hampden-Turner go on to show how these different types are shaped by technology and markets, and also, critically, by the work process required to facilitate the organisation's goals. However, they are also influenced by the preferences of those who design them and work in them. For example, the guided missile culture is appropriate where job roles are fluid and changing. It is also useful when professionals are required to join short-lived project groups. Trompenaars and Hampden-Turner give the example of an advertising agency as the type of work environment where a guided missile culture would be useful and effective – and where therefore it could often be found. Figure 5.1 adds a cross-cultural dimension as Trompenaars locates countries within his organisational culture types.

Figure 5.1 Trompenaars' organisational cultures ascribed to countries

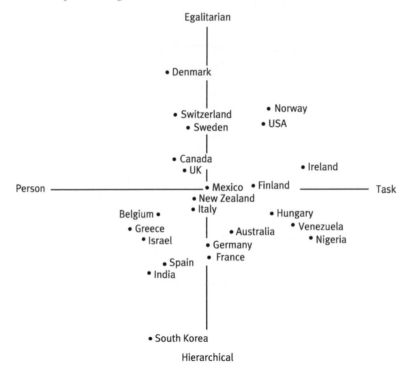

It should be pointed out that the authors expressed caution when locating societies along these dimensions. They state in this context (1997, p179) that, 'In France, for example, smaller companies tend to be family and larger companies Eiffel Tower. In the USA guided missile companies may dominate among large corporations but the archetypal incubators are to be found in Silicon Valley.' Notwithstanding these caveats, Trompenaars provides us with a model in which structure is a function of organisational culture which, in turn, has been shaped by societal-level culture. For Trompenaars, culture is not merely one factor influencing structure (or indeed any other business process) – rather, it is at the core of any explanation of how organisations develop and function.

Preceding analysis of Geert Hofstede's work (see Chapter 3) would also lead readers to anticipate that he viewed culture as a strong influence on organisation structure. This is indeed the case. Two points are particularly relevant when considering Hofstede's contribution in this area. Firstly, his substantive research focused on one organisation: IBM. In a sense this method is an extension of the matched pair comparison used by Child and other researchers. The attempt to isolate cultural influence by holding other variables constant is taken to its logical end point by Hofstede through the selection for research purposes of a single organisation – and one, furthermore, with a strong corporate culture. Hofstede has argued that differences uncovered in his research must be the result of cultural factors intervening, and he has gone on to construct a model showing how individuals socialised within a particular culture, and with specific 'software of the mind', can shape organisational processes by acting on their internalised preferences and values. Secondly, two of Hofstede's dimensions of culture – power distance (PD) and uncertainty avoidance (UA) – appear to have the potential to relate very strongly to the topic of organisation structure.

Hofstede's findings did, as we have seen in previous chapters, illuminate significant differences between the national sites within IBM. In countries with high PD scores, hierarchies were steeper and contained more layers, particularly at junior manager or supervisory level, and decision-making was typically centralised. When analysing the effect of the uncertainty avoidance dimension, Hofstede found that high UA countries exhibit more bureaucratisation in the form of written procedures and regulations. His 'cultural maps' locating countries along the PD and UA dimensions include in each quartile an evocative term which suggests the underlying characteristic of organisations in that location. In as much as an organisation can be referred to, for example, as a 'pyramid of people', this provides a meaningful description of its structure. Hofstede's typology is set out below (see also Mead and Andrews (2009) for a parallel interpretation of Hofstede's work).

- *Village market – low PD combined with low UA (Anglo-Nordic countries)*. Within this type of structure, people will feel more able to interpret their work roles flexibly, bypass formal reporting procedures both vertically (hierarchy) and horizontally (cross-departmental) and have recourse to greater informal and personal influence within the organisation. In effect this village market model is a 'looser' form of bureaucracy than depicted in the original ideal type.
- *Family – high PD and low UA (Asian societies)*. Here one finds direct control and close supervision by, or on behalf of, a central leader figure who is typically referred to on the basis of his or her social position or personal attributes rather than their organisational role. In this case we see a model which deviates sharply from the original concept of bureaucracy.
- *Well-oiled machine – low PD and high UA (Germanic cluster)*. In such organisations, professionals with technical expertise rank highly in the hierarchy, work procedures are standardised while all employees share common workplace facilities (true of Germany, for example) and mechanisms are in place to foster consensual decision-making; for

example, the legally based systems of co-determination or joint decision-making found in countries within this cluster.

- *Pyramid of people – high PD and high UA (Latin countries).* This model comes closest to the ideal of a full bureaucracy and we find impersonal and standardised roles, reporting relationships and authority together with a fixed and steep hierarchy. As might be expected, members are comfortable with the hierarchy in place and seek to avoid ambiguity in their working lives.

From this model it can be argued that national culture impinges in a fundamental way on preferred organisation structures within societies through culturally derived values of key players, primarily organisation designers and managers. The result is a proliferation of one organisational type within the specific cultural cluster. Once more, it should be noted that Hofstede's conclusion is one of relative prediction, allowing for both individual- and universal-level influences.

Hofstede's work taken together with that of Trompenaars concludes our journey through explanations of similarities and differences in classical organisation structure. In all cases researchers allow for real-life differences between structures in organisations in different locations. Whereas the culture-free approach says that relationships between variables such as size of organisation and structure will be stable in all societies, the adapted contingency view proposes that culture is one of a number of determining factors impacting on organisational structure, both through individual intervention and the effect of institutional arrangements, eg labour markets. This approach also highlights the important point that formal structural arrangements can mask significant differences in how people interpret their roles and how they behave in reality. Trompenaars and Hofstede, finally, place culture at the absolute centre of an explanation of variations in structure: for them it is the major determining force in this regard.

INDIVIDUAL ACTIVITY 5.2

Continuity and change in indian culture

Guirdham (2009) provides an extensive overview of relations between culture and business in selected Asian countries. Her conclusion regarding business in India is that it is characterised by the following features:

- status acknowledged by deference
- tall hierarchies based on 'master–servant' relationships
- top–down personalised decision-making.

Importantly, Guirdham found evidence of both diversity and change in her research. In India there is a very marked difference between the cultures of large public sector and large private sector organisations, with the latter encouraging originality, entrepreneurial talent and creativity. This resulted in a markedly different attitude toward work and career. In the public sector there is a far greater

employee focus inwards on the traditions of that single work organisation and little expectation of rapid promotion. Guirdham also suggests that business culture in general was viewed as changing with increasing professionalisation of management in small businesses evident, together with a greater focus on meritocratic deadline-based strategies and procedures. There is also some suggestion that the growing Indian middle classes will become more entrepreneurial and less inclined to seek secure salaried public sector employment. We have already noted the close inter-woven relationship between an organisation's culture and its structure, so there are clear implications for the structure of Indian organisations if we follow Guirdham's analysis of current Indian business and future trends.

1 Locate Guirdham's depiction of Indian business within both Trompenaars' and Hofstede's models of national and organisational culture.

2 With reference to any one named Indian private sector organisation, assess the extent of movement away from the traditional model of business in India. (Use published company sources, eg from corporate websites, as a basis for your answer.)

5.10 CONTEMPORARY AND EMERGING STRUCTURES

Much of the preceding commentary on the relative influence of national- or societal-level culture on organisational arrangements refers to research undertaken from a 30-year period following the 1960s. One result of this chronology, which is entirely to be expected, is that the debate regarding cultural influence has been applied to the dominant organisational forms of the time. In particular, it can be seen that many studies investigate the ways in which organisations in diverse societies deviate from the bureaucratic model, but bureaucracy is, of course, assumed to be the paradigm.

It is self-evidently true to say that work organisations operate in very different environments in the early twenty-first century. In as much as globalisation is often cited as a major influence upon organisations' operating arrangements, we can anticipate that culture itself has been a central influence on the development of new organisational forms. We now identify some characteristic trends in organisation structure apparent at the time of writing, and put forward suggestions on how far they are open to cross-cultural analysis. In the case of the first trend mentioned there is, of course, no doubt as to its relevance in this respect!

5.10.1 INTERNATIONALISATION

In Chapter 1 it was noted that this phenomenon is not new, nor has it been limited to specific periods of time in the past. However, it is recognised that the pace and extent of globalisation since 1990 has required many more organisational designers and managers to confront the structural implications of increased international activity. Although our focus is on the nature of multinational or transnational organisations, it should also be recorded that a range of strategies may be adopted which stop short of establishing a full-time physical presence in more than one country. These include franchising, by which a franchisor is involved in the set-up and monitoring of a foreign outlet or unit but is not necessarily involved in day-to-day management. The use of agents in other countries similarly allows the major part of an organisation's activities to continue in the home country while maintaining representation in other locations.

Mead and Andrews (2009) note that transnational companies are typically preoccupied with the issue of control. They can use a number of different instruments for control including those based around technology or budgets and other financial instruments or staffing policy (we examine this aspect in far greater detail in Chapter 10). Another instrument for control is the structural relationship between company headquarters and its subsidiaries. When examining ways in which organisations seek to establish large-scale operations across national boundaries, Bartlett and Ghoshal (1998) identify the following strategies typically underpinning supranational operation. As can be seen, each strategy contains certain in-built assumptions regarding structure:

- *International* – In this strategy core products are developed for the original (home) setting and sold in other countries. Products may then be adapted for local markets. This strategy holds the most potential for variation in structure with a mix of standardised structures – for core activities – and scope for local variation in other more peripheral areas.

- *Multi-domestic* – The characteristic feature of this strategy is decentralisation, the national units (or subsidiaries) retaining high levels of autonomy in terms of overall strategy and, importantly in this context, ways of structuring their operations.
- *Global* – A global strategy implies centralisation of production methods, which in turn very likely requires standardised structures with little scope for local adaptation.
- *Transnational* – In this case a range of structures are possible – regional or product-based, or both combined in matrix form. However, the chosen structure will reflect a corporate culture based on shared goals and values, allowing for local variation while seeking a high degree of co-ordination across countries. Structures therefore facilitate horizontal communication, even at the expense of hierarchy, in order that knowledge is jointly developed and shared.

The transnational strategy is the most complex in terms of prescribing structural arrangements because the overriding principle in a firm adopting this approach is one of synergy and the ways in which this can best be achieved will emerge within the structure. It is also pertinent to record that this strategy critically appears to demand reconciliation of culturally derived values, in this context relating to preferences regarding organisational structure. The stress on reconciliation in this respect has echoes of Trompenaars' work in his emphasis on the need for successful international managers to reconcile their own cultural views with their actual experience. This subject is examined again in greater detail in Chapter 9. However, it should first be recorded that empirical evidence for the existence of transnational firms is limited and such a firm may exist more at the level of an idealised construct at present. Overall, whichever strategy is chosen, Bartlett and Ghoshal's work helps us to appreciate both the range of available structures when companies 'internationalise' and the importance of this topic area in understanding the nature of international strategies.

5.10.2 NETWORK STRUCTURES

In previous chapters we have examined the work of Holden (2002), who envisaged a new role for cross-cultural management in facilitating knowledge transfer and continuous learning. This focus would seem to be predicated on suitable organisational arrangments allowing such sharing to take place. A suitable network structure would not resemble the traditional top–down centralised bureaucracy; rather, it would instead be based on multi-level systems of communication with dispersed autonomy and power to implement decisions. Broeways and Price (2011) suggest that the networking implied in such a model means that the setting in which it would occur would be that of a learning organisation. A learning organisation would, by its very nature, have a distinctive – essentially fluid – structure since the definition of such an entity involves it transforming itself through its core purpose of encouraging the learning and development of its members (Mullins 2013). If and as cross-cultural management evolves away from a preoccupation with cultural difference to a role centred on knowledge management, the stage in which it plays out, namely the organisational setting, must itself change to reflect this new reality.

5.10.3 DOWNSIZING AND DE-LAYERING

One result of globalisation has been a trend for the owners of organisations to review both overall staffing levels and the deployment of employees. Readers resident in the UK since 2000 will almost certainly be familiar with this phenomenon in the light of its widespread coverage in the national media. Nonetheless, as we shall see, the practice is evident across a range of countries. The received wisdom emanating from media coverage is that in the face of international competition – manifested in alternative skilled and educated workforces who are comparatively cheap to employ – there has been an outflow of particular types of job from Western societies. To take a Western perspective would be parochial (and against the spirit of this book) but also misleading, since it would ignore the profound impact downsizing in Western societies has had in others; for example, in countries in the Indian subcontinent.

One specific trend that can be observed when analysing the job migration phenomenon is the strategy of shifting 'back office' jobs to new country locations. In March 2006, for example, it was reported that Deutsche Bank planned to relocate almost half of the jobs in its sales and trading functions to India. One such report in the online journal *Banking Business Review* (2006) indicated that this movement of jobs would result in a tripling of the German bank's offshore staffing establishment to 2,000 workers. Such a substantial restructuring is likely to bring several new strategic concerns into view, including the issue of trust. It is suggested here that the topic of trust is likely to re-emerge as an increasingly important issue both for academic study and management attention, given very large-scale relocation of business operations exemplified by Deutsche Bank. One could expect further studies along the lines of Mohr's (2003) paper focusing on business relationships between alliance partners in China and Germany, which indicated that cross-cultural ventures could necessitate a review of the balance between trust and control within such relationships. The work of Fox (1974) identifying low- and high-discretion work patterns based on trust relations might usefully be re-interpreted within a cross-cultural perspective.

There is also scope for further cross-cultural study as additional countries become involved in the outsourcing trend. A European Commission-funded project entitled Emergence has concluded that whereas India has benefitted from a period in which it was a major net importer of back-office jobs, it is likely to be replaced in this regard by Indonesia, Sri Lanka, Thailand and Vietnam, while India is, in turn, already an outsourcer of jobs to Bulgaria, Hungary and Russia. The cultural profiles of these countries will in part determine the structural arrangements within the new locations when the jobs coalesce into formalised work organisations.

Overall, the back-office exporting trend has the potential for significant structural change if whole areas of organisations' activities are to be increasingly located in different areas of the world. Once again, however, one should be wary of assuming – or even implying – that trends within international business and cross-cultural management, more specifically, are irrevocable or subject to a fixed logic. There is some evidence that the offshoring trend may be past its peak. In February 2014 it was reported that the mobile phone company EE was planning to return its call centre operations to the UK (initially Northern Ireland) from the Philippines, while other organisations including the UK-based building society Nationwide had expressed a strategic intent to retain its back-office operations in the UK. There has been some suggestion that rising labour costs in Asia may have led companies (for example EE) to consider whether aspects of their operations – for example, customer service centres – should be 'returned home'. Cost considerations would be, of course, a quite normal consideration in such decisions. The entire phenomenon is, in short, ongoing.

Fiat and Chrysler – a new alliance

The global financial crisis and prolonged recession from 2008 to 2014 had a very serious impact on the automobile sector worldwide. One of the many casualties was the US Chrysler Group, which, according to media reports, had been down to its last dollars before government intervention and Chapter 11 bankruptcy, intended to stave off the company's collapse. In June 2009, it was announced that the Italian car-maker Fiat would henceforth run a newly constituted Chrysler group. The incoming CEO was announced as Fiat Chief Executive Sergio Marchionne. At the time of writing it was not clear how Marchionne would structure the new company; however, that month's edition of *Business Week* speculated that Marchionne would not run Fiat and Chrysler as two separate companies but would, instead, centralise operations in Italy with designers and engineers working in Michigan, USA. *Business Week* drew attention to the precedent of the Ford Motor Company, which, in a change of strategy, currently ran global product development from Michigan following years of placing key staff on different continents.

This episode clearly illustrates the important structural dimension of such global ventures. Consider the range of options available to this company's new executive board with reference to the models set out in this chapter. They are numerous and potentially critical to the success of the new venture. Interestingly, Sergio Marchionne himself recognised the key role played by structural arrangements. *Business Week* quoted him as follows: 'Five years ago, I stepped into a very similar situation at Fiat. It was perceived by many as a failing, lethargic automaker that produced low-quality cars and was stymied by endless bureaucracies. But most of the people capable of remaking Fiat had been there all along. We created a more efficient company while investing heavily in our techologies and platforms. And, importantly, we created a culture where everyone is expected to lead.'

5.11 CONCLUSION: CULTURE AND STRUCTURE – A COMPLEX AREA

Many textbooks in the field of international or cross-cultural business include closing sections in individual chapters weighing up the degree of convergence and divergence between cultures in the relevant subject area. It would be especially problematic to do so here because the issue of cultural similarity and difference is complex, multifaceted and potentially changing. In this chapter we have seen some evidence of worldwide harmonisation of organisational structures, partly via the impact of universal contingencies, while at the same time there is also clear evidence of significant difference between organisations operating in specific societies. The challenges faced by firms operating within global or transnational strategies further add to the range of possible outcomes when we examine the relationship between culture and organisation structure. Schneider and Barsoux (2003), reporting the findings of a study by Hofstede and Bond (1988) focusing on Asian businesses, even question the received wisdom that organisations do have to adapt to contingencies in order to survive and prosper. Schneider and Barsoux note (p111) that, 'companies in Hong Kong, Japan and Singapore where the hierarchy remains firmly in place have performed well in industries such as banking which are facing turbulent environments. Here, other value orientations, not readily apparent in Western business, may be at work, ie Confucian dynamism, thrift, persistence and a long-term perspective, which may account for the competitiveness of the Five Asian Dragons: China, Hong Kong, Taiwan, Japan and South Korea.' This last point, concluding the discussion of culture and structure, highlights once again the enduring role that culture plays in analyses of business, and also shows how Western models which are shaped by their own, and consequently culturally bound, dimensions of culture can only partly explain events across the world.

CASE STUDY 5.2

OUTSOURCING IN DIFFERENT DIRECTIONS

In 2005 Dutch bank ABN Amro announced that it was to outsource its global IT operations to the USA and India, with a net loss of 1,500 jobs. Such a development was in itself not unusual at that time, but what was more distinctive was the bank's strategy to outsource to two contrasting countries at different stages of economic development.

In a €1.8 billion deal, ABN Amro planned to transfer its core IT systems management to the US company IBM, while at the same time outsourcing support and development functions to four other businesses, including three Indian firms: Infosys, Patni and Tata Consultancy Services.

The five-year deal was intended to result in a saving to ABN Amro of approximately €260 million in each year.

The bank had conducted a fundamental review of operations within its highly competitive environment with a view to achieving significant cost reduction. In terms of staffing, the US outsourcing venture, which also involved Accenture, was planned to result in 1,500 job losses in the period to mid-2007, coupled with a transfer from the Netherlands of a further 2,000 employees to the other partner organisations.

Infosys and Tata Consultancy were to take over software maintenance within this new agreement, while software development was planned to pass to Accenture, IBM, Infosys, Patni and Tata Consultancy.

Questions

1 With reference to the work of either Geert Hofstede or Fons Trompenaars and Charles Hampden-Turner, list anticipated differences in attitudes towards organisation structure among the partners in this Dutch/American/Indian joint venture.

2 Explain how both a global and transnational strategy in this venture could influence the organisational arrangements underpinning the ABN Amro deal.

NOTES

1, 2 ROSEN, E. (2014) Pope Francis promotes collaborative structure. 30 April. Available at: http://collaborationblog.typepad.com/collaboration/religion [Accessed 16 October 2014].

REVIEW QUESTIONS

1   Summarise the arguments which minimise the role of culture in explaining organisation structure.

2   Identify the potential usefulness of either Trompenaars' or Hofstede's explanation of how culture can impact on organisation structure.

3   Assess the relevance of the topic of organisation structure within the study of cross-cultural management.

FURTHER READING

AYCAN, Z., KANUNGO, R. N. and MENDONCA, M. (2013) *Organizations and management in cross-cultural context.* London: Sage. These authors provide another contribution to material covered in this chapter and extend the discussion to the effect of culture on organisational change.

LINSTEAD, S., FULOP, L. and LILLEY, S. (2009) *Management and organization: a critical text.* 2nd ed. Basingstoke: Palgrave Macmillan. Chapter 4 of this text comprises a reflective review of the nature of organisation structure and the ways in which thinking on this topic has developed over time.

MULLINS, L. J. (2013) *Management and organisational behaviour.* 10th ed. Harlow: FT Prentice Hall. The topic of organisation structure is covered in Chapter 15 in a clear and comprehensive fashion and is recommended as an introduction to the topic.

Visit this book's companion website (**www.cipd.co.uk/olr**) to find further exercises including self-assessment questions and also weblinks to media and academic journal articles.

CHAPTER 6

Intercultural Communication and Negotiation

LEARNING OBJECTIVES

After reading this chapter you should be able to:

- identify the elements of the intercultural communication process, including potential barriers to intercultural communication
- appreciate the key significance of communication in analysing culture and cultural difference
- consider ways in which intercultural communication can be enhanced
- highlight the importance of culture in negotiation processes.

6.1 INTRODUCTION

The title of this chapter indicates a departure from terminology used in previous sections in that the term 'intercultural' is, in some places, used in preference to 'cross-cultural'. The word 'intercultural' is often used in this chapter because the topic of communication within the cross-cultural management area largely focuses on developing and sustaining supportive relationships between people. The word 'intercultural' might be regarded as more accurately reflecting this interpersonal dimension. However, intercultural and cross-cultural can be viewed as interchangeable terms separated only by nuances of meaning.

In Chapter 5 we examined the extent to which formal organisational arrangements could be subject to the influence of culture and consequently differ across cultural boundaries. While in an important sense organisations can, on the surface, look similar across the world, as we saw there is also convincing evidence pointing to cultural variation. We now turn to look at the impact of culture on several organisational processes, beginning here with a discussion of the topic of communication.

Readers might anticipate at the outset that we are entering into a subject area rich in potential for intercultural analysis. If formal structure can be subject to cultural difference, it is even more likely that an interpersonal process such as communication will be too.

For many of us the very first experiences of encountering people from other cultures involves an attempt to establish a connection – in short, to communicate with them. The extent to which we communicate effectively in turn colours our relationships: if communication fails, no relationship will be possible. In this chapter we consider both factors which could harm intercultural communication and the ways in which these can be addressed. One specific aspect of communication is negotiation and we will identify the ways in which culture impinges on people's views on the nature of negotiation and some consequent differences in preferred negotiation style and desirable outcomes. We also, in more general terms, reinforce the view set out in Chapter 3 that cultures are in part characterised by the ways in which their members communicate. This being so, it is necessary to understand distinctive communication styles in order to demarcate and classify cultures, both of which are necessary in order to fully understand them.

6.2 THE NEED FOR AWARENESS

'It is useless discussing Hindus with me. Living with them teaches me no more. When I think I annoy them, I do not. When I think I don't annoy them, I do. Perhaps they will sack me for tumbling onto their doll's house; on the other hand, perhaps they will double my salary. Time will prove.'

These words spoken by Dr Aziz, a character in E. M. Forster's 1924 novel *A Passage to India*, perfectly capture the perplexity and frustration experienced when people cannot comprehend the values and behaviour of those from other cultures. In this type of situation, other human beings appear alien and no true interaction is possible.

To what extent can a futile situation, as depicted in this novel, be seen as a likely occurrence in a business setting? In Chapter 3 we noted the multinational bank HSBC's advertising campaign intended to highlight the bank's stated objectives both to recognise local difference within a global business environment and to respect cultural diversity. Advertisements watched by television and cinema audiences were based on cultural misunderstandings scenarios and the negative consequences these engendered. Our selected example in the earlier chapter featured an (apparently Western) businessman attending a dinner arranged by Asian hosts. In an attempt to appear polite the Western guest finishes each dish placed in front of him. However, the hosts interpret this as meaning that insufficient food has been provided. The upshot is that the guest consumes increasingly outlandish food which he has no desire to eat. Neither the hosts nor the guest are aware of the cultural misunderstandings underpinning the encounter and, as a result, are trapped in a vortex of misunderstanding.

This example shows the potential importance of perceptual barriers in intercultural communication. Neither party can move on to communicate effectively if they initially fail to perceive relevant differences. Guirdham (2011) introduces the notion of group difference in inter-group communication, noting that modern work generally involves meeting or working with individuals from different backgrounds. We differ along many different dimensions; for example by age, socio-economic group (or class), level of education and professional and occupational status. Guirdham suggests that when we communicate with others, we do so not only as individuals with unique personalities and attributes but also in an important sense as representatives of social groups.

Likewise, the concept of inter-group communication is key within the overall approach taken in this book, in that awareness of (in our case, intercultural) difference is necessary for individuals who encounter people from other backgrounds in business contexts. Nonetheless, it is also important to recognise dangers (for example, over-generalisation) when gaining such awareness. A delicate balance is called for in this regard.

6.3 STEREOTYPING REVISITED

In Chapter 2 we alerted readers to the ample scope for stereotypical findings within cross-cultural writing, at the same time indicating ways in which researchers in the field had sought to minimise these within their work. It was also suggested that stereotypes were not entirely negative in that they could contain elements of truth and might provide a necessary underpinning for more precise delineation of cultural difference, particularly if the stereotypes were consciously held.

In the context of intercultural communication, stereotyping emerges once more as an important concept. In particular it has frequently been put forward (see, for example, Huczynski and Buchanan 2013) as a significant barrier to good intercultural communication. A more evaluative approach was taken by Schneider and Barsoux (2003, p15): 'The problem with stereotyping is that it conjures up an image [from die-casting] of stamping the same type on every blank face. It may be more useful to think of prototypes which allow for variation around a set of core characteristics.' In both cases the danger highlighted is essentially one of over-simplification and hence inaccurate judgement when perceiving individuals from other cultural groups. We might add at this point that a further error is to assume that specific behaviour will be exhibited by an individual from within the identified group; eg if you held a stereotypical belief that Dutch people were argumentative and that an individual Dutch citizen was therefore also argumentative, would you be right in predicting that he or she would make points in an especially robust way during contractual negotiations?

Stereotyping – a term coined by Lippman in 1922 – can be understood with reference to some basic principles of perceptual selection and organisation. In processing the infinite number of stimuli bombarding our sensory apparatus, certain stimuli are filtered for our attention and perception. It is simply not possible to internalise or take in all stimuli; rather, stimuli are selected according to particular principles, including contrast and novelty, both of which are highly applicable to our area of study. In Chapter 9, for example, we examine the phenomenon of 'culture shock', a model setting out sequential psychological processes which may occur when we find ourselves in a new culture. Factors in the new cultural setting which are very different from the original context are selected for attention and loom large in the consciousness of the new arrival. Similarly, an employee from another culture or a different ethnic group may stand out from his or her colleagues due to contrast (and conceivably novelty).

Perceptual organisation is also relevant within the cross-cultural area. This principle explains how we attempt to interpret stimuli, including our perception of others, into a meaningful and complete picture. Wertheimer, in establishing the Gestalt principle of perception in the 1920s, showed how individuals seek closure when interpreting external stimuli: what is seemingly disorganised and incomprehensible must be given meaning. One way in which this may occur is through categorising an individual by focusing on limited criteria, including his or her cultural background. In this sense stereotyping can be seen as a rational attempt to take a short cut to understanding an unfamiliar individual. Whether through selection or organisation, the (usually flawed) logic of stereotyping involves locating an individual within a pre-existing group, referring to the assumed characteristics of that group, and attributing them to the individual in question.

Stereotyping is unlikely to facilitate good and effective intercultural communication. An impression of another person based on incomplete or irrelevant information may lead us to filter out aspects of that individual which do not conform to the stereotype(s) used. In these circumstances we are unlikely to recognise that individual's unique personality or value systems, and by failing to do so we are arguably guilty of diminishing his or her essential humanity. In commonsense terms we will hear and see only what we expect to hear and see – which is certainly at the very least unprofessional behaviour. Because our stereotypical perceptions will not be value-free, we also run the risk of developing and perpetuating prejudiced attitudes. In the area of perception the terms 'halo effect' and 'horns effect' illustrate the positive and negative – or angelic and diabolical – connotations of perceptual judgements. Thompson and McHugh (2009, p266) point to possible wider social consequences of stereotyping: 'Stereotyping, then, is one of the mechanisms through which racism and sexism are socially enacted and given ideological justification.' We are here making an assumption that people involved in cross-cultural management would not wish, for a variety of reasons, to be party to prejudiced or discriminatory practices, so once again the term 'stereotyping' should sound a warning note.

GROUP ACTIVITY 6.1

Minoriteam

Minoriteam is an animated television programme first shown on a US cartoon network in November 2005. The basic premise of the programme involves the adventures of five 'superheroes', each appearing initially as a stereotyped figure, who in typical superhero vein battle against a group of villains that include the White Shadow, the Corporate Ladder and the Standardized Text (depicted as favourably biased towards white people). The superheroes are:

● Dr Wang, Chinese human calculator
● Non-Stop, an Indian convenience-store owner
● Jewcano
● El Jefe, a Mexican crime-fighter

● Fasto, the world's fastest man and an African-American.

Several of these characters have non-stereotypical alternative existences – for example, El Jefe is a senior executive for an oil company, and Fasto is employed as a Professor of Women's Studies!

1 Invent two new stereotypical characters for inclusion in Minoriteam. Show the bases for your thinking in inventing the characters. Create a non-stereotypical alternative existence for the two new characters. Provide an imagined example of how one of your new characters would regard one of the existing superheroes, and how this might affect communication between the two.

6.4 OTHER BARRIERS TO INTERCULTURAL COMMUNICATION

In addition to highlighting the specific dangers of stereotyping and prejudice when considering how we communicate with people from other cultures, it is also useful to reconsider fundamental aspects of the communication process *per se* in order to guard against other potential barriers. The classic perception of interpersonal communication views it as a linear process comprising a series of steps (essentially: encoding, transmission, decoding and feedback) which, when completed, result in the successful transmission of a thought from the sender to the receiver. The elements within this linear model are thus:

● *The sender*: the person or group intending to communicate.
● *Encoding*: the sender translates the thought for transmission into a code which the recipient(s) can understand.
● *The message*: the result or output of encoding, which is then transmitted.
● *The medium of communication*: the mode of transmission– as we will see, a great deal of communication occurs non-verbally, so the chosen medium may only partly convey the intended meaning.
● *Decoding*: the receiver interprets the meaning of the communication (an important aspect in intercultural or cross-cultural communication, since we may decode in different ways).
● *Feedback*: the receiver at this point becomes a sender (if only to acknowledge transmission); genuine feedback should enable the originator of the communication to judge the effectiveness of transmission.

This classic model of communication can justifiably be criticised in that the apparently sequential stages may occur virtually simultaneously in reality, and furthermore, the feedback depicted as completing the communication loop is required at each stage; ie each step of the process must be reciprocal if effective communication is to occur. However, our purpose is not to call into question an established model at this stage, rather to see how it can be applied in the cross-cultural context. In this respect the possibility of disruption at each stage of the process in the form of 'noise' – a technical term borrowed from radio technology and used to describe all forms of distortion – is particularly worthy of examination.

Taking the elements of the model in the sequence presented, the first possible difficulty in intercultural communication emerges when the sender encodes, that is to say, chooses a medium for transmission. One very obvious potential problem relates to language itself, a problem that becomes very quickly evident if the recipient of the message fails to understand the language used. In intercultural communication one fundamental decision is therefore which language to use. Another concern from the sender's viewpoint should be whether the recipient will be able to register nuances of meaning if his or her first language is different from that used in the message. Even when the sender and recipient share a similar linguistic facility, words can still be used differently. There are, for example, a number of examples of different usage in the English spoken in the UK and in North America (to take just a few, the words 'curb', 'pants' and 'boot' have different meanings in each setting). It may also be that when a phrase becomes slang or a cliché in one country, its precise meaning may not be apparent to speakers of the same language in another country: 'Garbage in, garbage out' was something of a technical term in computer usage as it emerged in the USA but might well not initially have been understood for a time elsewhere. The word 'mansion' denotes a modest-sized apartment in Japan, far removed from the image conjured up by a British person encountering the same word. Finally, books and articles in the field of international marketing are full of (mostly) amusing product names with inappropriate meanings for other cultures. One such episode occurred when an advertising slogan for the soft drink Pepsi originating as 'Pepsi brings you back to life' had the original literal translation of: 'Pepsi brings your ancestors back from the grave' when used in the Chinese market.

Cultural differences as manifested through language are not confined only to vocabulary: the structure of a language is both a reflection of culture at a deep level and serves to reinforce the culture through the expression of its members. Gao (2005), in examining the relationships between language and other aspects of culture in Japan, identifies several interesting points for consideration in this regard. Indirectness as one element of Japanese values is for Gao manifested in language. For example, the cultural value of harmony can be reflected in a number of ways including careful choice of words and indirect speech. She also suggests that in Japanese culture it is normal to take time to gauge other people's emotions before venturing an opinion when conversing with them, and furthermore that there will be a desire to avoid disagreement as far as possible. Gao goes on to show how in Japan language is used to avoid making categorical statements, which are regarded as a sign of egotistical behaviour.

In the same article she then shows how the unique structure of languages may render them more or less amenable to cross-cultural communication. Whereas Chinese and English are 'synthetic' languages in which a change in word order may considerably affect the meaning, Japanese is a strictly 'agglutinative' language in which word order is relatively insignificant and the concluding word in a sentence generally defines the emotional stance of the speaker. Chinese and English are syntactically fairly similar, so that a person speaking in English but using Chinese word order can apparently communicate reasonably understandably with another English-speaking person. However, a combination of Japanese word order using either Chinese or English words would result in incomprehensible communication – in Gao's own term, 'gibberish'. In summary, the choice to encode a message in a particular language has definite implications which go beyond mere considerations of vocabulary. That choice will unravel the interdependence between culture and language, and it is also important in that the specific language will be more or less amenable to cross-cultural communication.

The media in which language is used to transmit messages should also be reviewed when considering communication between cultures. It has frequently been stated that new technologies (for example, the use of email) have enhanced intercultural communication, certainly in terms of speed and in enabling 24-hour communication across the world's time-zones. It is also plausible to view standardisation of software as contributing to worldwide convergence in communication. It remains the case, however, that one should not assume familiarity with all methods of transmission. Morgan (1989) reproduces the story emanating originally from Marshall McLuhan's work of a group of Western volunteer workers who showed an educational film on the subject of water sanitation to African aid workers. These local viewers, on being asked to summarise the film's main points, thought that it was basically about a chicken, due to the fact that such an animal had appeared very briefly in one corner of the screen. Their attention had been drawn to the fastest-moving image in the film, and being untrained in constructing reality from the communication medium of film, they were at the time unable to perceive the intended messages. The implication for our purposes in this chapter is to highlight the need to check that transmission media are appropriate for the intended recipients of communication and not to make culturally based assumptions.

6.5 MIXED MESSAGES AND NON-VERBAL COMMUNICATION

It might be assumed from reading the previous sections that communication is essentially based on the exchange of messages through language. Any brief perusal of the communication literature would dispel such a view, however, and quickly alert the reader to the crucial importance of non-verbal communication (NVC). Bloisi et al (2006) note that a very high proportion of the meaning exchanged between people in face-to-face communication can come from non-verbal channels. In that 93% of meaning is transmitted in this way, NVC is, they claim, more reliable than verbal communications, should the two modes of communication impart different meanings. Bloisi et al indeed propose that NVC can be used as an informal lie detector, helping an active listener to interpret another person's words. In addition to the generic importance of NVC, this aspect of communication is especially pertinent in the cross-cultural area when we consider some of its functions as set out below:

- *Reinforcement of written or spoken communication* – When communicating with others less proficient in our own first language, we may find it helpful to strengthen our message in non-verbal ways – try to describe a spiral staircase without using hand movements, for example!
- *Symbols* – Gestures have specific and vastly different meanings across the world, and it is important to be aware of not all or even a fraction of these but rather of the potential cultural variation *per se*. A leading British organisational behaviour textbook (Buchanan and Huczynski 2004) began a section introducing comparative material by referring to the training of airport employees in terms of recognising the cultural significance of body movements – putting together the tips of the thumb and forefinger can, for example, signify anything from jocular agreement to vicious insult.
- *Signifying attitudes and emotions* – One should note firstly that this aspect of non-verbal communication may occur at different levels. Writers in this area, including Michael Argyle in his seminal work of 1967, have suggested that NVC can be understood in part by viewing it as vestigial childhood behaviour. For example, an adult hearing something not to his or her liking might touch an ear – the equivalent of a child cupping both hands over its ears when hearing an unwelcome message. Vestigial behaviour of this sort can occur below the level of conscious thought. Awareness of this may therefore be particularly useful in interpersonal encounters where it can, for a variety of reasons, be difficult to interpret spoken words. As previously suggested, the non-verbal cue, if understood, may provide a more accurate gauge of how the sender really feels.

More than this, Guirdham (2011) proposes that non-verbal communication behaviour itself varies between cultural groups. In order to pursue this important idea we now examine significant types of non-verbal communication.

6.5.1 KINESICS

This refers to body movements including posture, gestures and facial expression. One can expect these to vary considerably in their received meaning across the world. A website devoted to business etiquette in Indonesia[1] includes the following exhortations for business travellers unfamiliar with that country:

- Do not crook your index finger to call someone over. That gesture is offensive.
- Never stand with your back to an elderly person or a high-ranking official.
- Never show the soles of your feet or shoes, nor touch anything with your feet.
- No physical contact between men and women is made in public, except a possible handshake.

As indicated, one particular variant of kinesics is facial expression. In this context, Francesco and Gold (2005, p76) note that 'the smile usually indicates happiness or pleasure, but for Asians it may also be a sign of embarrassment or discomfort'. Even allowing for the possibility of 'fixed' or uncomfortable smiling in Western cultures, it appears that there may be a specific – and important – meaning to the smile in Asian cultures, which could fundamentally affect intercultural communications involving this group. Later in this chapter we link this and other aspects of NVC to wider concepts and models of cultural difference.

In a similar vein, oculesics, or eye contact, may also be perceived differently. It is possible that eye contact could denote untrustworthiness to Chinese people.

6.5.2 CHROMATICS

This form of NVC relates to the significance of colour in terms of its perceptual impact on the receiver. There is clearly ample scope for sending unintended messages if the sender is unaware of the meaning a colour holds for members of a particular society. While the author was aware of the Chinese view that red is an auspicious colour – evidenced by the vivid profusion of red at Chinese New Year – he had not known that red is associated with death in the Hindu religion until asked by a student not to write comments in red on her draft coursework. This is another area where business etiquette guides excel in alerting us to potential pitfalls. However, useful though such knowledge may be, one might reasonably assume that host cultures are at least partly tolerant of unintended faux pas. Would people in the Czech Republic really assume romantic interest if presented with red flowers by a visitor from another culture, for example? For our purposes it is sufficient to recognise that colour is bound up with non-verbal communication, which may be by no means obvious to someone approaching the area.

6.5.3 PROXEMICS

Proxemics refers to how space is used – either intentionally or unintentionally – in communication. The importance of this aspect of NVC was recognised in the influential work of Michael Argyle, who noted that physical proximity was a cue for intimacy, and that there were other tacitly approved 'zones' for social and business interactions. Argyle (1967, p38) also recognised that, 'The normal degree of proximity varies between cultures.'

With the more recent trends in globalisation leading to increasing cross-cultural interactions, several writers have expanded on this basic theme. Schneider and Barsoux (2003, p106), in examining office layouts in Japan, note that, 'This use of physical space and the consequent patterns of interaction, are cultural artefacts which reveal different beliefs regarding the optimal degree of hierarchy, formalisation and levels of participation.'

Guirdham (2011), focusing on the more interpersonal aspect of proxemics, concludes that Arabs and Europeans differ in terms of comfortable distance when talking to someone, with other significant differences evident in terms of facing, touching, voice tone and eye contact.

Proxemics is an interesting area within cross-cultural study in that it is manifested at a deep level of culture and conveys deeply held values and attitudes (see Chapter 2 for a discussion on the levels of culture). We return to this point later in the chapter when applying the topic within established models of culture.

 WHAT DOES IT MEAN TO BE GREEN?

CASE STUDY 6.1

'It's not easy being green.' These words sung by Kermit the Frog, a character from the 1970s television programme *The Muppet Show*, who was himself green, might serve as a signal of the complex and varying interpretations of colour in different cultures. Green has some widespread and commonly held significance as the colour symbolising nature, ecology and new beginnings across much of the world. However, there are important differences too. Green is associated with inexperience and jealousy in Western cultures (Shakespeare's 'green-eyed monster'), while it is linked to disgrace in China where, we are told, a man whose partner was cheating on him could be identified by him wearing a green hat! In the USA there is a particular association with money (the dollar is nicknamed the 'greenback'), while in North Africa green symbolises corruption. The hidden meanings of colours range from the profound – green is the sacred colour of Islam – to the trivial and obscure, as in the perception in the UK in the 1960s that green was an unwise choice when buying a car because it was unlucky.

Questions

1   Choose any one colour and show how its meaning and significance varies between different cultures. You may refer to business etiquette websites in your search.

2   Indicate how differences in perception of colour can reflect the different levels of culture (surface, middle and core) set out in Chapter 2.

3   How important do you think it is to recognise the cultural significance of colour (eg if you are male would you wear a green hat in China?) Give reasons for your conclusions.

6.6 ENHANCING INTERCULTURAL COMMUNICATION

If there are potentially important barriers to intercultural communication which could realistically vitiate the quality of interaction with people from other cultural groups, it is clearly relevant to have an awareness of those barriers as a first step to clearing the way for effective communication. This could be regarded as a merely defensive strategy, however, and it is preferable to take a more proactive role when seeking to enhance the value of intercultural encounters. How can this best be achieved?

It is suggested here that one way of enhancing intercultural communication is to have a thorough awareness of cross-cultural differences *per se*. Following our summary of some of the key models set out in Chapter 3, we will revisit the models with a view to extracting elements relevant to this topic area. Before undertaking this exercise, it should also be noted that a range of interpersonal attributes can also assist in facilitating positive communication:

- *An open, non-judgemental attitude* – It will be difficult to communicate effectively if 'noise' exists in the form of pre-formed negative attitudes towards a cultural group and therefore the representatives of that group (see our earlier discussion of stereotyping).
- *Self-awareness* – This covers both one's individual personal impact on an encounter, including posture and tone of voice, and knowledge of one's own cultural characteristics, eg American direct style of communication.
- *Resourcefulness and taking responsibility* – Readers can consider how they would communicate as foreign tourists faced with a lack of linguistic ability; finding alternative ways to communicate while not making assumptions about ambiguous messages could be useful tools, and this sense of resourcefulness applies equally to business settings.
- *Empathy* – In part an extension of the non-judgemental approach, empathy is also a personal characteristic. The psychologist Carl Rogers has argued that true listening – achieved by putting oneself in another person's position – is the key to overcoming misunderstandings in communication. The (difficult) skill of empathetic listening may be critical in the intercultural context.

Lewis (2004), in the course of an extended analysis of how best to communicate across cultures, has identified a series of 'weapons for empathy'; in other words, behavioural tools or states of mind, which he claims help an individual approach an intercultural encounter. They include:

- tact
- politeness
- calm
- patience
- warmth.

Guirdham (2011) suggests, finally, that intercultural sensitivity tends to lead to the use of elaborated codes when communicating. An elaborated code would typically involve use of a densely verbal style containing considerable explanation and elaboration in an attempt to avoid making assumptions as to what is understood. Noting that adopting this style is something of a 'double-edged sword' in terms of effective communication, Guirdham records that using an elaborated code might be necessary but can mean that intercultural encounters are marked by excessive formality. Such formality could have the unintended consequence of hindering relationship development. People from some cultures, eg North Americans, might also interpret the formality as unfriendliness. In conclusion, however, one can only commend the use of elaborated codes within the spirit of cultural sensitivity, as an aid to understanding.

The individual psychological aspects of communication, listed above, are important in that they provide a basis for effective communication. For example, self-awareness can indeed be plausibly seen as a prerequisite to positive communication. It should be noted that only one level of communication – the interpersonal – is relevant when considering this 'micro-level' of communication: others, including mass communication, are highlighted briefly later in the chapter. There is also a suspicion that attributes such as tact and/or patience relate primarily to the presentation of a message. If the content of the message is problematic, good presentational skills may not be enough to guarantee a successful interpersonal encounter. Nonetheless, as we shall see again in Chapter 9, skills and behaviours do have an impact on effective cross-cultural dealings, and we should acknowledge their importance.

6.7 CROSS-CULTURAL THEORY AND COMMUNICATION

At this point we examine selected elements within theories of cultural difference to explore their potential usefulness in elucidating the topic of communication, beginning with an analysis of Hofstede's contribution. As set out in Chapter 3, Hofstede initially identified four dimensions of culture (later joined by a fifth) along which individual societies can be compared. Although all of the dimensions can plausibly link to communication, the specific focus taken here is on power distance (PD).

Do the wide fluctuations in PD scores in Hofstede's work take effect in business communication both within and between societies? Material contained in a website devoted to Hofstede's work[2] points to significant divergence in this regard. For example, in a low PD country such as Israel, Hofstede's model indicates the prevalence of participative, two-way communication styles. This can be explained by a willingness on the part of subordinates to question the authority of senior figures within hierarchies, and, on the reverse side of the coin, a need for a more democratic management approach manifested in informal styles of communication.

Other ways in which Hofstede's power distance concept links to communication centre on non-verbal aspects. The United Arab Emirates (UAE) scores high in terms of PD. One implication noted in the website is the need for business visitors to the country to dress formally in order to communicate respect and decorum. Another interesting application of PD emanating from the UAE example concerns decision-making. We are informed that the real decision-maker(s) can be identified by lack of participation in verbal communication: they will, rather, remain silent during meetings. This finding is a more arcane aspect of the link between PD and communication, but important, nonetheless, and highlights the desirability of an awareness of academic models of culture in explaining practice.

It is important to recognise that Hofstede's conception of culture is an integrated one in which all four dimensions combine to produce a country's cultural profile. In the area of communication it is quite possible that the dimensions, or more specifically, the country's scores along the dimensions, will result in a mixed or paradoxical picture. Hofstede informs us that the USA's low PD is likely to lead to managers adopting consultative styles of communication, while at the same time the country's high score on individualism results in managers asserting their individual right – based on achievement of their position – to 'sell or tell' decisions (this last point emphasising top–down communication).

In Chapter 2, finally, it was proposed that the way societies regard gender and gender relations should be considered an inherent part of their culture. Gender in the form of the 'M' or masculinity dimension is an important element of culture for Hofstede. In terms of communication, in a more feminine society women will have higher representation in managerial roles, and it is frequently suggested that female managers exhibit distinctive communication styles. The Hofstede resource website previously referred to indicates that communication in business etiquette can also be affected by considerations of gender. In providing tips for communicating in the UAE (and other Arab countries), the aforementioned guide informs its readers that the subject of women should not be raised in discussion, even in enquiring about the health of female relatives. This may well present an ethical dilemma (see Chapter 9) for some people outside that culture.

In earlier chapters it was suggested that the work of Fons Trompenaars is informed by the real-life experiences of managers operating across cultures and is partly intended as a guide to existing or putative international managers. It might be anticipated therefore that Trompenaars and Hampden-Turner's writings stress the very practical issue of communication as part of their model for cross-cultural understanding. Prominent in this regard is their distinction between affective and neutral cultures, a dichotomy analysed in Chapter 3. Trompenaars and Hampden-Turner (1997, p69) draw our attention to the centrality of communication within this dimension as follows: 'Members of cultures which are affectively neutral do not telegraph their feelings but keep them carefully controlled and subdued. In contrast, in cultures high on affectivity people show their feelings plainly by laughing, smiling, grimacing, scowling and gesturing; they attempt to find immediate outlets for their feelings.' There are clear opportunities for misunderstanding between members of affective and neutral cultures, particularly as we not only have different levels of expression but hold evaluative views on what is desirable in this respect. Trompenaars and Hampden-Turner provide many examples of how individuals may disapprove of, for example, expressions of anger or joy in the workplace, or even perceived excessive talking. For Trompenaars it is possible to discern clearly distinctive styles of verbal communication which link to the affective/neutral dimension of culture.

Figure 6.1 Tones of voice characteristic of specific cultures

Figure 6.1 depicts an illuminating comparison of significant differences in characteristic tone of voice in Anglo-Saxon, Latin and Oriental cultures. Again, it is important to record the emotive aspects to these patterns: in neutral societies such as China, people may disapprove of perceived exaggerated tones of voice. Trompenaars and Hampden-Turner also draw our attention to variations within societies, claiming for example (1997, p75) that in Oriental societies, 'Frequently the higher position a person holds, the lower and flatter the voice.'

6.8 THE CRUCIAL CONTRIBUTION OF HALL'S LOW- AND HIGH-CONTEXT MODEL

It has been seen in earlier chapters that theories of culture such as those formulated by Hofstede and Trompenaars, and which take values and behavioural categories as their focus for analysis, can be useful reference points when we approach the topic of intercultural communication. However, the major theoretical perspective that links the topics of culture and communication is provided by Hall (see Chapter 3 for a fuller analysis of his contribution). The key point to recognise at this stage is that for Hall, cultural difference is to be understood in terms of diverse underlying styles of communication within societies. In low-context societies such as the USA, the explicit content of messages is paramount; 'the interpretation people and behavior importantly depends on what is actually said or written' (McFarlin and Sweeney 2013, p105). The contrast with high-context societies such as China is that in the latter category the 'context' or overall situation surrounding the message assumes far greater importance.

There are several important implications of Hall's work for people engaging in intercultural communication, including those listed below:

● Particular care should be given to decoding messages in high-context societies since meaning is wrapped up as much or more in the wider social setting – for example, power relationships – than in the chosen communication code.

- Non-verbal communication is a particularly rich source of meaning when attempting to understand messages in high-context settings.
- High-context societies are associated with indirect styles of communication in which subtlety, conceivably taking the form of ambiguity, is valued, as opposed to the low-context practice of coming quickly to the point of the message. Earlier in the chapter we showed how, for example, it would be necessary to wait until the end of a sentence before responding to a Japanese speaker in order to fully understand the meaning, in the light of the structure of the Japanese language which both determines and perpetuates an indirect style of communication.
- In high-context situations information is likely to be more closely contained within networks; certain people will have greater access to information. Communication may therefore be highly restricted, and it may be difficult for an 'outsider' to gain access to the communication network. The notion of *guanxi* (see Chapter 4) could provide a relevant example of such a situation; we revisit this concept again below.

Note once more that all societies contain situations which can be located within the high-/low-context dichotomy. All four of the bullet points above would be relevant within a close family setting in a low-context society like the UK. Equally, Hall claimed that certain societies could themselves be categorised as high- or low-context, and their members (or those who grew up within them) would exhibit behaviours consistent with the style of communication inherent within that society.

There are wide-ranging implications of Hall's theory and scope for further research in many areas of business studies. One interesting recent study was carried out by Wurtz (2005), examining the content of McDonald's corporate websites in high- and low-context countries, with reference to Hall's typology. Her conclusions, confirming her original hypotheses, were:

- In high-context societies, human presence was a greater feature of McDonald's websites.
- The websites in high-context settings included relatively more imagery and less written text than their counterparts in low-context locations.
- Chosen imagery reflected values associated with the cultural category; for example, the use of family pictures in Asian countries.
- More technically, there was greater divergence in terms of page layout in high-context settings, low-context websites exhibiting greater levels of consistency.

 INDIVIDUAL ACTIVITY 6.2

Highlight the main features of Hall's high- and low-context model of culture. Identify four countries falling into each category.

Write a short briefing note for business travellers from low-context countries advising them on how to communicate effectively with people from high-context cultures.

Provide one example of business communication – for example, from a corporate website – which you think illustrates the characteristics of that society according to Hall's model.

6.9 CHINESE CULTURE

In Chapter 4 some doubt was cast on the validity of the bipolar dimensions approach to analysing culture epitomised by Hofstede, Trompenaars and Hall. As useful as these models are in helping to structure our thoughts when approaching this complex topic area, it is eminently possible to claim that they do not capture the uniqueness of individual cultures, each shaped by its own history, language, economic development and human interactions. Added to this generic concern is the fact that the most influential models of culture are put forward by Western researchers whose choice of cultural dimensions has implicitly been informed by their own cultural background. These points are highly relevant when considering the subject of communication. It is, for example, suggested that in Chinese cultures unique factors, which partly fall outside the aforementioned classic models of culture, do have a profound impact on both intracultural and intercultural communication. Fan (2000) identified 71 elements of Chinese culture, separated into eight sub-categories. For our purposes the following four are highlighted:

- *Harmony and group cohesiveness* – Largely attributed to the influence of Confucianism, these concepts lead in practice to a preoccupation with teamwork and group processes. The two elements combine in a concern with group harmony, which itself is achieved by avoiding conflict wherever possible. Hempel and Chang (2002, p87) claim that, 'The brilliant but socially difficult employee has no place in a Chinese organisation.' One can anticipate that the desire for harmony and concomitant tendency to avoid conflict can be reflected in communication styles. Crookes and Thomas (1998) went further in suggesting that Chinese personality orientations are towards conformity, submissiveness and introversion; if this claim is valid, there will again be an implication for how interpersonal communication is manifested in real-life situations.

- *'Face'* – The concept of 'face' has consistently been highlighted as an important aspect of Chinese culture (see, for example, Luo (1997), and Tang and Ward (2003)). To give face to another person means that one has demonstrated respect for him or her. Conversely, if an individual loses face, he or she also suffers a loss of pride and may experience shame. Tang and Ward (2003, p18) state that 'face serves as the lubricant necessary to maintain harmony amongst those living in situations where moving away is not an option'. Guirdham (2011), while recognising that face can be applied universally, considers that in collectivist cultures members of social networks should help others keep face in support of the fundamentally important cohesion of the group and the individual's place within groups. In terms of communication, face can lead to an avoidance of criticism – and where this is not possible, critical comments will be muted and expressed in relatively indirect ways. There are implications for hierarchical communication. Crookes and Thomas (1998) note that giving face to a superior employee is a common phenomenon (we might say worldwide!), although absence of constructive feedback on a superior's performance can have the unintended consequence of inhibiting organisational effectiveness.

Gao (1998) concludes that there are two distinctive components of face in Chinese culture: *lian* and *mian*. *Lian* is defined as a person's sense of integrity and moral character, whereas *mian* refers to projected public image, a classical social-psychological concept earlier put forward by Goffman and Cooley, amongst others. Gao (p470), in looking specifically at Chinese personality traits, states that, 'A Chinese self is defined by relations with others. That is, a Chinese self tends to perform appropriate roles by assessing his or her relations with others in specific contexts. The importance of others, thus, explains the role of social expectations, social conformity, external opinions and personal achievement in the development of the Chinese self. "Other" influences and defines appropriate communication and interaction in various interpersonal relationships.' It is quite possible to refer to real or imagined examples which lead to social situations which could activate a sense of both *lian* and *mian*. It would also be illuminating to consider how these two elements of face (*lian* and *mian*) might affect interpersonal communication.

- *Guanxi* – This concept has been referred to on several previous occasions as involving webs of inter-relatedness. Individuals are linked to such webs through special relationships with others. *Guanxi* involves social connection, obligation and dependency. It links people together in a reciprocal relationship based on 'utilitarian' exchange. *Guanxi* is highlighted at this point to once again emphasise its effect on constraining communication networks: put simply, *guanxi* can have a significant effect on who you can communicate with (see also our earlier discussion of Hall's contribution to this subject).

● *Renqing* – Closely linked with *guanxi*, this concept refers to the affective part of *guanxi* exchanges. Chen (2001) suggests that *renqing* is more rational than emotional in that it suggests obligation or 'payback'. If someone within a *guanxi* network has benefited from a favour from another member of the network, the principle of *renqing* will invoke a need to respond with a favour of equal or greater value, thereby colouring the relationship with that other person and, crucially, the nature of communication between the two people.

The purpose of this extended analysis of aspects of Chinese culture – evident, of course, both within and outside China – is to reinforce the point that although the bipolar dimensions models of culture can be useful in identifying general patterns and styles of communication, it is also highly desirable to look in depth at features of particular cultures in order to gain a deeper understanding. We see here the value and applicability of the emic approach to culture within a specific topic area.

6.10 LEVELS OF COMMUNICATION

Much of the preceding analysis has focused on communication at the interpersonal or dyadic level, essentially assuming two participants in an encounter. In concentrating on this micro-level perspective, we have reflected the emphasis adopted within other textbooks such as Mead and Andrews (2009) and Francesco and Gold (2005). This is understandable, given the emphasis on intercultural competencies increasingly needed by managers who deal with people from other cultural groups. The interpersonal encounter for them may be a first, and crucial, step in effective management. However, at this stage several other levels of communication are briefly mentioned, together with pointers to some of their cross-cultural applications.

6.10.1 SMALL-GROUP COMMUNICATION

Social psychology examines the behaviour of individuals within small groups. There is certainly striking evidence to show how communication within groups can lead to unusual, even tragically inappropriate, decisions being taken – the phenomenon usually referred to as 'groupthink'. Several research studies including Merritt (1996) and Hayward (1997) have looked at the subject of safety within the transport industry, concluding that there were significant culturally derived factors which impacted on this inherently important area of work.

Merritt's study concluded that in 'non-Anglo' countries including Brazil, Taiwan and the Philippines, airline pilots were more comfortable with hierarchical command styles from the flight captain, and far less likely to speak out if they perceived a problem with the flight if the issue centred on a senior colleague. Hofstede's dimension of PD was taken to explain this finding. Hayward gave practical advice following on from this conclusion, suggesting that specific behavioural techniques should be introduced where there were dangers of over-acceptance of senior pilots' decisions including formalised cross-checking and assertiveness-building. Of course, where flight crew came from different national backgrounds there would be even more need to ensure a complementary approach that would not compromise safety.

This group of studies shows how cross-cultural theories and research in the area of communication can usefully move beyond the dyadic level to focus on structured small groups in formalised work situations.

6.10.2 ORGANISATIONAL COMMUNICATION

Earlier in the chapter our analysis of applications of the work of cultural theorists such as Hofstede and Hall revealed that these theorists, in addressing cross-cultural aspects of communication, provide insights that are relevant at the intra-organisational level. For example, Hofstede's dimension of power distance translated in practice to varying leadership and communication styles. In Chapter 5 we noted the potential for wide differences in organisational arrangements, including structure, as a result of the culturally derived preferences of key organisational actors. It can be seen therefore that differences regarding attitudes to communication may take effect in the ways organisations are structured, which in turn reflect and reinforce preferred patterns of communication.

Clegg et al (2011, p313) provide one of many possible examples of the organisational implications of cultural differences in communication: 'A study conducted by MIT focused on the difference between Japanese and American ways of producing cars, and it revealed that Japanese employees were more actively involved in the definition and refinement of car manufacturing process improvements. US industry, however, was still mainly organised according to concepts derived from Taylor, making such communications difficult. This difference in the management of communication was one of the determinants of the success of Japanese corporations during the 1980s.' In alerting us to the practical impact of intra-organisational communication, this example highlights the desirability of examining this aspect of communication within cross-cultural studies of business – once again moving beyond the interpersonal or dyadic level of analysis.

6.10.3 THE KEY AREA OF NEGOTIATION

Negotiation has long been depicted as an important aspect of international business, and many 'airport-style' guides to business etiquette in individual countries devote significant attention to this aspect, reflecting both the importance of the subject area in international business and the scope for problems in closing a deal with a partner in a new country. In academic terms, Koen (2005, p83) summarises these twin issues: 'Negotiation processes may be ubiquitous in general; they are an even more salient characteristic of international business, and levels of complexity and uncertainty in the international arena are also greater.' In previous chapters we have seen that cross-cultural (or intercultural) concerns also apply within organisations in any one cultural setting given the multicultural make-up of many workforces, so a focus on the impact of culture on negotiation will be important in domestic settings too. What are the most important cultural dimensions of this topic area?

In the most fundamental sense it may be that the entire concept of negotiation is perceived differently by people from particular cultures. Western human resource management textbooks characteristically view negotiation as a process in the course of which conflicts are firstly identified, followed by discussion in order to resolve these with a view to arriving at an acceptable solution. Torrington et al (2008, p716) provide a clear exposition of this central idea: 'the essence of the process is to find not just common ground between two parties but a new relationship with greater constructive potential than the one that preceded it.' While these authors do recognise the potential for differences across cultures, their essential approach to negotiation sees it as a problem-solving activity involving a sequence of events such as agreement on an agenda, exploration of arguments by both sides, decision-making, recapitulation and finally formal agreement. However, this is only one (culturally dependent) interpretation of the process. Broeways and Price (2011) refer to previous findings suggesting that Japanese business culture does not even contain the idea of a meeting as a forum for proposing rational arguments which then form the basis of a compromise decision. They go on to paint an alternative picture of meetings in Japan as, instead, comprising a setting to give the formal seal of approval to a decision that has already been made in other forums. Sebenius (2002) came to a similar earlier conclusion, suggesting that in Japan a negotiating table would not be an appropriate place to actually change anyone's mind. This is because decisions are reached by consensus within a group and changes to an agreed position would therefore be highly time-consuming. This is not to suggest that negotiating meetings in Western countries are not sometimes rubber-stamping or *fait accompli* exercises where the real decisions have been taken elsewhere. There is, however, a suggestion that the notion of negotiation as a formal rational decision-making activity with ritualistic set stages is, in itself, a construction arising from a particular cultural setting.

If we assume that there is agreement on the nature of negotiation – which, as we have seen, might be a questionable assumption – then there could still be significant cultural variations in other respects. For example, consideration of traditional models of cultural difference would lead one to anticipate real and meaningful differences in negotiating style. Hall's categorisation of high- and low-context societies provides a case in point. We have seen that in high-context societies, a very high proportion of a message is coded in non-verbal communication, so there is scope for a distinctive low-key style of negotiation and more subtle ways of showing emotion in a negotiating encounter. Moran et al (2014), in a summary of global leadership and negotiations, propose a number of implications of such differences for their readers, suggesting, for example, that Indian negotiatiors may be reluctant to articulate disagreement and that the phrase 'no problem' should not be taken literally. German negotiators, contrastingly, might be expected to use 'frank and realistic' language in the course of negotiation. One can similarly apply Trompenaars' distinction between neutral and affective cultures as a relevant dimension. As Trompenaars and Hampden-Turner (1997, p79) point out, in a neutral culture, 'the entire negotiation is typically focused on the object or proposition being discussed, not so much on you as persons,' while, contrastingly, in affective cultures, 'the entire negotiation is typically focused on you as persons, not so much on the object or proposition being discussed'.

Guirdham (2009) reported research indicating a link between negotiating style and Schwartz's value dimensions, summarised in Chapter 3 of this book. For example, Tinsley and Pillutla (1998) identified differences in style arising from Schwartz's dimensions of self-enhancement versus self-transcendence and conservatism versus openness to change. This study compared Hong Kong Chinese negotiators with their US counterparts, with the former giving higher priority to equality when negotiating, as opposed to the American negotiators who stressed joint gain. However, Guirdham's own research in this subject area found some differences between negotiating styles in Asian countries. These are summarised as follows:

- *Japan* – Negotiations are part of a relationship-balanced approach.
- *India* – Hard bargaining; the aim is to beat the other side.
- *China* – Holistic, rational, interpersonal, not unfair, but there is no 'getting to yes'.
- *Taiwan* – A link is a pre-condition. The aim is to win; 'face' issues are paramount.

Guirdham's findings, which deal with the overall approach to negotiating *per se* as well as negotiation styles, are interesting in that they indicate differences between countries which, although they can in part be related to traditional models of culture, also point to subtle variation which can best be explained by an emic in-depth exploration of the specific culture in question. However, in summary, one can certainly identify meaningful differences in negotiating style across the world, and it is relatively straightforward to link these existing models of cultural difference.

Another way in which negotiation could vary by culture is in the negotiating context. Gelfand and Dyer (2000) refer to proximal situational conditions as factors which will influence a negotiator's perceptions. These situational conditions include the following factors:

- *Roles* – In collectivist societies a negotiator is more likely to be part of a group, while cultures high on autonomy (such as the USA) will tend to put forward individual negotiators on the basis of their past achievements or expertise. In contrast, in China one would expect greater incidence of negotiators being chosen because of ascribed characteristics; for example, age or social class. More generally, there could be a closer link between role and negotiation outcomes in some cultures; for example, in societies with high PD there would be a stronger emphasis on roles *per se* and as a result roles would be a clear predictor of success or failure in the negotiation. Gelfand and Dyer propose in summary that the prevalence of particular proximal conditions (in this case negotiating roles) will vary across cultures.

- *Relationships with constituencies* – This factor relates to the people who represent a party in negotiation (the negotiators themselves) and the relationships between them and their constituents. Cultural differences could be linked to Schwartz's distinction between embeddedness and autonomy. In cultures that 'embed' the self, for example Indonesia, negotiators would feel more closely bound by instructions given by a constituent or, as Gelfand and Dyer term it, 'have their hands tied'. Societies characterised by high levels of autonomy (eg the UK) would, contrastingly, see negotiators feel less bound by constituents' instructions and more likely to be influenced by the process ensuing in the course of negotiation.

- *Deadlines* – Scwhartz's distinction between mastery and harmony was also a moderating factor in terms of perceptions of negotiation and subsequent behaviour and outcomes. In societies that emphasise mastery there would be less time afforded for negotiation. Gelfand and Dyer equate this notion with the 'time is money' attitude to be found in many Western countries, where time can be spent, saved or wasted. Cultures emphasising harmony would, for opposite reasons, be more likely to allow negotiations to grow into the time needed to secure harmonious agreement.

Usunier (2003) provides a model of cross-cultural aspects of negotiation which encompasses the following elements of the topic:

- *Behavioural predispositions of the parties* – Differing prior beliefs on the importance of harmony or self-interest, power differentials and risk-taking would mean that a negotiator approaches a negotiation event with particular orientations which will influence their attitudes and behaviour. It is possible to relate these beliefs to existing models of cultural difference, eg Hofstede. Note, however, that the different dimensions of culture may interact in a complex way in the area of negotiation. If we applied Hofstede's dimensions to Singapore, we would anticipate Singaporean negotiators only taking decisions if they were sufficiently high up in the hierarchy or, alternatively, referring decisions upward if they were not (PD dimension). On the other hand, uncertainty avoidance in this culture for Hofstede was low, implying a greater willingness to take risks in negotiation – although possibly only with the support of senior colleagues.

- *Underlying concept of negotiation*– Earlier in the chapter we noted differences in this regard, which we find again in Usunier's framework. For example, the concept of negotiation as a process which would ideally lead to an outcome acceptable to both parties is only one of a number of models, although it is considered normal in the Western context. We also find under this heading differences in how time is regarded in negotiation – which, again, we have already noted.

- *Negotiation process* – Usunier here refers to two key areas: firstly, potential differences in negotiating styles and, secondly, variability in how outcomes are perceived.

Usunier's focus on outcomes is echoed in other contributions to the cross-cultural negotiation canon. Moran et al (2014) make one such comparison between the typical situation when dealing with Indian negotiators (who will, they claim, require detailed agreements when concluding negotiations) and Brazilian negotiators, who prefer verbal agreements ('a handshake and words of honour' (p82)) followed up by details formalised by lawyers. Broeways and Price (2011, p322) put forward a comment on the specific nature of agreements with Chinese negotiators: 'Rather than being the last word on the deal, a contract is a formal moment in the development of a relationship; further negotiations will take place on the basis of the goodwill and friendship established.' In summary, one can say that cross-cultural or intercultural negotiations are infused with the influence of culture from the preparation stage through to the final (or not-so-final) outcome.

APPLYING THEORY TO PRACTICE 6.1

In late April 2009, Chinese Commerce Minister Chen Deming visited the US cities of Washington DC, San Francisco and Chicago, in the course of which he signed more than 30 business contracts with American-based firms including FedEx, Dell and Linovo. However, commercial ties between the two nations had at that time been adversely affected by the global financial crisis, with figures showing that trade between the two countries had slumped by nearly 7% and US investment in China had declined by almost 20% between September 2008 and March 2009. Nonetheless, Mr Chen noted that the need to foster positive international business links had never been greater and called on both countries to 'step up co-operation in trade and investment issues, and explore and establish new possibilities for co-operation in such areas as agriculture, new and high technology, finance, energy and the environment.'[3] He also recorded a view that, 'History tells us that the more serious a crisis becomes, the more committed we must be to openness and co-operation.'

There can be little doubt that any such positive links and openness can only be built on successful negotiation between these two countries.

6.10.4 MASS COMMUNICATION

Although it is beyond the scope of this book, one should also recognise a cultural component to mass communication. Mass communication is characteristically one-way communication, often on behalf of a large organisation such as a corporation or government, to a mass audience. In the business setting there are very clear implications for the marketing area. It is important to appreciate that mass communication can differ across societies and that cultural theories can usefully inform understanding in this regard. Daechun (2006) attempts to link the theoretical frameworks of Hall and Hofstede within a study of Internet advertising and culturally derived responses: this study may be of interest to readers who wish to explore the role of culture in marketing communications. Our brief summary of Wurtz's (2005) work contained earlier in the chapter is also relevant in this regard.

6.10.5 VIRTUAL COMMUNICATION

One very important trend in intercultural and, indeed, all forms of communication is that of virtual communication. Email has emerged as an especially significant medium and is particularly relevant to cross-cultural communication. Francesco and Gold (2005, p80) conclude that, 'Email accounts for 75 to 80% of virtual team communication. Because of the asynchronous nature of email, compared to face-to-face meetings or telephone conversations, team participants who are not communicating in their native language often find it easier to be effective.' The rise of email as a communication tool raises interesting issues, not least that of possible convergence in communication style worldwide due to its widespread use in cross-cultural communication. On the surface it may appear that cultural misunderstandings and mistakes could also be easier to avoid when using email: for example, should one person expose the soles of his or her feet when communicating in this way, no offence would be taken because they would not be seen by the recipient.

However, email has developed its own etiquette, and one cannot assume that considerations of cultural sensitivity are no longer of importance – such a view would in any case be anathema to the spirit of tolerance and respect needed in intercultural communication. Brooks (2009) summarises research by Sproull and Kieser (1991), concluding that these writers provide evidence that electronic media have the intrinsic potential to open up or democratise communication, with participants tending to communicate more explicitly and equally. Nonetheless, some cultural differences may remain. McFarlin and Sweeney (2013) propose that an American using email would 'probably' keep the text short and use personal pronouns while a French person would 'probably' be less precise and stress the third person. These recent writers clearly see a role for traditional cultural difference in a contemporary mode of communication.

This is an emerging area of study and it will be interesting to see whether the increasing use of email does result in any significant convergence of communication style between different cultures (for example, high and low PD societies) or whether the variations identified in this chapter largely remain intact.

6.11 CONCLUSION

It can be argued that intercultural or cross-cultural communication lies at the heart of cross-cultural management. Establishing a connection with someone from another culture is the first step in building a relationship; without effective communication this cannot happen. Consider too the notion that communication binds existing cultural groups. If communication across cultures exceeds that within a single group, then the whole essence of the initial group as a distinctive culture may be called into question.

The classical model of communication involving sender, coding/decoding, medium, message and feedback contains within it certain intrinsic barriers to intercultural communication including stereotyping and misintepretation of non-verbal elements such as symbols or kinesics. Intercultural communication can be enhanced through an appreciation of principles such as adopting an open attitude, self-awareness, resourcefulness and empathy.

It is possible – and useful – to understand intercultural communication with recourse to both traditional models of cultural difference such as Hall's low-/high-context typology and also Hofstede's work, while the in-depth emic approach too has the potential to increase knowledge, as can be seen from an analysis of distinctive features of Chinese culture.

One important aspect of communication in business is negotiation. We have seen that there are potentially very significant cultural differences in the most basic aspects of negotiation; in terms of predisposition to the essential concept, negotiating style and views on what constitutes an outcome. One could reasonably equate these issues to the core questions of 'how', 'why', 'what', 'where' and 'when' when approaching the topic. The extent of cultural difference will impact on the negotiation strategies chosen by each party and the degree of familiarity with any difference is likely to have practical implications; for example, if there is relative unfamiliarity then a third party may need to be involved, possibly to the extent of them actually undertaking the negotiation or maybe having a more indirect role of advising the parties.

CASE STUDY 6.2

IMAGE-CONSCIOUS: CROSSING CULTURAL BARRIERS AT AXA

Creating an employer brand can be tricky when you are a global insurance conglomerate such as AXA. When the company originally thought up a brand name, it came up with the word élan, which means 'leap forward' in French. But in Canada the word more commonly refers to a moose. Unimpressed with this image, Canadian employees understandably objected, and the name was quickly discarded in favour of 'AXA' in 1985.

This was just one of the cultural and linguistic barriers that the company had to be sensitive to when creating a global employer brand.

AXA started out as French insurer Mutuelle Unis, but grew rapidly over 20 years into a global conglomerate providing financial protection and wealth management solutions. By 2003 it employed 140,000 people across 50 countries following a series of acquisitions, including the US company Equitable, Guardian Royal Exchange in the UK and Nippon Dantai in Japan.

The challenge for the group has been to create an employer brand and a workplace culture that crosses cultural, language and social barriers, according to Françoise Colloc'h, senior executive vice-president of HR, brand and communications, and a member of AXA's management board.

'It has been more about taking the best of each company to make that part of the AXA culture, rather than destroying the past of those companies and saying there is only one way – the Mutuelle Unis way,' Colloc'h says.

Part of creating that employer brand was to establish a set of values representing the way it wanted to behave towards clients, shareholders and employees. The company did this in 1990, after its purchase of Equity & Law in the UK.

'We started discovering that cultures were very different. We needed to share the ethics that were supporting our core business,' says Colloc'h. AXA initially came up with seven values: loyalty, pride, courage, ambition, realism, imagination and integrity. But she admits that the company made a mistake by having a French team think up these values, because they failed to take cultural differences into account. 'The more global we became, the more we discovered that these values were reflecting French, rather than a global, culture.'

One example of different interpretations of values concerned the word 'loyalty' which, in Japan, could in some circumstances imply committing hara-kiri, a form of ritualised suicide. 'We discovered that some of our wording was not adaptable in some cultures,' Colloc'h adds.

As a result, the head office in Paris decided to rework AXA's values. Employees from seven countries, including the UK, Japan and USA, were chosen to make up ten focus groups and discuss the relevance of the values to different cultures.

The feedback resulted in the identification of five values that would surmount cultural barriers and reflect clients' expectations of AXA. These were professionalism, integrity, team spirit, innovation and pragmatism.

Yet having an employer brand and a set of global values was not enough to create a global culture. The firm realised that its staff had to embody the behavioural traits associated with its five values; in other words, they had to 'live' the values. It has tackled this issue by recruiting and appraising staff against behaviours linked to values.

But has AXA been successful in creating a global brand? Paul Walker, employer brand consultant at TMP Worldwide, believes that AXA has done a great job in creating a uniform brand across all its business. At the same time, he warns that although most of the values could be interpreted in the same way in parts of the world with a broadly Western culture, the company has to be aware of differences in interpretation.

'For example, in China AXA could encounter real problems trying to define what "professionalism" means in a country where the professional cadre was largely removed by the Cultural Revolution,' he says.

The company has sought to address issues of cultural confusion by letting individual countries interpret the values. AXA also uses pictograms – a form of visual alphabet – to illustrate behavioural concepts and management style in 28 forms.

'It's significant that it has adopted a graphic, rather than verbal, expression of its values in an attempt to sidestep any cultural booby traps,' says Walker. AXA believes that these pictograms cross cultural barriers, especially in Asia. 'It creates a common language,' says Andrew Burk, director of organisational development and reward, AXA UK.

Le droit a l'erreur   Courage   Être positif

AXA uses pictograms, known in the company as 'AXAgrams', within the organisation to illustrate behavioural concepts and management styles. The AXAgrams above represent encouraging employees to be honest and not afraid of speaking up.

Adapted from an article in *People Management* (6 February 2003) by Karen Higginbottom. Pictograms were still used in AXA strategic management development programmes as late as 2008.

Questions

1. In what ways have issues of communication affected AXA's attempts to create a global brand?

2. What would you see as the advantages and disadvantages of using graphic forms of communication in the context outlined in the article?

3. How might a knowledge of Ed Hall's work on high- and low-context cultures help a manager or consultant to improve communication within a global conglomerate such as AXA?

NOTES

1   Indonesia Business Etiquette & Culture. Available at: www.cyborlink.com/besite/
    indonesia.htm [Accessed 1 May 2006].

2   www.geert-hofstede.com/hofstede.shtml [Accessed 18 April 2006].

3   www.caltradereport.com/eWebpages [Accessed 19 June 2009].

 REVIEW QUESTIONS

1   Identify some typical barriers to effective intercultural communication and show how these
    can be overcome.

2   Assess the usefulness of Hall's typology of low- and high-context cultures to an explanation
    of intercultural communication.

3   Why should a cross-cultural negotiator be aware of cultural differences in negotiation prior
    to dealing with parties from other cultures?

FURTHER READING

GUIRDHAM, M. (2011) *Communicating across cultures at work.* 3rd ed. Basingstoke: Palgrave Macmillan. This is a comprehensive text covering both theoretical and practical aspects of the topic and recognising the complexities of the subject area.

LEWIS, R. (2004) *When cultures collide: leading, teamworking and managing across the globe.* London: Nicholas Brealey. This book contains many insights into cross-cultural communication in practice.

MORAN, R.T., ABRAMSON, N.R. and MORAN, S.V. (2014) *Managing cultural differences.* 9th ed. Oxford: Elsevier. Chapter 3 of this useful blend of theory and practice focuses specifically on negotiations in international business.

Visit this book's companion website (**www.cipd.co.uk/olr**) to find further exercises including self-assessment questions and also weblinks to media and academic journal articles.

CHAPTER 7

Leadership and Multicultural Teams

LEARNING OBJECTIVES

After reading this chapter you should be able to:

- assess the extent to which notions of cross-cultural difference can be applied to 'traditional' approaches to understanding leadership
- examine the potential impact of culture as a contingent factor affecting leadership style
- discuss how the topic of culture can be related to contemporary and emerging views on leadership
- evaluate the contribution of Project GLOBE to an understanding of this subject area
- identify key competencies of leaders who engage with multinational teams.

7.1 INTRODUCTION

In previous chapters we have characterised culture as a concept that is firstly made real at the level of people's attitudes and values, and that can subsequently impact on their preferred ways of operating within work organisations. We have also seen that major writers in this area, in attempting to classify cultures and demarcate cultural difference, have argued that people's perceptions of authority, independence and uncertainty are likely to vary according to their cultural background. All of this suggests that leadership is likely to be an area strongly affected by cultural variation, providing a rich source of data for cross-cultural researchers. It is also probable that actual or putative leaders may particularly benefit from cross-cultural awareness in carrying out, or preparing for, leadership roles.

As we will see, a particular concern of an increasing number of business leaders is to consider how one can most effectively lead multicultural teams.

A good deal of the current literature, particularly in the field of management studies, acknowledges that culture may have an important role to play in influencing leadership style. Nonetheless, such analyses are typically framed within an approach in which the essence of leadership is implicitly culture-free. Furthermore, because many writings in this field emanate from the USA, examples and other illustrations tend to relate to that particular context. Robbins and Judge (2014), in a global edition of a popular and influential organisational behaviour textbook, provide a good example of an approach which exhibits the aforementioned characteristics. Following a lucid overview of the development of thinking on leadership as applied to business, they go on to consider contemporary issues in leadership, including an evaluation of charismatic leadership, in which the cited examples are John F. Kennedy, Martin Luther King Jr, Bill Clinton, Mary Kay Ash and Steve Jobs. All of these figures are quite possibly charismatic; all are certainly American.

Robbins and Judge do, however, recognise that different forms of leadership will be more effective in specific cultures. Their conclusion is that culture is one of a number of contingent factors which leaders should take into account when operating within particular contexts. In an earlier work, Robbins (2005, p381) had set out this underlying logic, linking effective leadership style to Hofstede's cultural dimensions: 'For example, a manipulative or autocratic style is compatible with high power distance, and we find high power distance scores in Russia, Spain, Arab, Far Eastern, and most Latin countries. Participation is likely to be more effective in low power distance cultures as exist in Norway, Finland, Denmark and Sweden.'

Later in this chapter we will examine the contribution of the influential Project GLOBE study, whose researchers concluded that established styles of leadership would be more or less effective in different cultural contexts. That fundamental insight will be a major theme in this chapter.

More recently, McFarlin and Sweeney (2013) also concluded that particular leader attributes and behaviour frequently identified in management literature may be more or less successful in different cultural contexts. They note, for example, that some attributes such as decisiveness, honesty and intelligence are viewed as desirable in most cultures, while other types of leader traits and behaviour, including irritability and acting in an egocentric way, are universally derided by such leaders' followers. Interestingly, though, a third range of characteristics, for example sensitivity and risk-taking, are viewed differently across cultures.

Whether we are focusing upon leader attributes, styles or actual behaviour, there is clearly value in looking at the mainstream leadership models and applying them across the world to assess their relative validity for cross-cultural managers.

In this chapter, however, the aim is to go beyond an attempt to apply or fit existing models of leadership to cross-cultural study, useful though that might be. We attempt to dissect the concept of leadership, showing that it is inherently bound up with that of culture. For if different styles of leadership are more or less acceptable to 'followers' in the light of their culturally derived attitudes to, for example, authority, this highlights the essentially reciprocal nature of leadership. Leadership could therefore ultimately be viewed as a matter of perception. As pointed out by the sociologist Max Weber, writing in the late nineteenth century (so this is not a new idea), leaders can only lead if followers attribute leadership qualities to them or give them legitimacy more generally.

We also examine the extent to which the very meaning of leadership is constructed in different ways and, assuming the notion of construction of meaning is accepted, how it can be used to explain cross-cultural variations in leadership. Buelens et al (2006, p413) put an interesting slant on this central idea: 'Americans are the only people who talk so openly – sometimes obsessively – about the very notion of leadership. In America, leadership has become something of a cult concept. The French, tellingly, have no adequate word of their own for it. Germans have perfectly good words for "leader" and "leadership", but Hitler rendered them politically incorrect. Mussolini similarly stigmatised the word *duce*. The situation is even more extreme in the Netherlands or the Scandinavian countries, where leaders do not behave like leaders at all, at least not in the way described in American textbooks.' This last point is interesting in that it again highlights the link between culture and language set out in Chapters 1 and 4.

The idea that the perception of what leadership actually is varies between cultures continues to be explored. In one recent study Jonsson et al (2014) conducted research in the home furnishings company IKEA. They record how IKEA specifically identifies with 'Swedishness', with the company's founder Ingvar Kamprand quoted as saying that there is nothing more Swedish than IKEA, a notion which Jonsson et al link to business branding. Within IKEA the uniquely Swedish combination of participative, delegating and coaching-style leadership finds expression in day-to-day management of people. However, Jonsson et al found that non-Swedish employees found decision processes unclear and the leadership they experienced to be indecisive. The study raises questions concerning the strategy of multinational corporations, ie whether operating units in other countries should be run on principles emanating from headquarters (see also Chapter 10). In theoretical terms, the IKEA study points to the value of understanding leadership via an in-depth analysis of a single and unique culture, echoing our discussion of emic approaches to culture set out in Chapters 1 to 4.

The final section of this chapter focuses on the competencies needed by both expatriate or international leaders who find themselves in leadership roles in new countries, and global leaders – who have cross-border responsibilities – and who, it has been claimed, are characterised by a particular mindset. Of course, we examine both categories of leader and the relevant competencies more fully in that section. In particular, we will examine the specific competencies needed to lead multicultural teams.

A cross-cultural analysis of this area can also help us in shedding some light on the oft-cited confusion regarding leadership and management. Guirdham (2011) notes that the notion of management in the British concept is seen as an essentially interpersonal task (see also Mullins (2013) for a comprehensive account of management as an integrating activity based around managing the efforts of organisational members). In France, contrastingly, Guirdham notes that the roles of leader and manager seem more clearly separated, the work of management being characterised as an intellectual activity centring on the exercise of rationality rather than frequent involvement in interpersonal activities.

There are, of course, many other culturally specific views on the nature of management in work organisations. The relationship, or tension, between the two terms 'leadership' and 'management' is referred to throughout this chapter. As previously suggested, it may be that cultural definitions go some way to explaining different views on this topic. We now go on to look at an overview of traditional, or mainstream, thinking on leadership and, in particular, leadership effectiveness, showing how the cross-cultural dimension can, with hindsight, be perceived as central to each stage of the developing debate.

7.2 THE TRAITS APPROACH

It is often suggested that the earliest approaches to understanding the nature of leadership and leader effectiveness stressed the key importance of leaders' characteristics. The idea that leaders are born with inherited characteristics which result in their becoming 'great men' (there have been a dearth of references to 'great women') is routinely rejected in most modern writings, certainly in the field of business. However, a writer as influential as Peter Drucker (1989) could still claim, relatively recently, that leadership cannot be created, taught or learned. The decline of monarchical power, not to mention catastrophic military adventures presided over by 'born-to-rule' officers, has, however, been associated with a more general decline in the belief that leader characteristics are inherent from birth. Greater attention has instead been devoted to uncovering personality traits common to people found in leadership positions in contrast to non-leaders.

Schermerhorn et al (2009) are typical of authors writing in the area of organisational behaviour (OB) who cast doubt on the validity over time of this approach. They conclude that studies of leadership based on trait theories failed to account for differences between leaders and non-leaders; neither were they able to link traits with consistent leadership success. These writers, interestingly, suggest that the trait approach to leadership might be enjoying renewed popularity and influence. In this regard they contrast work carried out before and after 1990 as follows (p243): 'For various reasons including inadequate theorising and trait measurement, the [earlier] studies were not successful enough to provide consistent findings. More recent work has yielded more promising results. A number of traits have been found that help identify important leadership strengths. As it turns out, most of these traits also tend to predict leadership outcomes.'

One example of such 'recent work', in Schermerhorn et al's terms, is the research undertaken by Kirkpatrick and Locke (1991), whose findings did locate common leader traits. These are drive, incorporating both a strong desire for achievement and high energy levels; self-confidence, including an ability to make difficult decisions and to persevere in the face of setbacks; cognitive ability (perhaps unsurprisingly, it was found that leaders score above average on intelligence measures); and honesty and integrity. These traits were supplemented by knowledge of the context and desire to lead: the other traits would not be relevant without a desire on the part of the leader to actually lead.

Can the (possibly reviving) trait approach to leadership assist us in evaluating the extent to which leadership varies across cultures? At first sight it appears that traits identified among leaders by Kirkpatrick and Locke are universally applicable. There is no evidence to suggest that levels of energy or cognitive abilities are significantly different across the world. In earlier chapters we have demarcated the universal, cultural and individual levels of analysis when applied to human behaviour. It would appear that an analysis of leadership traits belongs firmly in the individual sphere. Bond and Smith (1996), in applying personality theory within a cross-cultural framework, found that the classic 'Big 5' model of personality which identified categories of extroversion, emotional stability, agreeableness, conscientiousness and openness to experience was valid across cultures, ie the categories captured personality traits, and consequent types, in all societies. In summarising this area of research, Guirdham (2011) also concluded that studies carried out in this area showed that distribution of personality traits across societies was stable. It appears at first glance that leadership traits – even if we accept that they impact on leadership role occupancy and success – are not subject to cultural variation.

The culture-free picture of leadership traits summarised above should, however, be modified in certain important respects. Despite confirming the universality of leadership traits, Guirdham notes that the study by Bond and Smith recognises the potential for cultural impact in that certain 'Big 5' dimensions may be highlighted at the expense of others, albeit acknowledging overall consistency in mean profiles. Bond and Smith's study, to take one finding, locates a relatively high use of the agreeableness category in China. We will see later in the chapter that the important GLOBE study on leadership also indicates that members of specific cultures express preferences for ideal leadership attributes when considering 'what should be' rather than 'what is'. This stress on ideal preferences has already been referred to in the summary of the GLOBE study in Chapter 3, and indicates scope for culturally derived differences in leaders' traits, and in their acceptability to followers. Put simply, there could be important culturally based differences in what people perceive as an ideal leader and the traits that such a person would possess must therefore also be different.

Finally, when considering the somewhat generalised traits identified by Kirkpatrick and Locke, we do not necessarily picture a leader in terms of the impact the leader has on us. To characterise Mahatma Gandhi in terms of intelligence, self-confidence and desire to lead does not portray the essence of this leader of the Indian independence movement, nor explain why he inspired followers in the 1940s (his perceived honesty and integrity might help us more in this regard). But Gandhi undoubtedly possessed traits which can, in part, explain his leadership success. We also posit that these traits resonated with his followers and were borne out of the societal context in which he and they lived. It is very much open to question whether Gandhi's leadership success would have been replicated in, say, Italy at the identical time where Mussolini was embodying his own version of the strong leader.

This brings us to the most important contribution that cross-cultural analysis can make to the debate regarding the importance of leaders' traits, namely, that leadership is essentially an attribution and that legitimacy may be conferred on leaders in part as a result of followers' culturally influenced perception of the leader's traits.

A MAN WHO ALWAYS KNOWS WHAT HE WANTS?

By 2014 the leadership traits of Russian President Vladimir Putin had become the subject of increasing and polarised discussion. Putin had drawn worldwide attention over the previous few years due to Russia's position, strongly articulated by its leader, on regional and global flashpoints. These included the events leading up to Crimea leaving Ukraine and joining the Russian Federation in March 2014.

Throughout this period, Putin had conspicuously displayed distinctive leadership traits. In an address broadcast from The Kremlin on 18 March 2014, Putin employed strong and decisive language when speaking of the situation in Ukraine: 'they have constantly tried to drive us into a corner for our independent stance, for defending it, for calling things by their proper names and not being hypocritical. But there are limits. And in the case of Ukraine our Western partners have crossed a line. They have behaved rudely, irresponsibly and unprofessionally.'

Vladimir Putin has also projected himself as a strong leader via a variety of high-profile physical pursuits ranging from judo and karate to shirtless horse-riding and whale shooting. Perhaps most strikingly, he was filmed on a hang-gliding expedition flying high in the sky alongside endangered Siberian cranes.

Subject to widespread criticism for his stance on international affairs, Putin has also drawn admiring comment from some Western commentators for his leadership qualities. Black (2013) suggested that 'Putin's most attractive trait is that he is a Russian nationalist at heart and is not afraid to say what he thinks – and what

he thinks often reflects on what most Russians think – hence his continuing political success. It's politics as it used to be, as it should be.'

Black's observations are supported in online comments submitted following his article. One online contribution from 'Katya' stated that, 'Putin is a genuine leader with very strong character [he is] a very clever man who always knows what he wants. And that's why it's obvious that in politics he will be the winner.'

Questions

1   Identify the leadership traits exhibited by President Putin. Why might these traits have appeared attractive to followers in this country at that time? Indicate how the traits might be perceived differently in other countries and give reasons for your conclusions.

2   Identify ten traits you think a leader should possess.

Share your thoughts within a small group. Make a list of the ways in which group members' views differ. If your group is multicultural, could differing views be explained by individuals' cultural background? If your group is monocultural, can you pick out any culturally linked differences? Identify other possible reasons why group members' views differed, eg their age, gender or occupation. Were there more similarities than differences when comparing group members' views on leaders' desirable traits, or more differences than similarities?

7.3 THE BEHAVIOURAL APPROACH

We have seen that doubts have been cast on the usefulness of trait theories of leadership, relating both to the difficulty of assembling meaningful traits which go beyond the very generalised, and the predictive validity of such traits in explaining leadership success. However, many of us may find it problematic to remove the leader from an analysis of leadership. The term 'leadership' continues to evoke the person occupying such a role and his or her attempts to carry out leadership tasks. From the 1950s onwards, researchers in the field, faced with adverse evidence on the applicability of trait theories, sought to extend their analysis to a search for models which identified appropriate leader behaviours. Closely linked to the notion of leadership as a function of behaviour is a preoccupation with leadership style.

There are a large number of studies that purport to identify particular leadership styles which are advocated in terms of both achieving set tasks and satisfying – or even inspiring – followers. For our purposes two such models are highlighted: the Ohio State Studies and Blake and Mouton's leadership grid. After a brief overview of both approaches, we attempt to place these, and similar studies, within the debate on the links between culture and leadership.

Commencing in 1945, the research carried out at the Ohio State University in the USA involved participants' identifying behaviours exhibited by leaders they had come into contact with. Participants in this study came from a very wide occupational background, including a number of ranks of the military services and employees from the manufacturing and educational sectors. The researchers went on to compile a list of such identified behaviours which reportedly grew to include 1,800 descriptions. The Ohio State researchers were able to pare down these descriptions to two underlying dimensions:

- *Consideration* – This dimension, as exhibited in leader behaviour, centres on attempts to grow and sustain positive relationships with subordinates, underpinned by respect and a concern for workers' welfare and feelings.
- *Initiating structure* – Within this contrasting dimension, leaders would orient their behaviour towards the tasks of work within an overall concern to achieve organisational goals.

The Ohio State Studies categorised these two dimensions into four types of leader behaviour: essentially leaders could be either high or low on both dimensions. The researchers concluded that the dimensions were not mutually exclusive, and that leaders with a high consideration/high structure style were likely to be the most effective through satisfying subordinates' social needs and meeting performance goals. This finding is by no means atypical of studies on leadership that emphasise the importance of leader behaviour and/or styles. However, the Ohio State Studies findings have not been universally accepted even on their own terms.

Bloisi et al (2003, p574) introduce caveats as follows: 'Although leaders high in both initiating structure and showing consideration tended to have better performance and satisfaction than leaders low in either or both, there were enough negative side effects (absenteeism and grievance) that the positive outcomes were not unconditional. Trying to predict group performance solely on the basis of a consistent leader behaviour turned out to be a futile endeavour.' Martin (2005, p351) identifies potential definitional and methodological drawbacks: 'It has been argued that these studies do not necessarily identify actual leader behaviour but reflect the perceptions of those completing the form. For example, leaders could answer on the basis of how they think they behave (or would like to), rather than how they actually do. Equally, a subordinate might complete the questions on the basis of personal feelings towards their boss rather than based on actual experience.'

Despite these retrospective criticisms, the original findings of the Ohio State Studies, emphasising a twin concern with people and tasks, informed business and management education at the time, and, we can assume, had some impact on leader behaviour on those actual and budding leaders who were exposed to the conclusions. Other studies followed, drawing similar conclusions, among them Blake and Mouton's (1978) managerial grid, subsequently re-entitled the 'leadership grid' (Blake and McCanse 1991).

The leadership grid contained five generic leadership styles (termed 'management styles') deriving from patterns of thinking relating to the relative importance of production achievements and concern for people:

- *Impoverished management* – involves low levels of consideration for both production and people, and perhaps unsurprisingly resulted in poor-quality outcomes on both dimensions. It was exhibited by leaders who sought to secure work targets at baseline level through gaining threshold levels of performance from subordinates.
- *Country club management* – where the leader's chief concern is to create a positive work environment and comfortable work targets. Production concerns are secondary to the desire to foster a convivial work environment.
- *Authority leadership style* – essentially task-oriented, with concerns for people's welfare 'below the radar' in such a leader's mindset. There is instead a belief that people need to be controlled and supervised closely.
- *Middle-of-the-road style* – also evocatively called 'dampened pendulum', this occurs when a leader engages in a mental trade-off between the two concerns and arrives at his or her own view of both acceptable performance levels and relationships with employees.
- *Team management* – within this framework, this is the ideal scenario, combining a drive for high production through the efforts of committed workers who are trusted and themselves identify with the aims of the organisation.

Revised on several occasions since its original appearance in 1964, the leadership grid enables leaders to identify their dominant style. It should be noted that Blake and Mouton recognised that many leaders could revert to a back-up style. Factors influencing leaders' styles have also been located supporting Blake and Mouton's original findings. These include personal experience, organisational practice and leaders' beliefs and values (this last factor could offer some scope for the addition of a cross-cultural perspective). However, it would not be unfair to record that the overwhelming thrust of Blake and Mouton's work is towards the adoption of the team style, which combines high concerns for both people and production, replacing in many cases the middle-of-the-road style which many leaders had developed as a compromise in the face of what they considered to be incompatible and indeed conflicting objectives.

Is there any sense in which behavioural and/or style theories of leadership can be usefully linked to a perspective that is 'culturally aware'?

The first point to record here is that there was little or no mention of international or cross-cultural concerns when the original studies were published. This is unsurprising since we have already noted in Chapters 2 and 3 that a cross-cultural slant to most business and management writings can, for the most part, only be discerned from the 1980s onwards, at which time increasing perceptions of a more 'globalised' business environment took hold.

The second point involves locating the precise origins of this school of thought, which lie within American Management Studies. The conclusions of both the Ohio State Studies and Blake and Mouton's work, in pointing to a concern with people's social and developmental needs at work, are representative of what has come to be termed human relations theory. We can identify a clear theme within the human relations tradition, namely, the desirability and practical benefit (in terms of increased output) of managing people in a humane way, through recognising workers' desire for autonomy and creativity (this theme is reinforced in our discussion of motivation in Chapter 8). It is often suggested that the human relations movement grew in reaction to the more mechanised approach of Scientific Management exemplified by the contribution of Frederick Taylor. The human relations school of management, in this reading of management theory history, sought to correct this perceived imbalance by emphasising the human dimension, referring to both research evidence and psychological theory to create a picture of thinking and feeling workers who would benefit from employee-centred leadership which, as we have seen, also focused on task or production considerations.

Some writers have gone further. Grey (2013) argues that the work of the human relations movement reflects a changing conception of personhood. He suggests that it was one more manifestation of a recognition of self alongside other branches of psychology – in this case related to people's working lives. He goes on to link the emergence of individual psychology (one can also plausibly add studies of group dynamics in this context) to a decline in organised religion and in particular a belief in an afterlife. However, if Grey is correct in this analysis, such trends are highly culturally specific, for as we have already seen in Chapters 2 and 3, any such decline in religious belief has not been uniform throughout the world. We seem to be moving towards a highly significant finding that the behavioural approach to leadership is very much anchored in time and space: the USA in the mid-to-late twentieth century.

Jacques (1996) has made much the same point in an even more precise way, concluding that the knowledge base of much management knowledge is derived from data centred on white, male North American workers from the 1950s and 1960s. The conclusion at this point is that the behavioural or style approach to leadership as it appears in many organisational behaviour or human resource management texts is of very little help to students or existing managers interested in the topic of leadership as applied to different cultural groups.

7.4 IMPLICIT LEADERSHIP THEORIES

Although the bulk of research examining the influence of leadership style can be seen to have emanated from the USA, therefore casting doubt on its applicability worldwide, some writers have sought to retain the central message that style is an important factor by identifying alternative implicit leadership styles from other cultures. Kakabadse et al (1997) conducted a study examining European countries, involving researchers from the Cranfield School of Management in the UK. The conclusion of this research was that different leadership styles were linked to particular countries and that leaders held contrasting views regarding appropriate styles. In other words, there were culturally derived variations in implicit views of leadership, ie what makes a good and effective leader. Fincham and Rhodes (2005) provide a summary of the Cranfield study's findings involving the following classification of leadership styles:

- *Leading from the front* – found in Ireland, Spain and the UK. Within this group of countries, stress was laid on the leader's competencies and even charisma; leaders were dominant and were expected to be self-motivated.
- *Consensus styles* – characteristic of Finland and Sweden, and within this typology leaders stressed the importance of communication and consensus, using 'open channels' to foster effective teamworking. In this style, attention to detail was also deemed to be very important.
- *Common-goal leadership* – associated particularly with Germanic societies where technical expertise, clarity of role and effective systems were seen to be to the fore.
- *Managing from a distance* – the predominant style found in France, where leaders were ideally regarded as conceptual thinkers absorbed with strategic concerns. However, communication was felt to be less than effective as a consequence of this style.

Significant attention has also been directed to establishing whether it is possible to identify a distinctive Asian implicit view of leadership. Westwood (1992) put forward the paternal model of leadership, concluding that this is the characteristic form of leadership evident in South-East Asia. Key points from Westwood's model are:

- *Social distance* – leaders seek to maintain a psychological distance from followers thereby establishing a paternal relationship.

- *Concern with harmony* – an essential role within leadership is to maintain harmony – itself a core principle of Asian religions and philosophies such as Taoism and the Confucian ethic.
- *Humane leadership* – the leader should have concern for followers, show 'heart' and avoid loss of face amongst subordinates.
- *Personal authority* – leaders will stress personal relationships in preference to formal rules.

Moran et al (2014) set out the cultural context in which characteristic and acceptable leadership styles are formed and sustained. When analysing South Korea they note (p447) 'there is little concept of equality in relationships. . .in relationships it is often necessary to appear to lower oneself in selfless humility and give honor to other people. To put oneself forward is considered arrogant and worthy of scorn.' Such a cultural backdrop has clear implications for the exercise of leadership at work, in particular on the leader–follower dynamic. Leaders may feel obliged to stress their superior status, which will then play out in the (limited) extent to which they consult lower-level employees. In a similar vein, Chow (2005, p220) highlighted Chinese cultural influences on leadership, concluding that 'Cultural norms state that leaders should exercise power on behalf of the collective, not on the grounds of self-interest, and maintain harmonious relationships within the group, to display the virtues of human-heartedness, respect, mutual obligation and reciprocity, to exhibit face sensitivity and to uphold a moral dynamic that has been labelled as "paternalistic" or "benevolent autocratic".' Guirdham (2011) made a similar point noting that in China, moral leadership emphasising selflessness and fairness was regarded as essential in a business context. When looking at the situation in India, Guirdham cited the research conducted by Pillai et al (2001). These writers concluded that successful leaders in Indian business settings paid attention to fairness, also known as procedural justice. A charismatic or 'transformational' style could be effective as it was associated with the group values (India is classified as moderately collectivist) of fairness and procedural justice. Taken together, these and other studies point to a distinctive Asian implicit leadership style which is far removed from that recommended by researchers emanating from the American human relations school who have played such a prominent role within the business and management literature.

INDIVIDUAL ACTIVITY 7.1

Refer to the findings on Asian leadership set out above and relate these to both Hall's and Trompenaars' models of culture summarised in Chapter 3.

How well do you feel these models explain differences in implicit leadership styles worldwide? To what extent do you think the concept of 'culture shift' could lead to changes in implicit views of culture? Give reasons for your conclusions.

7.5 THE CONTINGENCY APPROACH

The contingency approach to leadership has, as its central message, the suggestion that leadership styles and effectiveness will all depend on certain situational influences – that is to say, external conditions faced by the leader. This may immediately conjure up fruitful scenarios in the minds of readers: what if culture could be conceived as a contingent factor in this regard? This, in essence, was the approach taken by Robbins (2005), referred to at the start of this chapter. Identifying the potential importance of culture, Robbins (p381) notes that, 'National culture affects leadership style by way of the follower. Leaders cannot choose their styles at will. They are constrained by the cultural conditions that their followers have come to expect. For instance, Korean leaders are expected to be paternalistic toward employees; Arab leaders who show kindness or generosity without being asked to do so are seen as weak; and Japanese leaders are expected to be humble and speak infrequently.'

We could extend this line of reasoning by suggesting that different groups within nation-states may also have differing expectations, and that it appears that leaders attempting to lead in conditions of employee diversity may face their own special challenges. The contingency approach to leadership may offer them help in its basic premise that leaders need to adapt their styles, even to the extent of exhibiting different styles and behaviours concurrently.

Before examining the place of culture within a contingency view of leadership, it is relevant to examine a specific model which typifies the overall approach.

The work of House (1971) (see also House and Dessler 1974) provides a well-respected example of the tenets of contingency theory as applied to the area of leadership. House's path-goal theory identifies four generic types of leader behaviour:

- *Directive leadership* is where leaders give precise and unambiguous directions to followers. The followers – or subordinates, to use the hierarchical term – are then expected to adhere to these directions, having been made aware by the leader of what is required of them, of how to achieve the relevant goal(s) and of the intended results of their actions.
- *Supportive leadership* necessitates the leader's convincing the subordinates that he or she has a genuine concern for their needs and aspirations. This belief is to be achieved by adopting an appropriate (friendly) style and the promotion of a supportive working environment.
- *Participative leadership* involves leaders' consulting with subordinates and evaluating followers' views and proposals before making a decision.
- *Achievement-oriented leadership* requires that leaders set brave or challenging goals for subordinates, 'raising the bar' to ensure continuous improvement, while maintaining confidence in followers' ability to perform at a high level. This is normally associated with the design of meaningful 'enriched' work.

Clegg et al (2011) propose that House's work in more recent years points to the addition of two more recognisable leader behaviours. Firstly, networking leadership involves the leader actively seeking resources and increased influence at organisational level, for the benefit of his or her team or unit, while values-based leadership involves shaping and communicating vision – this might be regarded as similar to the transformational concept of leadership previously noted.

House's model is located within the contingency approach to leadership in that the different behaviours could profitably be practised by any individual leader in different settings; again, the crucial message is that 'it all depends'. In House's model the important contingent factors either were centred on the followers – their levels of experience, competencies and knowledge or, alternatively, aspects of their personality, such as desire for autonomy – or were linked to the task: that is, the degree to which it was routinised and highly structured.

As indicated earlier in this chapter, the contingency approach to leadership appears to lay the ground for a cross-cultural twist to the topic of leadership. We have already suggested that leaders themselves could adopt implicit leadership styles based on perceptions of the personal attributes and actual behaviours needed for appropriate and successful leadership of others (specifically, here, subordinates) within a work setting. The contingency view applied to leadership opens up the possibility of differences in the extent to which leader behaviour is viewed as acceptable, even legitimate and indeed effective, by subordinates themselves.

The notion that leaders may have to reconsider their behaviour or style in view of culturally influenced expectations of their followers can be found as a strongly developed theme within cross-cultural business research and textbooks. Denny (2003, p79), in applying Hofstede's framework to leadership as a 'vital management function', summarises leadership in French organisations (and, by inference, of French nationals working abroad) as characterised by 'Control based on authority. Roles ranked not people. Manager knows best. Subordinates expect to be told what to do. Emotional need for rules. Ideal boss = benevolent dictator.' The analysis of the concept of culture contained in Chapter 2 – specifically its multi-layered and changing nature – may counsel readers to exercise some degree of caution in the face of a very strong assertion of this sort. Nonetheless, this conclusion does once more point to the dangers of accepting recommendations on participative leadership deriving from the US context, and it also, paradoxically, implies that the contingency approach may have universal validity.

Importantly, the contingency model by definition acknowledges the reciprocal nature of culture. There is also an implication within the model that effective leaders will be those who are able to choose appropriate behaviours and styles. One is struck by the resultant picture of leadership as a behaviour which emerges from a cognitive appreciation of the situation within which leaders find themselves. Cross-cultural studies on leadership have played an important part in dispelling the earlier, and flawed, conception of it as a function of inherent personal traits or, alternatively, the adoption of prescriptive leadership theories. In as much as many leaders, certainly in the business context, will routinely encounter followers from different cultural backgrounds, conceivably within a single country, the contingency approach has much to recommend it in terms of both intellectual appeal and workplace applicability.

7.6 PROJECT GLOBE

In Chapter 3 we referred to the large-scale Project GLOBE research programme as an illustration of the underlying principles that have driven a good deal of cross-cultural research. We now turn to examining its very considerable significance within the area of leadership study. Commencing in 1991, the first and second phases of this project culminated in the publication in 2004 of a five-part book outlining the project and its findings. Project GLOBE (Global Leadership and Organisational Behaviour Effectiveness) continues to provide a source of data on cross-cultural leadership. Researchers have sought to apply the GLOBE findings to specific regions; for example Kabasaki et al (2012), in this case focusing on the Middle East. The GLOBE study itself was generating research material as late as 2013 (see Chokar et al 2013).

It should be stated at the outset that the scale of this project alone sets it apart from previous studies. The project's findings locate 62 societies along nine identified dimensions. This breadth of study is a marked departure from most previous writings which have typically focused on a smaller group of countries often comprising 'old favourites' such as Japan, Germany, the USA and the UK. The inclusion in GLOBE of countries which have not hitherto formed part of datasets emanating from large-scale cross-cultural business research, significantly enriches the scope of knowledge in this area and enhances topicality; for example, in the inclusion of newly capitalist states such as the Czech Republic and Poland.

The genesis of Project GLOBE can be traced back to the work of the late Robert House, who went on to become the principal investigator in the GLOBE study. House, on the basis of previous work in the field, hypothesised (reportedly in 1991) that the charismatic style of leadership and associated behaviour could be applied successfully across the world. One important concept underpinning this hypothesis is that effective leadership behaviour must be acceptable and therefore endorsed by followers, so the reciprocal nature of leadership was recognised from the outset in this influential cross-cultural study. At the same time, the researchers acknowledged the ongoing debate over the extent of cultural variation in organisational processes – in this case, leadership. House et al (2001, p3) note that 'the literature on this topic points to a major divergence of views regarding the universality of leadership patterns. Many researchers have argued for a direct impact of culture on leadership styles, arguing that specific cultural traditions, values, ideologies and norms are bound to differentiate as much as or even more than structural factors between societies.' By the time Project GLOBE began, House's original idea that aspects of leadership could be universally applicable had been incorporated within a research programme that sought to identify which leader behaviours and attributes would be effective (and therefore accepted) in all or merely some cultures.

The research conducted in the course of Project GLOBE is extensive in terms of both sample and subject matter. Data was collected from over 17,000 participants (mainly managers) from 950 work organisations operating in three sectors: financial services, food and telecommunications. Jackson (2005), in reviewing the GLOBE study and associated publications, identified 27 hypotheses contained within the study. The basic questions to which it was hoped GLOBE would provide answers are set out below (House et al 2001, pp492–493):

- Are there leader behaviours, attributes and organisational practices that are universally accepted and effective across cultures?
- Are there leader behaviours and attributes that are accepted and effective in only some cultures?
- How do attributes of societal and organisational cultures affect the kinds of leader behaviours and organisational practices that are accepted and effective?
- What is the effect of violating cultural norms relevant to leadership and organisational practices?
- What is the relevant standing of each of the cultures studied on all nine core dimensions of culture?
- Can the universal and culture-specific aspects of leader behaviours, attributes and organisational practices be explained in terms of an underlying theory that accounts for systematic differences across cultures?

In approaching their research relating leadership to culture, the GLOBE team highlighted nine dimensions of culture. These have already been referred to in the course of our discussion of culture as a concept in Chapter 3. The nine dimensions are reproduced again below, but see the section entitled 'Project GLOBE: tracing the bloodline' in Chapter 3 for further description of these categories and an account of the derivation of the dimensions:

- power distance
- uncertainty avoidance
- collectivism I
- collectivism II
- gender egalitarianism
- assertiveness
- future orientation
- performance orientation
- human orientation.

One very useful aspect of the GLOBE study was to distinguish between participants' views on how they viewed the actual situation with regard to these dimensions both in their own society and place of work, and how they wished things were – in GLOBE terms, *as is* with a view to *what should be*. The model of culture which emerges is therefore safeguarded from criticisms that it is idealised or prescriptive. The GLOBE researchers refer to the aspect of their methodology which attempts to capture both reality and aspiration as 'parallel culture items'. To take one example, the dimension of power distance (PD) was located by presenting respondents with statements to which they were required to respond along a seven-point scale. Three such statements are set out below:

- In this society followers should question their leaders when in disagreement/obey their leaders without question.
- In this organisation followers are expected to question their leaders when in disagreement/obey their leaders without question.
- In this organisation followers should question their leaders when in disagreement/obey their leaders without question.

The next stage of the GLOBE programme involved the identification of leadership styles or dimensions of leader behaviour. As a result of their empirical work, the following six dimensions were highlighted (see House et al (2004) for a fuller description):

- *Charismatic/value-based* – A leader within this category is defined as performance-oriented and decisive. Furthermore, as can be gleaned from the category title, he or she is characterised by high integrity and is visionary and inspirational. This type of leader also demonstrates altruistic behaviour where necessary, with a potential to self-sacrifice for the organisation.
- *Self-protective* – This leader type is status-conscious and self-centred. Described as 'conflict inducers', such leaders display face-saving behaviour and are very concerned with procedures.
- *Autonomous* – Autonomous leaders, in addition to displaying behaviour consistent with the category title, were viewed as independent and individualistic.
- *Humane* – As one might expect, leaders here adopt a humane orientation, but also, and importantly, exhibit the personal quality of modesty.
- *Participative* – House et al (2001) describe this type of leader as 'reverse-scored' on autocratic behaviour. Put positively, the leader in this case is willing to delegate and foster increased participation among subordinates.
- *Team-oriented* – This type of leader is a team integrator, has a collaborative style, is 'reverse scored' on malevolence (ie he or she is seen as benevolent) and is also viewed as highly competent.

When analysing the impact of the different leadership styles across the participating countries, the GLOBE researchers found that some leadership styles and attributes were 'globally endorsed' while others were regarded as 'universal impediments to effectiveness'. A third category were styles, behaviours and attributes which were subject to 'culturally contingent endorsement'.

Leader attributes that were universally supported within the GLOBE study centred on trust, integrity and vision, so it was concluded that charismatic/value-based leadership would be accepted and consequently would be effective across the world. A further conclusion was that leaders who build supportive teams would gain acceptance across cultural clusters. At the same time, self-protective leaders characterised by malevolence and face-saving, perhaps unsurprisingly, were clearly identified as universally unacceptable and, therefore, as an impediment to success in all situations.

The emergence of styles and behaviours that were more widely accepted in some cultures than in others led to the construction of country clusters. (As suggested in Chapter 3, this notion is very characteristic within cross-cultural research.) The specific clusters emanating from Project GLOBE are set out in Table 7.1.

Within this overall summary of the GLOBE project and findings, it is useful to look in greater depth at one cultural cluster in order to gain an impression of the intricacies bound up in the study. Bakacsi et al (2002) examine the Eastern European cluster, which added Greece to a number of ex-Communist countries, some of which were contained within the former USSR. These authors note that apart from the endorsement of charismatic and team-oriented leadership (which was universal) and the similar rejection of the self-protective style, there is moderate acceptance of humane and autonomous dimensions in this cluster. However, it is important to recognise the differences between countries in the cluster. Bakacsi et al record that Greek managers were far less favourable towards team leadership than those in other countries, while Hungarian managers displayed significantly less enthusiasm towards the autonomous style.

Readers should therefore delve into the specific GLOBE findings to identify individual countries' underlying views towards particular dimensions. Another important reason for 'drilling down' into the clusters is that further examination reveals a richness of data concerning socio-economic development and change. Bakacsi et al (2002, p79) provide an interesting example, noting that, 'Hofstede (1993) depicts the Russian cultural heritage as passivity, uncertainty avoiding and tradition. All known measures about the region tend to indicate avoiding rather than bearing uncertainty, positioning Eastern European countries to the uncertainty avoiding half of the world map. Yet on GLOBE uncertainty avoidance practice country rankings, Russia scores the lowest, Hungary is a close second, and Georgia, Greece, Kazakhstan, Poland and Slovenia are all in the last third.'

Other writers are now taking the GLOBE data and providing in-depth analyses of individual countries in an attempt to explain particular, and sometimes anomalous, findings. Keating and Martin (2004) – themselves GLOBE 'country co-investigators' – relate the GLOBE findings on Ireland to specific cultural and socio-economic phenomena. They account for Ireland's high score on the 'as is' part of the humane leadership style as being entirely predictable given that country's strong religious heritage and documented generosity in humanitarian appeals. They suggest that the even higher score (5.47) on the 'should be' element of the humane orientation may be explained more specifically (p9) as having been stimulated by the perception that the softer, gentler characteristics of life in this country were sacrificed to the 'Celtic Tiger' (Ireland's economy was booming at that time) with a zeitgeist emphasis on economic success, performance and individual achievement. Again, one is struck by how the new GLOBE data has captured the essence of culture as a dynamic concept amenable to significant rapid change within the volatile globalised economy. Readers are recommended to go beyond the standard summary of GLOBE found in many textbooks and to delve into the emerging, and fascinating, material examining specific clusters and individual countries.

The final part of the Project GLOBE study to record is the conceptual model which followed the extensive research programme documented here. House et al (2001, p499) categorise their own model as 'an integration of implicit leadership theory, value/belief theory of culture and structural contingency theory of organisational form and effectiveness'. The same writers state that a central theoretical proposition underpins the model: that the particular attributes and entities which delineate one culture from any other will predict the organisational arrangements, and specifically the types of leadership to be found at organisational level. Culturally influenced leader behaviour will be prevalent, accepted and, once again, effective within work organisations in that culture. This central proposition comprises 13 propositions, several of which have already been noted and discussed in Chapter 3.

1   Societal cultural values and practices affect what leaders do – Within this proposition it is suggested that leaders within organisations, having been selected by the founders of those organisations who are themselves immersed in a particular culture, will be influenced by dominant norms and values of their culture.

Table 7.1 Societal clusters by country

'Anglo' cluster	Latin America cluster
England	Costa Rica
Australia	Venezuela
South Africa (white sample)	Ecuador
Canada	Mexico
New Zealand	El Salvador
Ireland	Colombia
USA	Guatemala
	Bolivia
	Brazil
	Argentina

Latin Europe cluster	Sub-Saharan Africa cluster
Israel	Namibia
Italy	Zambia
Portugal	Zimbabwe
Spain	South Africa (black sample)
France	Nigeria
Switzerland (French/Italian)	

Nordic Europe cluster	Arab cultures cluster
Finland	Qatar
Sweden	Morocco
Denmark	Turkey
	Egypt
	Kuwait

Germanic Europe cluster	Southern Asia cluster
Austria	India
Switzerland (Germanic)	Indonesia
Netherlands	Philippines
Germany (former East)	Malaysia
Germany (former West)	Thailand
	Iran

Eastern Europe cluster	Confucian Asia cluster
Hungary	Taiwan
Russia	Singapore
Kazakhstan	Hong Kong
Albania	South Korea
Poland	China
Greece	Japan
Slovenia	
Georgia	

2 Leadership affects organisational form, culture and practices – This points to an enduring influence on the part of leaders.

3 Societal cultural values and practices also affect organisational culture and practices – Organisations are microcosms of society with implicit views that are framed by the cultural context of that organisation.

4 Organisational culture and practices also affect what leaders do.

5,6 Societal culture and organisational form, culture and practices all influence the processes by which people come to share implicit theories of leadership.

7 Strategic organisational contingencies affect organisational form, culture and practices and leader behaviours – Contingent factors such as the size of organisation or the environment it operates in (eg level of turbulence inherent in that environment) exert an influence on its internal operations, such as structure and other *modi operandi*.

8 Strategic organisational contingencies affect leader attributes and behaviour – Here there is acknowledgement that the logic of the contingency model of organisations applies to the area of leadership.

9 Relationships between strategic organisational contingencies and organisational form, culture and practices are moderated by cultural forces – To take one example, in an environment that would imply a highly directive leadership style in House's path-goal theory, the degree of preferred PD in a society might mean that a leader retained some degree of informality and a more participative style. We examined similar arguments in Chapter 5 when dealing with the topic of structure.

10 Leader acceptance is a function of the interaction between culturally endorsed leadership theories and leader attributes and behaviours.

11 Leader effectiveness is a function of the interaction between leader attributes and behaviours and organisational contingencies – In this case we are reminded that effective leaders are likely to be those who dampen their preferred style to take into account the context within which the organisation operates.

12 Leader acceptance influences leader effectiveness.

13 Leader effectiveness influences leader acceptance – This final point points to a virtuous circle whereby successful leaders, and their style and behaviours, become self-perpetuating.

7.7 EVALUATION OF PROJECT GLOBE

The blend of implicit leadership theory, clearly developed model of culture and contingency-style analysis means that Project GLOBE has resulted in the most systematic perspective on the topic of cross-cultural leadership to date. We should also acknowledge the scale of this piece of work, which continues in its third phase – seeking out links between leaders' style/behaviour and followers' attitudes and performance – at the time of writing. It would not be unreasonable to state that the GLOBE research has very significantly raised the bar for others working in the field. Most importantly, it provides a framework for those who occupy (or aspire to) leadership positions, helping them to understand their own situation and providing a platform for improved performance.

It is still, however, possible to identify some areas of criticism, or at least pointers to enhance future work on cross-cultural aspects of leadership.

● In Chapter 2 we alerted readers to the possible dangers of studying culture primarily at the level of nation states. The GLOBE writers were fully aware of this potential pitfall. House et al (1999, p42) note that, 'National borders may not be an adequate way to demarcate cultural boundaries, since many countries have large subcultures. It is impossible to obtain representative samples of such multicultural nations as China, India or the United States.' House et al go on to show that they have, where possible, allowed for the effect of subculture by sampling more than one or by examining the subculture with the greatest amount of commercial activity. Nonetheless, the potential inherent problems of what is primarily a national focus remain.

- The oft-voiced criticism that cross-cultural business research is conducted mainly at managerial level can also be levelled against this large-scale project. However, as we have seen, the GLOBE research focuses on what subordinates would like to happen, thus mitigating this criticism somewhat.

- Jackson (2005) indicates that the GLOBE research does not deal with the manifestations of leadership attributes. Although charismatic leadership is endorsed worldwide, would it be perceived in the same way in Canada, Thailand and Nigeria? In Chapter 3 we have suggested that this point – the framing of research constructs in ways which may reflect the culturally influenced perceptions of the researchers – has affected earlier studies. Can it also be said to be true of the multicultural GLOBE research effort?

- There is, finally, scope to expand on the dynamic processes of culture; for example, showing how leadership styles could possibly synthesise when leaders from different backgrounds work together.

APPLYING THEORY TO PRACTICE 7.1

The Australian *Herald Sun* newspaper, based in Melbourne, published a series of articles in 2008 contrasting the attitudes held by successive generations of Australians.[1,2] The differences put forward were certainly drastic in nature. While so-called war babies, born in the 1930s and 1940s, were characterised as conservative and security-conscious, exhibiting significant long-term loyalty to their employing organisations, subsequent generations were depicted as radically different in outlook. Generation Z children born after either 1995 or 1998, depending on which article you read, were in contrast seen as shaped by a world dominated by achievement and outcome. The Generation Z children had a different conception of community, many having been brought up in single-parent or same-sex families. These children were seen as both bombarded by information and highly selective in receiving messages from multiple sources of technology. The recession of 2008/09 would be a major determinant of attitudes and behaviour for the more affluent children within this generation, as they had only previously known a prosperous era. They would be the most educationally qualified generation ever (this of course also applies to previous generations) and also socially aware of certain single issues (such as climate change) although less tribal in political affiliation. The *Herald Sun* articles posited that these children would be measured, reserved and conservative as adults but would also be technologically sophisticated, using techonology and social networks in an attempt to 'make a difference'.

This picture of changing generational attitudes and behaviour holds considerable implications for leaders in business organisations. Contingency theories of leadership tell us that if the characteristics of followers change, then so too will leaders' styles and behaviour if they are to remain effective. The generational changes outlined here are common to many cultures, so there is some suggestion that leader behaviour may be influenced by similar social trends in all societies. In earlier chapters, we also saw how different societies were evolving at different stages of development, hence exhibiting meaningful difference, so effective leadership in work organisations is likely to be subject to both global convergence and individual society effect in future.

7.8 THE INSTITUTIONAL LEVEL

Much of the cross-cultural leadership literature, from the work of Hofstede through to Project GLOBE, takes as its primary focus the notion that cultural impact takes place at the level of individual preference in terms of norms, values and practices. The chief premise is, or is assumed to be, that individuals are socialised into their own culture and that this socialisation results in their internalising attitudes (for example, regarding authority) which then influence patterns of behaviour when or if they come to occupy leadership roles. Crucially, the same attitudes and beliefs are held by followers emanating from the same culture, resulting in a reflective process of selecting leadership behaviour that is likely to be accepted by the followers. This reciprocal logic reinforces the particular norms and values which are then perpetuated over a longer timeframe. However, these individual choices are in reality influenced by a range of factors which impinge at a higher institutional level; for example, the legislative framework regarding managerial prerogative and the extent to which subordinate employees are required to either be consulted on certain decisions or actually play a part in joint decision-making.

The Project GLOBE conceptual model takes this notion on board in its Proposition 11, which describes the role of organisational contingencies in shaping leader behaviour. This is potentially a significant finding, because formal systems of worker consultation can, for example, be found within a number of European states and exist, to a lesser degree, at a pan-EU level. Perhaps the most extensive system of employee participation is the German system of *mitbestimmung* (co-determination) in which all but the smallest work organisation would (if requested by workers) operate a works council comprising both management and worker representatives. The works councils have three rights, depending on the particular items on the agenda: the rights of information, consultation and co-determination. This last right of joint decision-making applies to a range of HRM issues; for example, relating to working conditions and holiday arrangements.

The key point here is that the leadership literature typically identifies autocratic, consultative and democratic styles with the assumption of choice on the part of the leader. However, in German work organisations, style is partly determined by the legislative context; in this case, industrial democracy. If the German model is to be seen as culturally influenced, then it is at the macro, in this case legal, rather than the individual, level of managerial choice or 'software of the mind'. Of course, we have already noted that the different levels of culture are interconnected. Nonetheless, in this example from Germany, leadership is very much framed within the existing 'middle layer' context of national values expressed in terms of policies.

In this context there is scope for an interesting debate on the role of culture on corporate governance (see Koen (2005) for one contribution to this growing area). In the specific topic area of leadership we are reminded again of the multi-layered nature of culture: the German system of industrial democracy is indeed influenced by that country's culture, which, in turn, is framed by its economic and political history.

7.9 GENDER, CULTURE AND LEADERSHIP

In previous chapters we have counselled against neglecting the topic of gender within any credible analysis of cross-cultural management. This is certainly the case when we examine leadership as there are a number of interesting linkages between culture, gender and leadership. We should, firstly, recognise that much conventional thinking on leadership has ignored gender, or, as Hopfl and Case (2007) suggest, 'subsumed' women in discussions of leadership. French et al (2011, p469) link the neglect of gender with the source of data as follows: 'Much leadership theory and research originates from a North American context and has focused primarily on masculine models of leadership. Given the globalization of business, the increasing diversity of domestic societies, the ageing of the workforce and the importance of women in the workforce and in the community, this is a significant gap in leadership studies.' How can cross-cultural studies of leadership encompass gender in future?

At the most basic level, we could begin by comparing the proportion of men and women in senior leadership positions in different societies. In the Anglo-American context, such comparison has frequently revealed under-representation of women in senior management, attributing the phenomenon in large part to the existence of a glass ceiling or invisible barrier which inhibited women's progress up organisational hierarchies due to unstated views of women and their roles at work. A 2012 European Commission report (Reding 2012) identified major imbalances in occupation of senior corporate roles across EU member states. Reding found that 96.8% of boardroom chairs were male, attributed in part to a continuing glass ceiling effect. There is some evidence that attitudes differ between cultures (see Ryan and Alexander 2005), with greater numbers of women in senior public service jobs in Sweden and New Zealand. Moreover, Sinclair (1998) notes the possible impact of anti-discrimination legislation which should affect all disadvantaged groups as such laws spread across many areas of the world – although the European Commission report cited above casts doubt on this conclusion, as such laws had been in place in the UK for over 30 years. Even in countries with a reputation for fostering gender equality there are still differences in gender representation in senior roles. A Grant Thornton report in 2013, for example, found that 27% of senior managers in Sweden were women; a figure which might surprise some as Sweden is commonly believed to be in the forefront of gender equality.

Nonetheless differences between countries do exist. There are significant variations in the amount of paternity leave that men can legally take across European states, ranging from two days in Spain to four weeks in Norway. It is quite possible to attribute differences of this kind to manifestations of culture set out in the classical models of culture. Norway was one of the 'feminine' cluster of countries in Hofstede's classification scheme, and the finding on paternity leave (encouraging fathers to take greater child-care responsibility, thereby freeing up mothers for a return to work) might be seen as a vindication of his model. The aforementioned Grant Thornton report found a leap in women's occupancy of senior management positions in mainland China from 25% in 2011 to 51% in 2012. So we should once again beware of assuming that cultures are static or of drawing false assumptions based on older literature and 'classical' models of culture.

If we nonetheless find more women in senior leadership roles in some societies, will this in turn impact on the prevailing leadership style found there? There is conflicting evidence for us to consider. Rosener (1990) conducted research which involved asking both female and male managers to consider and locate their own style of managing. She concluded that women were more likely to adopt a transformational leadership style which stressed positive interpersonal behaviour such as motivating and persuading others, and encouraging their commitment and participation. In direct contrast, men were more associated with transactional leadership, which Rosener depicts as characterised by leading through exchange, ie by reinforcing subordinates' good behaviour and punishing the bad. Rosener also found that male leaders would cite their position power (normally equating to their place in the hierarchy) when justifying decisions and managing others more generally. This finding has been qualified elsewhere. Scase and Goffee (1990) concluded that preferred styles are dependent on the wider context within which leaders operate, not just leaders' own characteristics. They noted that in the 1980s, when tough, 'macho' management was in vogue in the UK, 88% of female managers surveyed claimed to be assertive and aggressive in style. We should also recognise that the appropriateness of transactional and transformational leadership will, in any case, be determined by the particular situation faced in any one workplace, by any manager. Gender-based preferences should therefore be firmly placed in the wider context. Broeways and Price (2011, p188) locate Rosener's study in comparative terms as her research was conducted in a number of culturally diverse countries. They attempt to link leadership, gender and culture, noting that, 'differences between genders in one culture are also found in other cultures. Male and female leaders, it appears, display differing behavioural tendencies whatever their country of origin.' Broeways and Price conclude that cultural differences in leadership override the influence of gender, as the latter is associated with consistent differences in all cultures. The relationship between the demographic factors of culture and gender are therefore complex in nature and can usefully form the basis of future research work in order that they be further unravelled and illuminated.

7.10 EMERGING TWENTY-FIRST-CENTURY APPROACHES TO LEADERSHIP

The study of leadership has been associated with a series of paradigm shifts in terms of prevailing models, schools of thought and orthodoxies. The search for the great leader in terms of identifying such a character's idealised traits was replaced by a preoccupation with highlighting appropriate styles, which, as we have seen, frequently advocated that leaders combine task- and people-oriented approaches. In both cases the resulting leadership models were often constructed within the North American cultural framework, albeit with exceptions such as the work of Westwood and Kakabadse, which have already been identified. The dominance exerted by contingency models of leadership offered greater scope for the influence of culture and, most importantly, painted a more realistic view of the beliefs and behaviour of leaders worldwide. However, the field of leadership is constantly evolving and alternative conceptions of the topic continue to emerge.

Fulop and Linstead (2009) identified a series of trends within the business environment, including the flattening of organisational hierarchies, which have contributed to a questioning of the role of leaders *per se*, and in particular the continued relevance of the transformational or 'heroic' variety. Interestingly, another of the factors cited by Fulop and Linstead (p507) was 'internationalization and globalization of businesses making it increasingly difficult to centralise power, hence leadership in the head office of the organization'. A focus on post-heroic leadership may soon take on a cross-cultural slant. This could conceivably emphasise the increasing convergence of business across national boundaries, resulting in a global spread of what Boje and Dennehey (1999) have referred to as the 'postmodern leader', whose role is serving the people who serve customers. On the other hand, Boje and Dennehey's categorisation of postmodern leaders as empowering participation through democracy may still be subject to cultural variation in the light of the differences set out in Project GLOBE.

One approach to leadership which has been growing in influence is leader–member exchange theory (LMX), associated with Graen and Uhl-Bien (1995); see also Liden et al (1997) and Wayne et al (2002). The distinctive contribution of this approach is to question whether leaders display a consistent style and behave in a similar way towards all subordinates. LMX research shows that in reality there is evidence of leaders interacting more with some workers, in particular what has been termed an in-group, than with others. The quality of relationship could also vary in that one leader can enjoy open and constructive relationships with some subordinates, and poor interpersonal relations with others (the out-group). LMX theory (see, for example, Christy 2013) states that leaders choose who will fall into the in-group category partly on the basis of similarity. So in-group members who are similar to the leader in terms of personality, attitudes held or demographic characteristics will comprise the in-group. This last point opens up a cultural dimension to the LMX approach, with the possibility of leaders favouring subordinates from their own culture where there is a diverse workforce. There are important discriminatory overtones if such behaviour occurs, since within LMX theory, leaders will support their in-group members, resulting in the latter group performing better, thus creating a self-fulfilling prophecy whereby the in-group category or categories continue to be favoured over time. Graen and Schliemann (1978) conducted research into LMX in

Confucian cultures, noting in-group and out-group dualism where patriarchal leadership styles occurred. This finding points to the impact of particular cultural values affecting LMX and there is scope for more cross-cultural exploration of this model and its implications.

Finally, we could consider Bolman and Deal's (2003) work proposing that leaders use frames to make sense of the world and inform their actions. Whether leaders conceive the organisation as, to use Bolman and Deal's terms, a machine (structural frame), a family (human resource frame), a political arena (political frame) or a symbolic temple (symbolic frame) will determine whether they, as leaders, are basically concerned with goals and objectives, people, political games or symbolic organisational culture. Bolman and Deal propose that all four frames can be used by all people irrespective of cultural background, but it would be interesting to conduct further research to find out whether particular frames were, to any significant degree, associated with individual cultures or cultural clusters. The findings of any future research in this direction could cast more light on whether it is realistic to view leadership as a construction that can vary across cultures.

In summary, the history of cross-cultural explanations of leadership is not yet written, and the continuing importance of the international dimension in business is very likely to result in the emergence of still more innovative perspectives of interest to both students of business and those actively engaged in shaping organisational life.

7.11 LEADING MULTICULTURAL TEAMS

In previous chapters we have noted the importance of multicultural teams within cross-cultural management. Multicultural teams exist when organisations operate outside national boundaries, but also are a fact of life where multicultural workforces co-exist within any one national location (see the discussion of twenty-first-century London in Chapter 1). We have also seen that diverse cultural groups have powerful advantages for organisations, offering enhanced levels of creativity through the varying backgrounds of team members. The 'wisdom of crowds' effect can be a powerful tool in all sectors of business. However, multicultural teams need to be allowed to flourish, which shines a spotlight on the role of leaders of such groups. Before going on to look at the attributes needed by multicultural team leaders, we should firstly recognise that there are differences in how people from specific cultures view authority and leadership in work teams. Kirkman and Shapiro (1997) concluded that nationals from high-PD countries, eg Malaysia, will not react well (at least initially) to delegated responsibility, while those from low-PD backgrounds are more comfortable in bypassing their boss and generally accepting of high levels of responsibility. Furthermore, Kirkman and Shapiro's research revealed that people from 'doing' cultures (such as the USA) are more willing to set their own goals than those from 'being' cultures (eg Malaysia). The third cultural variable identified by these researchers is the distinction between 'free-will' cultures (eg the USA), whose citizens are happy to make changes within a work team, as opposed to 'deterministic' cultures (again, Malaysia provides an example) where there is greater reluctance to engage in self-management. Overall, Kirkman and Shapiro's work is significant since it indicates that people's underlying views of the nature of teams can vary across cultures. In the USA the combination of characteristics prevalent in that society would make it far easier for leaders to set up self-managing work teams. Their conclusion is that such self-managing teams would be far harder to even initiate in Malaysia, and by inference, they would require a more interventionist leadership approach (thus negating their essential character) if they were to be successful.

Assuming that a leader is aware of deep culturally derived perceptions of what it means to work in a team, what competencies does a multicultural team leader have to possess him or herself? Adler and Gundersen (2008) stated that the key to successful leadership is the ability to bring out the advantages of a multicultural team, eg its potential for creativity while maintaining cohesion. This last point is crucially important given the widely diverging ways in which people prefer to work within teams *viz* the aforementioned research by Kirkman and Shapiro. Davison and Ekelund (2004) identify a series of sources of difference in global teams showing how these firstly offer opportunities, secondly where the differences take effect, and thirdly how they are experienced and finally how the team must find an appropriate response to the process differences. To take one example, differences in preferred leadership styles provide an opportunity to seek out an acceptable and effective style and to change and align expectations in this regard. Such differences have an effect on the quality of decision-making and levels of satisfaction in the team, while they can be experienced as frustrations and disappointments. The appropriate responses take the form of awareness of different styles and expectations and identification of conflicts and ways of resolving them.

The twin themes of awareness and adaptability set out in Davison and Ekelund's work are echoed in other analyses of competencies required by multicultural team leaders. Brewster et al (2011) reviewed the nature of global leadership skills in managers. They begin by highlighting two attitudinal aspects: attitudes and values, and mindset. Attitudes and values centre on so-called international orientation, based on the extent and quality of international experience. Changes in this respect feed through to the mindset (defined as a cognitive structure) which, they found, became more global in line with increasing international orientation. In other words, the new attitudes and values became set in the form of a mindset, which then governed subsequent behaviour. Graen and Hui (1999) argued that organisations must develop global leadership through enhancing leaders' 'transcultural skills'. Such skills include those of a 'sensitiser', which involves a leader taking an outsider's view of norms, being attuned to the behaviour and attitudes emanating from another culture, and then reading and conforming to new cultural norms. Another transcultural skill is that of 'synthesiser', which, as the term suggests, involves an ability and willingness to synthesise different cultures either by incorporating elements of both or developing a third culture to which members of the other two can relate.

In addressing the nature of multicultural teams and strategies for leading them, Brewster et al remind us that multicultural teams are no different from mono-cultural teams in many respects. They go through clear stages in formation – to use the terms from Tuckman's (1965) model, forming, storming, norming and performing – and also need to consider task and process issues if they are to work together effectively. However, Brewster et al also indicate specific issues around group formation within multicultural teams which demand attention from the leader. They suggest that differences are frequently played down in the start-up phase, resulting in problems surfacing later. One example given is that teams might stress what they have in common; for example that they are highly educated professionals at the outset. However, after that (2011, p370), 'With depressing regularity, team dynamic problems surface later, when the pressure of work kicks in. Complaints of non-inclusion by those from high-context, neutral cultures are greeted with shocked surprise by UK and US members who view their time-and task-focused approach, combined with an assertive manner, as the "right" approach to teamwork.' The recommended way of dealing with these process difficulties for Brewster et al is to introduce intercultural awareness sessions with a particular emphasis on team-building in multicultural teams.

One concept which can have some relevance when considering leadership of multicultural groups is cultural intelligence, which was put forward by Earley and Mosakowski (2004). These authors claimed that leaders trained to develop cultural intelligence could interpret new behaviour or even non-verbal communication – as could someone from the same cultural background as those exhibiting that behaviour. They claim that it is both a frame of mind and practical skill which enables people to operate effectively in a multicultural setting. Cultural intelligence has four elements:

- knowledge of new cultures
- desire to persevere and a belief in one's own ability to succeed (self-efficacy)
- development of culturally appropriate behaviour mirroring that of the other culture
- learning strategies; for example on how to interpret new and unfamiliar behaviour.

Cultural intelligence is the latest in a series of skills and attributes which it is suggested will assist leaders of multicultural teams. In earlier chapters we have counselled against over-generalising cultural differences and of focusing on superficial aspects of culture which might then change. So any training in cultural intelligence should provide both a comprehensive and in-depth understanding of culture, in all its complexity; otherwise it could prove to be spurious and even harmful. We might also question whether cultural intelligence is inherently different from intercultural competences more generally, as set out, for example, by Dowling et al (2013). We look at such intercultural competences again in Chapter 8. One should also be mindful of the danger of exacerbating difference. In Chapter 11 it will also be argued that the best way of managing diverse groups might be to treat them equally, although cultural intelligence training need not preclude equal treatment.

7.12 CONCLUSION

Culture infuses the topic of leadership. There is an abundance of research showing that the concept of leadership itself is constructed in very different ways across the world. People will also attribute desirable characteristics of leaders in widely varying ways: as the GLOBE study concluded, leader acceptance is influenced by culturally endorsed leadership theories. While some leadership styles are universally welcomed by followers (and some are nearly always seen as undesirable), there is considerable evidence that distinctive leadership styles will be particularly effective in specific cultures. Culture can thus be viewed as a contingent factor in leadership; in other words, what works in one setting may be ineffective in another. Acceptable leadership behaviour derives from the preferences of both leaders and followers, but is also constrained by institutional macro-level factors; for example, the degree of authority afforded to business leaders by law. There is a complex multilayered relationship linking culture, leadership and other demographic factors such as gender. Leaders of multicultural teams can, finally, draw upon a number of sources which set out key drivers of effective leadership in this regard, including the emerging concept of cultural intelligence.

CASE STUDY 7.2

LEADING NATIONAL FOOTBALL TEAMS ACROSS THE WORLD

The Dutch football coach Guus Hiddink has been described as having a 'special place in the latest stage of football's history. In the twenty-first century he has been the world's leading exporter of football know-how from Western Europe to the margins of the earth.'[3]

Born in 1946, Hiddink became a player and coach in Dutch club football. A successful career followed, which also involved spells as coach of clubs in Spain and Turkey and a move into international management with the Dutch national team. His cross-cultural coaching career

really took off in his mid-50s, though, when he became manager of the South Korean national side. At that time South Korea, who were due to co-host the 2002 World Cup tournament, had never won a single match in that competition. Their participation in 2002 was, however, a considerable success and the country unexpectedly reached the semi-final.

More success followed for Hiddink when he coached Australia in the 2006 World Cup and Russia in Euro 2008. Hiddink's globetrotting football coaching career was scheduled to come full circle with his appointment as Netherlands national team manager following the 2014 World Cup.

How does Hiddink himself account for his success in leading foreign nationals? He firstly respects the local way of life, saying that, 'I don't go to work on the culture of the country. I just leave it, I respect it. I only do something about the conditions that they need to perform on the pitch. And of course, there are a couple of things off the pitch that do influence that.'[4]

However, Hiddink, while respecting local culture, has not been afraid to change what he perceives to be its dysfunctional aspects. He found that status attributed to players because of their age was holding back the development of the South Korean team and installed a younger player as captain, contrary to the prevailing cultural norms. He also engendered greater responsibility in the team, stating that the mindset of Korean players needed to change: 'They are used to thinking, I'm a soldier, I'll do what's

asked of me. And you have to go a step further if you want to make a team really mature. You need people who can and will take the team in their hands.'[5] What Hiddink was doing was bringing in a new cultural style of playing, based on the flexible notion of 'total football' pioneered in the Netherlands in the 1970s.

While Guus Hiddink's career as an international coach meant that he did not work with multicultural teams at any one time, his experience is, nonetheless, an interesting guide to some of the issues encountered in leading people from different cultures.

Questions

1   Identify the key competencies displayed by Guus Hiddink in his leadership of footballers from different cultures.

2   To what extent do you think that Hiddink is 'culturally intelligent'? Give reasons for your conclusions.

NOTES

1   WALLIKER, A. (2008) Generation Z Comes of Age. *Herald Sun.* 25 February.

2   BEATTY, R. (2008) It Pays To Know Your XYZ. *Herald Sun.* 10 June.

3,4,5 KUPER, S. and SYMANSKI, S. (2009) *Why England Lose and Other Curious Football Phenomena Explained.* London: Harper Collins.

REVIEW QUESTIONS

1   What do you understand by Westwood's notion of 'paternal leadership', said to be prevalent in South-East Asia? How does this leadership style differ from participative leadership?

2   The GLOBE research study concluded that leader acceptance was a function of an interaction between culturally endorsed leadership theories and leader attributes and behaviour. Show with the use of examples what you understand by this statement.

3   If there are comparatively high proportions of women in senior leadership roles in some societies, in what ways can this be seen as an indication of the cultural characteristics of those societies?

FURTHER READING

BREWSTER, C., SPARROW, P., VERNON, G. and HOULDSWORTH, E. (2011) *International human resource management.* 3rd ed. London: CIPD. Chapter 3 of this book examining culture and organisational life includes a clear and up-to-date summary of cross-cultural leadership, multinational teams and cultural intelligence.

HOUSE, R., HANGES, P., JAVIDAN, M., DORFMAN, P. and GUPTA, V. (eds) (2004) *Culture, leadership and organisations: The GLOBE study of 62 societies.* Thousand Oaks, CA: Sage. This volume, containing a wealth of material from the GLOBE studies, is essential reading for those who wish to reach greater awareness of this important project.

MULLINS, L.J. (2013) *Management and organisational behavior.* 10th ed. Chapter 10 of this best-selling textbook offers a clear and authoritative summary of schools of thought on leadership in a more general sense.

Visit this book's companion website (**www.cipd.co.uk/olr**) to find further exercises including self-assessment questions and also weblinks to media and academic journal articles.

CHAPTER 8

Motivation and Exchange in a Cross-Cultural Context

LEARNING OBJECTIVES

After reading this chapter you should be able to:

- evaluate the extent to which US content and process theories can explain workers' motivation in diverse societies
- assess the contribution of comparative research studies which focus on the meaning of work worldwide
- appreciate how social factors, including culture, shape individuals' psychological contracts and orientations to work
- recognise the trends in contemporary business that may lead to convergence in motivation theory and practice

8.1 INTRODUCTION

The topic of motivation has attracted considerable attention within the study of organisational behaviour and, indeed, management education more generally. Its ubiquity in this regard can be attributed largely to the problematic nature of employee motivation and commitment. In other words, these are not easy to secure, and should certainly not be taken for granted. We also frequently hear that managers must be aware of how best to motivate their staff in order to align workers' efforts to achieve the goals and objectives of the employing organisation. It cannot, however, be assumed that increased motivation will pay off in terms of improved productivity (however measured) and enhanced organisational performance. There are many other factors which affect work organisations' relative success. The twenty-first-century economic downturn saw the end of many hitherto successful companies with highly motivated workforces. Nor is it necessarily true that unhappy employees cannot work effectively: as Thompson and McHugh (2009, p310) note, 'working hard to make the time go faster in an unsatisfying job or just to forget about one's troubles is a familiar experience to many of us'. Nonetheless, the consensus is that motivation matters; this notion works well on a common-sense level and is also supported by research. French et al (2011, p5) summarise this view of the fundamental ingredients of a successful organisation: 'its members are happy and engaged with their task; ideas are shared; workers are supported; and the organisation is delivering worthwhile services'. All of which suggests that the topic of motivation is likely to be of the utmost importance in business terms.

What are the cross-cultural dimensions of this topic? It might reasonably be assumed, firstly, that the concerns of securing high performance for the benefit of all organisational stakeholders are implicitly universal. However, textbooks on motivation typically include a very high proportion of material emanating from the USA: the well-known contributions of Maslow, Herzberg, McClelland, Lawler and Adams, to name just a few, appear with great regularity. This is not to decry the work of any of these theorists or cast doubt on the validity of American social science findings *per se*. The prevalence of contributions from the USA in the field of motivation can in any case be partly understood as a microcosm of the situation in management education more widely. Nonetheless, the sheer volume of American research and theory in this subject area is itself worthy of further elucidation. Furthermore, we should ask whether the precepts of motivation theory as put forward by these writers can be applied in diverse cultural settings.

Students approaching this subject area – certainly as taught in most business schools – appear to be faced with an implied choice of scenarios between either motivation theory, which is held to be universally applicable and 'culture-free', or an alternative in which mainstream models are viewed as culture-bound and therefore unable to explain real-life cultural variation. These observations should not be regarded as part of an arcane academic debate: on the contrary, the issue of potential culturally based differences in employee motivation is centrally relevant to managers within work organisations. For example, a Western manager may be schooled in the principles of job enrichment. If, however, workers in other societies – or those brought up with particular cultural values – do not respond positively to attempts to increase their levels of autonomy at work, job enrichment (at least in this specific guise) may lead to adverse consequences in the very areas it purports to enhance (eg satisfaction and turnover).

8.2 UNIVERSAL NEEDS?

'Motivation' as a term has typically been viewed as a dynamic concept, partly made up of an individual's drive to act in a particular way. It is closely associated with images of movement and even propulsion. Pinder (2008) characterises motivation as comprising energetic forces emanating both from within an individual and from the outside world. Such forces ignite work-related behaviour and pre-determine the form, direction, intensity and duration of that behaviour. This is an evocative summary of motivation, which alerts us to important supplementary questions: namely, in what ways is a person motivated, to what degree, and for how long? However, the core of the concept, as identified by Pinder, is rooted in driving forces that can be activated by a desire to satisfy a need or achieve a chosen goal. As we saw, Pinder's reading of motivation allows for drives that originate externally, that is, from an individual's environment. These external forces point to the possibility of differences in the outside world which could be linked to cultural variation. Both individual attitudes (beliefs and feelings towards specific situations) and values (underlying criteria which guide behaviour more generally) are very much influenced by a person's cultural background.

We return to this important point later in the chapter. At this stage we look more closely at the premise that internal forces, or needs, are an important source of a person's motivation.

Need theories of motivation are rooted in the discipline of psychology. They can often be seen as implying a sense of 'human nature' (although social scientists tend to avoid using this term explicitly because it can evoke ill-thought) through common-sense thinking. Nonetheless, this approach to motivation brings us very close to a picture of what people are truly like. Need theories of motivation are underpinned by the belief that human behaviour is driven by psychological needs, which are frequently biological in origin. Furthermore, if their needs are not satisfied then humans will experience tension or disequilibrium which they will try to rectify (Arnold et al 2010). When applied to the specific area of work and reproduced in the business and management canon, the needs approach to motivation is frequently termed 'the content approach'. Mullins (2013, p252) delineates theories within this tradition in overall terms as an 'attempt to explain those specific things which actually motivate the individual at work. These theories are concerned with identifying people's needs and their relative strengths, and the goals they pursue in order to satisfy these needs. Content theories place emphasis on the nature of needs and what motivates.'

But are those needs, and therefore the content of work motivation, the same for all people? In order to pursue this question we now examine several actual theories contained within this overall school of thought.

8.3 SELF-ACTUALISERS?

The work of Abraham Maslow (1970), dating originally from 1943, embodies the principles underlying the content approach to motivation and has been hugely influential in the subject's development more generally. Watson (2006) considers that Maslow's theory plays an iconic part in the study of organisational behaviour within management education, although he goes on to question (p23) the value of 'probably the most frequently taught and commonly remembered "theory" in the business and management studies curriculum'.

One reason for the enduring influence of Maslow's work is conceivably its visual impact: based on his view that human needs are organised in layers, his resultant model is commonly displayed in diagrammatic form as a pyramid. Within Maslow's pyramid the following human needs are identified. Firstly, at the base of the pyramid we find basic physiological needs such as for food and other bodily needs. Moving further up the levels of the pyramid we find (in turn) safety needs, social needs, the need for esteem and the need for self-actualisation. This last level, usually described as at the apex of Maslow's diagram (although other commentators identify further needs, including a need for freedom of expression), involves humans' supposed need to fulfil their potential. Maslow's most distinctive contribution to motivation was to locate these human needs within a hierarchy. As people become relatively satisfied within each level of the hierarchy, he claimed that they would then move up to encounter the next level of needs.

One of many misconceptions surrounding his work is that Maslow stated that we must be fully satisfied at each level before we progress up the need hierarchy. In fact, he proposed that the degree of need satisfaction required to move upwards declined at each level. For example, people might experience 85% satisfaction of physiological needs but only 40% in esteem needs, yet they could still seek the next level.

It is also wrong to believe that Maslow saw the hierarchy as fixed in all cases. He acknowledged that for some individuals esteem may be prioritised over love, whereas a loveless childhood could see the need for love, friendship and affiliation remain dormant, but the individual in question could still strive to realise self-actualisation. There are other potential examples of need reversal or level omission. Nonetheless, the overriding theme within Maslow's theory is a developmental one, with 'higher-order needs' at the apex of most people's needs hierarchy. McFarlin and Sweeney (2013) conclude though that the needs that Maslow identified do not conform to a fixed hierarchy in every culture. This insight is in itself crucial within the field of cross-cultural management, as it introduces culture as a variable within what is commonly supposed to be a strictly universal model of motivation.

Another important feature of Maslow's theory is the attention he gave to psychological well-being – an important concept within his humanist philosophy. Self-actualisation for him would involve realisation of the human need to lead a life of optimal fulfilment. Although Maslow did not originally set out to develop his theories for a business setting, his work has subsequently had profound implications for how employees are managed in general terms and specifically for work organisations' motivation strategies.

Bunting (2004) reiterates this point in the following way: 'Take a look around some of the employers regularly cited as good companies to work for, and you see that some of their most striking characteristics can be traced back to American psychologist Abraham Maslow. His journal about observing a Californian factory over the summer of 1962, *Eupsychian Management*, never became a bestseller but it is arguably one of the most influential management books of the twentieth century...Maslow was also one of the inspirations behind the human potential movement – what we now call the New Age – and it is his thinking that lies at the crux of the role work now takes in many people's lives. He revolutionised the Victorian work ethic: instead of work being about duty and responsibility, he articulated it in terms of "the ultimate aim of human existence: self-actualisation". He neatly fused self-development, the growing preoccupation of the sixties, with the work ethic. The task of management was to nurture and stimulate a kind of heroic self-realisation through hard work.'

The writer who most clearly took Maslow's theory and applied it to work organisations, following further research, was Frederick Herzberg. The 'two-factor' theory of motivation developed by Herzberg identifies a series of motivator factors which, as the term indicates, serve as positive motivators for employees. These factors can essentially be seen as deriving from work itself: they include responsibility, a sense of achievement and personal growth. Herzberg was keen to stress the importance of environmental or hygiene factors, including pay, working conditions and relations with management. However, although these were critical to the experience of workers, they were for Herzberg more likely to lead to dissatisfaction – if such factors were improved, there would be less dissatisfaction but not positive motivation, which was instead a function of the work undertaken within the job.

Herzberg did not claim that all jobs could provide a source of motivation in terms of offering meaningful, responsible and autonomous work, but he was an important proponent of the principle of job enrichment, which implies the attempt to optimise levels of skill exercised by job-holders, increase their decision-making and 'expand' the job, ie by enabling workers to complete whole tasks, or at least a wider range of tasks than typically contained within the often fragmented blue- or white-collar work. If jobs could be enriched in these ways, workers would have their psychological higher-order needs satisfied through work; in other words, they could achieve psychological growth through their job content.

It is prudent to record at this point that other commentators have stressed more prosaic advantages in job enrichment schemes. Thompson and McHugh (2009, p312), for example, suggest that, 'No matter what the intent of consultants and practitioners in the area in terms of increasing job satisfaction and the elusive quality of working life, to management these techniques are effectively technologies of regulation aimed at increasing control over behaviour and performance.' Even allowing for this alternative interpretation that emphasises how job enrichment must be seen to work in managers' and organisations' interests (should we really be surprised by this?) the influence of psychological theories stressing individual well-being remains strong in the human needs or content approach to motivation. Once again, there is a broad inference within this school of thought that implementing aspects of job enrichment will pay off, for both workers and employing organisations, in all societies.

8.4 IS THE CONTENT APPROACH TO MOTIVATION CULTURE-BOUND?

In evaluating the degree to which the content view of motivation is relevant to all workers irrespective of their cultural background, one should firstly recognise the context within which this approach has been framed. The psychologist Oliver James locates the emergence of positive psychology in the developed (Western) world, with its stress on happiness and self-actualisation, by stating that in the early twenty-first century people in advanced societies were in general no more happy than in the 1950s when they were far less affluent. James noted in 2003 that, 'A typical 25-year-old today is between three and ten times more likely to suffer major depression compared to the 1950s. It seems that when you reach a certain level of income, an annual salary of around £15,000, (£20,600 in 2014 based on inflation calculator), increasing affluence has no impact on whether you are likely to be happier. In fact, the more you earn, the less likely you are to be happy.' Happiness in such a situation is seen as being associated with living a meaningful life, moving beyond a desire for comfort, security and material well-being. This conclusion actually echoes the essential rationale of Maslow's hierarchy of needs: if you are dying of starvation, threatened by plague or destitute, you will not experience a need for self-actualisation or personal growth. If, on the other hand, you have achieved a satisfactory baseline standard of living, you will experience, and be motivated to satisfy, higher-order needs.

It follows, therefore, that we should question the degree to which needs theories of motivation can be applied to workplaces across the world. It may be that attempts to enrich jobs will be better received in more affluent societies. We are reminded of Inglehart and Baker's (2000) thesis (summarised in Chapter 2), which predicts a shift towards values emphasising self-expression and quality of life in economically advanced societies which had provided economic security for many of their citizens. A similar idea was earlier put forward by Strauss (1976), who pointed to the effect of the baby-boomer generation in the USA – these were defined as people born between 1945 and 1960, who were perceived as being more suspicious of, and resistant to, authority and less concerned with economic security, having grown up in the post-war boom. As a result the baby-boomers were predisposed to place a high value on self-fulfilment, sustaining an agreeable lifestyle, doing meaningful work and controlling their own destinies in all areas of their lives including employment. French et al (2011) summarise work which locates other distinctive generations of workers ('Generation X' born after 1964 and 'Generation Y' born after 1978). In both cases these generations seek improved quality of life, meaning that they look for and value new forms of reward at work; for example, flexible working patterns and health and well-being programmes. These workers also display less intrinsic loyalty to their employer and expect to have a series of jobs and multiple careers over the course of their (increasingly extended) working lives.

In cross-cultural terms the advent of changing needs, expressed by new generations of workers, is interesting on several counts. In the first instance it points to the influence of the social setting on people's work-related needs, as had been acknowledged by Maslow. This in itself allows for cultural variation. Inglehart and Baker (2000) record differences in how a concern with quality of life can play out in diverse societies, noting that such concerns were manifested in a desire to engage with new forms of spirituality in North America and Western Europe, while in Eastern Europe and other parts of the world, people have returned to traditional religious values. So the baby-boomers of, say Poland, are both the same as, and different from, their counterparts in the US, in that they too are concerned with non-material values but express them in a different way. It is also the case that people's needs and values reflect the particular economic and business epoch reached by the specific society. Routine, repetitive Taylorist-style work may not ever fulfil workers' needs for self-actualisation. In Western societies, however, a lower proportion of workers might be engaged in such work over time, and we have, of course, in recent years seen much factory production switched from the West to China and significant outsourcing of routine white-collar work to India. We look at this historical dimension again in the section 'Job characteristics: a universal link to motivation?' below.

The period from 2010 to 2014 saw a series of reports citing instances of adverse working conditions in Chinese factories, coupled with some extreme examples of worker distress. One example was cited in a report in the British *Daily Mail* newspaper on 11 January 2012. The report detailed the threat by 150 workers at Foxconn's Wuhan plant to die by throwing themselves off their factory roof. Moore (2012) claimed that the incident was part of a pattern of similar events, with a 'suicide cluster' at Foxconn plants in 2010 resulting in 14 deaths. Following these earlier tragic events, Foxconn managers had reportedly installed netting to prevent similar plunges and, more proactively, hired counsellors to help workers. The January 2012 protests reportedly began after 600 workers were told to move to a new production line. One employee was quoted as saying that people were 'put to work without any training and paid piecemeal...the assembly line ran very fast and we all had blisters and the skin on our hand was black. The factory was also really choked with dust and no one could bear it.' A spokesman for Foxconn said that the incident was 'successfully and peacefully resolved after discussions between the workers, local Foxconn officials and representatives from the local government.' He went on to assert that, 'the welfare of our employees is our top priority and we are committed to ensuring that all employees are treated fairly.'

Questions

Undertake a search for incidences of suicide or attempted suicide in Chinese workplaces after 2010. Gather supporting information from workers, employee associations and company spokespersons and consider the following questions:

1   Referring to the work of Abraham Maslow and Frederick Herzberg, assess the extent to which workers' needs have been neglected in these factories.

2   Would you expect younger Chinese workers to be more prominent in protests against perceived poor working conditions than their elders? Give reasons for your conclusions.

8.5 POSITIVE PSYCHOLOGY AND ENGAGEMENT

Positive psychology is a recent school of thought closely bound up with the topic of motivation at work. Associated with the work of Martin Seligman, president of the American Psychological Society in 1998, this approach notes the importance of positive emotions in accomplishing work tasks by thinking in a more open-minded way and dealing constructively with others. West (2005, p38) concludes that 'the most important barometer of positive feelings and attitudes at work is job satisfaction. Research shows that feeling positive (which includes being satisfied with one's job) is significantly correlated with work performance. The association with average levels of employee satisfaction in organisations and organisational performance is particularly strong.' In his summary of positive psychology, West notes that HR managers can and should both tackle issues within organisations that are affected by negative emotions such as anxiety and anger, and actively foster a workplace culture of positive emotion.

Seligman and Steen (2005) state that a classification of character strengths and virtues would apply across the world, noting (p411) that research by Park et al (2005) 'discovered a remarkable similarity in the relative endorsement of the 24 character strengths by adults around the world and within the United States. The most commonly endorsed ("most like me") strengths in 40 different countries from Azerbaijan to Venezuela are kindness, fairness, authenticity, gratitude and open-mindedness.' Having identified the strengths and virtues that underpin human happiness, Seligman and Steen go on to promote a series of interventions to increase happiness. One can anticipate an increasing focus on identifying such positive interventions at work, and it will be interesting to see whether such interventions are in the event shown to be culture-bound. Kim and Markus (1999) had earlier found that in China individuals who supported group norms (and therefore promoted group harmony) were regarded positively whereas interventions which required employees to act in individualistic ways were less favourably received. Nonetheless, the character virtues referred to in Seligman and his colleagues' work should be accepted universally and recall the desirable leader attributes mentioned by different cultural groups in Project GLOBE (see Chapter 7).

Another recent contribution to the motivation literature can be found in the emerging concept of engagement. Holbeche and Matthews (2012) put forward four drivers of engagement:

- *Connection.* Workers feel connected – and hence engaged – if they have a sense of identification with, and pride in, the employing orgainsation. Identification and pride occur when there is a common purpose and shared values are evident within the orgainsation.
- *Voice.* This aspect of engagement is fostered by managers keeping other employees informed about progress and change and also listening to their views.
- *Support.* Employees should feel they are valued, receive a 'fair deal' and believe the employer is concerned with their well-being. If workers perceive those things to be true, they will feel supported.
- *Scope.* Work should be purposeful, allowing employees opportunities for growth and accomplishment, within a climate of mutual trust.

Engagement can be summarised as the willingness of employees to commit to the organisation and therefore to 'go the extra mile': Huczynski and Buchananan (2013). It is a new concept which, although linked to motivation and job satisfaction, implies psychological commitment to the employing organsation. The literature has emerged from the UK (see Arkin 2011) and is currently culturally specific. However, there is clearly scope to expand the concept to include cross-cultural comparison and one can anticipate that notions of group orientation and power distance (PD) could mean that engagement is more readily achieved in some cultures than others.

8.6 JOB CHARACTERISTICS: A UNIVERSAL LINK TO MOTIVATION?

It is also the case, as we have already seen, that the Western preoccupation with meaningful work – at least in the motivation literature – is related not just to increasing overall affluence and the emergence of specific movements such as positive psychology, but to the changing nature of work patterns within these societies. Hutton (2006), commenting on the situation in the UK, highlights the part played by so-called knowledge workers: 'Over the past ten years we have seen rising employment and greater numbers of workers employed in knowledge work – everything from building Formula One racing cars to writing software programs for trading financial derivatives. The higher our living standards, the more we want our products and services customised, and customisation, whether of our haircut or mobile phone ringtone, involves knowledge.'

The same author goes on to characterise the attitudes such workers will display in respect of their employment, claiming, amongst other factors, that, 'They have to be led and managed by persuasion, rather than by *diktat*. They want flexible working patterns that allow them to build relationships outside work – in particular, with their children.' Hutton claims that workers outside the knowledge sector (his examples are factory or supermarket workers) also have a desire for flexible working which can be achieved via creative shift-working or building up extended leave. However, if knowledge workers value such motivating factors as autonomy and meaningful work, then their actual jobs will undoubtedly affect the extent to which they can achieve satisfaction in meeting these needs or aspirations.

This brings us to consider another strand of motivation theory: namely, that of highlighting the effect of job characteristics.

Hackman and Oldham's (1980) model provides a useful illustration of this approach. These writers firstly identify five core job characteristics (listed below). If present in jobs, these characteristics lead to positive psychological states which in turn result in improved motivation, increased satisfaction and optimal performance.

- skill variety
- task identity – this is defined as present if the job results in a tangible and complete result
- task significance – the degree to which the job has an impact on others either inside the organisation or in the wider environment
- autonomy – the extent to which a job facilitates expression of freedom, independence and discretion both in organising and completing the job
- feedback – this refers to clear information fed back to the worker on how well he or she is doing the job.

Parker et al (2001) provide an elaborated model of job design which extends Hackman and Oldham's model in order to accurately capture the nature of twenty-first-century work. They incorporate additional characteristics, such as whether a job is compatible with home commitments and whether the job demands emotional labour (that is, a display of – possibly scripted – emotion in order to empathise with customers or clients). Parker et al also query the extent to which the term 'job', with connotations of fixed duties, is still appropriate in a (Western) context of role flexibility and adaptation to customer needs. Buelens et al (2006), in evaluating the job characteristics model, record that overall analyses of the job characteristics approach are supportive of the basic hypothesis in that employees who are located in enriched jobs are generally more motivated, are more satisfied and perform better than those who are not.

The job characteristics model is at first sight culture-free. As stated previously, the core job characteristics listed above are said to lead to positive psychological states. However, this happy sequence of events will only take place if workers have overall satisfaction with other parts of the working context (eg pay and co-workers), if they possess the requisite competencies to perform the job effectively, and if, finally, the individual worker has strong growth needs. If these conditions are in place and, in particular, if growth needs do not vary consistently between cultural groups (this is addressed below under the heading 'Needs and job characteristics models in different cultures – some evidence') the job characteristics model of motivation is universally applicable. Culture only becomes a significant factor if particular societies are clearly associated with different types of work, or if workers from specific cultural groups are shown statistically to be over-represented in certain jobs or types of work more generally. However, this caveat is critically important, because, as mentioned earlier, there is evidence that in many Western societies both routine manual and white-collar work is increasingly being outsourced to low (or lower) wage countries, where routine tasks are carried out by local workers at vastly lower costs to the employing organisation.

In this context Bond (2004) notes that, 'Indian call centres are 40% cheaper to run than British ones and the number of outsourcing staff in the subcontinent is expected to grow tenfold in five years'. Bond quotes a 22-year-old female call-centre worker from Bangalore, who refers to her customer adviser role as a 'dream job'. Her salary of £40 per week is twice what an Indian teacher earned at that time, and roughly the same as that of a newly qualified doctor. Unsurprisingly, her main stated motivation is the salary, which she describes as 'absolutely fantastic'. It is also noteworthy that this high salary is seen as a source of prestige within an increasingly consumerist society. So could we be facing a situation in which many workers in Western societies exhibit a desire for meaningful enriched work – or are assumed to by managers and academics – while those in other parts of the world take on jobs less amenable to self-actualisation or task significance? Meanwhile, within more affluent countries there are documented instances of migrant workers taking on work it would be difficult to regard as intrinsically motivating. It is debatable whether they have any real choice in this regard – certainly their experiences of work are very different from those of most local employees.

 GROUP ACTIVITY 8.1

The invisible workforce

In 2006, Reflex, a taskforce set up by the UK Government to report on organised immigration crime, concluded that there were likely to be up to half a million illegal workers in Britain, comprising both illegal immigrants and others not permitted to enter the officially recognised workforce, such as people with student visas. It can be argued that the presence of this unofficial labour force has mixed benefits for all concerned. This duality is by no means atypical when we consider the profound implications of aspects of globalisation (see, for example, Morgan (2007) for a double-edged assessment of the Nike Corporation's activities). So in the case of the UK's illegal workforce it has been claimed that over £3 billion is lost each year to the economy in terms of non-payment of income tax and National Insurance contributions, together with even less quantifiable consequences such as that arising from VAT fraud.[1]

On the other hand, people living in the UK can, possibly without realising the fact, be grateful to this 'reserve' workforce for supporting their consumer lifestyle. A BBC online news report from 2004[2] concluded that many things taken for granted by the British general population (eg cheap supermarket food and designer clothes) were conditional on the presence of migrant labour in the country, in many cases working in (by UK standards) very poor conditions. One farmer who supplied major supermarket chains

expressed the view that it was, in reality, difficult to avoid using illegal labour in his own sector, while another farmer drew attention to the very much lower wages that could be paid to workers from Eastern Europe (often way below the statutory minimum wage) and stated that if illegal labour was not present in the UK, food prices in shops would, in his view, have to rise significantly.

Illegal workers are not only underpaid by UK standards, but may operate in sub-standard and possibly dangerous conditions. George Brumwell, of the construction industry union UCATT, was quoted in the above-mentioned BBC news report identifying the scale of this problem: 'Of the 200,000 building workers in London, probably 40,000 are migrants and a fair proportion are illegals. It's a dirty, physically tiring job – perhaps you might say the last big manual heavy industry in Britain.' He went on to highlight the economic factors that could see a continuation or even worsening of this situation, namely, the key role of the construction industry in driving the economy at that time compounded by a skills shortage of home-country workers in the sector.

1   To what extent could the trends depicted above be explained with reference to both content theories of motivation and Inglehart and Baker's modernisation thesis?

2   Should jobs undertaken by illegal workers in farming and construction be 'enriched'? Give reasons for your answer.

8.7 TOTAL QUALITY MANAGEMENT

A number of commentators (see Watson 2006; Linstead et al 2009; Thompson and McHugh 2009) draw attention to negative effects of jobs designed within principles of scientific management, often traced back to the work of F.W. Taylor in the early twentieth century, and further developed in Henry Ford's assembly line system. Scientific management led to prescribed job roles typically broken down into standardised tasks. These tasks were normally narrow in scope and the work would mainly be repetitive in nature. Taylor believed that breaking down work in this way would secure operating efficiency. On the other hand, from the earliest work conducted by Taylor onwards, there was evidence that some workers found this regime boring and unattractive. Unintended consequences of scientific management included high rates of absenteeism and staff turnover, poor quality work and informal disruption of work, ie through sabotage. From the 1920s onwards various systems emerged with the underlying aim of humanising work in order to secure worker efficiency while eliminating the negative symptoms associated with Taylor's model. One such system was Total Quality Management (TQM). Although associated with the American management writer W. Edwards Deming, TQM has been particularly linked with Japanese organisational practices. This came about through Deming's work in Japan in the immediate post-Second World War period and also because TQM is underpinned by Japanese concepts, most notably *kaizen*, which can be translated as gradual but continuous evolutionary change. TQM is centred on process controls intended to improve organisational performace; however, it contains important human elements and undoubtedly seeks to foster high levels of motivation and commitment amongst employees.

Linstead et al (2009) set out principles of TQM, including inspirational or heroic leadership, a clear customer focus, zero tolerance of errors and a commitment to fact-based decisions, involving a wide range of decision science techniques. For our purposes, the most relevant principles are those of teamwork and the building of trust within a work organisation. In this regard, within TQM, teams of workers were required to contribute to improved performance, this constituting a major departure from the individualised division of labour advocated by proponents of scientific management. It should be stressed that the emphasis on teamwork did not emanate solely from Japan: other schemes such as that pioneered by Volvo in Sweden were also apparent. However, TQM, with its emphasis on teams, commitment and trust, gained significant ground in the Japanese collectivist culture (Hofstede 2001). Linstead et al (2009) record how TQM initiatives emerging from Japan laid an especially strong emphasis on consensus and conformity. Linstead et al (p432) claim that, 'at its extreme, TQM recasts the notion of employee satisfaction to one that depends on a complete subordination of the individual to the collective whole, be it the team, the organisation or the culture'. We see here a particular response to problems of motivation and control shared by many societies, which elicited a response rooted in the national culture of one society: Japan. We can note, finally, that TQM has not always been successfully transplanted to other cultures; as Schermerhorn et al (2009, p398) state, 'when Deming's ideas were not generally accepted in the United States, he found an audience in Japan. Thus, to some managers, Deming's ideas appear in the form of the best Japanese business practices.' It has indeed been claimed that the aspects of Japanese working practices which were most transferable were technological principles such as lean production (exemplified by Toyota), rather than the more interpersonal elements focusing on motivation through conformity, groups and team-working. These aspects, one can reasonably surmise, were not as amenable to the local cultural values in place.

8.8 NEEDS AND JOB CHARACTERISTICS MODELS IN DIFFERENT CULTURES – SOME EVIDENCE

Several research studies have focused on the question of whether workers' needs and/or job characteristics do in practice motivate people in a uniform way irrespective of their cultural background. It is useful at this stage to review some actual findings in order to anchor the topic in reality and move the focus away from the speculative application to theorists such as Hofstede found in other textbooks.

Fisher and Yuan (1998) undertook a study of a large number of Chinese hotel workers employed in the same establishment in Shanghai (the researchers looked at usable data returned by 785 workers). Supervisors at the hotel were also asked which job factors they felt their subordinates would most value. This data was then compared with material emanating from previous studies carried out in other societies, including the USA. One interesting theme of this research was a cross-cultural comparison of how accurate superiors were in predicting the expressed preferences of their subordinate employees.

In this study, Chinese workers were found to rate interesting work as far less important than American employees (the US comparison was related to work carried out by Silverthorne (1992)). The Chinese sample also attributed great significance to good wages and working conditions, which were scored as first and second out of a list of ten factors, compared to fifth and sixth in the American study. The Chinese workers laid greater stress on personal loyalty (from superiors) than in the US research and also a Taiwanese study. However, Fisher and Yuan concluded that Russian workers (again, based on a previous study) also appeared to value such loyalty highly.

Fisher and Yuan draw attention to the influence of a number of extrinsic factors when explaining their findings. For example, they locate the emphasis on the importance of pay in their Chinese sample within specific socio-economic trends in that country, the following quote (1998, p519) pointing to the specific and complex range of factors involved: 'Today, with an end to the security of the "iron rice bowl", increased variability in income, high inflation in the early 1990s, and strong competition for qualified employees in major cities, employees may see good wages as being an extremely important and attainable job attribute.' These contemporary social trends are contrasted with the unavailability of entrepreneurial and performance-based rewards prior to the 1980s, and the enforced egalitarian wage policies harking back to the Cultural Revolution period.

Likewise, the lesser importance attached to job security in China was, for Fisher and Yuan, partly to be understood by the historically higher levels of security in the country, leading employees to worry less about their future employment prospects. The fact that the specific research sample worked in a Western-managed chain hotel was also relevant as employees qualified to work in such an environment were in short supply at the time of the research study and therefore in a favourable position in the labour market. The authors recognise that because extrinsic factors influence employee motivation, the factors will obviously change and in turn affect workers' views of their jobs. They speculate that younger Chinese workers, less affected by the Cultural Revolution and its aftermath, could be increasingly concerned with intrinsic job satisfaction in future.

Two further conclusions from this study are worthy of detailed consideration at this stage. Firstly, Fisher and Yuan show (1998, p524) how Chinese managers were 'much more accurate at anticipating employee preferences than US superiors were at anticipating US subordinates' preferences'. This raises the intriguing possibility of Western managers' habitually misinterpreting the work preferences of their employees – certainly in the case of blue-collar employees, conceivably due in turn to the managers' immersion in US-based motivation theory – and also questions how close they are to their workers in reality. The second conclusion is closely related to the same finding: that culturally influenced values on how work should ideally be perceived are also relevant. As Fisher and Yuan indicate,

US respondents may be more hesitant to admit the importance of money within their overall motivation to work, at least when prompted to discuss their attitudes to work within surveys undertaken to assess their motivation.

Roe et al (2000) conducted research into causes and consequences of job involvement and organisational commitment (attitudes assumed to have a motivational component) amongst workers in three countries: Bulgaria, Hungary and the Netherlands. Data for the study was collected in the mid-1990s, using samples of white- and blue-collar workers from a variety of sectors. The sample was also held constant for comparative purposes by gender, age and job level. Using sophisticated statistical measures, the researchers concluded that there were differences in both the antecedents and consequences of job involvement and feelings of commitment to the work organisation. When using Hackman and Oldham's job characteristics model, Roe et al conclude that, in the case of Bulgaria, feedback is not particularly important and extrinsic factors emerge as key sources of commitment. At the same time, involvement in the job emerges as a key factor for Bulgarian workers along with availability of opportunities to satisfy higher-order needs. In the case of Hungary, the second former Communist country studied, an alternative picture emerged; for example, involvement in the job proved to be relatively unimportant for the Hungarian workers in the research study.

Roe et al propose that their findings for the three countries can be explained by using a mix of frameworks. In analysing the Hungarian data, the researchers point to variation which suggests that the impact of job characteristics is mediated by culture, stating (2000, p678) that, 'The fact that, unlike in the Bulgarian model, the opportunity to satisfy social needs and climate plays a significant role, may be seen as an expression of the greater collectivism in Hungary.' At the same time, specific economic factors were also perceived to play a part, with job factors less likely to link with performance and propensity to leave in Hungary, these causal links being attributed to the economic conditions prevalent in that country. When analysing data from the Netherlands, the authors again attribute the characteristic pattern that emerged there as partly the result of cultural factors; for example, clear preferences for autonomy (a job characteristic) are claimed to reflect the high individualism noted by Hofstede and Trompenaars within Dutch society. The economic circumstances present resulting in low job security also played a role in explaining commitment, the Dutch sample emphasising lifetime career self-development.

One important general conclusion of Roe et al's research concerns the motivational process itself covering stimuli, behaviour and performance. The authors summarise this finding as follows (2000, p679): 'Based on our results we would hypothesise that the environment that people are in produces differences in what motivates them, while the consequences of motivation tend to be universal.' This is in itself a vitally important insight for managers worldwide: they should all be concerned with workers' motivation because the concept links in practice to performance, satisfaction and turnover levels irrespective of the cultural context.

Sagie et al (1996) sought to ascertain the applicability of one particular content theory of motivation: David McClelland's learned needs model across the USA, Hungary, Israel, Japan and the Netherlands. McClelland (1985) put forward the view, based on research undertaken since the early 1960s, that there are four main motives, activated by arousal (but also learned) which influence human behaviour. These are:

- *Achievement* – Individuals with a strong need for achievement ('n-Ach') exhibit a preference for challenging tasks, seek out personal responsibility, tend to be innovative and have a need for very clear and quick feedback on their work.
- *Power* – A need for power could be expressed positively, with a focus on persuasion and influence, or negatively, which would imply a desire to control and even subjugate others.

- *Affiliation* – This need is centred on a desire to develop and sustain social relationships. People with a strong need for affiliation will seek out collaborative rather than competitive situations.
- *Avoidance* – Avoidance of failure is the main need in this category and individuals who score highly here will not look for gratification in the other three areas as this more negative need is dominant.

McClelland was of the view that the need for achievement was essential in the USA to sustain economic growth and success. He was particularly concerned to identify the characteristics held by high achievers and to assess how each of the categories linked to success in management. Sagie et al put an interesting twist on to McClelland's work, firstly by showing how people's preferences for tasks would indicate their own preferred category, and secondly applying the model to the five countries previously mentioned.

Sagie et al's conclusions again point to an interplay between needs, environmental (in this case related to tasks) and cultural elements when explaining motivation. In focusing on the various components of the achievement (n-Ach) category, these researchers found that in the USA task preferences were more for activities which were uncertain, difficult, autonomous, risky, creative and success-oriented. The need for achievement as demonstrated by these task preferences was *pro rata* strongest among US citizens followed by people from the Netherlands, Israel, Hungary, and finally Japan. Japanese managers who might have been expected to have high needs for achievement were instead found to have strong needs for affiliation. In this way culture can once again be seen to intervene in a model of motivation which took as its starting points individual needs and task characteristics.

The aforementioned research studies have been selected in order to provide a more in-depth analysis of work in the field. They are by no means the only significant contributions in the field; see also studies by Ajila (1997), Erez (1997), Harvey et al (2000), Ronen (2001), Earley (2002), Sue-Chan and Ong (2002) and Scholtz et al (2002). In some respects one can find potentially conflicting evidence regarding the extent of cultural differences in motivation. Ronen's research provides support for the universal applicability of Maslow's motivational strata, whereas Ajila and Harvey et al's studies unravelled differences in need order across the world, both of these researchers concluding that the hierarchy of needs should be reconsidered for African workers. As we have already seen, however, Maslow was himself open to this degree of reformulation of his work. Overall, the conclusions of this group of studies, together with those analysed in greater depth in this chapter, provide clear evidence of the important role of cultural differences in motivation, most clearly evident in the antecedents of motivation. A range of factors can lead a person to satisfy culturally influenced needs or to consciously work towards chosen outcomes at work. However, differences can also in part be explained by the prevalence of particular types of work within particular societies at certain times, suggesting that identified differences in motivation across cultural groups may be transitory.

8.9 HOW ARE PEOPLE MOTIVATED? ORIENTATIONS TO WORK ACROSS CULTURES

We have examined evidence which assesses the validity of content (needs) and job characteristics models of motivation in the cross-cultural context. Many organisational behaviour and management texts cast doubts on the currency and explanatory potential of content theories, however, and instead advocate adopting alternative perspectives. Clegg et al (2011, p151) note, for example, that, 'Content theories do not sufficiently explain why people are motivated to behave in certain ways. To answer such questions we need to consider what processes are involved in motivation. Some argue that the process is one of expecting that behaving in a certain way will realise certain outcomes.'

This process view of motivation has an underlying premise that people, rather than being driven by needs, will make conscious choices regarding their behaviour based on their assessment of both the processes involved in achieving an outcome and the desirability of that outcome. Individuals might, for example, ask themselves whether they could achieve promotion at work by working harder, and if they in any case valued that anticipated reward. They might even question whether the anticipated trade-off between effort and reward was on balance positive from their own point of view. Organisational behaviour textbooks frequently capture the essence of the process approach as an emphasis on how individuals are (or are not) motivated. Watson (2006, p312) recommends a further and wider application of the process view, as follows: 'We need to stop focusing on people's "motives" and look at what people are thinking and doing within the broader context of the strategic exchange relationships between employing organisations and employees.' He goes on (p313) to claim that the strategy 'of the employee can be understood as their basic orientation to work. This is something much more subtle, much more complex and much more dynamic than "motives".'

As we have already seen, research studies indicate that individuals' culturally derived values influence their choices underlying motivation at work, these in turn being affected by the external context within which they operate. It is quite possible, therefore, that a framework encompassing notions of strategic exchange and orientations to work may offer a fruitful way forward in explaining cross-cultural aspects of motivation.

The concept of orientations to work was first put forward by Goldthorpe et al (1968) following a large-scale study of different categories of workers partly carried out in a car production plant. The study revealed that white-collar workers in the plant appeared to exhibit greater commitment to the organisation and were more concerned with career advancement, whereas the factory-floor workforce in many cases had chosen their jobs – in a favourable labour market – for the comparatively high pay offered, having turned away from more intrinsically satisfying (but less well-paid) job opportunities. In an important sense this study drew attention to widely divergent values concerning the place of work within a person's life. This analysis took socio-economic groups as its main factor for comparison, but one can easily reformulate this to focus on national culture.

In Chapter 3 we introduced the work of Shalom Schwartz and his basic human values model. At that time we highlighted the relevance of his and his team's perspective that emphasised the role of work values – expressions of fundamental values on life as realised in the work arena – to an understanding of topics such as motivation and commitment. The relevance of work values extends beyond an examination of how the particular values of intrinsic, extrinsic, social and prestige play out in the workplace. Each of the values would, very importantly, also determine the importance of work within people's lives more generally. As we saw in Chapter 3, where there was a preoccupation with mastery and hierarchy deriving from intrinsic and prestige values, work itself is likely to take on a centrally important role in life (the USA provided just such a composite picture for Schwartz). We have here the possibility of locating cultural differences in motivation with reference to orientations to work which vary systematically across different societies and/ or cultural groups. However, we should also keep in mind the original source of the concept of orientations to work as rooted in workers' occupation. Rao and Kulkarni (1998) found that among bank employees in India, officers gave greater importance to psychological growth than did clerks – this finding appearing to corroborate Goldthorpe, Lockwood et al's conclusion regarding the central importance of a person's occupation in framing his or her particular orientation.

One study that looked explicitly at the centrality of work across cultures was the Meaning of Work (MOW) project published in 1987 (England 1986). This study focused on possible differences between societies in terms of work centrality (ie the general importance of work within one's life) and work goals (ie preferences expressed regarding people's actual working lives). In terms of work goals, interesting work was rated highly in all the countries covered by the research, and good physical working conditions were deemed to be comparatively less important in all participating countries. However, there were also differences: good interpersonal relations at work was the second most important factor mentioned in the Israeli sample, but only the seventh by those in the USA group. In the Netherlands, autonomy was the most important work goal, whereas this was rated eighth most important in neighbouring Germany.

The MOW study identifies a mixed picture in terms of conscious evaluations of desired work outcomes, some items relatively consistently rated in terms of importance together with some discrepancies. Some differences were also evident when the study explored the role of work within people's lives, the Japanese sample scoring 25% higher than that in the UK. Nonetheless, the picture that emerges overall is of the relative importance of work within individuals' lives. Francesco and Gold (2005, p136), after dissecting the MOW data, found that 'An interesting finding is that in the eight countries studied, 86.1% of all individuals said they would continue to work even if they no longer had any financial need. Even in Britain, which had the lowest percentage, 68.9% said they would continue to work.'

Returning to the differences which emerged from the MOW study, work itself might be seen as more of a motivating factor where countries score higher on the work centrality scale (for example, Japan and Israel), while maintaining a work–life balance might be an important motivator in societies with lower scores (such as the Netherlands and the UK). Again, one is struck by the possibility of time lags in research data: the MOW finding might be explained by the early stirrings of 'post-industrial' concerns with quality-of-life issues in the Western societies listed.

In summary, the MOW data examined views and choices regarding the place of work within people's lives in different societies. We can therefore plausibly interpret this study's findings as showing how individuals' orientations to work are to some limited degree affected by the cultural context in which they operate.

APPLYING THEORY TO PRACTICE 8.1

Karoshi

Karoshi is a Japanese compound noun that literally means 'death from overwork'. It has become something of a technical term used to describe cases of sudden death in service. The word has special significance in Japanese culture because it also has historic connotations of ritual suicide, but it is now primarily applied there when the death is caused by stress-related conditions such as heart disease and strokes (which are major killers across large parts of the globe).

The first 'business' case of *karoshi* was reported in the late 1960s following the death from a stroke of a 29-year-old male employee who had been working for a major Japanese media company. Some 20 years later this specialised use of the term was popularised after the sudden and premature deaths of a number of senior managers. The Japanese media then highlighted the deaths as examples of a serious and newsworthy phenomenon, and death through overwork (ie stress-related collapse) became the subject of considerable debate within Japanese society, understandably leading to some degree of alarm. The Japanese Ministry of Labour has published statistics on *karoshi* from 1987, partly in response to serious public concern.

A variety of factors have been used to explain Japan's significant economic growth from 1945 through to the financial crises of the 1990s. These include comparatively high levels of investment, particularly in technology, and the emergence of government import controls leading to overwhelming domination of home markets. However, explanations of this strong performance over a prolonged period have also commonly recognised the role played by particular workplace values and practices (Needle 2010). Qualities of loyalty, teamwork and harmony, together with the effect of Hofstede and Bond's long-term orientation are perceived as important factors that have contributed to Japan's rise after the havoc wreaked at the end of World War II. Williams et al (1992) nonetheless also record the important role played by a long-hours and hard-work culture, and the resultant cost advantages for Japanese companies. In other words, the strictly non-miraculous factor of sheer hard work was key in explaining the Japanese 'economic miracle'.

The unintended consequences of Japan's long-hours work culture, conceivably in tandem with employees' conscientious attitudes deriving from a strong sense of loyalty and duty, can now be seen in mental and physical strain resulting, in extreme cases, in *karoshi*. It will be interesting to see whether the concept becomes more widely recognised in other countries (within Europe the UK exhibits a pattern of long working hours) and whether the phenomenon also occurs within Japanese-owned companies operating in other locations.

Within Japan, *karoshi* has been cited in legal cases, lawyers seeking compensation in proven cases for surviving partners and relatives. However, before compensation can be awarded, a designated government official must first acknowledge that the death was work-related. This can involve a lengthy process in order to establish whether the government is liable for *karoshi* compensation. In the light of the subjectivity involved in attributing the causes underlying a recorded cause of death, the whole area remains controversial.

Read the above *vignette*, and respond to the following, either on your own or as part of a group.

1   Undertake a web search of the term *karoshi*. Referring to at least three sources, assess the prevalence of this phenomenon and state the degree to which you think it should be a matter for concern. Give reasons for your findings.

2   With reference to theories of cultural difference and motivation, explain why this phenomenon was first identified in Japan. To what extent is it likely to be noted in other societies in the future, and why?

8.10 OTHER 'PROCESS' MODELS OF MOTIVATION

In the previous section the concept of orientations to work was located alongside process theories of motivation as an approach which emphasises the conscious exercise of choices on the part of workers when forming attitudes towards their work and employer. Within a work orientations perspective, the term 'motivation' is used in the wider context of strategic exchange ,whereby a range of factors including cultural influences shape the way an individual comes to view his or her work. The approach also implies that the meanings people attach to work and, consequently, their actions and behaviour, are likely to change. There are a number of more commonly cited models which also fall within the process paradigm in the motivation literature, and we now consider some of them and assess their potential for explaining motivation in cross-cultural terms.

At the outset it might be expected that process models of motivation would be more amenable to cross-cultural analysis than either the content/needs or job characteristics approaches. This is because process theories, in addressing the question of how people are motivated, do not propose generic lists of things (eg 'enriched' work) which, it is claimed, will motivate all people. Instead, as the name implies, they focus on the processes through which humans choose to direct their actions based both on their perceptions of how likely they are to achieve outcomes and the value they attach to the outcomes themselves. This last point is crucial, since it allows for individual difference.

Earlier in the chapter we noted the premise that motivation was linked to both attitudes and values. In both cases these are influenced by an individual's cultural background. Process theories of motivation acknowledge individual differences in attitudes and values and thereby implicitly accept the possibility, or even likelihood, of cultural variations in motivation.

8.10.1 GOAL-SETTING THEORY

Goal-setting theory has its roots in the work of Edwin Locke. Originally published in 1968, Locke's underlying premise is that individuals' goals will play a vital part in determining their behaviour. Goals in this context are conceptualised as accomplishments, objects or aims which, it is anticipated, will follow one or more actions. In responding to needs, values and their situational context, people will, according to this view of motivation, set goals and develop strategies in order to reach the goals. The goals will in turn affect work performance and lead to potential positive consequences, including valued feedback. Initially seen as a motivational technique with important implications for managers, research findings point to the possibility of a virtuous circle linking goals, performance and reward. Latham et al (2002) showed how rewards obtained through goal realisation lead both to satisfaction and high self-efficacy: defined as an individual's confidence that he or she can meet future challenges through the pursuit of ever higher goals.

There are several caveats regarding the positive effects of the goal-setting process which should be recorded at this point. Goals, firstly, should be specific, such as a deadline or defined performance level. Locke and Latham (1990) also show that whereas difficult goals lead to improved performance, this positive relationship (usefully depicted as an inverted U curve) founders if goals are perceived to be impossible. One is reminded of the similar logic inherent in the topic of stress: a certain amount of stress is needed for effective working, but someone overwhelmed by stress burns out and fails to perform effectively. Finally, feedback performs an important role within goal-setting theory in terms of reinforcing performance; it also constitutes a good way of checking progress in goal attainment.

Can the logic of goal-setting theory be applied worldwide? Buelens et al (2006, p219) state that, 'Research has consistently supported goal-setting as a motivational technique. Setting performance goals increases individual, group and organisational performance. Further, the positive effects of goal-setting were found not only in the USA but also elsewhere, as in Australia, Canada, the Caribbean, England and Japan.' However, once again this general statement should be qualified in the light of alternative findings. Fang et al (2004), when conducting a US/Chinese comparative study, found that the impact of goal difficulty and specificity on worker's motivation varied in these two societies, and these writers conclude that managers should take individuals' cultural context into account when designing and implementing goal-setting programmes. Erez and Earley (1987) found that participation in goal-setting (ie by the workgroup rather than management) was more appreciated, and led to better performance, in low PD societies (using Hofstede's classification). Similarly, group participation in goal-setting was welcomed more in countries scoring highly on Hofstede's group dimension. Francesco and Gold (2005) suggest, finally, that because self-efficacy (an individual's perception that he or she can actually undertake a task successfully) forms a key concept within goal-setting, cultures in which self-efficacy may play a weaker role could be less receptive to the tenets of the goal-setting approach. They note, for example (p132), that, 'in China, a collectivist country, it is often important to use *guanxi*, a special relationship to accomplish certain tasks. As a result, if a person lacks *guanxi*, for a particular task, self-efficacy could be low regardless of personal talents or ability.'

In conclusion, however, and despite the foregoing valid points, goal-setting offers considerable scope for understanding motivation in all cultural contexts. A contingency approach to goal-setting which allows for variation in preferences for either self-set or directed goals – these preferences are, of course, potentially linked to cultural difference – has the potential for offering a locally effective framework for ensuring high levels of motivation while keeping the underlying principles of the model in place.

8.10.2 EXPECTANCY THEORY

Expectancy theories of motivation have been extremely influential in the field of business and management education, certainly in the Western context. The theories can be seen in part as a reaction to the universal needs models of motivation proposed by Herzberg and others. The essence of expectancy theories is found in the premise that individuals are influenced in their actions by their perception of anticipated consequences. With that premise, expectancy theories are firmly located within the process school of thought regarding motivation. Victor Vroom (1964) was the first writer to put forward an expectancy model of work motivation. Vroom indicated that the extent of motivation or its force will be dependent upon an expectancy that expending effort will in reality lead to anticipated outcomes linked to an individual's performance (termed 'first-level outcomes'). The valence (defined as anticipated satisfaction) to be derived from those outcomes will also affect a person's level of motivation, as expressed in motivational force. So-called 'second-level outcomes' will determine valence and, in turn, influence the choice to expend physical, mental or emotional effort. These second-level outcomes are achieved via first-level performance outcomes, and are based on needs; for example, for feedback, money, status or interaction with others. In choosing between alternative courses of action, an individual will consider not just the valence associated with outcomes but also the likelihood of achieving them, so motivation is in essence a function of the interplay between valence and expectancy.

Porter and Lawler (1968) provide another more intricate model which can be understood within the tenets of expectancy theory. Additional features within Porter and Lawler's model are abilities and traits, which mediate the connection between effort and good performance; role perceptions (individuals may differ in the ways they interpret how to approach their work; and finally, perceived equitable rewards); the essential view people hold regarding their rewards; and the extent to which these are congruent with the status and demands of their job. There is a link with Vroom's model and, indeed, expectancy theory more generally, in the fundamental connection (albeit arranged in a complex sequence) between effort, performance and outcome and the exercise of conscious consideration of outcomes of actions and their perceived attractiveness.

Expectancy theories of motivation appear to be both sufficiently generalised in their overall process logic to indicate their applicability across cultural groups, and, paradoxically, with enough scope for individual interpretation within their models (for example, differences in valence) to allow for cultural adaptation. However, there is an important sense in which their universal use can be questioned. Adler and Gundersen (2008) note that an important assumption within expectancy theory is that individuals believe that they can to a large extent influence or even control their own environments. Vroom and Porter and Lawler's models, with their inference that individuals will choose x in order to achieve y, exemplify this underlying rationale. Adler and Gundersen note that in reality there are significant differences in terms of whether people in some cultural groups do actually possess this belief. She notes that in Chinese culture a more fatalistic sense that events may be less than completely under humans' control casts the validity of expectancy theory within that culture into doubt.

Aycan (2002), in listing the characteristics of motivation in developing societies, also records that individuals in this cultural context have a low sense of control, while fatalistic thinking can result in (comparatively) less personal initiative at work. Finally, Steers and Sanchez-Runde (2002), in examining Muslim cultures, conclude that expectancy theories have very little relevance in a context where people may believe that the majority of occurrences in life are out of their own control.

One particular model of motivation which is normally grouped within the 'expectancy' heading is equity theory. Developed by Adams (1965) in the USA, equity theory proposes that workers will gauge the fairness of their work outcomes in comparison to others. If they believe that there is inequity in this regard, they will experience a sense of discomfort and will be compelled to remove this unpleasant feeling. So the drive to eliminate this feeling will itself manifest itself in a motivating mindset, with the individual choosing from a number of strategies including changing their own inputs (for example, reducing their effort), changing the point of comparison or even leaving the situation (in its most extreme manifestation, resigning their post). Adams noted that it would be possible to experience positive inequity when someone feels that they have received relatively more than another individual or group (and that this is unfair), as well as the more obvious case of felt negative inequity. It is possible to anticipate cultural variation in feelings of inequity, particularly when one considers that PD was one of Hofstede's dimensions of culture and that both Trompenaars and Hall identify cultures in which members put a particular stress on maintaining close and harmonious relationships. Guirdham (2009, p254) provides a recent exposition of this idea in her work on culture and business in Asia noting, 'equal distribution is associated with solidarity, harmony and cohesion, so it fitted with the values of people in collectivist cultures.' Guirdham goes on to contrast this concern with equality with a preoccupation with equity (between individuals) in individualistic societies where the prime concerns are productivity, competition and self-gain. There are considerable implications for organisational reward systems if we follow this logic. French et al (2011) suggest that in Eastern cultures the group rather than the individual will be the focus of equity comparisons, so individually based rewards and incentives will not be as successful there as in a Western setting. This area is considered in greater detail in Chapter 10. Once again, we should also consider whether culturally derived values obtain in a new culture outside the country of origin.

8.10.3 PSYCHOLOGICAL CONTRACTS AND THE SELF

Expectancy theory focuses on the relationship between a person's attitudes, behaviour and anticipated consequences of that behaviour. As we have seen, if this logic is accepted then the extent to which a worker is motivated will depend on a calculation they make regarding the likely consequences of increased effort in terms of enhanced performance and the value attached to any consequent reward. Such a calculation invokes the concept of a psychological contract (Rousseau 2000), in which an individual will develop an informal (ie unwritten) expectation of what they will give to, and receive from, an organisation. If this psychological contract is in equilibrium, for example an employee's contributions such as time, effort expended, and loyalty are felt to be justified by the inducements they receive (eg pay, status and praise), then there will be a perceived balance and a healthy psychological contract. However, the psychological contract, as with so many other models, is a construction arising out of Western thought and which has taken its place in the Western business studies canon. In Chapter 4 we examined the contribution of Triandis (1989) to an understanding of cultural difference. Triandis located differences in the extent to which a private, public and collective self was manifested, depending on the degree of individualism, complexity and looseness of the culture in question. Crucially for our purposes, Triandis (1989, p517) noted that, 'the more they [people] sample the private self, the more their behaviour can be accounted for by exchange theory and can be described as an exchange relationship'. The implications of this claim are profound in that the notion of expectancy and psychological contracts may be more applicable to the individualist societies of the West. In other less complex, group-oriented and homogenous or tight societies (for example Japan), the basic precepts of the psychological contract may be less important in that members are more concerned with communal relationships rather than focusing on individual cost-benefit style exchange calculations.

INDIVIDUAL ACTIVITY 8.2

Select a country of your choice. With reference to both content and process theories of motivation, identify the factors one should take into account in drawing up and implementing a strategy for motivating workers within that country.

8.11 GLOBALISED MOTIVATIONAL STRATEGIES

We end this chapter by examining an emerging phenomenon: the encroachment of what have hitherto been regarded as Western-style incentives (for example, performance-related pay) across the world. It is suggested that global organisations may strive for consistency across their subsidiary units in their human resource management policies (although such a global strategy is by no means the only one available). If such a trend is evident, and even accelerating, it may be that standardised reward policies based on existing motivational models, which as we have seen are almost exclusively Anglo-American in origin, will increasingly spread across different cultures. One should express caution regarding any perceived inevitability in this regard, however. Leung (2001) concluded that motivational strategies, whatever these might be, had more effect on employees in cultures with – again using Hofstede's model – high PD. In other words, the very effect of adopting a motivational strategy *per se* could vary, which is a potentially key insight within the field of international human resource management. Koen (2005) examined human resource practices in six countries: Germany, Japan, Sweden, the Netherlands, the USA and the UK. She concludes (p243) that 'the evolution of human resource features in the countries discussed reveals a mixed picture of cautious and slow changes as a result of the resilience and continuity of the relevant societal context'. The ability of managers in particular societies to exercise culturally based choice in the field of motivational strategies should not be discounted. We examine this issue more fully in Chapter 10.

8.12 CONCLUSION

We have seen that although content need theories and explanations of motivation centring on job characteristics can, to an extent, be applied to different cultural groups, there is significant evidence which points to the impact of culture as an intervening variable, thus questioning the universal applicability of these models. It is also the case that many of these models have been developed in Western societies and therefore reflect the specific concerns of those societies at particular times. It may be, for example, that enriched work will come to be seen as a motivator in developing societies in the future if and when they move into post-industrial mode with an associated critical mass of knowledge workers and associated jobs. But this does not seem to be the case at present.

On the other hand, process theories of motivation allow for the possibility of a range of factors, including culturally held beliefs, influencing an individual's motivation or strategic exchanges at work. Both in their preoccupation with how people come to be motivated (or not) and their consequent emphasis on differences between people, process views are more amenable to meaningful discussion of the impact of culture on motivation. Nonetheless, Adler's critique of the cross-cultural relevance of expectancy theory highlights the underlying Western perspective of this group of theories too. We have seen how Triandis's distinction between different aspects of the self imply that the basic principles of expectancy theory and the psychological contract may only apply within certain social settings. This is a potentially profound finding in the area of motivation.

In a recent attempt to tie together strands of motivation theory in order to construct a model of motivation that explains the role of culture – rather than offering a mere critique of existing schools of thought – Steers and Sanchez-Runde (2002) proposed that national culture affects the following sources of motivation:

- individuals' self-concepts incorporating personal needs, beliefs and values
- societal norms, including work ethic and achievement
- environmental factors incorporating education and legal systems and overall levels of prosperity.

This model appears to offer the possibility for further exploration of the topic and is aligned with the view of culture as being manifested at different levels (a recurrent theme in this book), emerging in a wide range of individual topic areas (see also Chapter 5 on structure and Chapter 7 on leadership). One might also wish to place the role of culture in context. As has been made evident throughout the chapter, there are many influences on work attitudes and experiences which take effect in all cultures (for example, the impact of the job itself) and a whole range of biographical influences that make up an individual's unique orientation to work.

CASE STUDY 8.2

BONUSES AND LONG-TERM INCENTIVES GAIN MORE WIDESPREAD ACCEPTANCE ACROSS THE WORLD

Pay-for-performance advances in Asia and Latin America

Today's successful global companies are increasing their use of performance-based pay and are also moving to customised incentive pay packages by region, according to the Towers Perrin 2005–2006 Worldwide Total Remuneration study. The study highlights compensation and benefit practices in 26 key locations around the world.

'Based on the success of performance pay in North America and Europe's developed economies, Asian and Latin American companies are now instituting similar practices that tie employee compensation to business results,' said Martine Ferland, principal and head of Towers Perrin's HR Services Business Global Consulting Group.

The study also found that multinational companies are deriving advantages by applying a global framework to their pay and benefit programmes while adapting actual mix and level to regional standards. This kind of approach can help companies cut costs and bring more consistency to their reward practices worldwide, at the same time remaining competitive by varying performance pay and other types of remuneration by country and region based on regulatory and cultural differences.

'As companies continue to shift the pay mix in favour of performance pay, it implies that an HR strategy should – at a minimum – articulate the company's desired pay mix and competitive positioning against the market. It should also state whether target levels will be set locally, regionally or at a global level and identify how performance will be measured,' said Ferland.

Performance-based (variable) pay as a share of total remuneration for chief executive officers (CEOs) worldwide range from 14% in India to 62% in the United States. Variable pay as a share of total remuneration for accountants worldwide had a much smaller variation, ranging from 0% in countries like Sweden, Switzerland and Venezuela to about 10% in Mexico and South Africa.

Performance-based pay consists of bonus pay-outs and long-term incentives (LTIs), which generally come in the form of stock options or some other type of equity compensation. Successful companies employ a methodology that ties bottom-line results to the compensation of nearly every employee. This is most effective when it is part of a total approach to employee remuneration that includes cash, equity and benefits like retirement and health care.

'The size and frequency of stock and other long-term incentives are on the rise in most parts of the world, although we are seeing a decline in the use of stock options in some developed economies, particularly the United States, as a result, among other things, of new accounting rules and increased scrutiny by institutional investors looking to protect the dilution of capital,' said James Matthews, Towers Perrin principal and consultant in the Global Consulting Group.

Part of the performance pay package, bonuses are being used more widely and to more eligible employees in global companies. 'We are seeing annual bonuses, which used to be reserved for the professional-level employee, being used more broadly in lower levels in the organisations, represented in our study by the manufacturing employee,' said Matthews. 'For the first time, in countries like Canada, France, Korea, Mexico and the United Kingdom, year-end bonuses for this group are the norm and not the exception.

'Furthermore, in Asian countries such as Taiwan, Malaysia, China (Shanghai) and Singapore, annual bonuses are in the range of 10% to 15% of salary at the professional level. This is more than 5% to 10% of salary that is common practice in North America and Europe for this group.'

Extracts from Towers Perrin press release, 11 January 2006.

Read the case study above, and respond to the following.

1   How can we account for the increase in the use of perfomance-related remuneration in countries outside the UK and the USA?

2   With reference to cultural theories, describe the extent to which you anticipate resistance to the implementation of performance bonuses from workers in cultures outside the Anglo cluster.

NOTES

1   www.this_is_London.co.uk/news/article-23369243 [Accessed 15 October 2006].

2   How illegal workers are propping up our lifestyle (2004) *BBC news online*. 10 February. Available at: http://news.bbc.co.uk/1/hi/magazine/3475147.stm [Accessed 12 September 2006].

FURTHER READING

ADLER, N. J. with GUNDERSEN, A. (2008) *International dimensions of organisational behaviour.* 5th ed. Mason, OH: South-Western College Publishing/Thomson Learning. This book examines the topic of motivation within an integrated cross-cultural perspective present throughout the text.

BUELENS, M., VAN DEN BROEK, H. and VANDERHEYDEN, K. (2006) *Organisational behaviour.* 3rd ed. Maidenhead: McGraw-Hill. This is one of a large number of organisational textbooks which cover the topic of motivation. It is recommended because of its international focus, including some insightful vignettes drawn from different cultures.

MULLINS, L. J. (2013) *Management and organisational behaviour.* 10th ed. Harlow: Pearson. It should be very useful to read this current chapter alongside Mullins' encyclopaedic and authoritative coverage of the widely-researched area of motivation.

Visit this book's companion website (**www.cipd.co.uk/olr**) to find further exercises including self-assessment questions and also weblinks to media and academic journal articles.

PART 4

MANAGING ACROSS OR WITHIN CULTURES

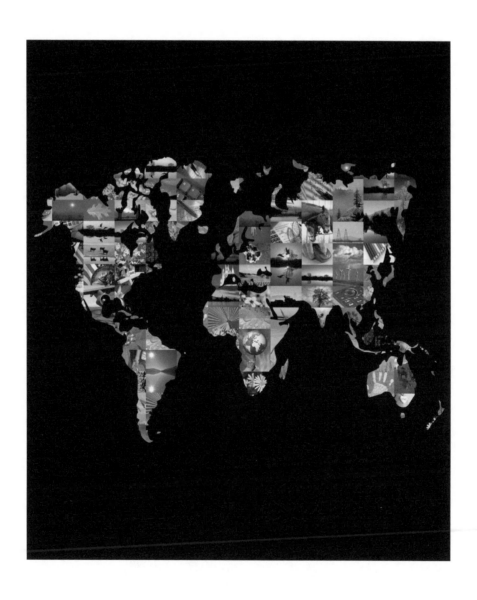

CHAPTER 9

Intercultural Competencies, Training and Ethics

LEARNING OBJECTIVES

After reading this chapter you should be able to:

- list desirable intercultural competencies put forward in existing cross-cultural management literature, and assess the value of additional competencies in view of changes within business settings
- appreciate the importance of cross-cultural training in enhancing managers' competencies, and evaluate the value of such training in reality
- identify links between culture, ethics and managerial competencies
- evaluate the impact of intercultural competencies on successful cross-cultural management.

9.1 INTRODUCTION

We now move from an understanding of culture and the cultural dimensions of particular business and management topics, to focus on the competencies needed by successful cross-cultural managers. In order to be effective, they need more than an awareness of the latest academic knowledge and topical issues: rather they must be able to perform their roles successfully in different settings and when dealing with people from diverse backgrounds. The title of this chapter again brings into view the distinction between intercultural and cross-cultural management (see also Chapters 1 and 6). When we examine the existing literature on expatriate managers' competencies, we find a particular focus on those managers' interpersonal encounters when working abroad. I have attempted to record this tradition faithfully for readers' benefit in this section of the book, and have therefore opted for the term 'intercultural competencies' because it seems to most accurately reflect the real-life experiences of such managers. Much of their role, we are told, involves building and sustaining successful interactions between individuals. Nonetheless, as will be seen, the development of intercultural sensitivity involves taking a comparative view of cultures more generally, beyond individual encounters between people. Evaluative awareness forms an inherent part of cross-cultural management, so the two terms are in reality very closely linked.

Intercultural or cross-cultural competence has emerged as a topical area for study within business and management literature in the twenty-first century, although as we will see, some contributions can be traced back to previous epochs. The preoccupation with such competencies reflects the increasingly global nature of business which we have referred to in previous chapters. This trend has resulted in many employees routinely working abroad and, in particular, many more managers have been sent on international assignments. Williams et al (2013) locate the following reasons why companies use international assignments:

- Companies may have job vacancies in a foreign subsidiary and an international assignee might be dispatched to fill such a vacancy.
- International assignments fulfil an important purpose in developing global competencies within a management team, in order to strengthen a company's competitive advantage. Assignments, in fostering global competencies, also enhance individuals' career prospects, ensuring that both the assignee's and organisation's goals are met.
- Assignments aid the process of knowledge transfer within a company. This can involve the assignee transferring knowledge to a subsidiary. It can also take the form of knowledge transfer from a subsidiary to the 'home' organisation and, once again, the assignee can be the conduit for such transfer.

International assignments – unsurprisingly in view of their importance– have formed a topic of interest since the 1970s (see Zhang and Iles 2013). There is clear evidence, however, that such assignments can be problematic. For example, Gribben (2006) found that around 40% of employees returning from an international assignment left their employer within a year of their return, resulting in significant problems for that company, including the loss of valuable cross-cultural knowledge. There is therefore a clear implication that such assignments need to be managed effectively. We will go on to look closely at the phenomenon of culture shock, which is often cited as a reason for expatriate failure, and the measures which can be taken to reduce its effects. In human resource management terms more generally, it is proposed that expatriate management should be integrated within an organisation's overall HR strategy (Dowling et al 2013). One cannot assume that international assignments will be successful without careful planning and, where necessary, making rapid interventions during the assignment.

Working with and managing people from other cultural groups is an activity with inherent ethical undertones. It can be argued that tolerance of difference – a key attribute for successful cross-cultural management – in itself is an ethically loaded stance. There are key moral and ethical questions to address when managing diverse groups, concerning degrees of expected integration by that group and acceptance of new and different behaviour. In 2007 an English schoolteacher working in the Republic of the Sudan was convicted of insulting religion, inciting hatred and showing contempt for religious beliefs under Sudanese criminal law. This followed a complaint by a school employee that the teacher had allowed a class of children to name a teddy bear Muhammad. The teacher was released from prison after five days following intensive lobbying by the UK Government.[1] The case, albeit in an unusual scenario, brings out some important ethical debates. Should the teacher have been aware, or made aware via cross-cultural training, of the particular religious sensitivity of her actions? Should the legal process have allowed for ignorance as a defence and how would one in any case regard the charges against her? Should the maxim 'when in Rome do as the Romans do' always apply? The section 'Ethics and the cross-cultural manager' later in this chapter introduces some of these issues and attempts to (inevitably partially) provide some guidelines for those involved in managing people from other cultures.

9.2 OVERCOMING CULTURE SHOCK – THE CORE INTERCULTURAL COMPETENCY?

'All the world's queer save me and thee – and sometimes I think thee a little queer.' This pithy quote, which has been attributed to a Quaker saying originating in the English county of Yorkshire, might have been designed as an introduction to a cross-cultural adjustment programme. It evokes a sense of bewilderment, not to say alienation, in the face of perceived differences with others. As we saw in earlier chapters, there are some potentially wide differences between cultures so it would not be surprising if managers operating across cultures were to find these differences disorienting. Culture shock has been widely recognised within the field of cross-cultural business studies (see, for example, Ferraro 1994 and Hickson and Pugh 1995). Holden (2002) refers to work by Oberg published in 1960 recording anxiety experienced by people in new cultures who lose familiar signs and cues on which they are dependent for their peace of mind.

It continues to be a subject of analysis. For example, Perkins and Shortland (2006, p64) claim that, 'It is therefore expected that most people will experience culture surprise when interacting with other cultures, and culture shock, to some degree, particularly when living and working in another country. Culture shock is a normal and predictable phenomenon, although those experiencing it may feel that they are inadequate or weak, even believing that they are suffering some form of mental illness.'

Schneider and Barsoux (2003) set out an extended summary of the area of cultural adjustment, focusing particularly on the experiences of expatriate managers. They suggest that culture shock affects not only individual managers but, even more importantly, their partners and/or families, because culture shock occurs outside work too and may be even more keenly felt away from the manager's employment setting. The process of culture shock is depicted by Schneider and Barsoux as a U-curve, implying an initially positive stage followed by a downward plunge or trough from which the manager and their loved ones may (or may not) ultimately emerge feeling adjusted to the new environment – if so, providing a case of a 'happy ever after' scenario. Adler (2002) indicates that the recovery stage can take place three to six months after arrival, while Perkins and Shortland (2006) indicate that the overall evidence points to all of the stages within the culture shock process, including adaptation, taking place within six to eight months. Within the overall process specific symptoms can also be delineated, reflecting some of the stages depicted within the U-curve model:

- a sense of euphoria and optimism in the initial stage (sometimes referred to as the 'honeymoon' period)
- confusion and frustration felt when people fail to comprehend their environment and when their own tried and tested ways of behaving fail to achieve desired results
- 'fight or flight' symptoms – eg complaining about local customs or withdrawal into a cultural ghetto (or even oneself), respectively
- falling in love with the new culture, coupled with rejection of the original culture (sometimes termed 'going native').

None of the aforementioned symptoms are viewed as indicators of healthy adjustment which, if and when it ultimately occurs, is felt in a more emotionally neutral way, accompanied by perceptions of competence and possibly mastery of the new cultural setting. It is also important to realise that much the same process takes place on the travellers' return to their indigenous culture. Schneider and Barsoux (2003) propose that the so-called 'reverse culture shock' can be all the more shocking because it is so unexpected; they adopt the phrase *jamais vu* to express feelings of disorientation experienced upon returning home.

Several other aspects of the culture shock phenomenon are worthy of mention at this point. It is not first experienced as a sudden shattering event; rather, more as an accumulation of minor events. Craig (1979) described these as the 1,001 stress-producing events causing the eventual shock. It would furthermore be misleading to regard the phenomenon in wholly negative terms. Francesco and Gold (2005, p163) state that, 'Although it may seem logical that expatriates who adjust well should perform effectively, this may not always be true. In some cases, people who have trouble adjusting and experience the most culture shock may be the most effective performers.' This apparently paradoxical finding can be explained by conscientious expatriate managers' seeking greater exposure to the new culture and therefore exacerbating culture shock. Thomas

(1998) identified traits leading to excellent expatriate performance which included interpersonal sensitivity. Again, this trait can plausibly be seen to both aid intercultural interaction and, at the same time, heighten vulnerability to feelings of culture shock.

While acknowledging the validity of views which see the effect of culture shock as a 'double-edged sword', the symptoms experienced in the 'low stage' of the cycle should be seen as potentially serious for the person suffering them. Guirdham (2011) identifies symptoms of irritability, rigidity in behaviour, loneliness and depression from her survey of prior literature. Furthermore, when those experiencing culture shock do not progress through the documented stages and remain in a negative mindset, the consequences are dire for all concerned. Tarique and Caliguiri (2004, p284) summarise as follows: 'Expatriates who are not prepared to confront the challenges [eg] to cope with culture shock find it difficult to adjust and hence incur, and impose on others, costly implications. For example, expatriates who are unable to adjust are more likely to perform poorly. Poor performance on the assignment has costly implications for expatriates (such as low self-esteem, low self-confidence and loss of prestige among co-workers), for the parent firm (such as lost business opportunities), and for the host company (such as damaged company image).'

Selmer (2005), in conducting research on international adjustment among Western expatriate managers in mainland China and the Hong Kong Special Administrative Region (SAR), casts doubt on some existing received wisdom on culture shock. Approaching his own research study, he laments the lack of actual empirical studies in the area, suggesting that much of the material on culture shock is anecdotal, emanating from what he terms the popular business press. Selmer also refines the concept of international adjustment, distinguishing between sociocultural and psychological adjustment. Sociocultural adjustment refers to an individual (and/or a partner's) ability to integrate into the new culture and the ways he or she deals with everyday situations there, particularly those of an interpersonal nature. Psychological adjustment deals with the subjective affective component of adjustment, ie symptoms such as anxiety experienced in the unfamiliar culture. Selmer proposes that the two aspects are related. His own findings indicate that there is a stronger relationship between the two when expatriates are better adjusted in the sociocultural sense. However, merely interacting with host nationals did not lead to more positive psychological adjustment, conceivably due to language difficulties. Selmer finally concludes that the effects of culture shock can occur later than popularly suggested. He notes (p252) that in his study, 'the expatriates did not start to experience any culture shock until after 17–18 months, indicating a delayed effect when on assignment on the Chinese mainland. It is not evident why this discrepancy occurs, but it might be speculated that many Western expatriates on the Chinese mainland are to a certain degree barred from sociocultural interactions with host nationals, thus delaying their culture shock.'

Interestingly, a further conclusion from Selmer's research is that although the expected U-curve pattern was evident in sociocultural adjustment, it could not be seen in the case of psychological adjustment. This can be explained by discrepancies between the cognitive and affective elements of adjustment: put simply, an expatriate might be well aware of cultural differences and become more skilled in dealing with them. He or she may, however, not be well disposed to the differences in attitudinal terms. Selmer's research is timely in drawing our attention to the fact that adjustment, and culture shock more specifically, is a more complex and multi-dimensional phenomenon than sometimes suggested in the business and management literature. His work also provides living proof of the value of empirical research in the field rather than recourse to anecdotal material or, even worse, data resulting from mere assertion.

The influx of overseas footballers into the English Premier League is generally perceived as having improved the quality of play and has arguably made some of its leading clubs into a global brand. However, the process of cultural adjustment among players has not always been smooth, and there are documented examples of the psychological trough associated with culture shock.

In the late 1990s, the Dutch player Brian Roy and Macedonian Georgi Hristov provided two examples. Roy, shortly after moving from Hertha Berlin to Nottingham Forest, commented, 'Berlin has everything. It is a cosmopolitan city with theatres and the people are open-minded. They are not as narrow-minded like the people in Nottingham.'[2] Even more prosaically, Hritsov noted, 'the local girls are far uglier than the ones back in Belgrade or Skopje, the capital of Macedonia, where I come from. Besides, they don't drink as much beer as the Barnsley girls, which is something I don't like at all.'[3]

More recently, the Serbian footballer Nemanja Vidic, at that time a Manchester United player, made some unfavourable comments concerning aspects of life in the UK compared with Eastern Europe: 'In Russia and Serbia the people's way of life is similar. In England it's totally different. Here they just don't have time to feel the joy of life. Throughout the week they all work so hard. They only talk to people at lunch break. Then in the evening they come home and watch the telly, so they can get up early for work the next day.' Vidic also hinted that his transition from one employer to another, which as we will see can be managed proactively, added to his initial sense of disorientation: 'In England I had no one to talk to. The first month was especially hard. I lived alone in a hotel, which I only left for training. I thought I would go crazy inside those four walls.'[4]

However, work organisations are constantly seeking solutions to problems and football clubs have sought to make the process of transferring from one culture less traumatic. Conn (2012) identifies the very considerable steps that Manchester City, under Abu Dhabi ownership, have taken in this regard. This football club undertake a very sophisticated profiling exercise before signing new players, which crucially focuses on cultural adaptation. The club's hierarchy (which includes an HR department) also provides newly arrived players, and their families, with practical help in areas like their children's schooling.

We go on to look at ways in which orgainsations can alleviate culture shock later in this chapter.

9.3 THE SEARCH FOR EFFECTIVE INTERVENTIONS

The apparent prevalence of culture shock and its sometimes deleterious effects have led to a number of suggestions as to how its impact can be suppressed. Traditional approaches centred on the use of cross-cultural briefings containing advice (or *diktats*) on how to conduct business in country *x* or *y*. Schneider and Barsoux (2003) cast doubt on the currency of this approach, noting that the global manager's operating territory may be either in a neutral venue (ie he or she may well no longer conduct dealings with other cultures on a strictly bilateral basis) or, alternatively, in 'virtual' venues (eg via video-conferencing or email exchange). However, these authors continue to stress the importance of the expatriate's personal aptitudes to successful cross-cultural (or intercultural) management. Among the skills and abilities they list as important in this regard are: tolerance for uncertainty and ambiguity, flexibility, motivation to live abroad, ego strength and cultural empathy. Work organisations can in the following ways maximise the chances of their employees' firstly possessing these traits, and then putting them into effect.

In the first instance there is a need for an awareness and use of appropriate recruitment and selection measures. De Vries and Mead (1991) are among authors who identified 'adaptability factors' which partly predetermined success for, in their case, pan-European managers. These factors included a profile of cultural diversity in these managers' childhood: their parents may have been from different national backgrounds or they may have moved around the world due to their parents' or guardians' career commitments. This biographical information can, of course, be gleaned through the recruitment process, while other desirable attributes, such as ability to withstand high levels of stress and self-confidence, can, to a degree, be unearthed during actual selection, although there are no completely valid means of identifying these attributes, and in particular, predicting either their manifestation or behavioural consequences in specific situations.

The preoccupation with personal competencies is also reflected in a good deal of guidance on training and development and, indeed, in a preponderance of actual training programmes that have sought to alleviate culture shock. Gudykunst et al (1996) distinguish three interlinked goals of cross-cultural training: firstly, cognitive, including increasing knowledge and understanding of the new culture; the affective dimension, which deals with how attitudes and emotions are handled (highly relevant when dealing with culture shock); and finally behavioural goals, emphasising the development of intercultural skills such as negotiating and relationship-building. These distinct, but related, goals evoke Selmer's (2005) later distinction between sociocultural and psychological adjustment. One is left with the impression that training in this area often has an underlying theme of fostering and enhancing cross-cultural sensitivity among international managers.

In addition to devising suitable recruitment and selection and training interventions (language training should not be forgotten in this respect), organisations have also been advised to put in an infrastructure of support to help managers adjust to their new environment. Harzing (2004), in examining the issue of expatriate failure (which, she argues, should be the subject of more sophisticated research), concludes that it is frequently caused by the manager or his or her partner's failure to adjust. The proposed remedies put forward to reduce the incidence of poor adjustment include the provision of support systems by the employing organisation, not just from head office or the manager's country of origin but also at host country level. Harzing also advocates that the manager's partner (if such a person exists) should, crucially, be involved in training and support events.

One aim of this chapter is to identify what have been typically perceived as intercultural competencies held to enhance success in cross-cultural management. In reviewing the existing literature one is struck by the volume of material devoted to understanding the phenomenon of culture shock. It appears that many of the desirable intercultural competencies set out in cross-cultural management textbooks link back to culture shock, and the need both to recognise it and to 'rise above' its effects. Success in this regard has largely been associated with identifiable individual attributes. This aspect of cross-cultural management has also tended to emphasise cultural sensitivity – in particular its paradigm promotes the reconciliation of cultural differences.

The work of Trompenaars and Hampden-Turner, summarised in Chapter 3, provides an example of this viewpoint in that they both categorise cultural differences and put forward recommendations on how to deal with them. Their questionnaire-based research confirmed the hypothesis that managers able to reconcile different values (manifested in real situations) would perform better in their role. In reconciling difference, such managers would also avoid the tendency either to reject their own culture or to withdraw from the stressful process of adjustment altogether.

One of the earliest writers on culture shock, Craig (1979), characterised the above-mentioned adaptation behaviours as exhibited by the absconder (into the new culture) and the encapsulator types respectively. The absconder immerses him or herself in the local culture and has little or no contact with any expatriate community, while the encapsulator lives mainly within an enclosed expatriate community. For example, the British media have frequently painted a picture of UK residents who have moved to Spain but speak little Spanish and mostly interact with other British residents rather than the indigenous community: this is classic encapsulator behaviour. The third identified type – the cosmopolitan, who retains intimate contact with both the expat and local culture – is the most successful adjuster and performer. The novelist F. Scott Fitzgerald appears with hindsight to broaden out this philosophical approach in his 1936 quote that, 'The test of a first-rate intelligence is the ability to hold two opposed ideas in the mind at the same time and still retain the ability to function.' It would be wrong to see intercultural competencies solely with reference to the individual, however: they also vary according to the precise task(s) carried out and the organisational context – for example, whether a global or localised strategy is in place. I refer to this aspect in more detail in Chapter 10.

9.4 INTERCULTURAL COMPETENCIES AT HOME

In earlier chapters cross-cultural management was described as being of relevance to an increasing number of people, not simply those who physically travel to foreign countries. Ever more sophisticated technologies can mean that we interact with people from other cultures online, without face-to-face encounters. However, we still need to recognise culture as a factor in such situations, whether as a potential barrier to communication or as an opportunity to achieve synergy. In Chapter 1 it was pointed out that increasingly multicultural workforces in many parts of the planet resulted in many more potential instances of cross-cultural management, even in organisations operating in one society. In many respects this aspect of management is more problematic since we may be more attuned to differences while abroad – and hence more culturally sensitive – than when living in our 'home' environment.

With reference to culture shock, we should recognise that incomers to our own culture will also experience what has been regarded as a largely universal occurrence. Culture shock can be seen to be relevant in any new situation requiring adjustment to an unfamiliar situation in which existing knowledge and values are called into question. Either conscious downplaying of the potential effect of culture shock on incoming workers, through an explicit view that they just have to 'fit in', or mere unawareness of the phenomenon can lead to negative perceptions on the part of the new employees and lower performance – for that has consistently correlated with reduced motivation. Dismissal of culture shock and its effects can also be indicative of either a parochial or ethnocentric style of management, the dangers of both of which were pointed out in Chapter 1.

One area of work that has become increasingly more culturally diverse in the early twenty-first century is the university or higher-education sector, extensive international student mobility resulting in significant inflows of students into certain countries. Egege and Kutieleh (2004, p77) document the increasing internationalisation of Australian universities and the fact that academics in that country have, in many cases, been suddenly exposed to a diverse student population. These writers go on to identify differences in the core area of students' learning, noting that, 'If we are to accept that there are significant enough differences in learning styles and attitudes between different cultural groups to be problematic, then these need to be addressed or accommodated in order to facilitate successful transition.' However, they question views which promote assimilation and integration in order to achieve success and raise for debate the extent to which students should be expected to balance two cultural traditions as 'cultural colonialism'.

This last political point is interesting, not least in the way it is frequently ignored in much of the business literature where integration, reconciliation of values and synergy in diversity are put forward as apolitical concepts. Turner (2006, p3) examines the experience of a group of Chinese students in a UK university. She also records the significance of the 'internationalisation' of the UK university sector, terming it 'an almost tectonic shift from the culturally homogenous populations that dominated them 30 years ago to the diverse and multicultural constituencies that characterise them today'. Turner goes on to identify differences in societies' knowledge traditions which can impact on academic practices; in other words, what it takes to be judged as a good student.

Turner (2006, p9) describes how these differences are experienced by her studied group of Chinese students at the UK university: 'They were very aware that expectations of them as students and the ways in which learning and its articulation were constructed in the UK differed from what they had previously experienced in China. They arrived in the UK ready to adapt to the new situation but quickly discovered that the basic expectations that lecturers had of them were implicit.' It is important to note that in Turner's sample, students were not ultimately unsuccessful in their courses: some achieved distinction level. However, her research documents the difficulty the students had in their transition to UK study, particularly in the central area of teaching and learning. She also documents (p10) some level of under-achievement, not due to intrinsic ability but, 'because their work does not conform to culturally based academic conventions into which they have not been initiated and because cultural values within assessment criteria are highly implicit'. It is also possible that success was down to students' learning to complete work according to convention, and was thus a technical rather than a life-changing accomplishment.

9.5 IS CULTURAL AWARENESS SUFFICIENT?

The cross-cultural management literature frequently refers to the phenomenon of culture shock and the ways it can be overcome for the benefit of all parties. It may well be, though, that possessing cross-cultural sensitivity and awareness only partly predicts success in intercultural encounters. Other non-cultural factors may also have a major positive effect, and I now go on to identify some of these (the list is ultimately infinite). Before I do so, it is useful to cast a sceptical eye on the value of the concepts of awareness and sensitivity *per se*. Holden (2002, p307) proposes that what the Swedish anthropologist Hennerz has termed 'the culture shock prevention industry' has resulted in a focus on the management of cultural difference, which 'is less and less important than creating environments, structures and procedures for facilitating cross-cultural learning and knowledge-sharing'. Certainly we should guard against the exaggeration of cultural differences when we become sensitised to those that are undoubtedly there. Just as a parochial approach which does not recognise difference is doomed to failure when managing other cultures (or managing *in* other cultures), so it is possible to go too far in the other direction and paradoxically reduce the chances of people from other cultures working together. Holden (2002) also quite correctly documents a changing business world where email and other forms of virtual communication result in new ways in which people interact, and in which existing thought on culture shock and its resolution needs increasingly to be reframed.

It is also important to work with the most up-to-date material when designing and delivering cross-cultural management programmes. In Chapter 4 I put forward the case for a re-evaluation of the traditional bipolar dimensions school of cultural analysis, while recognising its usefulness in providing a basis for comparison. However, adopting an emic-style approach involving an in-depth understanding of individual cultures at a deep level, moving beyond surface etiquette, can provide a more meaningful way of perceiving how others think and behave, focusing as it does on the perceptions of how people view their own culture and how cultures reproduce themselves and change. In specific terms, attempts to comprehend Chinese culture in order to enhance (non-Chinese) managers' competencies could usefully refer to the work of writers such as Fan (2000), Tang and Ward (2003) and Chen (2004) as well as the comparative Western-derived work of Hofstede and Trompenaars.

Which other management competencies – beyond awareness of and sensitivity to differences – are relevant? One obvious, but sometimes overlooked, response is that to some degree it depends on the tasks to be undertaken. There are several elements to cross-cultural management frequently highlighted in the literature, one of which is negotiation. Competencies in this area can be once again related to cross-cultural knowledge, and I elaborate on the issue of differences in preferred negotiating style in Chapter 10.

More generally, if negotiation is regarded as a core part of cross-cultural management, it follows that anyone operating in the field should be adept within this sub-set of management activity. For example, they must follow the process of negotiation with its individual stages of preparation, relationship-building, presentation, persuasion and concession/agreement. Generalised competencies in this area include impact and persuasiveness. Watson (2006, p184) concludes that more able or competent managers 'have the personal presence and credibility to win support for proposed actions, values and strategies; they use persuasive arguments, symbols and rewards to gain support, and they win compliance through setting examples to others'. Intercultural competencies extend and apply general principles as outlined by Watson. For example, Cortes (2003) identifies cultural differences affecting the second stage of relationship-building, referring to the importance in Asian, Latin American and Arabic countries of building relationships before proceeding to negotiation. This point recalls the work of Trompenaars and Hall covered in Chapter 3. The relevance at this point lies in an illustration of how a well-established general management competency holds true but must be adapted to the specific cross-cultural context.

The management of teams is another assumed key area of cross-cultural management. The important textbook written by Schneider and Barsoux (2003) reflects this concern with managing multicultural teams by devoting an entire chapter to the subject. Trends within business identified in earlier chapters have led to a situation where multicultural teams are a fact of life, either via the construction of global networks of managers deliberately drawn from different parts of a business, or through 'normal' business processes within a multicultural society. Once again one is struck by the need to incorporate general management principles into this area and then apply them with reference to cross-cultural awareness. Watson (2006, p184), in his summary of the characteristics of competent managers involved in team leadership, building and maintenance, concludes that they 'work with teams they lead to build up a positive climate, an efficient allocation of tasks and they ensure that information is shared and that skills are kept up to date and directed towards efficient task achievement and continuous improvement'. Again intercultural competency in this regard is achievable through blending general principles with specific demands arising out of the situation in hand.

Schneider and Barsoux (2003), in their list of strategies for managing multicultural teams, make it clear that structuring tasks for team members is an integral part of the team leader's role, echoing Watson's concern with effective task allocation. However, they identify cultural determinants which affect how the strategies should be put into practice. Reference to whether an individual team member is from a high- or low-context society or how the person's country of origin scores on uncertainty avoidance will influence the extent to which a task should be clearly specified. Note at this point the possible dangers of this approach, however – namely, in focusing on cultural difference and seemingly relegating in importance non-cultural factors (eg an individual's personality).

9.6 CULTURAL INTELLIGENCE

Earley and Ang (2003) and Earley and Mosakowski (2004) are credited with bringing a new perspective into the cross-cultural competencies arena. They introduce the concept of cultural intelligence (CQ). CQ can be interpreted as the attitudes and skills that enable someone to deal effectively with situations involving cultural diversity. A person's CQ will be a predictor of their ability to adapt in a new cultural setting. Brewster et al (2011) conclude that CQ is an individual difference but unlike other such differences, eg personality, CQ can be developed and enhanced by organisational interventions. Early and Mosakowski (2004, p140) suggest that, 'Anyone reasonably alert, motivated and poised can attain an acceptable level of cultural intelligence.'

In terms of developing CQ, the following steps could make up a typical CQ programme:

- An individual reflects on their existing CQ strengths and weaknesses.
- That person then selects training which focusses on the identified weaknesses.
- The individual identifies the resources in their own organisation needed to support the chosen approach, eg who has the skills to conduct training?
- The relevant training is carried out.
- The individual then enters the new cultural setting and acts based on their (existing or developed) strengths.
- The individual re-evaluates their skills and how effective they have been.

What are the different aspects that make up cultural intelligence? Aycan et al (2014) locate the following components of CQ:

- *Knowledge.* This includes both general awareness of cultural difference (as set out in this book, for example) and more specific knowledge about a host country, as might be found in a business etiquette guide.
- *Skills.* These might include open-mindedness and flexibility as well as interpersonal skills such as emotional intelligence, including an ability to 'read' non-verbal communication.
- *Metacognition.* This aspect involves the ability to rise above a specific situation and maintain objectivity and control over one's feelings and behaviour.

In summary, Earley and Mosakowski (2004) claim that CQ is linked to emotional intelligence but also separate from it, as someone could be very effective in their own indigenous cultural setting but a 'fish out of water' in a new culture. If we have (or develop) high CQ we are able to see and demarcate the things which are true of all people, those unique to the individual and the attitudes and behaviour which vary across cultures and are the result of exposure to any one culture.

When putting forward the CQ concept, Earley and Mosakowski, finally, identified different types of people who approached new cultural situations in different ways. In common with similar typologies, the model works better if we recognise that people may exhibit characteristics of more than one type.

- The *provincial* type who was effective when working with people from similar backgrounds but who ran into trouble when required to deal with diverse groups.
- The *analyst* who preferred to decipher a new culture through learning.
- The *natural* who relied on their own intuition when dealing with new situations and who achieved some measure of success in this way.
- The *chameleon* who could be mistaken for a host national and possesses very high levels of CQ. They can achieve optimal results due to the combination of an insider's skills and outsider's perspective.

9.7 CULTURAL COMPETENCIES – REVIEW

Many writings on intercultural (and cross-cultural) management have put forward the view that the most important factor in predicting successful outcomes in the field is the possession and/or development of identifiable competencies. This chapter has summarised some of the pivotal contributions within this school of thought. There has understandably been less concentration on other aspects of management beyond those impinging on the intercultural encounter. It would be naive, however, to assume that intercultural competencies alone will guarantee a manager's, and by implication his or her employing organisation's, success. A manager concerned with inter- or cross-cultural issues must retain an overall view of corporate objectives; in other words, how his or her work contributes to organisational objectives.

Such managers will also be required to demonstrate functional ability and knowledge, whether in the area of marketing, logistics, finance, or whatever their own specialist area happens to be. A senior manager will also, one assumes, retain a strategic focus aligning cross-cultural activities within an overall longer-term plan(s).

There are other competencies which may also be relevant; for example, a willingness to play political games within the organisation in order to further an individual's or group's own career and other unofficial interests. These points may appear to be superfluous, even obvious, to the reader. However, there is a sense in which they are overlooked in many previous texts in which intercultural communication is assumed to be all-important. Holden (2002, p300) provides a notable exception to this trend by emphasising an alternative overriding business agenda: 'But if the cross-cultural manager is a genuine manager, then he or she needs a further competence: *business focus*. This is the sense of knowing where the company is going and why, and knowing how cross-cultural management activities relate to the organisation, its goals and aspirations. Business focus is the ultimate guiding light of these activities, the logic of last resort if they are to deliver value to the company and its stakeholders.'

A full analysis of managerial work and objectives is beyond the scope of this book, yet it is useful to set the area of intercultural competencies in context: it is only one part of cross-cultural management which in turn must be seen as an integral part of wider organisational and business concerns.

CASE STUDY 9.1

On 24 July 2014 a Malaysian Airlines plane, MH17, en route from Amsterdam to Kuala Lumpur crashed in the war zone of eastern Ukraine. All 298 on board were killed. (The tragedy unfolded as this chapter update was being written, so the full story behind the crash had yet to emerge, if that were ever possible.) There were allegations that the plane was shot down by pro-Russian rebel militia, while sources from that group blamed Ukrainian government supporters for the act. What was certain was that both international air crash investigators and journalists encountered resistance in entering the crash site. Keane (2014), reporting for the BBC, was confronted by an armed militiaman whom he claimed told the reporter that he was 'only here because foreigners are dead'. Keane pointed to a body bag that was open, revealing the naked corpse of a 'young man killed in the prime of his life'. Keane pleaded with the armed man to close the bag; he shrugged and then agreed and carefully rearranged the bag. There were numerous accounts of a very tense and aggressive atmosphere at the ghastly site. This was one example of a cross-cultural encounter, albeit one that we can all hope that we are never involved in.

Questions

1   How and to what extent might CQ help to resolve an extreme situation such as this?

2   Identify the components of CQ as they could apply in this case.

9.8 CROSS-CULTURAL TRAINING – OTHER CONSIDERATIONS

It is important when considering the area of cross-cultural training to recognise the wide range of interventions that could be chosen and the different times or stages in which these could be offered. Caliguiri et al (2005) distinguish between a number of initiatives, including:

- cross-cultural orientation (pre-departure stage)
- cross-cultural training during the foreign posting
- diversity training, including development of cultural sensitivity
- immersion in cultural experiences
- membership of cross-border global teams with debriefing
- global meeting coaching with debriefing
- international assignment by rotation
- language training which can support both cross-cultural and diversity training.

It may also be that aspects of formal national education systems can feed in to cross-cultural training; for example, international management courses (usually offered at post-school level). It is more common, though, for cross-cultural training to be designed specifically for a particular work assignment or study period abroad. Black et al (1991) draw the distinction between anticipatory adjustment and in-country adjustment, the latter category subdivided into work-related and more general adjustment. There is of course a clear implication of differences in the timing and sequence of these aspects.

Whichever initiative or group of initiatives is chosen, it is important to follow a systematic approach which incorporates principles of the training cycle. Tarique and Caliguiri (2004) accordingly identify the importance of determining needs, establishing goals and measures and evaluating effectiveness following delivery. All of these stages reflect those contained in the classical training cycle, here applied to the specific area of cross-cultural training.

Mendenhall and Oddou (1985) identified distinctive aspects of expatriate acculturation which they claimed could be linked to personality dimensions (these are listed below). Identification of these dimensions, they suggest, should form an important part of international recruitment and selection. However, the dimensions can also be referred to within cross-cultural training programmes. In terms of the personality dimensions themselves the distinction is made between self-oriented, others-oriented and perceptual dimensions.

- The *self-oriented dimension* focuses on personal skills and includes a person's ability to act differently in a new cultural location, his or her ability to deal with stress, and technical competence (seemingly an area often neglected in cross-cultural training).
- The *others-oriented dimension* refers to an individual and/or his or her family's ability to form relationships with people in the new culture.
- The *perceptual dimension* affects a person's ability to comprehend and respect new and unfamiliar behaviour, which in turn influences whether and to what extent a newcomer is separated or marginalised from the new culture, as opposed to being integrated or even assimilating (in extreme cases 'falling in love' with the new culture and rejecting their original culture).

Cross-cultural training programmes could be designed within the terms of Mendenhall and Oddou's framework, or at least be framed with an awareness of this model.

Tung (1981) introduced the importance of regarding adjustment and cross-cultural competencies more generally as a broader concept, and specifically the key role of partners and/or spouses in explaining success in international postings. In this context Brewster et al (2011) note that the 'coffee machine' system whereby expatriates are selected informally from a small pool and even a more systematic section based on psychological adaptability has the drawback of not bringing family problems into view. Such problems could be critical to the success of the international posting.

9.9 THE EFFECTIVENESS OF CROSS-CULTURAL TRAINING

Parkinson and Morley (2006) provide a historical overview of the perceived effectiveness of cross-cultural training based on the results of eight studies conducted over the 20-year period from 1981 to 2001 (their evaluation is also referred to in Chapter 10). Although Tung (1981) found little value in briefings, which were essentially informational, Earley (1987) showed how programmes combining cognitive with experiential elements could be effective in terms of preparing managers to work abroad. More recently, Eschbach et al (2001) found clear evidence of the value of cross-cultural training where it was deemed to be 'rigorous', while Selmer (2001) found that knowledge transfer could be poor; in other words, knowledge acquired before departure might not be put to effective use in reality. In summary, while the benefits of cross-cultural training may appear self-evident at first glance, actual research conducted in this area has resulted in a more complex and ambiguous picture. There is recent evidence pointing to the value of systematic coaching as an aid to 'acculturation' of expatriates (Abbott et al 2006); while mentoring has also been advocated as a potentially valuable form of support for people undertaking overseas assignments (Mezias and Scandura 2005).

9.10 REPATRIATION

Earlier in the chapter, we noted the tendency for large numbers of managers to leave their employer on return from an international assignment, or soon after (Gribben 2006). In reviewing literature on cross-cultural transitions, one can discern an increasing focus on the repatriation of staff to the home country. It has been argued that repatriated staff may occupy a particularly favourable place in the labour market (Lazarova and Caliguri 2001) because of their enhanced skills, including foreign language proficiency, exposure to alternative techniques and, finally, a more global mindset. This makes them attractive to potential new employers. Linehan and Scullion (2002) put forward the view that repatriation was more stressful than the initial outward transition (see also our earlier discussion on 'reverse culture shock'). Williams et al (2013) conclude that the literature on this topic points to a clear need for organisations to manage employee repatriation. These authors also note that the expectations of the employing organisation and the assignee may differ, highlighting a requirement to maintain ongoing communication. An example cited by Williams et al is that of the multinational bank HSBC, which assigns a sponsor to monitor the expatriate's progress through the assignment, including the important stage of repatriation, ensuring, for example, that a suitable job role is found for the returning worker.

 INDIVIDUAL ACTIVITY 9.1

Which of Caliguiri's cross-cultural training initiatives would you expect to be most important? List them in rank order, applying them to a cross-cultural scenario of your choice. Give reasons for your conclusions.

9.11 THE ETHICAL DIMENSION

Cross-cultural management is inextricably linked with ethical concerns, as is business and management more generally. Later in the chapter I pick out specific areas of a cross-cultural manager's work signifying the key importance of ethical considerations and the adoption of an ethical perspective. Before I do so it is necessary to highlight some fundamental issues in the broader field of business ethics.

The subject of business ethics centres on an examination of principles of conduct that influence decision-making. In the most general sense, ethics are linked to moral considerations of good and bad in actions (and outcomes). There has been little consensus in respect of what should be understood by the term 'business ethics', which in turn begs questions regarding the role and purpose of business organisations. The economist Milton Friedman consistently argued (see his 1970 work for a good example of his overall philosophy) that the essential purpose of a business organisation is to maximise wealth for the owners, paying particular attention to the presumed interests of shareholders. Businesses should, within this viewpoint, act legally and within accepted rules of conduct. Any wider conception of social responsibility is therefore, for Friedman, outside the scope of business objectives unless activities under this heading can be seen to link to profitability.

This view has been challenged by many other commentators; see, for example, Bennis (1996 cited in Hodgetts 1996) and Fisher and Lovell (2003) – and a widespread view currently exists that businesses do have obligations to the societies in which they have a presence. The term 'stakeholder' has come to denote individuals and groups affected by an organisation's normal operations (potentially a very great number), and stakeholder theory argues that organisations have responsibilities towards them. This notion of stakeholders refers both to those within an organisation and groups external to it, including not just clients/customers but the wider community. The concept of corporate social responsibility (CSR) has developed out of this more expansive view of a business organisation's role. CSR is defined by Bouckenhooge and Van den Broek (2006, p672) as: 'those responsibilities and obligations organisations attempt to pursue, so they can respond to economic, societal and environmental needs in a harmonious manner'. This quotation highlights the concern within CSR for organisations not just to take into account the interests and priorities of their stakeholders but also to hold them in balance when formulating strategies and taking decisions.

Rayner and Christy (2013) distinguish between the following perspectives on the study of ethics:

- *Deontological* – Where the stress is laid on the inherent goodness – or badness – in an act. This stance on the subject involves identification of duties to be carried out because they are morally correct. Equally, there are things one must not do because they contravene what the philosopher Kant, writing in the eighteenth century, termed 'categorical imperatives'. Examples would be lying and cheating, which if seen as bad could not occur under any circumstances. The deontological view sees ethics as universal, and not amenable to varying cultural interpretations
- *Consequential* – In which the concentration is on the (good or bad) effects and results of an act. This approach introduces some element of relativity into the ethical domain. While the deontological approach might regard murder as intrinsically bad, the consequential view would focus on the results, and possibly conclude that one of the assassination attempts on Hitler should with hindsight have succeeded. This perspective is not a recent insight and can be traced back to the work of the English philosophers Bentham and Mill, who wrote in the eighteenth and nineteenth centuries. The ideas contained within utilitarianism originated in their work, and had at their core the maxim that an action should be evaluated against the extent to which it resulted in the most benefit for the greatest number of people (Bentham) or most resulted in widespread happiness (Mill).

- *Character virtue* – This differs from the other categories in that good is associated with certain qualities residing in people. Ethical behaviour derives from how individuals conduct themselves having utilised these qualities; for example, courage, generosity and magnanimity (all these are balanced virtues: generosity lies between the extremes of meanness and wastefulness).

Ethics have also been associated with the concept of justice. Snell (2004) identifies a link between the two concepts in that ethical behaviour involves preventing and remedying injustice. Justice is in turn partly ensured by rights; for example, rights to fair treatment and even equal opportunities. Snell includes in his summary of categories of justice:

- *Procedural justice* – which implies a need for rules establishing agreements and dealing with grievances.
- *Distributive justice* – ensuring fairness of outcome; for example, in pay and promotion.
- *Interactional justice* – referring to the quality of interpersonal interaction and how far decisions are perceived as fair in the way they are presented.

The first inklings of a link between ethics and culture might emerge at this point. When considering the concept of distributive justice, one can link its essential focus on fairness of outcomes with the work of Adams (1965) and his equity theory approach to motivation. The essence of Adams' thesis is that individuals evaluate the relationship between their inputs and outcomes at work. If they feel they are working excessively hard for little reward, they are likely to experience a feeling of exploitation and their motivation (and conceivably their effort and productivity) will drop. Individuals also habitually compare their own input/outcomes ratio with those of others. If they do not consider that there is equity between their own and other people's ratios, a feeling of inequity ensues, with various negative consequences possibly following. In Chapter 8 evidence was presented that pointed to significant variations in employee attitudes across cultures which suggested that many influential motivational theories were in reality culture-bound and therefore of limited usefulness in some cultural settings, particularly those outside the Anglo-American cluster of countries. Is it therefore possible that culturally based differences in perceptions of an ethical construct like distributive justice could lead to variations in motivational levels, with all that potentially entails in terms of behaviour and performance?

Powell (2005) conducted research involving perceptions of equity among over 5,000 undergraduate students from 19 countries. The students were asked to consider a number of groups including doctors, maids/domestic helpers, alcoholics, university professors/lecturers, truck drivers, bankers and unwed mothers, with reference to three questions. The questions were: What contribution did the group make to society? What were their input/outcome ratios? And should they receive help from others? Powell found that students from Western Europe and North America placed great stress on equity as a norm, with special concern on the input/outcome relationship as a measure for judging fairness within societies. He concluded (2005, p69) that when considering the equity motivational model, 'other potentially important distributive fairness criteria such as equality, obligation, identity, altruism, and/or reciprocity norms – which, in some non-Western cultures, are more central to everyday justice judgements – remain largely untapped'. Powell's work is a good illustration of the cross-cultural nature of ethical judgements. Ethics can be seen as means for giving expression to cultural norms and values. They represent one way in which these norms and values are transposed into codes of behaviour. Underlying Powell's research is the crucial insight that the perception of ethics – as expressed in norms like distributive justice – vary across societies: they are subject to cultural relativism.

Guirdham (2011) expresses a very clear view that adopting a relativist position is necessary in order to fulfil some roles within cross-cultural management, suggesting that authentic and ethical intercultural communication requires people to adopt a position of cultural relativism. This involves the parties shifting away from a position in which the norms, roles, values, and behaviours into which they were socialised are seen as uniquely valid. In contrast, people should view others' norms, roles, values and behaviours as equally valid in themselves, possibly beneficial, and even eligible for adoption. Of course this statement will in reality evoke some hard choices and dilemmas for managers, as set out later in this chapter.

9.12 ETHICS AND THE CROSS-CULTURAL MANAGER

Ethical considerations can arise within any part of a cross-cultural manager's role or duties. However, certain aspects of their work or, indeed, their own identity (for example, gender) may particularly lend themselves to an ethical focus. These are set out below.

9.12.1 MANAGING A DIVERSE WORKFORCE

There are a number of strategies (either explicit or unstated) that can be adopted in this regard (see also Chapter 7). These include assimilation, the central premise here being that all employees must learn to conform to the values and behaviour of the majority dominant group within the organisation. Earlier in the chapter we saw that expatriates can abscond into the new society (Craig 1979): this is an extreme form of assimilation, but it does show that incoming workers can indeed fit into their new environment. A strategy of assimilation will intensify and formalise the sense of fitting in through recruitment practices, induction or orientation programmes and via other more informal means of socialisation.

Buelens et al (2006) find assimilation to be among the least preferred ways of managing diversity (itself an ethically grounded statement) and instead promote the use of mutual adaptation, which is associated with the acceptance of difference. They do nonetheless acknowledge that not all organisations are ready for mutual adaptation.

All possible strategies either have ethical undertones or are formulated explicitly within an ethical stance. These ethical considerations can have implications in practical policy terms. Rumbles and French (2013) identify a number of employment measures taken by the retailer Asda within its 'opportunities for all' ethos: itself a part of Asda's corporate strategy. These include: religious festival leave, 'Benidorm leave' and/or grandparents' leave, and assistance in completing application forms; this last measure intended to assist applicants with disabilities.

If ethical considerations can translate into practical policy within diversity management, it is also true that philosophical underpinnings remain important, and should not be lost sight of. Robbins (2005) concludes that successful diversity management can only occur when principles of multiculturalism and the value of embracing diverse views are accepted not just at corporate policy level but throughout the organisation. The issue of ethics and diversity can raise many areas of controversy. In 2006 a British university lecturer was suspended for membership of a racist political organisation and for reportedly expressing views supporting racial superiority. The affair brought into debate the question of whether students from non-white ethnic groups could be expected to receive fair treatment from the lecturer (an intercultural management issue), while the principle of free speech formed an important part of the very heated debate that ensued.

9.12.2 CORRUPTION

Cross-cultural management textbooks have highlighted the relevance of corruption as a topic area for students, including Schneider and Barsoux (2003), Francesco and Gold (2005) and Koen (2005). There is a clear inference that cross-cultural managers should be aware of the topic area and have recourse to coping mechanisms should they encounter real-life examples of corruption. Corruption is a generalised concept referring to impairment of integrity or a specific principle. It is also commonly used to denote improper conduct or the subverting of an existing system (for example, by breaking the law). It does not necessarily relate to financial impropriety. Snell (2004) suggests that media reporting of global corruption has highlighted bribery, gifts and nepotism as salient issues affecting cross-cultural management. If managers operating in different societies or among diverse cultural groups are exposed to bribery, to take just one example, it will undoubtedly impact on their intercultural competencies.

The existing literature points to very different views on what constitutes corrupt practice across cultures. There are also significant variations in people's perception of the relative level of corruptness endemic in individual countries. Transparency International (TI), an organisation formed with the aim of exposing and addressing corruption worldwide, produces an annual summary of surveys listing just such perceptions of corruption. The 2013 TI ranking, produced from up to 16 surveys, identifies Denmark, New Zealand, Finland, Sweden, Norway and Singapore as the now six least corrupt countries under this perceptual measure, whereas the six most corrupt countries listed are Somalia, North Korea, Afghanistan, Sudan, South Sudan and Libya. The complete ranking can be found on Transparency International's website.[5] One obvious lesson for cross-cultural managers involves assessing the likely extent of corruption within a specific society, although TI's prediction in this respect may not match reality.

Schneider and Barsoux (2003) present findings from a comparative study of US and European managers, showing that three times more French managers felt that bribery could be a necessary consequence of conducting business than their American counterparts. The scandals involving the Enron and WorldCom corporations in 2001 and 2002 are nonetheless examples of significant corruption in US organisations, albeit in a separate area of corruption (namely, institutionalised accounting fraud). So research examining perceptions of corruption elsewhere and attitudes towards it in general terms should be treated with scepticism.

Likewise, it is tempting in the light of the extensive literature on cultural classifications to claim that corruption is more linked to particular types of society. A major scandal involving several top-level Italian soccer clubs, uncovered in 2006, in which one club was shown to have influenced the appointment of referees to matches, might be claimed to be emblematic of a society classified as a relationship culture. However, this would conveniently ignore a scandal involving at least one referee actually receiving money to fix matches in Germany (a rule-based society) the previous year. In short, managers should be alive to the possibility of corruption in all societies, with perhaps some particular sensitivity to its potential in cross-cultural settings.

9.13 GENDER ISSUES AND ETHICS

Brewis and Linstead (2009), in examining the subject of gender globalisation, point to ways in which gender and cross-cultural aspects of management interact. These authors report research by Calas and Smircich (1995) indicating the overwhelmingly high proportion of males among the global management cadre. This research found that as male American managers embarked on global assignments, they were often replaced by a 'reserve army' of domestic female managers. It is interesting to note that this female workforce could also act as cross-cultural managers within their own society. Nonetheless, there is a stark difference between the operating terrains of male and female managers if, as is suggested by Brewis and Linstead (p118), women 'care for the home-based workforce while the promotable males are sent overseas to grow and develop the business – to do battle with the competition in the global marketplace'. If true, this gendered international division of labour contains an inherently ethical, and political, dimension.

In Chapter 2 I referred to the work of Forster (1999), who identified under-representation among women in overseas management postings, in part due to perceived adaptability in other cultures. Brewis and Linstead (2009, p74) also make reference to Forster's work, going on to suggest that Western female managers face lack of acceptance in 'more patriarchal cultures like those of the Middle East or Asia'. One should not automatically accept that such lack of acceptance is widespread or will in any case continue. Napier and Taylor (2002) looked at actual experiences of Western women managers working in China, Japan and Turkey. The women concerned had developed strategies to overcome initial resistance which was manifested in issues of credibility within the work setting. They had in reality experienced greater problems in the non-work parts of their lives, involving documented cases of isolation and loneliness. Harris (2004, p371) reports a complex picture when summarising issues faced by Western women working abroad, concluding that, 'One can then question the validity of the argument put forward by very many companies that women will not perform successfully in expatriate management positions as a result of host-country cultural sanctions against females.' Harris then goes on to conclude that women are potentially better performers in cross-cultural management roles due to superior communication skills and in the interpersonal sphere more generally.

While recognising the complex and dynamic interplay between gender and cross-cultural management issues, one can nonetheless still envisage ethical dilemmas arising out of contrasting cultural beliefs concerning the role and place of women at work. The dilemmas would, of course, be experienced by individuals on both sides of the debate. Interestingly, the ethical issues can arise as much within the home culture as abroad. Linehan (2005, p187), reviewing reasons for the low number of female international managers within Western organisations, concludes that, 'It seems that one of the most difficult aspects of an international assignment for women, either married or single, is obtaining the assignment in the first place. The practice (intentional or incidental) of selecting only a small number of women for international assignments may be contributing to the already existing workplace phenomenon known as the "glass ceiling", whereby one finds fewer and fewer women the higher one looks in the organisational hierarchy.'

9.14 DEALING WITH ETHICAL DILEMMAS

What, then, can we do when faced with an ethical dilemma arising out of a cross-cultural business encounter? Kohls et al (1999) conducted research which involved presenting 113 students (87% of whom were US nationals) with different scenarios requiring the students to deal with situations in which another party acted in ways contrary to approved ethical standards. The researchers beforehand identified six ways of dealing with ethical conflicts:

- *Avoiding* – turning a blind eye to the conflict.
- *Forcing* – making the other party, by whatever means, do things your way, or conceding under duress to doing things the other party's way.
- *Educating* – using rational argument or appeals at an emotional level.
- *Negotiating* – working out and agreeing compromise on both sides.
- *Accommodating* – conceding at least partly to the ethical position of the other party, and/or getting him or her to concede at least partly to yours.
- *Collaborating* – both parties working jointly and proactively together in order to achieve a mutually satisfactory outcome that meets everyone's needs.

Kohls et al list three variables that they claim determine which of the six strategies will be used, all three relating to perceived feasibility and appropriateness. The variables are:

- *Moral significance* – This factor is subdivided into an evaluation of how important the ethical value is within a person's home culture, and secondly, how widely held it is within the home culture's population.

- *Power* – What influence does an individual have within the cross-cultural situation? For example, if power is evenly distributed, it will more likely lead to the use of either the negotiation or accommodation strategy.
- *Urgency* – How quickly does a decision have to be made? If there is less urgency, negotiation or collaboration are more feasible options.

It is, of course, possible to relate these suggested strategies to the intercultural competencies outlined earlier. If a cross-cultural manager does not possess awareness and sensitivity, not to mention resourcefulness and a high stress threshold, he or she may not be able to evaluate the six options or be in a position to identify which is most feasible and appropriate in the specific situation.

One important finding from Kohls et al's research is the potential for personal development in terms of dealing with ethical conflicts. The authors state (1999, p47) that, 'Students exposed to the training were significantly more likely to demonstrate flexibility in their responses to situations involving cross-cultural ethical conflict and to recommend solutions more consistent with expert provision.' Ethical dilemmas could therefore be made part of either or both of the selection and training of cross-cultural managers. To claim that increasing experience in dealing with ethical dilemmas will, and should, result in greater flexibility is relatively uncontroversial. However, it is necessary to deconstruct the assumptions underlying the expert solutions to ethical conflict scenarios (are the experts taking a deontological or consequential approach?) and, most pertinently, one should also ask whether the solutions are formulated within the philosophical stance of ethical relativism. If so, flexibility could be equated with emotional maturity and cultural empathy. Ultimately, no training in this area can eliminate the possibility of a real ethical conflict which a manager cannot reconcile due to his or her own deeply held beliefs, and which he or she is compelled to deal with within the parameters of his or her work role.

9.15 NON-NEGOTIABLE MORAL ISSUES

Much of the existing literature on intercultural competencies and their associated ethical dimensions stresses the need for cross-cultural managers (or indeed anyone involved in an intercultural encounter) to develop and nurture such qualities as flexibility, adaptability and cultural empathy. An individual who possesses these qualities (or competencies) is likely to increasingly adopt a relativist mindset in which his or her normal *modus operandi* when dealing with people from different cultures will be to interpret the other person's attitudes and behaviour with reference to that other person's cultural background. But although embracing a relativist perspective can plausibly be seen as crucial to enhancing intercultural communication and the effectiveness of cross-cultural management more widely, it carries certain hazards.

Firstly, it requires the individual to reflect on and question his or her own ways of thinking and acting, and the reasons for those. While such profound self-questioning can be a life-enhancing experience, it may also lead to a deep re-evaluation of life values – in psychological terms, a possibly painful process. Just as a person experiencing culture shock may suffer a loss of identity, so taking on board the principles of cultural relativism can result in disorientation and a questioning of fundamental principles and previous life choices. It is not surprising that another personal trait often mentioned as important is strong self-image. Schneider and Barsoux (2003, p208) claim that, 'International managers have to consciously manage concerns regarding personal boundaries and control. They have to be sure of their own identity, to let others know where they stand. Having a strong sense of self is required to be able to acknowledge the identity of others. Having secure personal boundaries enables us to interact comfortably with others.' Cultural relativism might, though, be a highly risky philosophy should an individual not have this strong sense of self.

Cultural relativism is not synonymous with ethical relativism, an approach which does not recognise any universal sense of right and wrong. Guirdham (2011) identifies flaws in this relativist stance including the fundamental point that the mere existence of differences in beliefs and practices does not in itself mean that they are all right. She goes on to identify an alternative approach whereby parties from different cultures seek a consensus on an 'ethical minimum'. Schneider and Barsoux (2003) also offer up some possibly universal ethical standards: honesty, integrity and the protection of stakeholders. They locate others, including reciprocity or gift-giving, within a group of culturally specific standards. Broeways and Price (2011) refer to the work of Martin et al (2001), who identify three principles which could be used when applied to discussion between people from different cultures. The first principle is humanness, in which peace, respect and empathy are put centre stage. The next principle is termed dialogic. This principle stresses mutual support in relationships and includes acceptance of mutual equality. The final principle is termed speaking 'with' and 'to' – rather than speaking 'for' and 'about'. This relates to ways of communicating and is predicated on dialogue and active listening. Broeways and Price consider that this framework offers the possibility of a 'meta-ethic'; in other words building blocks that can form the basis of an ethical approach acceptable in different cultures.

Any classification of ethical norms and behaviours in this way is by definition subjective and intensely controversial. Guirdham (2005, p217) offered a solution to a difficult area as follows: 'Ethical issues are among the most problematic in intercultural work. Ethical relativism, which evades ethical issues by the contention that no moral system is better than any other, appears to be logically flawed. Consensus-building by fair and open communication based on cultural relativism, finding a way to increase the power and voice of weaker stakeholders and having a deep concern for others' value systems are among the suggested ways to achieve ethical intercultural work communication.'

If it is not possible to achieve such an ethical consensus – or if an individual is not able to instigate such a process – then people must ultimately resolve any ethical dilemma on their own. They could refer to existing models to inform their decision – such as Kohls et al's (1999) framework. These models may be found to provide only a restricted choice of action, however. The aforementioned framework does not, for example, list 'leaving the organisation' as an option. Any individual might in any case choose to take a bolder course of action based on his or her own 'ethical minimum', such as withdrawing from a transaction with a partner organisation who refused to deal with female managers or when offered a bribe in exchange for a preferred contract.

A final point is that should one be wary of focusing exclusively on existing cross-cultural managers when considering responses to ethical dilemmas. An applicant for a cross-cultural management job could also encounter ethical dilemmas if the future employer used suppliers who were associated with sweatshop labour. One response could simply be to discontinue their application. However, given the scope of this book, the focus has been on how ethical considerations link with cross-cultural management within work organisations and the choices existing managers could make when confronting ethical dilemmas as part of their working lives.

GROUP ACTIVITY 9.2

There is no definitive template of agreed ethical principles to which cross-cultural managers can refer when seeking help with ethical dilemmas arising from their work. Within the terms of cultural relativism, ethical standards are mostly fluid. The cross-cultural manager, in following this approach, should appreciate the ethical norms of a new country and adhere to them, even if they go against accepted standards in his or her home culture.

- Identify any two forms of behaviour in business that you consider to be universally wrong – ie they should not occur in any culture – and two that you think you would tolerate in another culture even though they were not normally accepted in your home culture. Give reasons for your choice.
- Discuss your findings within a small group (of two to four people). How can you account for similarities and differences in your views?
- To what extent do you think cultural empathy is the most important competency that a cross-cultural manager should have? Refer to the relative importance of other competencies in preparing your answer.

9.16 CONCLUSION

In previous chapters we have proposed that effective cross-cultural management is linked to an understanding of the complex and fluid concept of culture, together with an appreciation of the cultural nuances of specific business and management topic areas; for example, organisation structure, leadership and motivation. We had already noted that effective intercultural communication plays a key part in successful interaction with people from different cultural backgrounds. In this chapter we have moved the debate squarely on to the field of intercultural competencies. Deep knowledge of other cultures is not enough to ensure success in cross-cultural management: the manager must be effective in a cross-cultural role if they are to flourish and fulfil both their own and an employing organisation's needs.

Since 2003 we have had the emerging concept of CQ to guide our thinking on this topic. A person's CQ is made up of our knowledge about both cultural difference in general and specific cultures, plus our own skills (eg of open-mindedness) and, finally, the relative ability we have to control our own thinking and behaviour. However, one should not forget the importance of more general competencies such as an individual's personal presence, credibility and the ability to win support for their actions. These are important in any context.

We have seen that an understanding of the nature of transitions and, in particular, culture shock is a valuable resource for a cross-cultural manager, together with an ability to cope in such a potentially stressful situation. A work organisation can do much to facilitate successful transitions, including addressing the crucial repatriation stage. However, it remains the case that personal attributes also play a significant role in completing a successful foreign assignment. Beyond this, a successful cross-cultural manager is likely to be able to reconcile cultural dilemmas (echoing the work of Trompenaars covered in previous chapters). Cross-cultural management also carries an inherently ethical component. While a sense of cultural relativism is undoubtedly necessary when engaging with other cultures, it may not always be possible to reconcile certain attitudes, values and behaviour, even if one can identify 'meta-ethics' to guide one's own principles.

CASE STUDY 9.2

MIRANDA'S STORY

Miranda Fung was born and brought up in Wuhan, China. Her given name is Li Hua Fung: she gave herself the Western name on arrival in the UK. Miranda enrolled on a bachelor's degree in business administration at a Welsh university in 2004. Her father is a senior manager in the chemicals industry, and Miranda is ambitious to progress to a managerial position in the future, preferably within the financial services sector. Approaching her three-year stay in the UK, Miranda was keen to learn about the new culture, feeling that this would give her self-confidence and enhance her career prospects. She enjoyed her induction programme, which included organised trips to London and Stonehenge, and quickly made friends with other students whom she met via the Chinese society at the freshers' fayre.

In her first few weeks of study, however, she experienced some difficulties in many of her subjects. Although she quickly emerged as a star performer in her statistics module, in other subjects – particularly marketing and organisational behaviour – she found that she equally quickly fell behind. Although she enjoyed the subjects, Miranda was unused to working with other students on case studies. In China she had experienced a far greater input from the teacher. Her schooling in China had accustomed her to taking copious notes from classes, which were mostly taken up by the teacher talking. In her new environment, she found herself experiencing a sense of loss of familiar teaching and learning styles, and while she knew that she had to adapt to the less didactic approach evident in the UK, in moments of reflection she had to admit that she found the Chinese model better.

There was also strange behaviour to confront outside the classroom. The

British students in her hall of residence made too much noise for her liking, mostly but not only at weekends, and she was frankly appalled by the levels of alcohol consumption among both male and female UK students. When a group of her Chinese friends asked the British students to be a little quieter, on more than one occasion the response had been to invite Miranda and her friends to join the party. After four weeks, following an unsuccessful all-night attempt to take notes from a recording she had made of a lecture, Miranda found herself breaking down in tears during a telephone call to her parents. Her first term of study from September to December, she would later recall, was largely spent in a haze of distress.

With hard work and perseverance, Miranda progressed to her second year of study, where she found events to be more under her control. She had learned to seek advice from lecturers regarding her study methods, and took on board lessons from feedback she received on her written work. However, she tolerated rather than embraced group seminar work, and still could not see why she had to constantly reference academics' work in her essays because she felt that it stopped her expressing her own ideas. In an email to an old school friend in Wuhan, Miranda confided that she had now learned what the expectations were of a student in a British university, and was able to adapt her behaviour to these in order to achieve some measure of success. She had become more and more focused on completing her qualification as a means to advancing her career and earnings potential. Pressed by her friend as to whether she felt a changed person, Miranda replied that she did not.

Questions

1   Read the case study above, and respond to the following.

2   Which (if any) of Craig's (1979) adaptation behaviours is displayed by Miranda, according to her own account of culture shock? Give reasons for your answer.

3   Should a university put measures into place in order to alleviate potential culture shock as felt by overseas students – and if so, what could these be?

4   To what extent are Miranda's initial reactions to her first term at university the result of her cultural background? Could a British student experience similar reactions – and if so, why?

NOTES

1   Teacher speaks of Sudan 'ordeal' (2007) BBC News online. 4 December. Available at http://news.bbc.co.uk/1/hi/7126162.stm [Accessed 16 October 2014].

2,3   Top 20: Great Football Insults (2009) *Telegraph*. 30 January. Available at http://www.telegraph.co.uk/sport/football/teams/newcastle-united/4398209/Top-20-Great-Footballing-Insults.html?mobile=basic [Accessed 16 October 2014].

4   Manchester United on the defensive over 'misquoted' Nemanja Vidic article (2008) Telegraph. 26 August. Available at: http://www.telegraph.co.uk/sport/football/teams/manchester-united/2627983/Manchester-United-on-the-defensive-over-misquoted-Nemanja-Vidic-article-Football.html, 27 August 2008 [Accessed 11 August 2009].

5   www.tranparency.org [Accessed 28 July 2014].

 REVIEW QUESTIONS

1   What are the commonly identified stages in culture shock? Identify the different ways in which an individual might respond to the experience of culture shock.

2   Why do many employees leave their job after being repatriated to their home country, and what can employers do to minimise staff turnover at that time?

3   How might the deontological, consequential and character virtues perspectives on ethics be applied to cross-cultural management?

FURTHER READING

CLEGG, S., KORNBERGER, M. and PITSIS, T. (2011) *Managing and organizations*. 3rd ed. London: Sage. Readers interested in the topic of ethics are recommended to look at Chapter 11 of this book, which provides a full summary of topical thinking beyond the cross-cultural arena.

DOWLING, P. J., FESTING, M. and ENGLE SNR, A. D. (2013) *International human resource management*. 6th ed. Andover: CENGAGE Learning. Readers may be interested to read more about international training, development and careers and Chapter 7 of this book takes a more in-depth and specialist look at this topical area.

GILMORE, S. and WILLIAMS, S. (eds) (2013) *Human resource management*. 2nd ed. Oxford: OUP. Chapter 15, written by Steve Williams, Liza Howe-Walsh and Peter Scott, contains an overview of the important area of international assignments and how these might be effectively managed.

Visit this book's companion website (**www.cipd.co.uk/olr**) to find further exercises including self-assessment questions and also weblinks to media and academic journal articles.

Culture and Human Resource Management

10.1 INTRODUCTION

The focus of this book is on cross-cultural management in work organisations. As culture is manifested in values, attitudes and behaviour, much of cross-cultural management is therefore intrinsically bound up with the management of people. Within many work organisations this human dimension is the domain of HRM, whether interpreted as the responsibility of all managers, or a specialist HRM function, or more likely a combination of both. Many of the issues and topics raised in this book fall within the responsibility of HR managers; for example material contained in Chapter 8 on the topic of motivation has implications for remuneration strategies as they are devised and implemented within different cultures. As the global context of HRM has assumed greater importance there has been a plethora of writing on international human resource management (IHRM) in recent years, including specific IHRM books authored by Brewster et al (2011), Dowling et al (2013), Harzing and Pinnington (2014), Hollingshead (2010) and Iles and Zhang (2013). More general HRM textbooks have also included chapters on IHRM (see, for example, Gilmore and Williams 2013), while books examining themes and contexts affecting HR managers have highlighted the significant international dimension (eg Hall et al 2013).

Within the aforementioned extensive literature a distinction has frequently been made between international and comparative HRM. IRHM has been understood as essentially addressing the ways in which work organisations deal with people management issues occurring in more than one national context. For the most part the subject has concentrated on businesses' attempts to internationalise by establishing a presence in one or more foreign countries. However, as we have seen in earlier chapters, we do not need to travel abroad to be concerned with cultural difference. Once again, this time in the HRM area, we should recognise that IHRM issues can also affect activities in the home country context; for example, when organisations employ migrant labour. Comparative HRM is a related area concerned with analysing the extent to which national or regional HRM practices diverge, and where this is the case, the reasons for identified differences. Garavan and Carberry (2012), in examining the specific area of human resource development, apply their work to both an 'international trajectory' (focusing on multinational corporations (MNCs)) and a 'cross-cultural trajectory', which takes a broader view on the influence of culture on HR in general terms. International and comparative HRM are therefore separate terms which are often linked in practice. Both perspectives draw on the same academic work as a resource for understanding culture and Hofstede's contribution is frequently cited.

10.2 IHRM IN CONTEXT

Scullion (2005) set out the main reasons for the rapid growth of interest in IHRM since 1990. In this context he refers to the growth of MNCs in this period with attendant labour mobility and problems in expatriate manager performance. Both issues have been addressed in earlier chapters. Scullion also puts forward other reasons for the perceived growing importance of the field including the following (a full list can be found in Scullion 2005, pp8–10):

- Success and failure in cross-border business have been closely linked to effective HRM. Harris et al (2007) concluded that this area was a major determinant of business performance.
- Evidence that HR strategies have an especially significant impact in terms of their implementation in international companies (Scullion and Starkey 2000). Success of transnational or even global strategies has been associated with the development of diverse organisational cultures (Bartlett and Ghoshal 1998), which is identified as a core HR issue.
- Suggestions that HR systems should be realigned in order to support global organisational learning, in particular through facilitating cross-border teamwork in order to secure competitive advantage (Bjorkman and Xiucheng 2002).
- HRM can play an important role in enhancing knowledge management within the company by capturing knowledge held by organisations' subsidiary units (Foss and Pedersen 2002; Gooderham and Nordhaug 2003).

The increasing interest in international aspects of HRM has been associated with increasing numbers of businesses internationalising their operations. More specifically, writers on IHRM including Bartlett and Ghoshal (1998), De Cieri and Dowling (1999) and Schuler et al (2002) point to differences in HRM policy and practice depending on the level of internationalisation involved, ie whether the company in question is involved in a multi-domestic or global venture. Budhwar (2003), in reviewing previous literature including Schuler et al (1993) and Dowling et al (1999) on international HR staffing, highlighted four generic approaches to the area (see below.) Collings and Scullion (2006) link these approaches back to the work of Perlmutter (1969), who claimed that the extent to which an international firm was oriented towards foreign ideas and resources in both central and country specific operations would determine its 'multinationality'.

- *Ethnocentric* – Under this strategy senior managers who operate out of a clearly defined headquarters are drawn from the organisation's home country. As important decisions are made by this group of managers, home country practices are prevalent and subsidiary country units comply with centralised directives.
- *Polycentric* – Local managers are employed to implement strategies and subsidiaries are allowed to operate in more diverse ways, including in the HR field.

- *Geocentric* – Staffing is undertaken on a worldwide basis. The HR practices which emerge have the stamp of staff from both headquarters and subsidiary units. Although there is more cultural flexibility contained in these practices they are implemented consistently.
- *Regiocentric* – This is a variant of the geocentric model; however, in this case, managers are recruited regionally and HR practices are consistent within specified regions.

The approaches to staffing identified by Budhwar are similar to Adler and Ghadar's (1990) model of phases of internationalisation more generally. This model is underpinned by the premise that culture will progressively influence HR policies and practices as the organisation moves through the identified phases. Scullion and Paauwe (2005) show how Adler and Ghadar's work builds on Vernon's life-cycle theory (1966), which described the international product life cycle. Adler and Ghadar took Vernon's phases of development and showed how they would take effect within HRM. Adler and Ghadar's phases are set out below:

- domestic
- international
- multinational
- global.

In the first domestic phase, managers take an ethnocentric (or even parochial) approach and will not consider, or be aware of, other cultures, which in consequence will not be perceived as affecting their organisation. In the second international phase, managers will take cognisance of cultural differences and, in particular, seek to align product design, marketing and production to the new country or countries with reference to their perceived relevant cultural characteristics. In some cases production itself could be transferred or outsourced there. The major concern within the third multinational phase is to take advantage of varying production costs in the different countries or regions. While financial considerations are to the fore at this point, Scullion and Paauwe (2005, p25) note that within this phase, 'it is, however, important that a certain internal sensitivity or awareness develops of the various cultural differences (cultural diversity) within the global concern'.

Finally, within the fourth global phase, Adler and Ghadar suggest that a company's products and services are expected to meet or even exceed quality standards, so cost is no longer the only preoccupation. As a concern with quality involves adapting a product or service to 'new culture' preferences or standards (either expected or legally specified), cultural awareness is once again necessary.

Adler and Ghadar then show how the different phases of internationalisation are associated with the use of specific HRM 'instruments'. From Phase 2 onwards, international or cross-cultural aspects become increasingly evident with managers assigned to foreign postings, therefore needing to be aware of differences in the new location, as an integral part of their role, which is in turn governed by the organisation's overall strategic focus. Recruitment, selection, induction and training of such managers should in consequence concentrate on identifying and developing competencies identified in Chapter 9; for example, adaptability and cross-cultural awareness. Alternatively, the company could consider the appointment of host-country nationals to specified management positions. In Phase 3 the company is more likely to develop a cadre of managers who will share corporate values, irrespective of their nationality. As far as the HR function is concerned, management development will loom large as a priority area and cross-cultural and intercultural training will be needed in order to achieve integration and mutual understanding. Finally, in Phase 4, when a large measure of cultural diversity has become apparent both in the external environment and within the company (bearing in mind the multinational management group now in place), the organisation will seek to use this diversity to allow organisational learning and to secure competitive advantage. The role of IHRM at this stage is to facilitate continuous learning throughout the organisation.

Another perspective on the development of IHRM is provided by De Cieri and Dowling (1999). These authors identify two categories of influencing factors: endogenous and exogenous. Endogenous factors (those originating from within the organisation) include level of previous experience in international business, organisational and industry life cycle (echoing Adler and Ghadar's work), structure of its international operations and corporate and business level strategies. All of these will influence the organisation's strategic approach to IHRM. However, existing HRM strategies and practices will also have an influence on the ways in which an organisation approaches IHRM issues. The endogenous factors reflect, and in turn influence, more general concerns and goals regarding the organisation's own conception of competitiveness, efficiency and flexibility.

De Cieri and Dowling's exogenous (external) factors are:

- industry characteristics
- country-regional characteristics
- inter-organisational networks and alliances (for example those fostered by the EU single market project in the early 1990s).

All of these factors affect IHRM activities in MNCs and also have a clear influence on the wider concerns and goals of the organisation; De Cieri and Dowling (1999) cite the effect of the recession in Asian countries post-1997 as an example of how regional factors can lead to a reappraisal of concerns regarding competitiveness.

The list of exogenous factors should not be viewed as final or definitive. Merlot et al (2006), when conducting research on non-governmental organisations (NGOs), add two further exogenous factors which they claim will influence this particular type of organisation: funding resources (the nature of donors) and international pressure groups. However, this updated contribution from a group of researchers including one of the original authors essentially supports De Cieri and Dowling's finding that a mix of internal and external factors reflecting both HR and strategic management concerns will affect the nature of any organisation's strategic IHRM activity.

   SELECTION IN A GLOBAL COMPANY

CASE STUDY 10.1

A Nigerian candidate is looking for work as a marketing manager within an MNC. A local recruitment agency forwards his curriculum vitae to UOPB, a bank headquartered in Chicago. UOPB's selection processes were developed in the USA, although this particular vacancy is in Singapore. The Singapore office identifies a senior manager (who is Australian) to conduct a structured interview using a Skype link. This manager had no previous experience of international recruitment. A senior HR manager at Chicago HQ then asks the local office in Singapore to administer a psychometric test. They have no previous experience of interpreting such tests and so a consultant is hired from the Norwegian-based firm who devised the test. The test results are sent to one of their senior consultants, a Dutch psychologist who is based at the consultancy's office in Madrid. He sends the interpretation back to the interviewing manager. After reviewing the evidence she decides to reject the candidate's application.

The candidate is unhappy with the decision and intends to challenge it on legal grounds as he suspects that he may have been unfairly discriminated against due to his ethnicity.

Questions

1   Assess the events outlined in the UOPB case study in the light of both:

(a)   Budhwar's approaches to international HR staffing

(b)   Adler and Ghadar's phases of internationalisation.

2   What has gone wrong in the selection process, and how would you advise UOPB to proceed in similar cases in future? Give reasons for your recommendations.

Case study by Ray French adapted from Searle (2003).

10.3 VARIETIES OF CAPITALISM

One very important part of the context within which HR policies and practices are developed and operationalised is the macro level of the nation state. Iles and Zhang (2013, p6) refer to this area as comprising, 'capital, labour and financial systems and the route taken by different countries to industrialisation and modernisation'. So-called national business systems can explain divergent types of capitalism and very different frameworks for managing people. Hyman (2004), in similar vein, identified differences in the social context of industrial relations based on varieties of capitalism. He locates four dimensions of social relations, the first of which is the property regime denoting ownership and economic governance; for example, the relative extent of private and public ownership of resources. The production regime refers to characteristic systems of work organisation (for example, skill levels); while the welfare regime deals with health care and other social protection – who provides it and how generous is it? Finally, the gender regime centres on male/female patterns of employment. Hyman provides a four-way classification scheme which locates groups of societies along the dimensions, acknowledging that this is a simplified classification; indeed, Hyman immediately goes on to refine the model as applied to European societies as we shall see. The original four categories are:

- *Anglo-American* – Here there are liberal property and welfare regimes, a Fordist production regime and what is termed a formally egalitarian but in practice patriarchal gender regime.
- *Northern European* – There are two variants of this model: the Nordic and the Germanic. Overall, the property regime is highly regulated, the production regime status-based, there is an extensive welfare regime, and the gender regime is relatively egalitarian.
- *Southern European* – A regulated property regime, status-based production regime, less developed welfare regime and traditional patriarchal (with recent changes) regime characterise this model.
- *Japanese* – This type is depicted as containing a regulated property regime status-based production, conservative welfare regime and patriarchal gender regime.

Hyman makes allowance for variation within societies. For example (2004, p414), he notes that: 'within any country, production regimes can differ between firms, partly reflecting the requirements of different industries and services, but also in line with employers' strategic choices. To take another familiar distinction, there is a "low road" and a "high road" to competitive success: many firms may attempt to compete on the basis of low cost or high quality.' Over and above variations within societies, Hyman continues to recognise significant similarities between grouped societies along the aforementioned dimensions. Readers will recognise arguments familiar from earlier chapters regarding the nature of categorisation, but more importantly highlighting the macro-level manifestation of societal difference. In this context, Hyman relates these differences to the strategies used in employing and managing people. Differences are seen to occur not only between specific employment practices but in underlying philosophical approaches to the area. Hyman (p421) notes variances in discourse suggesting that, 'in most of western Europe, the English term "industrial relations" is commonly understood through the notion of "social affairs" or some analogue. Employment is perceived as a social relation, not a simply contractual issue. Partly as a corollary, industrial relations is an area for collective actors: trade unions and employers' organisations are described in much of Europe as "social partners".' Hyman continues his analysis by examining the relative influence of forces of convergence and divergence noting evidence for both trends. His conclusion is that there is likely to be continued diversity in the ways in which capitalism is interpreted leading to differences in the industrial relations contexts of individual societies, which in turn will influence managers' employment strategies, policies and practices.

Needle (2010) locates three broad models of capitalism: Anglo-Saxon; social market (also known as the Rhineland model; Albert 1993); and Asian capitalism. When applied to the industrial or employee-relations elements of business, the Anglo-Saxon model, prevalent in the UK and USA, allows for the existence of trade unions but typically curtails their powers through legislation. The social market model is identified in Germany, France, the Netherlands and Scandinavian countries (although there are important differences in how the models takes effect between countries in this group). Overarching principles which characterise this as a unified category concern the role of trade unions who are seen to have an important role in decision-making, and the key concept of significant employee representation at company level, epitomised by the German system of *mitbestimmung* (co-determination). In Asian capitalism (within which there are again important variations), trade unions are weak and often organised by companies rather than being truly independent bodies. However, in the Asian model, long-term employment is viewed as desirable and significant efforts are made to protect workers' tenure in low points within the economic cycle. Again, we have an example of national differences or macro-level system effects having a potentially profound influence on how HRM is conceived as an activity and, of course, in actual policies and procedures involving the management of people.

One should regard models such as those listed above with a certain amount of caution as, on closer reading, do the authors themselves. The picture in any one country can firstly change; on occasions in a sudden and dramatic way. There is scope for far-reaching and relatively sudden developments in political philosophy leading to a revolution in employee-relations practices, as seen in the rapid changes in the UK under the neo-liberal policies adopted by the Thatcher administrations (arguably continued to a degree by subsequent governments), in the course of which the UK moved away from a 'Rhineland' model of employee relations towards the American model. Such trends are not irreversible and there is some level of opposition to the neo-liberal model, as evidenced by anti-capitalist movements.

Complexity of change was also found by Needle (2010), who recorded that transitional economies (those changing from centrally planned to market economies) can follow different paths both in terms of pace of change and in actual policies (he cites Poland and Hungary as contrasting examples). Needle also points to the role of joint ventures in transitional Chinese economy, resulting in a tendency for China to follow Western models of capitalism rather than the Asian model with which it is much more closely related. Chen (2004) also provides an in-depth account of the intricacies of Asian management systems in the early twenty-first century, once more identifying a range of complex variations between societies. In Chapter 2 we examined the work of Inglehart and Baker and their modernisation thesis which pointed to a range of different ways in which individual countries (and their citizens) could respond to global trends.

It is also prudent to acknowledge pressures leading to convergence in employment practices. For example, in both the Rhineland and Asian models of capitalism, workers' employment is in theory strongly protected. However, this does not mean that widespread job losses do not actually occur in societies associated with this approach: recent examples include the car maker Renault's plans to cut 7,500 jobs (14% of its workforce) in France between 2013 and 2016; and a number of Japanese companies, including Sony, reducing staff in 2014. There is a further complicating twist when job losses in Anglo-American societies occur within foreign-owned companies, with claims that operations in these countries are chosen to bear the brunt of employment reduction because the legal framework makes this easier to achieve. One example of this phenomenon occurred in 2013 when Ford closed its van assembly facility in Southampton, England with production switched to Turkey.

10.4 CULTURE AND HRM

Overall, the preceding section points to clear evidence that HRM differs between societies due to distinctive institutional features within individual countries, which can in turn be explained in the light of wider philosophies broadly shared by groups of countries and/or regions. One should not ignore the influence of educational systems as manifested at the micro level of individual subject traditions in this regard. Schneider and Barsoux (2003, p149) provide an illuminating example noting that: 'the approach to HRM in the United States and Europe has evolved from different disciplines, psychology and sociology, which have different assumptions regarding the nature of the relationship between people and organizations. In the United States, HRM has its roots in psychology, its prime concern being the improvement of worker motivation.' One can therefore see the effects of such educational differences on the very concept of HRM. Equally, the existing literature proposes that managers should recognise that HRM strategies need to be chosen with reference to their likely success in particular contexts. Boxall and Purcell (2011) identify both a 'best practice' model which puts forward universally applicable HR principles and a contextual view implying national variation in practice. These authors advocate a hybrid model combining a survey of internal strengths and weaknesses (similar to the 'resource-based' view assuming that internal processes can be easily adapted to market conditions) with an external analysis of opportunities and threats; this latter exercise allowing for an analysis of national-level features. Tatli (2005, p89) summarises what is a widely held view that strategic IHRM cannot provide universally applicable solutions to people management issues, suggesting rather that, 'its valuable contribution is the emphasis on contextuality regarding the applicability and efficiency of strategies themselves. It presumes the multiplicity of contexts and best strategies, so it is the role of human resource managers to creatively find the best fit between an external business environment and the internal organizational setting, so as to shape the company's human resource strategy which is also organically bound to its corporate strategy.'

The view of IHRM put forward so far, gleaned from existing writing on the topic, is essentially contextual. One could plausibly argue that the term 'ethnocentric', used to locate corporate approaches to HRM, could be applied to the academic field too, with so much writing on international and/or comparative HRM emanating from a Western (and specifically Anglo-American) background. At any rate, managers schooled in its main body of work will adapt their actions to identified aspects of the pre-existing national or regional employment setting. In as much as culture is mentioned (some contributors including Hyman do not actually use the term) it is referred to at the macro institutional level, rather than in terms of internalised norms, attitudes and values.

Koen (2005), who has provided an in-depth analysis of the concept of culture in all its multi-dimensional form, provides an example of this phenomenon when considering the specific area of HRM. Koen identifies several factors within Swedish society that can account for the widespread existence of autonomous work groups, namely the advanced nature of technology in some sectors of Swedish industry; its education system, which delivers an autonomous, flexible and employable workforce; modernised factories; and employers' ability to move workers between comparable jobs. There is no reference here to Sweden's position on classification measures such as power distance or femininity, or of how individual attitudes affect this method of working, although one has to assume that workers are willing to engage with the levels of autonomy afforded to them within such a system of work. Koen (p201) does, however, indicate that managers' own cultural preferences form part of the process of change in HR systems, noting, 'an explanation of change must incorporate constraints by external institutions; especially in the form of previous human resource policies, which exercise inertial forces, management values as shaped by norms accepted in the society, legal constraints and unions' bargaining agendas.' The interplay between contingent factors such as an organisation's size, market position and cultural location and the level of choice available to managers in shaping strategies and putting them into action is a matter of ongoing debate within the study of organisations; see Watson (2012).

Budhwar (2003) identifies the following five ways in which national culture finds expression in HRM policies and practices:

- the socialisation process shaping managers
- basic assumptions underlying managers' behaviour
- common values (behavioural norms and customs)
- influence of country-specific social elites or pressure groups
- management logic reflecting wider national business systems.

The list is drawn from previous research findings and comprises a blend of factors based on managers' characteristics and structural features of the country in question. One can also surmise that HRM practices must have wider credibility and so the values of employees and other stakeholders also become relevant. For example, when discussing recruitment and selection practices we will see that the 'face validity' or general acceptability of techniques like graphology can vary widely even between neighbouring countries.

In the specific field of cross-national differences in HR, Sorge (2004) concludes that the systems and mental programming approaches to understanding and explaining culture are in any case inter-related. He states that the choices that individuals make are bounded by existing structures and 'rules of the game', while those individuals will learn to view certain choices in an especially favourable way. Sorge (p133) states that in this reciprocal sense, 'we now see institutions created, modified or held in place through the mental programming of actors; and we also see the latter as emerging through the confrontation of actors with fairly robust and stable patterns'. Giddens' (1984) concept of structuration had earlier made this point in more general terms, showing how individual actors have pre-existing systems in mind when approaching choices and decisions, while systems only exist in terms of the meanings given to them by actors. The interplay between the values and systems approaches to culture can be seen in practical application when examining specific areas of HR policy which follow in the next section.

 GROUP ACTIVITY 10.1

Working in a small group (two to four people) select one country and using De Cieri and Dowling's framework identify three country characteristics showing how these could affect approaches to HRM in that country.

1   Where would the country be located within Hyman's varieties of capitalism model?

2   How would you characterise the country's production and gender regimes within this model and how could these influence employment relations within the country?

10.5 CULTURE AND THE FUNCTIONAL AREAS OF HRM

One core area within HRM is recruitment and selection. This involves firstly establishing and clarifying a staffing need, using appropriate techniques in order to attract appropriate candidates to a post (recruitment) and selecting and hopefully appointing one or more persons from a group of applicants (assuming aggressive recruitment (headhunting) is not the method used). A systematic approach is usually advocated which includes continuous evaluation of practice based on experience. Recruitment and selection is viewed as an important area. Pilbeam and Corbridge (2010, p155) state that, 'The recruitment and selection of employees is fundamental to the functioning of an organisation and there are compelling reasons for getting it right. Inappropriate selection decisions reduce organisational effectiveness, invalidate reward and development strategies, are frequently unfair on the individual recruit and can be distressing for managers who have to deal with unsuitable employees.' In Chapter 9 we saw how the recruitment and selection of expatriate managers was a particularly sensitive area in which an attempt would be made to identify particular personal and managerial competencies. What other cross-cultural dimensions are likely to affect this important sub-set of HRM work?

Perkins and Shortland (2006) report that particular selection methods are used more or less frequently in different societies, citing the example of psychometric testing. UK and US nationals may be more used to undertaking such tests, raising the issue of equity as other nationals will not be as familiar with them. This point in turn leads to questioning of whether selection measures are culturally biased; this criticism has long been levelled against IQ tests, in particular their verbal reasoning elements. As fairness will be one goal of a recruitment and selection process, it is clearly important to choose selection methods which do not disadvantage any cultural group. Likewise it is important to recognise cultural norms as they are exhibited in behaviour during the selection process. In Chapter 6, we saw that there were important cultural differences in non-verbal communication (NVC), manifested in body posture, degree of eye contact and even nodding and smiling. In certain Asian cultures eye contact is regarded negatively and therefore minimised. As this along with other manifestations of NVC occur partly at the sub-conscious level, it is incumbent upon the person(s) involved in selection not to misinterpret the emotions underlying the behaviour. Perkins and Shortland give a real-life example of a Korean interviewee who chose to delay answers within an interview in order to demonstrate respect for the interviewer. However, this choice was open to cultural misunderstanding; without awareness of the significance of such behaviour it could easily be interpreted as mere 'slowness'.

There has been some suggestion that different cultures stress varying attributes when embarking on recruitment and selection of employees. Francesco and Gold (2005, p149) relate this notion to status and whether – as in Trompenaars' classification scheme – this is essentially achieved or ascribed, suggesting that, 'when making a hiring decision, people in an achievement-oriented country consider skills, knowledge and talent,' while contrastingly, 'in an ascriptive culture, age, gender, personal relationships and family background are important, and an organization selects someone whose personal characteristics fit the job.' Schneider and Barsoux (2003) make a similar point related to how companies recruit staff, noting that in individualist societies a match between the person and job description will be of paramount importance. This concern is contrasted with that in collectivist societies where the authors posit that (p156), 'nepotism is a natural outcome of the logic of interdependence. When an employer takes on a person, a moral commitment is established. There is implicit understanding that the employer will look after the employee and quite possibly his or her family too.' In both cases one can relate recruitment and selection practices to existing models of cultural difference, showing their practical relevance within the world of work.

It is necessary to qualify the effect that culture can have on the supposedly systematic area of recruitment and selection. Sue-Chan and Dasborough (2006) conducted research investigating the role of 'particularistic ties', ie friendship in recruitment and selection practices in Australia and Hong Kong. Their conclusion was that personal subjective elements could be seen in both contexts. This finding concurs with others' views on the importance of *guanxi* in Chinese societies (see Chapter 4 for a full explanation of this concept). That this occurred in the Australian context too in the form of what Sue-Chan and Dasborough termed 'mateship', is on the surface more surprising. One explanation is that recruitment and selection is in reality a less objective or quasi-scientific exercise (as put forward in textbooks) in all societies. Just as countries' scores on cultural classification schemes are probabilistic rather than definitive, so we can expect some of the behaviours associated with ascriptive or collectivist societies to be displayed in both achievement or individualist countries, but maybe not to the same extent in each. One should also be mindful of possible convergence in behaviours. Chen (2004) points to pressures to reduce incidences of *guanxi* resulting from economic development and modernisation in Chinese societies and predicts the gradual combination of *guanxi* with market rationality. One can speculate that this 'new rationality' will take effect in HR policies and practices.

Finally, recruitment and selection can be seen to be affected by culture in several other ways. In Chapter 2 we saw how institutional society-wide factors combine with norms and attitudes to form culture. One such institutional factor is a country's legal framework. The USA has a series of laws seeking to protect the rights of individuals at work, including a range of measures in the equal opportunities area. These apply to the selection or non-selection of potential employees. This strong legal framework, coupled with what is sometimes seen as a litigious culture, has been one reason why US employers have sought to develop and operate objective measures of job-related ability within recruitment and selection in an attempt to distinguish fairly between applicants; in other words, to discriminate in a valid way. In the course of selection, employers are prohibited by law from basing decisions on group characteristics such as gender or religion and are likely therefore to adhere strictly to measures which predict individual task-related achievement.

Earlier in the chapter reference was made to the 'face validity' of selection methods: do they, on the face of it, appear reasonable to the general population? Face validity will vary across cultures. The CIPD (2004) offers an expert view on the efficacy of graphology (handwriting analysis) as follows, 'Employers considering the use of graphology should be aware of the limitations of the technique, its unreliability and the potential harm this could cause to their business. At present we can find no viable argument why graphology should be seen as a real alternative to properly validated personality assessments.' Unsurprisingly, given this critical slant put on the subject by the national professional body, graphology is not highly regarded as a selection tool by most companies in the UK. However, its use is far more widespread in France, the reasons seemingly deriving from the birth of modern graphology in the mid-nineteenth century in that country. In as much as graphology is a well-known and prevalent method in French business culture, its cultural face validity is high (its proponents continue of course to also stress its predictive validity as a selection tool).

Another important core area within HRM is training and development. As with recruitment and selection, this core aspect of HRM is affected by culture in several different ways. Training and development of employees (and potential workers) is particularly closely linked with culture at the macro institutional level as national philosophies regarding, for example, vocational education, differ greatly and are given expression in a multiplicity of training systems. At the start of this chapter the distinction was made between international and comparative HRM and it is the latter focus which comes to the fore when we consider systems unique to a country or cultural group.

Koen (2005) makes the important point that characteristic philosophies on training should be linked back to more general notions of desirable work relationships incorporating views on job classification. Koen states that the typical version of job design in US organisations involves a 'Taylorist' division of labour, with many discrete jobs. She notes that this has been reinforced by a low status accorded to vocational education which in any case offers narrow training resulting in relatively little worker flexibility. Training infrastructure was only one reason for this characteristic working pattern (the role of unions in devising job classification schemes was another), but macro-level training initiatives are seen to play a significant role in shaping workplace practices. In contrast, Koen points to the extensive training of workers in Germany, where there is a long tradition of vocational education, most famously embodied in nationally standardised apprenticeships enabling workers to proceed to master craftsman or engineer status. In respect of cross-cultural management, the comparative focus on this aspect of HRM is primarily informational; any business intending to deal with a new country should be aware of traditions and practice in the important area of training. One can also gain valuable lessons from abroad when comparing national training systems. These are certainly very diverse; see Cervino and Bonache (2005) for an illuminating picture of practices in Cuba after a lengthy period of communist rule.

The cross-cultural training of managers is also of great significance (see also Chapter 9). There is an extensive literature outlining the types of training available together with evaluation of the efficacy of different methods; see Caligiuri et al (2005), Dowling et al (2013), Gudykunst et al (1977), Selmer (2001), Zakaria (2000) and Zhang and Iles (2013). There are a number of interlinked factors which explain likely efficacy. Parkinson and Morley (2006) conclude that success in cross-cultural training is a function of the rigour of a programme, that is the mental involvement and effort required of the trainee and trainer, combined with the specific requirements of the trainee's assignment. This suggests that a contingency perspective, involving the adaptation of methods to the precise situation, would be especially valuable. However Parkinson and Morley (p132) note conflicting findings on the value of cross-cultural training *per se*, concluding, 'while there is an empirical literature questioning the value of CCT and its effectiveness in facilitating intercultural transitional adjustment, some work does point to its value in composing an international staff.' It is likely, though, that training will continue to occupy a prominent place within cross-cultural management in future, encompassing both area briefings and other cognitive techniques, and experiential methods such as role plays, 'look-see visits' and immersion programmes. In such a fast-moving area, cross-cultural training must address new and changing concerns of cross-cultural managers. Scullion and Collings (2006) identify global virtual teams with team members communicating primarily via electronic media as an increasingly important feature within international business. Such teams face issues of communication, relationship-building, managing conflict and leadership. This is just one new area for cross-cultural training to address; the field is nothing if not fast-moving, although there is identified consistency in certain aspects, eg cross-cultural sensitivity where well-established models of cultural difference form the staple academic background.

There are suggestions that cultural differences are manifested in the ways people prefer to learn (Aycan et al 2014; Moran et al 2014) and that the differing preferences in this regard reflect some of the 'classical' dimensions of difference put forward by Hofstede. Moran et al contrast preferred learning processes in Europe and North America where these include dialogue, interaction and idea exchange with that evident in China where learners prefer to work with the data and task. The authors also point to ideal approaches taken by a trainer; for example, in China individual leaders should not be singled out as there is a danger of losing face (see also Chapter 4). In an earlier study, Marquardt and Engel (1993) examined the cross-cultural aspects relationships in training and development. For example, in the Middle East and North Africa, trainers are highly respected and there is a desire for formality; however, trainees will hope for a friendly relationship with the trainer. In North American societies the trainer can act in an informal way and trainees will challenge them, which in itself would not be seen as disrespectful. In Latin America, Marquardt and Engel's finding was that the trainer's personal attributes assumed great importance, with a charismatic style preferred.

Schneider and Barsoux (2003) report interesting findings on the comparative value of different learning and training methods. Kolb (1984) identified different individual preferences which led to people having preferred learning styles. Some individuals, for example, favour active experimentation in which learning involves applying principles through problem-solving and decision-making. This is reminiscent of case study methods of learning, which has been characterised as an American approach. Schneider and Barsoux report that European managers have often reacted negatively to such methods, viewing them as atheoretical. Kolb's classification scheme might suggest a preference for abstract conceptualisation, ie the transposing of observation into sound theories among European managers. It is therefore possible to apply models of cultural difference to actual learning situations (allowing for personality-based differences), with an implication that trainers should be able to adapt their styles of delivery where possible and be sensitive to differences before, during and after training events. One should not only refer to bipolar models when considering the cultural dimension of training and learning. As we saw in the work of Moran et al (2014), in Chinese societies it is important to maintain participants' face, so, for example, feedback should be given in a constructive way, preferably away from a group situation, in order that an individual is not seen to lose face.

Concerns relating to face can also be manifested in performance management. Fenwick (2004) records evidence showing that performance appraisal (a specific aspect of performance management) is perceived differently across cultures – it may be regarded with distrust in certain cultures – and as a result she concludes that appraisal practices probably need adapting in different cultural contexts. Noting that cultural variations in the area encompass both how people should be appraised and by whom, Fenwick identifies the cultural roots of some methods; for example, the relatively widespread usage of multi-rater or 360-degree appraisal in Australia and the USA. It is eminently plausible to go on to link differences in performance appraisal to models of cultural difference and to provide examples from particular countries. Schneider and Barsoux (2003) provide several such examples. They note that in collectivist societies and where there is a preference for 'being' rather than 'doing', the concept of performance appraisal sits uncomfortably with character assessment. Problems in this respect are according to these authors to be found in Asian societies and France.

One has also to assume when setting up a performance management system that goals can accurately be set, achieved through performance and measured. However, in Chapter 2 we saw that one of the core assumptions within the innermost layer of culture dealt with the issue of the degree to which people can ultimately control their environment. If this belief is in doubt, as has been suggested, for example, in Asian societies, the fundamental acceptance of performance management will be called into question. To what extent are such differences likely to endure in a more global interconnected business world? Schneider and Barsoux (2003) give some indication of blurring of cultural distinctions, noting that in India performance appraisal had been welcomed as a new, fresh, meritocratic approach, while one study of Chinese–Western joint ventures showed adoption of performance appraisal mechanisms in China despite doubts and actual initial resistance.

The reality of change in this regard is characteristically complex: it would be wrong to state that Western approaches to performance management are spreading unchecked in an inevitable sweep of progress. Individual features of cultures can take effect in more unpredictable ways, ie not related to the classical models of cultural difference. Schneider and Barsoux (2003) cite as one such example Russian managers reacting against the imposition of objectives within performance management due to their associating these with the preoccupation with target-setting expressed by previous communist regimes. Once more, the lesson for cross-cultural managers is to exercise cultural sensitivity but to be prepared to go beyond prescriptions arising from the standard literature.

The final area within HRM to consider within a cross-cultural perspective is pay and reward. Widely viewed as one of the core areas of HRM, sometimes within the wider area of employee relations, effective reward strategies are seen as key in terms of attracting, retaining and motivating staff, thereby contributing to the enhancement of organisational performance. Pilbeam and Corbridge (2010, p254) note that pay and reward is 'a turbulent area characterised by contextual complexity and tension. Universal reward solutions remain elusive and at best the choice is one of compromise between sometimes competing reward alternatives. For contingency theorists there is no such thing as best practice in reward, only best fit.'

We can pose the question of how and in what ways an awareness of cultural difference can inform managers' choices when devising reward strategies. In Chapter 8 we saw that workers' motivation could be affected by culture in terms of differing personal needs, beliefs and values. At the same time, culture could impact on motivation through societal norms on such items as work ethic and achievement. A third way in which culture could be significant in affecting motivation was via the impact of elements of an individual country's institutional arrangements; for example, its educational system. One important area for consideration when evaluating the likely effectiveness of rewards was the overall level of prosperity within a society: we saw how concepts like self-actualisation and job enrichment had emerged from highly developed economies, in particular the USA, casting doubt on the universal relevance of such terms.

In summary there is considerable evidence suggesting variation between sources and manifestations of motivation in different cultures, so that in Pilbeam and Corbridge's terms culture could arguably be an important contingent factor, which should influence both the initial choice and ultimate success of an organisation's reward strategies. However, at the same time, we also noted in Chapter 8 that there is clear evidence of convergence of practice in remuneration practices; for example, transference of performance-based pay (characterised as endemic to individualist cultures) across the world to new areas like Asia and Latin America. What is the current evidence base concerning links between reward and culture and what lessons can managers draw from the picture which emerges?

Lowe et al (2002) conducted a comparative study of reward practices in ten locations. In a similar vein to the approach taken by the GLOBE study (see Chapter 7), the researchers in this study examined both current practice and obtained the views of participants on 'what should be', ie in an ideal situation, locating disparities between current practices and employee preferences in an attempt to suggest some ways forward for compensation practice. In an introduction to their findings these researchers highlighted some counterintuitive findings emerging from their work, once again pointing to the complexity of this subject area. For example, one might expect there to be a high incidence of group or organisation-wide performance incentives in collectivist societies, but this was found not to be the case in Lowe et al's study. Furthermore, when asked whether such group incentives should form a bigger part of reward practices, respondents from Mexico and Taiwan agreed – which might be expected from our knowledge of Hofstede and Trompenaars' work – but so did those for the USA, which is, for the same reason, a more unexpected finding.

When examining the prevalence of incentive-linked pay, Lowe et al found limited evidence for its implementation worldwide: including in the classic individualist cultures of Australia and the USA. To counterbalance the unusual nature of some findings, a more predictable result arose when respondents were asked whether they would welcome more performance-related pay incentives. It is noticeable that respondents from North America felt that this form of incentive should assume a greater importance than was the case at that time. Perhaps we are seeing here one example of the oft-quoted gap between 'rhetoric and reality' in HRM: at any rate a fuzzy picture emerges from this cross-cultural study in its attempt to capture real-life similarities and differences.

Other writers identify a more direct relationship between culture and employee reward. Schneider and Barsoux (2003) relate fundamental questions contained within the area of compensation and reward to classical dimensions of culture. To take three examples, they conclude that the question of 'who gets what?' varies across cultures depending on the relative preoccupation with equity as opposed to equality, while the degree to which pay links to performance will differ according to whether the society in question has a 'being' or 'doing' orientation. Preferences for financial or non-financial aspects of reward are linked to where the society is placed along a masculine/feminine continuum.

The first two aspects – allocation of reward and association with performance – can for Schneider and Barsoux (2003, p166) be placed firmly within the American context as follows: 'The dominant influence in American managerial thinking is the principle of equity, that individuals are rewarded according to their individual contribution and if not, are prepared to move on. This reveals cultural assumptions of individualism, control over nature and achievement...and the sky is the limit! In fact, there may be no upper limit on salary, which means that star performers could be earning up to 200 percent of their core wage.' Later, in their summary of the links between culture and remuneration, Schneider and Barsoux claim that in Sweden employees are likely to opt for time off from work in preference to a monetary bonus and go on to explain this finding with reference to Hofstede's characterisation of Sweden as a country high on femininity – supposedly manifested in a greater concern with quality of life and, by inference, maintaining a work–life balance (assuming, of course, that one accepts the particular conception of gender differences contained within Hofstede's work).

Schneider and Barsoux recommend that managers need to consider whether HR policies can be successfully transferred across cultures or if, contrastingly, they are unsuitable for the local cultural context (assuming one does not want to change it). They list alienation and poor morale as some potential negative consequences when alien and therefore inappropriate policies and practices are imposed. In the specific area of reward, they identify problems when US-designed policies were either proposed or introduced in countries as diverse as Denmark, Switzerland, Indonesia and Russia. Given the preponderance of American or British writing in the topic of remuneration one should consider not only whether Anglo-American policies align with different cultures but also their probable varying effect and sometime negative consequences when introduced outside Anglo cluster countries. To balance this negative view, we have seen that policies such as pay for performance might be welcomed as desirable innovations in certain societies, with all the predicted benefits in terms of higher levels of motivation that this implies.

Finally, one should acknowledge one remaining factor when considering international and cross-cultural aspects of employee reward. This is the trend towards increasing migration of workers across national borders. This is not a new phenomenon, but at different times specific patterns of migration impact on labour markets – and hence pay and other rewards – to a significant degree. In early 2014, the UK media was preoccupied with a possible influx of workers to the UK from Bulgaria and Romania following the end of transitional controls on free labour movement after those countries' accession to the EU seven years earlier. The debate echoed that on inward migration from other Eastern European states after 2004. The (stereotypical?) figure of the 'Polish plumber' had become lodged in the popular imagination as an industrious figure, willing to work long hours and also highly skilled. It has been suggested that such new workers have had an effect on wage rates in this and similar occupations initially in London and increasingly in provincial cities, prompting a debate on the advantages and disadvantages of this level of labour mobility for the national economies of both the UK and Poland (there are, of course, double-edged arguments to be put forward, depending in part on one's own personal interests). The purpose of inserting this vignette at this point is to remind readers of the economic backdrop to debates on reward and HRM more generally: the power of the global market should not be underestimated in this regard. There is also an interesting potential area of research investigating whether such workers bring and retain their own culturally derived assumptions on the nature of reward into the new culture, over and above the very great differences in rates of pay which drive their mobility.

10.6 THE EFFECT OF CULTURE – A MIXED PICTURE?

There is certainly value in looking for reasons for differences in HRM practices by referring back to traditional models of culture. However, one should be mindful of possible limitations in taking this route, not least if it leads to the false assumption that countries are culturally homogenous. In Chapter 8 we saw evidence of the spread of Western-style individual incentives to other parts of the world, so it is very important to remain alert to changes in practices with some measure of convergence possible. Convergence can occur due to the influence of MNCs as previously outlined and may also be initiated at a political level. Zhu and Warner (2004) trace developments in Vietnam, focusing in particular on the so-called reform period in that country since 1986. From this time onwards, state-owned enterprises (SOEs) have been transformed into new capitalist forms of organisation, with government support. Vietnamese governments have been concerned to set new frameworks for HRM within a changed economic philosophy. Relevant changes have included relinquishing state control over recruitment and selection, and the promulgation of a new employment system based on contract. In the field of reward, there has been a concerted attempt to reform wage systems from that based on tenure to a revised model linking payment with corporate and individual performance.

The Vietnamese example emphasises the importance of macro-level factors on international and comparative HRM, as well as the potentially sudden and far-reaching changes affecting the area. However, Zhu and Warner (2004, p214) also highlight the continuing effect of culture as expressed in norms and values, noting, 'there is a mixed pattern of HRM in Vietnamese enterprises. The influences of cultural traditions as well as political, economic and historical factors are reflected in several dimensions, such as adherence to rules, common values and norms, less individual-oriented pay and harmony. Even FOEs [foreign-owned enterprises] adopt certain localised strategies in order to fit into the social/cultural environment.'

Zhu and Warner's work on Vietnam paints an intriguing picture of both cross-cultural convergence and culturally specific forces in dynamic interplay. Their work provides support for the view that culture as expressed through norms, values and core assumptions, can continue to exert an influence in the HR area. Fang Lee Cooke (2005, 2011) presents evidence concerning trends in work and employment in China since the 1980s and shows how these are both reflected in and shaped by HR initiatives. The data referred to in her study is drawn from official statistics, government reports, media publications, academic research including her own work, and her personal experiences of living and working in the country. As such, this recent evidence provides us with a rich source of data and in-depth analysis, although the author voices her own concerns regarding topicality given the speed of change in Chinese businesses and the economy more generally.

Cooke, in tracing the development of HRM in China, records that the term emerged out of the activities of MNCs through joint ventures and via academic collaborations between Chinese and Western universities. While the term is now well established, the way it is distinguished from personnel management is less clear (this perhaps reflecting earlier semantic debates in the UK). The study goes on to conclude that HRM is becoming more visible in larger, Chinese organisations (the situation was very different in the very important small business sector) as, 'these organizations are beginning to adopt Western practices of HRM, notably in job analysis and description, recruitment and selection, training and development, and performance management and reward' (2005, p191). These involve greater flexibility in the deployment of workers and more extensive use of financial incentives (see also Chapter 8).

Cooke goes on, however, to introduce an important caveat as her research indicates that Chinese managers, while welcoming the advent of Western HR practices in principle, found them difficult to implement in reality. Cooke also warns against uncritical use of such techniques without reference to context and, indeed, critical evaluation in terms of their effectiveness. Nonetheless, Cooke's work lays stress on an increasing convergence of HR strategies in larger organisations.

In the case of private small firms. Cooke also notes similarities across societies concluding (2005, p168) that, 'the findings draw our attention to the fact that there is a high level of similarities between the Chinese small businesses and their counterparts in other countries in terms of their business environment and employment practices and that there may be some generalizable patterns at the international level.' Cooke also notes the trend for many younger Chinese managers to exhibit more individualistic behaviour (see also Ralston et al 1999), many of whom have been trained in Western countries. This trend might also reasonably predict still more HR convergence with Western societies, or at least attempts in that direction. Coupled with Needle's (2010) observation that Chinese business has been strongly influenced by the experience of engaging in international joint ventures, Cooke's research in China indicates the emergence of a 'Westernised' HR model in one of the key players in the twenty-first-century global economy.

INDIVIDUAL ACTIVITY 10.2

Present evidence to indicate the extent to which Chinese cultural values are seen to influence HRM strategies, policies and practices in that country. At the same time gather evidence showing convergence of Chinese HR along the Anglo-American model.

Which evidence appears to be more compelling to you and why?

Are the two underlying propositions of cultural specificity and convergence reconcilable?

Give reasons for your conclusions.

REVIEW QUESTIONS

1   What is the 'life-cycle' approach to understanding the internationalisation of HRM? Provide one academic model and one example from actual practice to illustrate your answer.

2   Identify three ways in which recruitment and selection practices can differ between countries and account for these differences.

3   Choose any one country and assess the embeddedness and diffusability of characteristic policy and practice in any one area of HRM.

FURTHER READING

BREWSTER, C., SPARROW, P., VERNON, G. and HOULDSWORTH, E. (2011) *International human resource management.* 3rd ed. London: CIPD. The authors provide an overview of current theory and practice in IHRM, together with a discussion of new developments in the area.

ILES, P. and ZHANG, C. (2013) *International human resource management: a cross-cultural and comparative approach.* London: CIPD. This book includes a range of valuable contributions on issues surrounding comparative HRM and also a summary of the context influencing HRM in selected countries and regions.

Visit this book's companion website (**www.cipd.co.uk/olr**) to find further exercises including self-assessment questions and also weblinks to media and academic journal articles.

LOOKING TO THE FUTURE

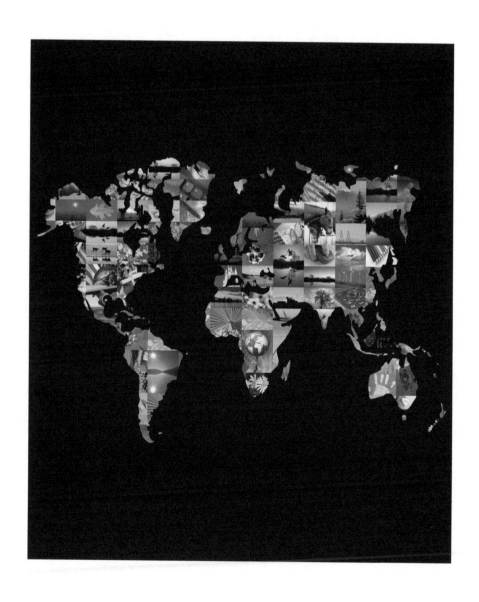

Conclusions

11.1 COMPARING CULTURES – ENDURING EVIDENCE

Culture matters. In Part 1 of this book, we saw how people's divergent values and meanings have led to cultural differences – although there is much that we have common too as human beings. It is certainly the case that identified dimensions of culture purport to focus on fundamental life questions so profound that one could reasonably surmise that they are they common to all people, hence universal, and also largely unchanging.

In Chapter 3, for example, we saw how the pioneering work of Kluckhohn and Strodtbeck (1961) had influenced the contributions of later writers on culture, including in the business and management area the pivotal work of Geert Hofstede. It is worthwhile reiterating the essential nature of Kluckhohn and Strodtbeck's dimensions of culture, based on underlying problem areas which, the authors claimed, were faced by all societies. One dimension centred on attitudes towards nature, the key question here being whether people saw themselves as subjugated by nature, merely content to maintain a harmonious balance with it, or able to go further by exercising mastery over nature. Rapp et al (2011) find that this dimension of culture, characterised by Hofstede as undertainty avoidance, continues to underpin business research. These writers note (p6) that there is 'continuing influence of Hofstede's uncertainty avoidance (UA) construct on international research. His initial work has engendered a significant stream of research that has examined cultural difference in a variety of disciplines...it is used in a variety of ways: as a means for definition, as a construct for measurement, and as a basis for the development of additional instruments.'

Another of Kluckhohn and Strodtbeck's universal problem areas related to human relationships. In this category they contrasted views stressing individual independence and responsibility, with those emphasising more family or group or hierarchically dominated perspectives on the nature of relationships. McFarlin and Sweeney (2013) locate this basic dichotomy in Hofstede's 'I' dimension and Trompenaars and Hampden-Turner's distinction between individualist and communitarian societies. We saw in several chapters how differences in this regard could be profound, as exemplified by Chinese *guanxi*, viewed as a central tenet of business by an increasingly influential population.

In summary, existing models of culture have dealt with some of the most basic and important areas of human existence and sought to compare societies in these terms, both in general terms and, more specifically, in the business domain. Such philosophically oriented material underpins much of the writing on cross-cultural management, and one could anticipate that findings emerging from methodologically sound research studies in the field should be relevant, accurate and enduring. In this book corroboration for the theoretical insights of Hofstede and other traditional writers has been found in the areas of leadership (GLOBE study), motivation (Broeways and Price 2011) and organisation structure (Aycan et al 2014); see also Lasserre (2012) for a more general application to the cultural background of potential international business partners. While it should be noted that when examining actual research one can find both counter-intuitive findings (ie opposed to what might be expected from a reading of the standard literature) and country-specific factors which fall outside the predetermined dimensions, there is evidence that the tradition of cross-cultural analysis stretching from Kluckhohn and Strodtbeck through Hall, Hofstede, Schwartz, and Trompenaars and Hampden-Turner continues to capture meaningful cultural differences in a reliable and valid way.

Another aspect of culture that should be stressed is the notion that it must be understood as comprising distinct layers. As discussed in earlier chapters, the outer layer or strata consists of explicit observable differences, either in individuals' behaviour, or in cultural artefacts. As we saw in Chapter 9 in our discussion of culture shock, it is important to recognise and deal with these surface-level features. This is followed by a second, deeper layer comprising norms or guidelines on appropriate behaviour. These norms in turn emerge from the core layer of culture, which is made up of the deeply embedded values and implicit assumptions embraced by individuals and transmitted across generations through processes of socialisation (it is also possible to locate values and assumptions in two separate layers). The work of Hall (1976), which identified differences in the context of communication, also promotes a deep view of culture in which fundamental beliefs influence people's perception of the world.

Much of the work exploring the nature of culture within the cross-cultural management literature lays down frameworks of culture which allow comparisons between cultures along core (universal) dimensions, based on societies' underlying values and assumptions. To what extent does this tradition within cross-cultural study continue to bring forward meaningful data that can usefully inform the work of cross-cultural managers in the twenty-first century?

The conclusion at this point is that cross-cultural managers should possess a good knowledge of work within this tradition as a basis for informing their view of culture and cultural difference as these impact on real-life work situations. The most influential writer on culture, Geert Hofstede, in his 2001 revision of his major text on the subject, re-emphasised the importance of five core value dimensions to an explanation of cultural difference. While adding new countries to his working database and recalculating societies' scores on the five (now six) dimensions, Hofstede has retained the dimensions themselves within his framework, noting (p455) that evidence points to, 'no international convergence of cultural values over time, except towards increased individualism for countries having become richer.' He goes on to claim (p455) that, 'value differences between nations described by authors centuries ago are still present today, in spite of continued close contacts. For the next hundred years, countries will remain culturally very diverse.' If we accept this finding, then the culturalist school of thought within business and organisation studies will most definitely maintain a key role, particularly as it provides a welcome counterpoint to the proliferation of supposedly universally applicable business and management solutions, which often turn out to be far from helpful in reality. An awareness of culture as a factor within business can at the very least lead to an explicit engagement with the topic – many business and management models and theories appear to be culture-blind, their authors seemingly unaware that their ideas have emerged in a particular time and place.

In as much as cross-cultural management theory deals with fundamentally important issues linked to core human values, it is unsurprising that the relevance of some models extends beyond the study of work organisations *per se*. There is ongoing scope for application to wider areas. To take one example, a report from the Center for Global Development (CGD) published in 2013 compiled a list of the 27 richest nations, ranking them according to how they improved lives in developing countries. Measures of their contribution in this regard included policies on trade, investment, migration and environmental protection, as well as direct aid. Four out of the top five countries ranked pro rata to their populations were: the Netherlands, Denmark, Sweden and Norway (the other was Luxembourg). The first group of countries mentioned, as we know, formed part of the small group of nations scoring highly on Hofstede's femininity index, which is associated with a concern with nurturing and the quality of life. There are other possible explanations for the prominence of these countries in the CGD listing, but the finding is strikingly reminiscent of Hofstede's work and suggests that his concept of culture, as understood with reference to distinctive dimensions and clusters, can be used outside the confines of managing people within work organisations.

INDIVIDUAL ACTIVITY 11.1

Read one of Hofstede's original contributions to the study of culture, business and management (for example those published in 2001, 2010 or 2014; see the References section of this book). We often rely on summaries of original work (and sometimes on summaries of summaries) when evaluating concepts and models within business and management studies. The core messages from the original author can be misinterpreted in the course of this process, or even lost altogether, and there is no substitute for looking at source material. Read Hofstede's work; appreciate its ambitious scope, and make up your own mind on its essential validity and applicability within the field of cross-cultural management.

11.2 CULTURAL VALUES – SOME FURTHER CONSIDERATIONS

To concur with the generic view that values-based differences between societies remain crucially important to an explanation of business processes and practices does not mean that all aspects of mainstream theories promoting this approach need be accepted uncritically. There are several specific conclusions – or assumptions – within such models which are worthy of further scrutiny at this point.

The focus on national culture first highlighted in Chapter 2 has by definition restricted the scope for comparison between other social groups (see also Patel 2014). The work of Hofstede, which underpins many subsequent studies, is particularly noteworthy in this regard. Hofstede (2001) recognised the limitations imposed by his essentially national focus, noting that while his dimensions of culture could also be applied to regional and ethnic cultures, and that his power distance (PD) measure could be used to differentiate occupations, the dimensions would not ultimately be suitable for making comparisons on the bases of gender, generation, social class and organisational culture. As we have seen, Trompenaars and Hampden-Turner do posit a link between national and organisational culture, finding that the latter is partly shaped by cultural preferences of leaders and other employees. However, once again their focus on national culture as an explanatory factor obscures the potential impact of other variables such as values and attitudes associated with socio-economic class (as defined by identifiable groups of people with shared characteristics in terms of wealth, lifestyle, status and power).

It is, of course, the contention of cultural theorists that national culture is the most meaningful determinant of attitudes, norms and ultimately behaviour. Yet a thorough reading of the main researchers into culture reveals that they do recognise the impact that other social factors could have on people's values. For example, Hofstede (2001) noted that people's social class would be a more important influence on their values than the organisational culture they were exposed to as an employee, since the former would impact on them early in life, as opposed to organisational culture which, because it took effect in adult life, would typically be less influential and impinge at the level of practices rather than deeply embedded values. Hofstede goes on to conduct an analysis of class-based differences between societies as a precursor to his PD dimension, so class is undoubtedly a factor within his overall academic stance, although the overall focus, as set out in earlier chapters, is on national cultural differences, as manifested in collective mental programming.

It is open to future researchers to attempt to highlight the place of social factors such as class within the overriding topic of culture and to assess in greater detail and depth whether class is a concomitant of culture, or alternatively if the reverse is true, or thirdly to identify any symbiotic relationship between the two entities.

A related point concerns the need to recognise the extent to which culture is dominant within cultural analysis. This may seem an odd point to make at this stage – one might think it self-evident that culture is overwhelmingly important within the classic work on the topic. However, one flaw within some earlier cross-cultural management literature is to summarise what are admittedly key cultural differences identified within existing models and frameworks without recording the caveats expressed by writers in their original work regarding the limits of culture's influence.

Once again, Hofstede's contribution provides us with an excellent example. In the 2001 revised version of his major work *Culture's Consequences*, Hofstede reviews the research material which formed the raw data for his original influential work. When reviewing a 1970 survey seeking to isolate a number of criterion variables influencing preferred manager behaviour, together with a range of attitudinal statements, Hofstede (2001, p50) records that, 'The fact that the nationality of the respondents, and sometimes the other criterion variables occupation, gender and age, affected the scores of these questions highly significantly does not mean, of course, that a respondent's answer was fully predictable from his or her nationality or any other identification. In fact, of the total variance in the answers of the 3,220 respondents in the variance analyses, only 4.2% was accounted for by their belonging to one of the ten nationalities in the sample. This, however, was 16 times as much as could be expected on the basis of pure chance.'

This illuminating point within Hofstede's analysis of culture shows his measured approach to the effect of culture and should be clearly taken on board by aspiring or actual cross-cultural managers. Another important, but often neglected, point is Hofstede's recognition that human programming takes place at an individual as well as a collective cultural level, with wide variations noted between individuals raised in very similar contexts – these accounting for uniqueness in personality and capabilities. Other human characteristics such as aggression formed part of a third universal set of factors.

There are two important conclusions to be drawn from a close reading of Hofstede's original work (as opposed to a bullet-point summary of his conclusions). Firstly, even the archetypal culturalist writer gives credence to the influence of non-cultural factors on human affairs, so maybe what is now needed is a revised cultural approach which allows a significant role for non-cultural explanations. Secondly, because few summaries of Hofstede's work go into any significant depth in terms of analysing his epistemological stance, one is reminded of the irreplaceable value of reading the original source material (see Individual activity 11.1). Overall, it is credible to state that national culture has been seen to exercise a potentially important influence upon individual members' values and attitudes. It is only one factor, however; albeit a key one, as depicted consistently in research studies. At the same time, one should also take a measured approach when considering the effect that culture has on business organisations in terms of their chosen *modi operandi*. Just as culture is one element among many to make up an individual person's characteristics, so organisations face a range of pressures from many different sources when selecting strategies, policies and practices. The cultural context(s) they operate in constitute only one factor influencing their chosen strategies, policies and practices. This point is addressed again later in the chapter.

It is also appropriate to remind readers of the less than direct link between a person's values, attitudes and behaviour. Social science tends to distinguish between cognitive, affective and behavioural components of attitudes. Ajzen and Fishbein (2000) show how the propensity to actually behave in a particular way is affected by attitudes towards that behaviour, subjective norms (social pressure to behave – or not – in a particular way) and perceived behavioural control (the relative ease or difficulty in behaving in the intended way). Because levels of behavioural control are not constant in all situations, attitudes and norms can only ever play some part in predicting behaviour.

In reviewing Ajzen and Fishbein's work, Buelens et al (2006, p100) state, 'The relative importance of attitudes, subjective norms and perceived behavioural control is expected to vary across situations and actions. For instance, sometimes only attitudes will have a significant impact on intentions, while in another situation two or all three determinants make independent contributions.' Once again Hofstede, the main proponent of the view that culture is made up of values and attitudes, is aware of the complex linkages involved, claiming (2001, p12), 'That value change has to precede behaviour change is an idealistic assumption that neglects the contribution of the situation to actual behaviour.' Moreover, any view of cultural classifications based on values, norms and attitudes is open to criticisms that the practical consequences resulting from actual behaviour are neglected within such a theoretical scheme. Hofstede (2001, p462) concludes that his own work's primary asset lies in the provision of a broad conceptual framework, and in making a plea for further research, expresses his wish that, 'most important, the consequences for organisational, national and international policy of a better insight into dimensions of national culture should be elaborated. My theory of cultural differentiation is like a product of the research laboratory which awaits the efforts of the development technicians to elaborate it into something of practical use.' This remarkably modest comment, given the quality and scope of Hofstede's work, nonetheless points to a need for future models of culture which derive from real situations experienced in day-to-day business life.

In Chapter 4 the cultural standards model put forward by Fink et al (2005) was examined as an interesting new approach that could illuminate cultural difference and inform future intercultural encounters. The model is predicated on the identification of cultural standards drawn from the past experiences of managers which were then interpreted by 'cultural experts'. Fink et al developed this approach in part as a reaction against the dominant view of culture based on values and anticipated behaviour. They note (p9) that, 'Value dimensions do not directly predict the actual problems emerging in business and management encounters. They do not explain how business encounters are perceived and how and why managers and staff react in a specific way. Guided by values, these reactions are chosen from the available repertoire of behaviours, but ill chosen modes of behaviour may produce undesired conflict and counter-productive results, if the valid norms of behaviour of counterpart cultures are not considered.' This practical orientation may well be characteristic of emerging approaches to the study of culture within business, and signifies something of a move away from the existing values-based approach which has constituted the orthodox school of thought since the 1950s.

11.3 MACRO-SOCIAL MANIFESTATIONS OF CULTURE

The values or meanings-based approach to culture has taken the individual psychological level as its main arena for study. Throughout this book I have pointed to the existence of an alternative perspective which locates differences between societies at the macro or institutional level. Although at first sight these are seemingly discrete approaches, it would, however, be wrong to regard them as irreconcilable views on the topic.

Sorge (2004) provides a clear summary of the ways in which the institutionalist approach contrasts with the culturalist view. He gives the example of how the institutionalist perspective explains the distinctive facets of Japanese business life, noting that this approach minimises the role of individual mental programmes and socialisation. Rather, Sorge (p122) claims that proponents of the institutional view would instead, 'argue that the specificity of Japanese practices resides in a different construction of professional careers, labour markets (lifelong employment), payment systems, industrial relations, etc. They would argue that if Europeans and Americans were to be transplanted into a Japanese-type context, they would reproduce or generate the same organisational patterns. The outcome would have to be traced back to the institutionalised rules of the game. Such proponents would also point to instances where Japanese-type management and organisational practices have been transplanted successfully to other countries.'

In this book macro-level institutional factors have been seen to intervene in important ways in terms of organisational structure (Chapter 5) and HRM strategies and practices (Chapter 10). The conclusion is that an exclusive preoccupation with the values and norms of individuals is unlikely to capture the essence of international differences in the business arena, because these can manifestly also be located in existing organisational and societal structures. In part, the different aspects of culture (values and institutions) are more or less associated with diverse areas of cross-cultural management, so in this sense the two approaches can be regarded as complementary. For example, in Chapter 6 we saw that an awareness of deep underlying values, possibly manifested in individual behaviour, would be very important when engaging in the area of intercultural communication. On the other hand, a business setting up in a new country might look for the effects of culture within institutional arrangements when formulating policy on employee training and development. In academic terms we saw in Chapter 10 how the two trends within the topic of cross-cultural business – culturalist and institutionalist – could also be regarded as complementary rather than competing. This reciprocal logic works if we conceive institutions and structures as the creation of 'mentally programmed' actors which in any case only exist in that they are given (culturally grounded) meaning by individuals and groups. This essential idea was further developed by Giddens in his notion of 'structuration' (see Chapter 2 for a fuller discussion).

Once again, a thorough reading of Hofstede's work reveals that even the arch-exponent of the values approach to culture was also aware of more macro concerns. It is sometimes overlooked that the sub-title of his work *Culture's Consequences* refers to 'values, behaviours, institutions and organisations'. Hofstede (2001, p20) argues that, 'Societal norms shape institutions (family, education systems, politics, legislation), which in turn reinforce the societal norms. They are the chicken and the egg. Institutions reflect minds, and vice versa.' Hofstede concludes as a result that the institutions-versus-culture dilemma is a non-issue.

APPLYING THEORY TO PRACTICE 11.1

Capping bankers' bonuses in Europe: a difference of opinion

In January 2014 the EU enacted a cap on highly paid bank executives' bonuses. Under a new directive, EU banks were restricted from paying more than one year's salary as a bonus without shareholder approval. The measure quickly brought out very major differences of opinion between member states. An article in the German magazine *Der Spiegel* anticipated British opposition when the measure was in planning: 'The City of London is the heart of the European financial industry, and the British are willing to resort to every shady trick possible to ensure that it remains that way...The British said they could agree to a compensation cap if the principle of regionalism were respected. This meant that the foreign subsidiaries of European banks would be able to continue setting their bonuses as they see fit. The other Europeans, quickly realising this as a potential recipe for abuse, rejected the British proposal' (Hesse and Pauly 2013).

As anticipated, there was indeed bitter opposition to the bonus cap from the British Government and London Mayor, Boris Johnson. Johnson was quoted as saying the EU proposals were, 'a vengeful and self-defeating attempt to pick on London. We don't try to cap the pay of oil executives or football players...this is an attempt to knock London off its perch and we're not going to let it happen. I hope Brussels will think again. It's not just hostile to the greatest financial centre on earth. It's hostile to growth across the EU. If this did succeed, people would just head off to New York or Singapore' (Aldrick 2013).

It is tempting to attribute such differences to cultural factors. We have seen that Anglo cultures exhibit far greater levels of individualism than those of mainland Europe. So it may be that the attitudes expressed by Boris Johnson on individual bonus payments reflect these culturally held preferences. However, what is also crucially important in this regard are the macro-economic conditions of the countries concerned. The UK's financial sector, particularly evident in the City of London, has become a key part of the overall economy, given its sheer size. Concerns have been expressed that London would lose its competitive edge if lower bonus payments resulted in employees moving elsewhere. Once again we see that cultural attitudes held by individuals converge with institutional factors in explaining real events.

11.4 NEW APPROACHES TO UNDERSTANDING CULTURE

In Chapter 4 we noted some emerging approaches to the analysis of culture within the field of cross-cultural management. These included a renewed interest in the emic approach to culture, which advocates viewing cultures in terms of their own distinctive essences, and in particular, through the meanings and definitions of their own members. Fang (2012) saw practical benefit in adopting an emic approach, claiming that it was only by attempting to understand a culture (in his analysis, China) from the inside, as opposed to placing it on a comparative scale, that one could comprehend its true nature. This insight, if correct, has considerable significance for existing or aspirant cross-cultural managers, suggesting that a good deal of the existing literature comparing cultures is limited in scope and practical application. It should be stated at this point that a single-culture focus should concentrate on all levels of that culture, not just surface-level etiquette as found in some 'airport-style' guides, if it is to result in the deep understanding which is a potential advantage of taking this approach.

The emic approach to culture has some existing proponents. D'Iribarne's 1997 study, very much within this tradition, is analysed in depth in Chapter 4. What is more striking in terms of the development of this approach is a nascent view, as expressed by Fang, that bipolar classifications of cultures – strongly associated with many etic models of culture – are in essence spurious. Fang's conclusion set out in Chapter 4 is that the *yin-yang* philosophy, emphasising a holistic and harmonious view of mankind, cannot be reconciled to a conception of culture which categorises societies in 'either/or' terms – individualistic or collectivist, etc. If we accept this premise, then a more inclusive perspective which sees emic and etic approaches as complementary is not possible; they must rather be mutually exclusive, given that one is fundamentally flawed. This runs counter to Hofstede's (2001, p26) conclusion that quantitative and qualitiative and etic and emic studies, 'represent two sides of the same coin, two ways of finding out about the same reality: they are both equally necessary and complementary'. What can be said in conclusion is that readers should at least be aware of work from both approaches as set out in this book, and always recognise the philosophical underpinnings of new contributions to the field of cross-cultural management that will most certainly emerge in the future.

Holden (2002) also expresses a clear view that models of culture which centre on comparison and difference do not help those involved in cross-cultural management roles, whose role it should be (p293) to, 'give direction to the cross-cultural activities of people and facilitate their interactions to achieve organisational goals.' Holden's view is that culture as exhibited in patterns of meaning is open to constant reproduction, so that the boundaries between culture will come and go. He categorises the majority of previous writers in the field (including Hofstede and Trompenaars) as viewing culture – composed essentially of core values – as being broadly stable and internally consistent. Holden criticises this approach as limited. He concurs with its validity in terms of categorising systems, but questions its ability to explain the ways that people from different cultures habitually interact ('clash and fuse'; see Chapter 4) with each other in the current business context.

Holden concludes his overview of the traditional view of culture which highlights sets of values and norms, by accusing it of over-emphasising difference and encouraging a ranking of cultures. This contribution is interesting in that it points to changes in organisational functioning in the twenty-first century, together with an altered role for cross-cultural managers, which need revised models of culture to adequately explain them.

Magala (2005) proposes that culture can usefully be viewed as a language in which meanings are transmitted and assumptons maintained. Holden (2008) and Holden and Tansley (2008) show how language is used to create and sustain meaning and can also – as in the case of Russia – constrain development, leading to new sub-languages developing in order to encapsulate business terminology. In summary, language is re-emerging as an area of study in cross-cultural management and will very likely inform new thinking in this area over the next decade.

In earlier chapters I have sought to address the subject of gender within cross-cultural management. In reviewing existing work in the area, the conclusion must be that gender has been relatively neglected in most previous research. In many cases gender is not explicitly referred to, or is sidelined due to models having been derived from overwhelmingly male research samples. One exception is found in the work of Hofstede (2001), who incorporated notions of masculinity and femininity in his analysis of culture within one self-standing dimension of cultural difference. This dimension has formed the basis for further studies applying Hofstede's work, with support found for his conclusion that gender-based differences do impact on national culture. Alves et al (2006) provide a recent example in their study of cross-cultural aspects of self-leadership. This research team concluded that femininity (in cross-cultural terms) was associated with values which promoted social relations and non-rational processes.

Support for Hofstede's masculinity/femininity distinction can, however, be set alongside a questioning of the assumptions which underpin it. Close reading of Hofstede's work reveals statements that are at the very least open to heated debate – as, for example, his conclusions on sexual norms and behaviour (p327) that, 'in masculine cultures, sex is more often experienced as performance; in feminine cultures, it is experienced as a way of relating'. Apart from Hofstede's potentially controversial incorporation of gender within his overall model, most attention to gender-based issues has been paid when analysing trends in the international division of labour (see, for example, the studies referred to in Chapter 9). The picture which emerges from research in this area (see, for example, Harris 2004 and Linehan 2005) indicates that acceptance of female representation in the cross-cultural management *cadre* is very much dependent on perceptions within the home organisation, and that assumptions regarding the role of the sexes within societies may be outdated.

The increasing feminisation of cross-cultural management may be a valid focus of future research because there is evidence that there is a changing context in this regard. Smith (2006), writing in *The Observer*, reports on increasing numbers of women taking on 'high-profile national roles in finance and commerce throughout the Arab world', and highlights 'the headway females are gradually making across the 22-nation Arab world'. Changing patterns of employment (underpinned by changing norms and values), together with the previously mentioned acceleration of interest in diversity, suggest that future work on cross-cultural management must incorporate a reinvigorated preoccupation with gender if it is to inform managers of the future.

11.5 CROSS-CULTURAL MANAGEMENT IN 'NEW' FORMS OF ORGANISATION

Throughout this book I have sought to locate academic contributions to cross-cultural management in time and space. In Chapter 1 we saw how many of the key insights underpinning theories were obtained from the late 1960s to the early 1990s. It can be questioned, therefore (see Jackson and Aycan 2006 and Holden 2008), whether research data based on the staple theories can be usefully applied to current work organisations, particularly in the light of the very rapid changes that have typically affected them in more recent decades. While the overall conclusion in this book is that central assumptions of cultural difference based on values traced back to the work of Kluckhohn and Strodtbeck are still valid, there is a growing need for cross-cultural management study to focus more explicitly on topical and changing aspects of organisational life. The following two areas are highlighted in this context; these, it should be stressed, form only a small proportion of an inevitably infinite list of changing trends.

11.5.1 FLEXIBLE STRATEGIES AND STRUCTURES

Kanter (2001 and 2009) is prominent among management writers who point to new challenges faced by organisations (and cities, regions and countries), especially challenges driven by globalisation and technological advance. She also analyses the more or less successful moves that organisations frequently make in order to confront and overcome them. These include increasing utilisation of what she terms 'horizontal ties', which involve organisations buying in services that were previously provided in-house (the classical 'make or buy' dilemma) and the formation of strategic alliances with suppliers and customers. This trend has resulted in both an increasing volume of inter-organisational relationships and a concern with the quality and effectiveness of such relationships.

In Chapter 5, we saw how inter-organisational arrangements could operate on a cross-cultural level with many forms of collaborative venture possible which fell short of the original partner establishing a full-time presence in another country. Such new forms of organisation are heavily dependent on mutual trust (see Powell 1990 for an analysis of how network forms of organisation require reciprocity), made up of perceptions of indebtedness and obligation in order to function effectively. For Powell, creating long-term commitment could result in the establishment of mutual interest and goodwill, so building up trust would be preferable to any attempt to enforce it. In Chapter 5 it was suggested that the increasing prevalence of inter-organisational networking across national boundaries was likely to result in additional cross-cultural studies focusing on the critically important topic of establishing and sustaining trust.

Fulop (2009) provides an exploration of the possible dynamics of cross-cultural networking. She suggests that the contribution of Hall, referred to at length in Chapter 3, could help in understanding cross-cultural interactions between organisations and their representatives. She notes that previous work (Fulop and Richards 2002; Child 1998) indicated that in high-context societies, as found, for example, in Asia, reliance on legal agreements will not guarantee trust which, within Hall's framework, is instead based on deep personal ties built up over a longer period through relationships. Fulop and Richards also concluded that the extent to which people trusted others would itself vary across cultures. These authors cite Shane (1993), who found that societies classified as high in PD and UA in Hofstede's terms were less likely to trust people from another group. Fulop and Richards also find confirmation of the cross-cultural variability of trust in Trompenaars and Hampden-Turner's classification scheme, showing how within particularist cultures, trust is ultimately gained through sustaining longer-term relationships in the business context. These findings are interesting in that they point to the enduring validity of established models of culture while transferring their findings to contemporary business concerns, in this case inter-organisational networking.

It is also illuminating to note an application of the emic tradition of culture in Child's (1998) study examining aspects of trust in China, with the conclusion that specific features of Chinese society – once more, *guanxi* proved to be important – influenced the strategies adopted by foreign companies when seeking to build up trust. Child offers practical alternatives to organisations when considering trust in the Chinese context; namely, either to adopt a low-trust strategy in which 'Western standards' are imposed by formal means, or to take a high-trust approach achieved by employing host-country citizens to deal with local officials and government bodies. Third-party intermediaries could also be used, although they have to be very carefully chosen if trust is to be maintained. The purpose of summarising Child's findings is to give a flavour of the topical and practically focused nature of his work. It is probable that other future work in the field of cross-cultural management will take the same approach, applying well-established models of culture within an emerging area of interest with a view to providing findings of genuine value to managers. Nonetheless, Fulop (2009) notes that Child's research is still culture-bound in that he uses a typical Western typology to explain what are inherently cross-cultural processes.

11.5.2 VIRTUAL ORGANISATIONS

Virtual organisations are set up on the basis of networked information communication technologies. To some extent the use of such technologies can lead to a diminution of face-to-face working relationships and their replacement by communication through electronic computer-based media. The extent of resultant virtual working varies from allowing work to be carried out while travelling to and from the employing organisation's premises, thus eliminating 'deadtime', through other forms of remote working such as teleworking, culminating in the possible wholesale abandonment of permanent physical locations and consequent creation of networks of dispersed individuals who then constitute the organisation (Huczynski and Buchanan 2013). There is also evidence that developments in information technology have resulted in more workers' redefining their relationship with organisations; for example, acting as self-employed suppliers of services rather than employees.

There has been some questioning of the extent to which such changes are inevitable. Grey (2013, p104), for example, records that, 'we must be wary of the extravagant, generalized claims of those who proclaim a new and unprecedented era of change within which organizations exist and to which they must respond.' However, ever more sophisticated communication technologies leading to the creation of virtual organisations have the potential to radically alter the character of cross-cultural interaction.

Electronic communication technologies have already contributed to the intensification of cross-cultural communication. The advent of email has enabled parties to communicate with each other 24/7, although not necessarily simultaneously. The medium is regarded as especially useful in allowing relatively swift communication across different time zones. Email is, by definition, an impersonal medium, so it is difficult to gauge reactions to messages in the absence of non-verbal communication cues in this asynchronous mode. This should not imply that cross-cultural sensitivity (see Chapters 6 and 9) becomes less important; the opposite may be the case. However, cross- or inter-cultural encounters change their character when electronic communication media are used: they are more impersonal, but culturally based differences as exhibited in reactions to messages will still manifest themselves. There is scope for further work to assist cross-cultural managers in decoding cultural signals from others even when one cannot see the people in question.

Although such a concern is not new – telephone conversations or fax communications contain the same essential problem – the rapid growth of electronic communication in cross-cultural encounters provides a good example of the need for the subject area to redefine principles within a changing twenty-first-century business environment. It is possible that virtual encounters will assume an even greater importance within international business if levels of international travel decrease in response to terrorist attacks on transport systems, although at the time of writing it was unclear whether concerns in this regard would consolidate into a significant and long-lasting trend. More significant still could be a preoccupation with climate change, which can also impact on people's views on international travel and ultimately feed through to their actual behaviour.

There is evidence indicating that cultural differences can take effect in interesting ways within virtual settings and encounters. Warschauer (1996) compared face-to-face and electronic communication patterns between Asian students enrolled in an American college. Although the Filipino sample in the study participated most actively in the standard classroom situation, Japanese students (who were less communicative in the classroom) became the most active participants when communicating online. Liang and McQueen (1999) compared reactions to computer-assisted learning methods between Asian and Western students, noting that the Western sample welcomed the interactive style of email communication more than their Asian counterparts. Kim and Bonk (2002) compared communication behaviours between Finnish, Korean and US students. These researchers concluded that there were noticeable and significant differences in levels of participation in collaborative encounters. American and Finnish students were far more task-focused when engaged in web-based conferencing, whereas the Korean students exhibited greater social interaction behaviour – in other words, they were more likely to share their personal feelings while communicating via this medium. Kim and Bonk make a persuasive case in linking this behaviour to Hall's (1976) classification between low- and high-context styles of communication. The high-context style, which Hall claimed would be characteristic of Asian cultures, came through strongly in this new form of communication, pointing to the enduring nature of Hall's distinction.

Kim and Bonk's work provides another example of future-oriented research which is both academically well grounded (showing the continuing relevance of a classical model of culture) and helpful to anyone operating in the quickly changing cross-cultural business world. One hopes that this topical, rigorous yet practical approach will be followed by other new studies in this and parallel subject areas.

11.6 DIVERSITY AND SYNERGY – THE FUTURE OF CROSS-CULTURAL MANAGEMENT

In Chapters 4 and 9 we saw that recent contributors to the field of cross-cultural management have sought to orient the discipline away from a concern with identifying cultural difference to focus more on ways to enhance cross-cultural interactions. Crucial in this respect are endeavours to eliminate intercultural communication barriers and to achieve synergy. It has been argued (Holden 2002) that existing literature in the subject area has itself played a part in exacerbating cultural separation through the identification of differences along value dimensions (this was not, it should be stressed, the intention of earlier writers). Holden claims that models of culture which view the concept as essence (ie something stable possessed by a society or organisation) are ill-equipped to explain what he sees as complex overlapping social networks which link people within the current business world. The same author notes (p59) that, 'the identified terrain of the management of multiple, networked cultures is awesome, complicated, subject to change and massively overlaid with technology. This is the new heartland of cross-cultural management, both as an operating domain and as a conceptual field for which the practitioners need new competencies and the academics need to develop more conceptual tools.'

This overview of the state of cross-cultural management at that time viewed it as an emerging area, responding to profound change within the business sphere – in particular, the emergence of diversity as a concept that can be used as a competitive differentiator. However, a new role for cross-cultural management centring on breaking down barriers and allowing new ways of approaching issues to create effective business solutions might usefully be supported by a developing academic paradigm which preserves the most enduring insights of existing models and theories, while applying them to situations that require collaborative working between diverse groups.

Throughout this book I have also stressed that cross-cultural management theory should be applicable at the level of individual workplaces – not just across national boundaries – given the increasingly multicultural workforces found within countries across parts of the world.

What are some of the other competencies and qualities needed by a successful cross-cultural manager, beyond an ability to foster synergy? One can argue, firstly, that such a manager should be aware of the contested nature of the term itself. He or she should also posssess an up-to-date knowledge of theory and research in the field and be aware of emerging work, which at the very least seeks to qualify the conclusions of much prior work in the area since 1980. It is also important to be able to apply concepts and models, locating where and how culture and cultural difference plays out in the setting of work organisations. We have also seen that cross-cultural management is a potentially stressful activity and have argued that managers would benefit from an ability not just to recognise difference but also to be comfortable with it; in other words, reconciling very different views of the world while still being able to function without incurring psychological damage. In recent years, there has indeed been a preoccupation with coping with stress as a means to understanding culture itself (see Tweed et al 2004).

If it is important to recognise the sources and nature of cultural differences, this should be balanced with an appreciation of more general principles of managing people. In Chapter 9 we noted the work of Martin et al (2001), who identified principles of humanness, which emphasised peace, respect and empathy, dialogic with its preoccupation with mutual support and equality and, finally, speaking with and to. It is often necessary to manage people in different ways in order to both meet subordinates' expectations and ensure effectiveness. However, the aforementioned principles can serve as guidelines for fair and ethical treatment of all employees within a multicultural work environment.

In recent years the concept of cultural intelligence (CQ) (see Chapter 9 for a fuller explanation of the term) has offered a framework for assessing our own competence and improving performance. The components of CQ (knowledge about other cultures; skills such as open-mindedness and metacognition; the ability to rise above a specific situation and keep a hold on emotion) offer a unified model that consolidates existing thinking in the area and can predict success in cross-cultural working (Aycan et al 2014).

11.7 NON-MANAGERIAL APPROACHES

Much of the work within the cross-cultural management canon, wholly unsurprisingly, approaches the subject from a managerial point of view. It is useful to recognise this point if for no other reason than that it is often assumed and unstated within existing cross-cultural texts. The underlying rationale of such managerial approaches is based on gaining knowledge and know-how intended to enhance the effective management of work organisations. Within business and organisation studies more generally, there is an established countervailing tradition of critical management studies whose proponents focus on the deconstruction of ideological assumptions inherent in the discipline of management, particularly those relating to the priority goals of organisations. This tradition is relatively underrepresented within the field of cross-cultural management studies.

Readers interested in cross-cultural analyses which also contain wider ideological concerns may wish to refer to Magala (2005), who takes a broader view of the subject area, claiming that cross-cultural competence can enable managers to go beyond managerialism by educating employees in creative community-building. Magala (pp204–205) concludes that cross-cultural competence depends on creativity and moral autonomy (the ability of cross-culturally competent individuals to exercise choice and evaluate alternatives) but also, crucially, criticism, 'in detecting ideologies and methodologies that lurk behind these [cultural] differences and which flow from the ongoing power struggles, the most sensitive processes of organising'. Criticism, Magala argues (p205), helps us 'to avoid a too one-sided selection of organisational solutions (which would dangerously reduce variety in our culture, as was the case in totalitarian societies of the twentieth century).'

On a more prosaic level, an excessive concern within cross-cultural management on managers themselves, their training, role and desired competencies, may result in concomitant neglect of the realities of working life for other organisational members. An increase in cross-cultural comparisons of 'non-rational' topics such as micropolitical behaviour, power, deal-making, humour and bullying could bring forward fascinating insights which both strengthen academic material on the nature of culture and result in a more rounded picture of the day-to-day experiences of everyone involved in a cross-cultural business setting. It is therefore hoped that cross-cultural management studies will increasingly (or at least occasionally) step outside a focus which has at its heart examination of purely formal aspects of work organisations. Trompenaars and Hampden-Turner's use of the unusual scenarios method and Fink et al's cultural standards approach, based on actual behaviour, could provide a basis for renewed study of culture in work organisations based on reality.

11.8 UNIVERSALISM OR RELATIVISM?

In Chapter 9 we examined how cross-cultural management necessarily connects with the concept of relativism. We saw how cultural relativism involves interpreting other people's attitudes and behaviour from the other person's culturally derived perspective. It is important to emphasise again that cultural relativism differs from moral relativism – the latter comprising a conscious position that one cannot and should not say that one idea or system is superior to another. Guirdham's (2011) notion of an ethical minimum agreed by partners from different cultures through a process of consensus-building (see Chapter 9) may offer a useful framework for resolving internal dilemmas and intercultural conflicts (real or anticipated). Nonetheless, ethics will continue to assume a key role within cross-cultural management.

One important question surfacing in many cross-cultural collaborative ventures is the extent to which home-country values or standards should be imposed on the partner. In some cases the point may be moot if such issues are bound up in the nature of the collaboration. In many franchise agreements, for example, procedures and standards are externally set by contract. The franchisor can therefore legitimately impose standards of behaviour, although the way this is done remains an important issue. In other forms of collaboration – for example, joint ventures – the rules regarding the upholding of standards, including expectations regarding quality, could be less clear. Agreements on ethical minimum conditions may not be easy to arrive at in reality, and all parties are likely to be aware of allegations of cultural imperialism – and the undesirability of being accused of, or even actually, acting in an imperialist fashion.

The ethical dimension of cross-cultural management remains a difficult area. In all cross-cultural encounters it is necessary to recognise the cultural specificity of one's own assumptions. Because these could relate to such emotive issues as democracy, indefinite detention without trial, gay rights or secularism, any of which could impinge on cross-cultural management, recognising and even reassessing such core beliefs may be a traumatic process. Once again it should be noted that where countries have adopted a philosophy of plural monoculturalism, involving cultural separation – via, to take one example, faith schools – then these issues could be raised within any one organisation in a single country. Schneider and Barsoux (2003) introduced a further complication by suggesting that different cultures approach aspects of ethical issues from diverse perspectives. They note (p316) that individuals may, for example, react to decision dilemmas in culturally distinct ways: 'Those from individualist cultures, such as Americans, will look within themselves, asking if they can personally live with the decisions taken. Those from collectivist cultures will look to those around them and ask how the others would live with them.'

These concluding remarks are intended to reinforce the key part that ethics play in cross-cultural management, and to offset any impression gained from a reading of Chapter 9 (where existing literature was reviewed) that solutions to ethical dilemmas and conflicts are easy. It remains the case, though, that the paradigm within the subject area is one of flexibility of approach when one is confronted with different and possibly conflicting cultural values. Neither parochial nor ethnocentric thinking is seen as helpful in terms of relating to people from other cultures, and there is general reluctance to consciously adopt a position, certainly within the sphere of business, in which one culture takes a dictatorial stance and demands that its values are imposed on another. As the twenty-first century takes shape, the extent to which such an approach should drive global politics is the subject of fierce ongoing debate, and it may be that business norms driven by the need to achieve mutually acceptable working solutions to problems could usefully inform cross-cultural relations at the macro-political level.

11.9 CONTINUOUS CHANGE

In this final section, it is appropriate to once again stress that cross-cultural management is pre-eminently a dynamic area. It must constantly evolve and reassess core principles and received wisdom if recent patterns of dramatic change continue. Such flexibility of approach is necessary if the subject is to adequately reflect on and analyse a business world, the nature of which is difficult to predict. Harries (2006), writing in the Singapore-based *Straits Times*, gives an interesting account of the past failures of commentators to foretell 'the big trends and events'. He records a dominant mode of thinking in 1910 that wars were becoming extinct and that forces of capitalism – including technological advance – were leading to a peacefully co-existing borderless world. This, of course, was within four years shown to be an entirely spurious analysis.

In 1989, the historian Francis Fukuyama announced the 'end of history' consequent on a widely held view that liberal democracy would no longer be challenged following the collapse of the Communist bloc in Europe. Fukuyama has since quickly reappraised this view. Harries (2006) predicts continuous uncertainty regarding the future, noting that, 'We are living at the beginning of an epoch whose essential character still awaits definition. At present several competing herds of independent minds are careering around, noisily insisting that their preferred label – "American hegemony", "Borderless world", "Rise of the Asian Giants", "Postmodern World Ecological Catastrophe", "War on Terror", etc – does the trick.' Harries' argument, that great change is difficult to foresee – and that intellectuals have a poor forecasting record in any case – has resonance within the field of business studies and, in our case, cross-cultural management. We have seen that there is some evidence of convergence of culture at the outer level of artefact (product and lifestyle), with continuing and in some cases diverging values at the deeper levels of culture. There is considerable debate over the outsourcing of jobs from Western countries to, among other areas, the Indian subcontinent – a trend that appeared irreversible a few years ago. It is commonly proposed that technological advance is leading to permanent change in the character of intercultural interaction, indicating that it will in future be dominated by 'e-communication', while continued migration of labour has resulted in increasing numbers of multicultural workforces. But none of these developments and trends can be assumed to be permanent, and experience suggests that they could, contrastingly, be quickly reversed.

Scholars of cross-cultural management and, of course, practising managers are faced with the task of disentangling data and theories which are enduring (Hofstede's work has been so identified in this book), while remaining acutely receptive to meaningful sudden changes, sometimes occurring with little advance warning, that have the power to profoundly affect their lives. Within the hubbub of a rapidly changing business world and the constant hurly-burly of activity we feel is necessary to carry out our own jobs in such a fast-moving environment, there is a particular challenge to recognise the deep-rooted currents which drive those changes. Those of us committed to the field of cross-cultural management, not least because it is a relevant and dynamic subject area, can be grateful that we live in such interesting times.

 ADVANTAGE INDIA?

CASE STUDY 11.1

With so much talk about the Asian Century, many Australian organisations are increasingly looking to India for growth opportunities. A report by the Australian Institute of Company Directors in 2014[1] highlighted some powerful potential drivers of business success in India. Stephen Manallack, who had spent over a decade dealing with Indian businesses, located the secrets of Indian success in particular mindsets, including:

- an acceptance of change as well as an ability to live in the moment, making

for very adaptable and opportunistic leaders

- Indian leaders building generosity into their personal and business lives
- a thought process which focuses on reaction to events, which Indian leaders see as more important than the events themselves
- while the West strives for simplicity and certainty, Indian business leaders know that life is like trying to find your way through a spider's web: where does it begin, where does it lead, who can tell?

An earlier article in *BusinessWeek*[2] noted that at that time the 'global sentiment' was highly favourable towards India. The article questioned whether Indian CEOs were better equipped to deal with such crises than their counterparts elsewhere. Professor Harbir Singh from the University of Pennsylvania was quoted as stating that, 'Indian leaders think in English, thanks to their Western educations, but act in an Indian context. They internalize Western best practices but adapt them to India.'

In the same article, R. Gopalakrishnan, an executive director with the Tata business group, stated that Indian leaders relied more on intuition than those in the West. Professor Singh also found that Indian business leaders believed that their role went beyond safeguarding their shareholders' interests to that of bringing positive transformation to society. To balance out these laudatory comments, some Indian CEOs had themselves drawn attention to their hierarchical nature (and cited this as a negative trend) while the most unique aspect of Indian leadership identified by Professor Singh, namely *jugaad* (a preference for a quick fix or make-do), was also seen as something both valuable and potentially dangerous.

Questions

1   Why might Indian business leaders be seen as well placed to succeed in the twenty-first-century business environment? What other factors could explain India's emergence as an economically powerful nation?

2   How appropriate is it to 'internalise Western best practices' in leadership and management?

3   How accurate do you expect the prediction of 'advantage India' to be? Give reasons for your conclusions.

NOTES

1   AUSTRALIAN INSTITUTE OF COMPANY DIRECTORS. (2013) Secrets of Indian business success. Available at: http://www.companydirectors.com.au/Director-Resource-Centre/Publications/The-Boardroom-Report/Back-Volumes/Volume-11–2013/Volume-11-Issue-2/Secrets-of-Indian-business-success [Accessed 16 October 2014].

2   MENON CARROLL, A. (2009) Advantage India: Are Indian CEOs Better than US Execs? *BusinessWeek*. 2 July. Available at: http://www.businessweek.com/globalbiz/content/jul2009/gb2009072_158349.htm [Accessed 16 October 2014].

REVIEW QUESTIONS

1 To what extent do you agree with Hofstede's prediction that countries will remain culturally very diverse? Would this be true by the year 2021? Give reasons for your conclusions.

2 Identfy the competencies and qualities needed by a successful cross-cultural manager.

3 How might advances in communication technologies alter the nature of cross-cultural management?

Visit this book's companion website (**www.cipd.co.uk/olr**) to find further exercises including self-assessment questions and also weblinks to media and academic journal articles.

REFERENCES

ABBOTT, G.N., STENING, B.W., ATKINS, P.W.B. and GRANT, A.M. (2006) Coaching expatriate managers for success: adding value beyond training and mentoring. *Asia Pacific Journal of Human Resources.* Vol 44. p295.

ACKROYD, S. (2002) *The organization of business.* Oxford: Oxford University Press.

ADAMS, J. S. (1965) Inequity in social exchange. In: BERKOWITZ, L. (ed.) *Advances in experimental social psychology.* Vol 2. New York: Academic Press. pp267–299.

ADLER, N. J. (2002) *International dimensions of organizational behavior.* 4th ed. Cincinnati, OH: South-Western College Publishing.

ADLER, N. J. and GHADAR, F. (1990) Strategic human resource management: a global perspective. In Pieper, R. (ed.) *Human resource management: an international comparison.* Berlin: Walter de Gruyter.

ADLER, N. J. and GUNDERSEN, A. (2008) *International dimensions of organizational behavior.* 5th ed. Mason, OH: Thomson.

AJILA, C. O. (1997) Maslow's hierarchy of needs theory: applicability to the Nigerian industrial setting. In *IFE Psychologia.* Vol 5. pp162–174.

AJZEN, I. and FISHBEIN, M. (2000) Attitudes and the attitude-behavior relation: reasoned and automatic processes. In STROEBE, W. and HEWSTONE, M. (eds) *European Review of Social Psychology.* New York: Wiley. pp1–33.

ALBERT, M. (1993) *Capitalism against capitalism.* London: FWEW.

ALDRICK, P. (2013) Boris Johnson Attacks EU Bonus Cap. *Daily Telegraph.* 6 March.

ALLARD, M. J. (2002) Theoretical underpinnings of diversity. In: HARVEY, C. P. and ALLARD, M. J. (eds) *Understanding and managing diversity: readings, cases and exercises.* 2nd ed. Harlow: Prentice Hall. pp3–27.

ALVES, J. C., LOVELACE, K. J. and MANZ, C. C. (2006) A cross-cultural perspective of self-leadership. *Journal of Managerial Psychology.* Vol 21 No 4. pp338–359.

ARGYLE, M. (1967) *The psychology of interpersonal behaviour.* Harmondsworth: Penguin.

ARKIN, A. (2011) Is engagement working? *People Management.* November. pp23–27.

ARNOLD, J., RANDALL, R. and SILVESTER, J. (2010) *Work psychology: understanding human behaviour in the workplace.* 5th ed. Harlow: Pearson.

AYCAN, Z. (2002) Leadership and teamwork in developing countries: challenges and opportunities. In: LONNER, W. J., DINNEL, D. L. and HAYES, S. A. (eds) *Online readings in psychology and culture.* Bellingham, Washington USA: Center for Cross-Cultural Research, Western Washington University. www.wwu.edu/culture

AYCAN, Z., KANUNGO, R. N. and MENDONCA, M. (2014) *Organizations and management in cross-cultural context.* London: Sage.

BAKACSI, G., SANDOR, T. and KARACSONY, A. (2002) Eastern European cluster: tradition and transition. *Journal of World Business.* Vol 37 No 1. pp69–80.

BANERJEE, S. B. and LINSTEAD, S. (2001) Globalization, multiculturalism and other fictions: colonialism for the new millennium? *Organization*. Vol 8 No 4. pp683–722.

BARTLETT, G. A. and GHOSHAL, S. (1998) *Managing across borders: the transnational solution*. 2nd ed. London: Random House.

Mourning sickness is a religion (2004) BBC News website. 13 February. Available at: http://news.bbc.co.uk/1/hi/uk/3512447.stm [Accessed 7 September 2005].

BJORKMAN, I. and XIUCHENG, F. (2002) Human resource management and the performance of western firms in China. *International Journal of Human Resource Management*. Vol 13 No 6. pp853–864.

BLACK, C. (2013) Vladimir Putin: an increasingly attractive political leader. *The Week*. 18 September. Available at: http://www.theweek.co.uk/world-news/55195/vladimir-putin-increasingly-attractive-political-leader [Accessed 12 November 2014].

BLACK, J. S., MENDENHALL, M. and ODDOU, G. (1991) Toward a comparative model of international adjustment: an integration of multiple theoretical perspectives. *Academy of Management Review*. Vol 16 No 2. pp291–317.

BLAKE, R. R. and MOUTON, J. S. (1978) *The managerial grid*. New York: Gulf Publishing.

BLAKE, R. R. and MCCANSE, A. A. (1991) *Leadership dilemmas: grid solutions*. New York: Gulf Publishing.

BLOISI, W., COOK, C. W. and HUNSACKER, P. L. (2003) *Management and organisational behaviour*. Maidenhead: McGraw Hill.

BLOISI, W., COOK, C. W. and HUNSACKER, P. L. (2006) *Management and organizational behaviour*. 2nd ed. Maidenhead: McGraw Hill.

BOJE, D. M. and DENNEHY, R. (1999) *Managing in the postmodern world*. Dubuque IA: Kendall-Hunt.

BOLMAN, L. G. and DEAL, T. E. (2003) *Reframing organizations: artistry, choice and leadership*. 3rd ed. San Francisco: Jossey-Bass.

BOND, C. J. and O' BYRNE, D. (2014) Challenges and conceptions of globalization: an investigation into models of global change and their relationship with business change. *Cross-Cultural Management*. Vol 21 No 10. pp22–38.

BOND, R. (2004) Call centre is my 'dream job'. BBC News website. April 14. Available at: http://news.bbc.co.uk/1/hi/england/norfolk/3623993.stm [Accessed 11 October 2014].

BOND, R. and SMITH, P.B. (1996) Culture and conformity: A meta-analysis of studies using Asch's (1952b, 1956) line judgment task. *Psychological Bulletin*. Vol 119 No 1. pp111–37.

BOUCKENHOOGE, D. and VAN DEN BROEK, H. (2006) Corporate social responsibility and ethics. In BUELENS, M., VAN DEN BROEK, H. and VANDERHEYDEN, K. (eds) *Organisational behavior*. 3rd ed. Maidenhead: McGraw Hill.

BOXALL, P. and PURCELL, J. (2003) *Strategy and human resource management*. New York: Palgrave Macmillan.

BRANINE, M. (2011) *Managing across cultures*. London: Sage.

BRATTON, J., CALLINAN, M. and FORSHAW, C. (2007) *Work and organizational behaviour*. Basingstoke: Palgrave Macmillan.

BREWIS, J. and LINSTEAD, S. (2009) Gender and management. In: LINSTEAD, S., FULOP, L. and LILLEY, S. (eds) *Management and organization: a critical text*. 2nd ed. Basingstoke: Palgrave Macmillan.

BREWSTER, C., SPARROW, P., and VERNON, G. (2011) *International human resource management*. 3rd ed. London: CIPD.

BROEWAYS, M.-J. and PRICE, R. (2011) *Understanding cross-cultural management*. 2nd ed. Harlow: FT Prentice Hall.

BROOKS, I. (2009) *Organisational behaviour: individuals, groups and organisation*. 4th ed. Harlow: FT Prentice Hall.

BUCHANAN, D. and HUCZYNSKI, A. (2004) *Organizational behaviour: an introductory text*. 6th ed. Harlow: FT Prentice Hall.

BUDHWAR, P. S. (2003) International human resource management. In TAYEB, M. (ed.) *International management: theories and practices*. Harlow: FT Prentice Hall.

BUELENS, M., VAN DEN BROEK, H. and VANDERHEYDEN, K. (2006) *Organisational behaviour*. 3rd ed. Maidenhead: McGraw Hill.

BUNTING, M. (2004) Faustian pact with your pay slip. *Observer*. July 11.

BURNS, T. and STALKER, G. M. (1961) *The management of innovation*. London: Tavistock.

CALIGIURI, P. M., LAZAROVA, M. and TARIQUE, I. (2005) Training, learning and development in multinational organizations. In: SCULLION, H. and LINEHAN, M. (eds) *International human resource management*. Basingstoke: Palgrave Macmillan.

CAULKIN, S. (2005) You call this best practice? *Observer*. 5 June.

CENTER FOR GLOBAL DEVELOPMENT (2013) Commitment to development index 18 November. Washington DC: CDG.

CERVINO, J. and BONACHE, J. (2005) Hotel management in Cuba and the transfer of best practices. *International Journal of Contemporary Hospitality Management*. Vol 17, No 6. pp455–468.

CHANALAN, J.-F., DAVEL, E. and DUPUIS, J.-P. (2013) *Cross-cultural management: culture and management across the world*. Abingdon: Routledge.

CHEN, C. C., CHEN, X.-P. and HUANG, S. (2013) Chinese guanxi: an investigative review and new directions for future research. *Management and Organization Review*. Vol 9 No 1. pp167–207.

CHEN, M. (1995) *Asian management systems: Chinese, Japanese and Korean styles of business*. London: Routledge.

CHEN, M. (2001) *Inside Chinese business*. Boston, MA: Harvard Business School Press.

CHEN, M. (2004) *Asian management systems*. 2nd ed. London: Thomson.

CHILD, J. (1998) Trust in international strategic alliances: the case of Sino-foreign joint ventures. In LANE, C. and BACHMANN, R. (eds) *Trust within and between organizations.* Oxford: Oxford University Press.

CHILD, J. (2005) *Organization: contemporary principles and practice.* Blackwell: Oxford.

CHILD, J. and KIESER, A. (1979) Organizational and managerial roles in British and West German companies: an examination of the culture-free thesis. In: LAMMERS, C. and HICKSON, D. J. (eds) *International and inter-institutional studies in the sociology of organizations.* London: Routledge and Kegan Paul.

CHOKAR, J. S., BRODBECK, F. C. and HOUSE, R. J. (eds) (2013) *Culture and leadership across the world.* Mahwah, NJ: LEA.

CHOW, I. (2005) Gender differences in perceived leadership effectiveness in Hong Kong. *Women in Management Review.* Vol 20 No 4. pp216–233.

CHRISTY, G. (2013) Leadership. In: REES, G. and FRENCH, R. (eds) *Leading, managing and developing people.* 4th ed. London: CIPD.

CHRISTY, R. and BROWN, E. (2009) Ethics and diversity in human resources management. In: RAYNER, C. and ADAM-SMITH, D. (eds) *Managing and leading people.* 2nd ed. London: CIPD.

CIPD. (2004) *Graphology.* Factsheet. London: CIPD.

CIPD. (2011) *Diversity in the workplace: an overview.* Factsheet. London: CIPD.

CLEGG, S., KORNBERGER, M. and PITSIS, T. (2011) *Managing and organizations: an introduction to theory and practice.* 3rd ed. London: Sage.

COHEN, N. (2009) *Waiting for the Etonians: reports from the sickbed of liberal England.* London: HarperCollins.

COLLINGS, D. G. and SCULLION, H. (2006) Approaches to international staffing. In: SCULLION, H. and COLLINGS, D. J. (eds) *Global staffing.* Abingdon: Routledge.

CONN, D. (2012) *Richer than God: Manchester City, modern football and growing up.* London: Quercus.

COOKE, F. L. (2005) *HRM, work and employment in China.* Abingdon: Routledge.

COOKE, F. L. (2011) The role of the state and human resource management in China. *International Journal of Human Resource Management.* Vol 22 No 18. pp3830–3848.

CORTES, A. C. (2003) Understanding the business protocol of bonding in establishing cross-cultural relationships: a US and Chilean example. *International Journal of Business.* Vol 8 No 2. pp 213–226.

CRAIG, J. (1979) *Culture shock.* Singapore: Times Books International.

CROOKES, D. and THOMAS, I. (1998) Problem solving and culture: exploring some stereotypes. *Journal of Management Development.* Vol 17 No 8. pp583–591.

CROWTHER, D. and GREEN, M (2004) *Organisational theory.* London: CIPD.

DAECHUN, A. (2006) A content analysis of multicultural advertisers' localisation strategy in web advertising. *International Journal of Internet Marketing and Advertising*. Vol 3 No 2. pp120–141.

DAHL, S. (2004) Intercultural research: the current state of knowledge. *Middlesex University Discussion Paper*. No 26.

DAVISON, S. C. and EKELUND, B. Z. (2004) Effective team processes for global teams. In: MAZNEVSKI, H. W., MENDENHALL, M. L. and MCNETT, J. M. E. (eds) *The Blackwell handbook of global management*. Oxford: Blackwell. pp227–249.

DEAL, T. E. and KENNEDY, A. A. (1982) *Corporate cultures: the rites and rituals of corporate life*. New York: Addison-Wesley.

DE CIERI, H. and DOWLING, P. J. (1999) Strategic human resource management in multinational enterprises: theoretical and empirical developments. In: WRIGHT, P. M., DYER, L. D. and BOUDREAU, J. W. (eds) *Research in personnel and human resources management: strategic human resources management in the twenty-first century*. Supplement 4. Stamford, CT: JAI Press.

DENNY, S. (2003) Culture and its influence on management: a critique and an empirical test. In: TAYEB, M. (ed.) *International management: theories and practice*. Harlow: FT Prentice Hall.

DE VRIES, K. and MEAD, C. (1991) Identifying management talent for a pan-European environment. In: MAKRDAKAS, S. (ed.) *Single market Europe*. San Francisco, CA: Jossey-Bass.

D' IRIBARNE, P. (1996/1997) The usefulness of an ethnographic approach to the study of organizations. *International Studies of Management and Organizations*. Vol 26 No 4. pp30–47.

D' IRIBARNE, P. (2009) National cultures and organisations in search of a theory: an interpretive approach. *International Journal of Cross-Cultural Management*. Vol 9 No 3. pp 309–321.

DORE, R. J. (1973) *British factory–Japanese factory*. Berkeley, CA: University of California Press.

DOWLING, P. J., FESTING, M. and ENGLE, A. D. (2013) International human resource management. 6th ed. Andover: Cengage.

DRUCKER, P. (1989) *The practice of management: economic tasks and risk-taking decisions*. London: Heinemann Professional.

DUPUIS, J.-P. (2014) New approaches in cross-cultural management research: the importance of context and meaning in the perception of management styles. *International Journal of Cross-Cultural Management*. Vol 14 No 1. pp67–84.

DYAS, G. P. and THANHEISER, H. T. (1976) *The emerging European enterprise: strategy and structure in French and German industry*. London: Macmillan.

EARLEY, P. C. (1987) Intercultural training for managers: a comparison of documentary and interpersonal methods. *Academy of Management Journal*. Vol 30 No 4. pp 685–698.

EARLEY, P. C. (2002) Redefining interactions across cultures and organisations: moving forward with cultural intelligence. In: STAW, B. M. and KRAMER, R. M. (eds) *Research in organisational behaviour: an annual series of analytical essays and critical reviews.* Kidlington: Elsevier.

EARLEY, P. C. and ANG, S. (2003) *Cultural intelligence: individual interpretations across cultures.* Stanford, CA: Stanford University Press.

EARLEY, P. C. and MOSAKOWSKI, E. (2004) Cultural intelligence. *Harvard Business Review.* Vol 82 No 6. pp139–146.

EGEGE, S. and KUTIELEH, S. (2004) Critical thinking: teaching foreign notions to foreign students. *International Education Journal.* Vol 4 No 4. pp75–85.

EGRI, C. P. and RALSTON, D. A. (2004) Generational cohorts and personal values: a comparison of China and the United States. *Organization Science.* Vol 15 No 3. pp210–226.

ENGLAND, G. W. (1986) National work meanings and patterns: constraints on management action. *European Management Journal.* Vol 4 No 3. pp176–184.

EREZ, M. (1997) A culture-based model of work motivation. In: EARLEY, P. C. and EREZ, M. (eds) *New perspectives on international and organizational psychology.* San Francisco, CA: New Lexington Press.

EREZ, M. and EARLEY, P. C. (1987) Comparative analysis of goal-setting strategies across cultures. *Journal of Applied Psychology.* Vol 72 No 4. pp658–665.

ESCHBACH, D. M., PARKER, D. E. and STOEBERL. P. A. (2001) American repatriate employees retrospective assessments of the effects of cross-cultural training on their adaptation to international assignments. *International Journal of Human Resource Management.* Vol 12 No 2. pp270–287.

FAN, Y. (2000) A classification of Chinese culture. *Cross-Cultural Management.* Vol 7 No 2. pp1–10.

FANG, E., PALMATIER, R.W. and EVANS, K.R. (2004) Goal-setting paradoxes? Trade-offs between working hard and working smart: the United States versus China. *Journal of the Academy of Marketing Science.* Vol 32 No 2. pp188–202.

FANG, T. (2003) A critique of Hofstede's fifth national culture dimension. *International Journal of Cross-Cultural Management.* Vol 3 No 3. pp337–368.

FANG, T. (2012) Yin yang: a new perspective on culture. *Management and Organization Review.* Vol 8 No 1. pp25–50.

FENWICK, M. (2004) International compensation and performance management. In: HARZING, A. W. and VAN RUYSSEVELDT, J. (eds) *International Human Resource Management.* London: Sage.

FERRARO, G. (1994) *The cultural dimension of international business.* 2nd ed. Englewood Cliffs, NJ: Prentice Hall.

FINCHAM, R. and RHODES, P. (2005) *Principles of organizational behavior.* 4th ed. Oxford: OUP.

FINK, G., KOLLING, M. and NEYER, A.-K. (2005) The cultural standard method. *EI Working Paper 62*, University of Vienna.

FISHER, C. and LOVELL, A. (2003) *Business ethics and values*. Harlow: FT Prentice Hall.

FISHER, C. D. and YUAN, A. X. (1998) What motivates employees? A comparison of US and Chinese responses. *International Journal of Human Resource Management*. Vol 9 No 3. pp516–528.

FONTAINE, R. and RICHARDSON, S. (2003) Cross-cultural research in Malaysia. *Cross-Cultural Management: An International Journal*. Vol 10 No 2. pp75–89.

FORSTER, N. (1999) Another glass ceiling? The experiences of women expatriates on international assignments. *Gender Work and Organization*. Vol 6 No 2. pp79–91.

FOSS, N. J. and PEDERSEN, T. (2002) Transferring knowledge in MNCs: the role of subsidiary knowledge and organizational context. *Journal of International Management*. Vol 8 No 1. pp49–67.

FOX, A. (1974) *Beyond contract: work, power and trust relations*. London: Faber and Faber.

FRANCESCO, A. M. and GOLD, B. A. (2005) *International organisational behavior*. 2nd ed. Upper Saddle River, USA: Pearson Prentice Hall.

FRENCH, R., RAYNER, C. and REES, G. (2011) *Organizational behaviour*. 2nd edn. Chichester: John Wiley & Sons.

FULOP, L. (2009) Interorganizational networking. In: LINSTEAD, S., FULOP, L. and LILLEY, S. (eds) *Management and organization*. 2nd ed, Basingstoke: Palgrave Macmillan.

FULOP, L. and LINSTEAD, S. (2009) Leadership and leading. In: LINSTEAD, S., FULOP, L. and LILLEY, S. (eds) *Management and organization*. 2nd ed. Basingstoke: Palgrave Macmillan.

FULOP, L. and RICHARDS, D. (2002) Connections, culture and context: business relationships and networks in the Asia-Pacific region. In: HARVIE, C. and LEE, B. C. (eds) *Globalisation and SMEs in East Asia: studies of small and medium-sized enterprises in East Asia*. Volume 1. Cheltenham: Edward Elgar.

GAO, F. (2005) Japanese: a heavily culture-laden language. *Journal of Intercultural Communication*. Vol 10. December.

GAO, G. (1998) An initial analysis of the effects of face and concern for other in chinese interpersonal communication. *International Journal of Intercultural Communication*. Vol 22 No 4. pp467–482.

GARAVAN, T. N. and CARBERY, R. (2012) A review of international HRD: incorporating a global HRD construct. *European Journal of Training and Development*. Vol 36 No 2/3. pp129–157.

GELFAND, M. J. and DYER, N. (2000) A cultural perspective on negotiation: progress, pitfalls and prospects. *Applied Psychology: An International Review*. Vol 49 No 1. pp62–99.

GELFAND, M. J., EREZ, M. and AYCAN, Z. (2007) Cross-cultural organizational behaviour. *Annual Review of Psychology*. Vol **5**. pp479–514.

GERHART, B. (2008a) Cross-cultural management research: assumptions, evidence and suggested directions. *International Journal of Cross-Cultural Management*. Vol 8 No 3. pp259–274.

GERHART, B. (2008b) How much does national culture constrain organizational culture? *Management and Organization Review*. Vol 5 No 2. pp241–259.

GIDDENS, A. (1984) *The constitution of society: outline of the theory of structuration*. Cambridge: Polity.

GIDDENS, A. (1990) *The consequences of modernity*. Cambridge: Polity Press.

GILMORE, S. and WILLIAMS, S. (eds) (2013) *Human resource management*. 2nd ed. Oxford: Oxford University Press.

GOLDTHORPE, J. H., LOCKWOOD, D. and BECHHOFER, F. (1968) *The affluent worker*. Cambridge: Cambridge University Press.

GOODERHAM, P. N. and NORDHAUG, O. (2003) *International management: cross-boundary challenges*. Oxford: Blackwell.

GRAEN, G. B. and HUI, C. (1999) Transcultural global leadership in the 21st century: challenges and implications for development. In: MOBLEY, M., GESSNER, M. J. and ARNOLD, V. (eds) *Advances in global leadership*. Stamford CT: JAI Press.

GRAEN, G. B. and SCHLIEMANN, W. (1978) Leader–member agreement: a vertical dyad linkage approach. *Journal of Applied Psychology*. Vol 63 No 2. pp206–212.

GRAEN, G. B. and UHL-BIEN, M. (1995) Relationship-based approach to leadership: development of leader–member exchange (LMX) theory of leadership over 25 years: applying a multi-domain perspective. *Leadership Quarterly*. Vol 6 No 2. pp219–247.

GREY, C. (2013) *A very short, fairly interesting and reasonably cheap book about studying organizations*. 3rd ed. London: Sage.

GRIBBEN, R. (2006) Rising stars who jump ship on re-entry. *Daily Telegraph*. 26 November.

GRINT, K. (1998) *The sociology of work*. Cambridge: Polity.

GUDYKUNST, W. B., GUZLEY, R. M. and HAMMER, M. R. (1996) Designing intercultural training. In: LANDIS, D. and BHAGAT, R. S. (eds) *Handbook of intercultural training*. 2nd ed. Thousand Oaks, CA: Sage.

GUDYKUNST, W. B., HAMMER, M. and WISEMAN, R. (1977) An analysis of an integrated approach to cross-cultural training. *International Journal of Cross-Cultural Training*. Vol 1 No 2. pp99–110.

GUIRDHAM, M. (2011) *Communicating across cultures at work*. 3rd ed. Basingstoke: Palgrave Macmillan.

GUIRDHAM, M. (2009) *Culture and business in Asia*. Basingstoke: Palgrave Macmillan.

GUPTA, V., HANGES, P. J., and DORFMAN, P. (2002) Cultural clusters: methodology and findings. *Journal of World Business*. Vol 37 No 1. pp11–15.

HACKMAN, J. R. and OLDHAM, G. R. (1980) *Job redesign*. New York: Addison Wesley.

HAJRO, A. and PUDELKO, M. (2010) An analysis of core competencies of successful multinational team leaders. *International Journal of Cross-Cultural Management*. Vol 10 No 2. pp175–194.

HALL, D., PILBEAM, S. and CORBRIDGE, M. (2013) *Contemporary themes in strategic human resource management*. Basingstoke: Palgrave Macmillan.

HALL, E. T (1959) *The silent language*. New York: Doubleday.

HALL, E. T. (1976) *Beyond culture*. New York: Doubleday.

HALL, E. T. (1990) *Understanding cultural differences*. Yarmouth, USA: Intercultural Press.

HANDY, C. (1989) *The age of unreason*. London: Business Books.

HARRIES, O. (2006) Suffer the intellectuals. *Straits Times*. January 27.

HARRIS, H. (2004) Women's role in international management. In: HARZING, A.-W. and VAN RUYSSEVELDT, J. (eds) *International human resource management*. London: Sage.

HARVEY, J., CARTER, S. and MUDIMU, G. (2000) A comparison of work values among Zimbabwean and British managers. *Personnel Review*. Vol 29 No 6. pp723–742.

HARZING, A. W. (2004) Composing an international staff. In: HARZING, A. W. and VAN RUYSSEVELDT, J. (eds) *International human resource management*. 2nd ed. London: Sage.

HARZING, A. W. and PINNINGTON, A. (2014) *International human resource management*. 4th ed. London: Sage.

HAYWARD, B. (1997) Culture, CRM and aviation. *ANZSASI Asia Pacific Regional Air Safety Seminar*. Brisbane.

HEMPEL, P. S. and CHANG, C. Y. (2002) Reconciling traditional Chinese management with high-tech Taiwan. *Human Resource Management Journal*. Vol 12 No 1. pp77–95.

HICKSON, D. J., HININGS, C.R., and MCMILLAN, C. J. (1974) The culture-free context of organization structure: a tri-national comparison. *Sociology*. Vol 8 No 1. pp59–80.

HICKSON, D. J. and PUGH, D. S. (1995) *Management worldwide: the impact of societal culture on organizations around the globe*. London: Penguin Books.

HILLS, M. J. (2002) Kluckhohn and Strodtbeck's values orientation theory. In: LONNER, W. J., DINNEL, D. L. and HAYES, S. A. (eds) *Online readings in psychology and culture*. Bellingham, Washington DC: Center for Cross-Cultural Research, Western Washington University. www.wwu.edu/culture

HODGETTS, R. M. (1996) A conversation with Warren Bennis on leadership in the midst of downsizing. *Organizational Dynamics*. Vol 26 No 2. pp72–78.

HOFSTEDE, G. (1980) *Culture's consequences: international differences in work-related values*. Beverley Hills, CA: Sage.

HOFSTEDE, G. (1996) Riding the waves of commerce: a test of Trompenaars' model of cultural difference. *International Journal of Intercultural Relations*. Vol 20 No 2. pp189–198

HOFSTEDE, G. (1997) Riding the waves: a rejoinder. *International Journal of Intercultural Relations*. Vol 21 No 1. pp 287–290.

HOFSTEDE, G. (2001) *Culture's consequences*. 2nd ed. Thousand Oaks, USA: Sage.

HOFSTEDE, G. (2002) Dimensions do not exist: A reply to Brendan Mc Sweeney. *Human Relations*. Vol 55 No 11. pp1355–1360.

HOFSTEDE, G. (2003) What is culture? A reply to Baskerville. *Accounting, Economy and Society*. Vol 28 No 7/8. pp811–813.

HOFSTEDE, G. (2011) Dimensionalizing cultures: the Hofstede model in context. *Online Readings in Psychology and Culture*. 2(1). International Association for Cross-Cultural Psychology. Available at: http://scholarworks.gvsu.edu/orpc/vol2/iss1/8/. [Accessed 12 October 2014].

HOFSTEDE, G. and BOND, M. (1988) The Confucius connection: from cultural roots to economic growth. *Organisational Dynamics*. Vol 16 No 4. pp5–21.

HOFSTEDE, G., HOFSTEDE, G. J. and MINKOV, M. (2010) *Culture and organizations: software of the mind*. 3rd ed. New York, NY: McGraw Hill.

HOFSTEDE, G. and SONDERGAARD, M. (1993) Transfer of management ideas to Eastern European business organizations. *Paper presented at the 11th EGOS Colloquium: The Production and Diffusion of Managerial and Organisational Knowledge*. Paris. July 1993.

HOLBECHE, L. and MATTHEWS, G. (2012) *ENGAGED: unleashing your organisation's potential through employee engagement*. Chichester: Wiley/Jossey Bass.

HOLDEN, N. J. (2002) *Cross-cultural management: a knowledge management perspective*. Harlow: FT Prentice Hall.

HOLDEN, N. J. (2008) Reflections of a cross cultural scholar: context and language in management thought. *International Journal of Cross Cultural Management*. Vol 8 No 2. pp239–251.

HOLDEN, N. J. and TANSLEY, C. (2008) Management in other languages: how a philological approach opens up new cultural vistas. In: TIETZE, S. (ed.) *International Management and Language*. London: Taylor and Francis.

HOLLINGSHEAD, G. (2010) *International and comparative human resource management*. Maidenhead: McGraw Hill.

HOPFL, H. and CASE, P. (2007) *Guest editorial*. In: HOPFL, H and CASE, P. (eds) *Journal of Organizational Change Management*. Vol 20 No 2 (Women and leadership: special issue). pp198–208.

HOUSE, R. J. (1971) A path-goal theory of leadership effectiveness. *Administrative Science Quarterly*. Vol 16 No 3. pp321–338.

HOUSE, R. J. and DESSLER, G. (1974) The path-goal theory of leadership. In: HUNT, J. G. and LARSON, L. L. (eds) *Contingency approaches to leadership*. Carbondale, IL: Southern Illinois University Press.

HOUSE, R. J., HANGES, P. J. and JAVIDAN, M. (eds) (2004) *Culture, leadership and organisations: the GLOBE study of 62 societies*. Thousand Oaks CA: Sage.

HOUSE, R. J., HANGES, P. J. and RUIZ-QUINTANILLA, S. A. (1999) Cultural influences on leadership and organizations: Project GLOBE. In: MOBLEY, W. H., GESSNER, M. J. and ARNOLD, V. (eds) *Advances in global leadership*. Stamford, CT: JAI Press.

HOUSE, R. J., JAVIDAN, M. and DORFMAN, P. (2001) The Globe project. *Applied Psychology: An International Review.* Vol 50 No 4. pp489–505.

HUCZYNSKI, A. A. and BUCHANAN, D. A. (2013) *Organizational behavior.* 8th ed, Harlow: Pearson.

HUTTON, W. (2006) At last: work isn't a dirty word any more. *Observer.* 21 May.

HYMAN, R. (2004) Varieties of capitalism, national industrial relations systems and transnational challenges. In: HARZING, A. W. and VAN RUYSSEVELDT, J. (eds) *International human resource management.* 2nd ed. London: Sage.

ILES, P. and ZHANG, C. (2013) *International human resource management: a cross-cultural and comparative approach.* London: CIPD.

INGLEHART, R. (1997) *Modernization and postmodernization: cultural, economic and political change in 43 societies.* Princeton: Princeton University Press.

INGLEHART, R. and BAKER, W. (2000) Modernization, cultural change and the persistence of traditional values. *American Sociological Review.* Vol 65. pp19–51.

JACKSON, B. (2005) The enduring romance of leadership studies. *Journal of Management Studies.* Vol 42 No 6. pp1311–1324.

JACKSON, T. (2011) From cultural values to cross-cultural interfaces: Hofstede goes to Africa. *Journal of Organizational Change Management.* Vol 24 No 4. pp532–538.

JACKSON, T. and AYCAN, Z. (2006) From cultural values to cross cultural interfaces (editorial). *International Journal of Cross Cultural Management.* Vol 6 No 1. pp5–13.

JACQUES, R. (1996) *Manufacturing the employee. management knowledge from the 19th to the 21st centuries.* Thousand Oaks CA: Sage.

JAMES, O. (1998) *Britain on the couch: why we're unhappier compared with 1950, despite being richer – a treatment for the low-serotonin society.* London: Arrow.

JAMES, O. (2003) *They f**k you up: how to survive family life.* London: Bloomsbury Publishing.

JOHNS, T. (2005) Foreword. In: RAYNER, C and ADAM-SMITH, D. (eds) *Managing and leading people.* London: CIPD.

JONSSON, S., MUHONEN, T. and SCHOLTEN, C. (2014) Illusive inclusion – construction of leaders and employees based on nationality. *Cross Cultural Management: An International Journal.* Vol 21 No 2. p55.

KABASAKI, H., DASTMALCHIAN, A. and KARACKAY, G (2012) Leadership and culture in the MENA region: an analysis of the GLOBE project. *Journal of World Business.* Vol 47 No 4. pp519–529.

KAKABADSE, A., MYERS, A. and MCMAHON, T. (1997) Top management styles in Europe: implications for business and cross-national teams. In: GRINT, K. (ed.) *Leadership: classical, contemporary and critical approaches.* Oxford: Oxford University Press.

KANTER, R. M. (2001) *Evolve! Succeeding in the digital culture of tomorrow.* Cambridge, MA: Harvard Business School Press.

KANTER, R. M. (2009) *Supercorp: how vanguard companies create opportunity, profits, growth and social good*. New York: Crown.

KEANE, F. (2014) MH17 disaster: standoff with militiamen at crash site. BBC News Online. 19 July. Available at: http://www.bbc.co.uk/news/world-europe-28384930 [Accessed October 12th 2014].

KEATING, M. and MARTIN, G. S. (2004) *Managing cross-cultural business relations: the Irish-German experience*. Dublin: Blackhall Publishing.

KIM, K. J. and BONK, C. J. (2002) Cross-cultural comparisons of online collaboration. *Journal of Computer-Mediated Communication*. Vol 8 No 1. p0.

KIM, Y. and MARKUS, H. R. (1999) Deviance or uniqueness, harmony or conformity? A cultural analysis. *Journal of Personality and Social Psychology*. Vol 77 No 44. pp785–800.

KIRKMAN, B. L. and SHAPIRO, D. L. (1997) The impact of cultural values on employee resistance to teams: toward a model of globalized self-managing work team effectiveness. *Academy of Management Review*. Vol 22 No 3. pp730–757.

KIRKPATRICK, S.A. and LOCKE, E. A. (1991) Leadership: do traits matter? *Academy of Management Executive*. Vol 5 No 2. pp48–60.

KITTLER, M. G., RYGL, D. and MACKINNON, A. (2011) Beyond culture or beyond control? Reviewing the use of Hall's high-/low-context concept (special review article). *International Journal of Cross-Cultural Management*. Vol 11 No 1. pp63–82.

KLUCKHOHN, F. and STRODTBECK, F. L. (1961) *Variations in value orientations*. Evanston IL: Peterson.

KOEN, C. (2005) *Comparative international management*. Maidenhead: McGraw-Hill.

KOHLS, J., BULLER, P.F. and ANDERSON, K.S. (1999) Resolving cross-cultural ethical conflict: an empirical test of a decision tree model in an educational setting. *Teaching Business Ethics*. Vol 3. pp37–56.

KOLB. D. (1984) *Experiential learning*. New Jersey: Prentice Hall.

KOLMAN, L. K., NOORDERHAVEN, N. G. and HOFSTEDE, G. (2003) Cross-cultural differences in central Europe. *Journal of Managerial Psychology*. Vol 18 No 1. pp76–88.

LAMMERS, C. J. and HICKSON, D. J. (1979) *Organizations alike and unlike: international and inter-institutional studies in the sociology of organizations*. London: Routledge and Kegan Paul.

LASSERE, P. (2012) *Global strategic management*. 3rd edn. Basingstoke: Palgrave Macmillan.

LATHAM, G. P., LOCKE, E. A. and FASSINA, N. E. (2002) The high performance cycle: standing the test of time. In: SONNENTAG, S. (ed.) *The psychological management of individual performance. a handbook in the psychology of management in organizations*. Chichester: Wiley.

LAZAROVA, M. B. and CALIGIURI, P. (2001) Retaining expatriates: the role of organizational support practices. *Journal of World Business*. Vol 40 No 4. pp 389–401.

LEUNG, K. (2001) Different carrots for different rabbits: effects of individualism-collectivism and power distance on work motivation. In: EREZ, M., KLEINBECK, U. and THIERRY, H. (eds) *Work motivation in the context of a globalizing economy*. Mahwah, NJ: Erlbaum.

LEWIS, R (2004) *When cultures collide: leading, teamworking and managing across the globe*. London: Nicholas Brealey.

LIANG, A. and MCQUEEN, R. J. (1999) Computer assisted adult learning in a multicultural environment. *Adult Learning*. Vol 11.

LIDEN, R. C., SPARROWE, R. T. and WAYNE, S. J. (1997) Leader–member exchange theory: the past and potential for the future. In: FERRIS, G. R. (ed.) *Research in Personnel and Human Resource Management*. Vol 15. pp47–119.

LINEHAN, M. (2005) *Women in international management*. In: SCULLION, H. and LINEHAN, M. (eds) *International human resource management: a critical text*. Basingstoke: Palgrave Macmillan.

LINEHAN, M. and SCULLION, H. (2002) Repatriation of European female corporate executives: an empirical study. *International Journal of Human Resource Management*. Vol 13 No 2. pp254–267.

LINSTEAD, S., FULOP, L. and LILLEY, S. (2009) *Management and organization: a critical text*. 2nd ed. Basingstoke: Palgrave Macmillan.

LOCKE, E. A. and LATHAM, G. P. (1990) *A theory of goal-setting and task performance*. Upper Saddle River, NJ: Prentice Hall.

LOWE, K., MILLIMAN, J. and DE CIERI, H. (2002) International compensation practices: a ten-country comparative analysis. *Asia Pacific Journal of Human Resources*. Vol 40 No 1. pp55–78.

LU, L.T. (2012) Etic or emic? measuring culture in international business research. *International Business Research*. Vol 5 No 5. pp109–115.

LUO, Y. (1997) Partner selection and venturing success: the case of joint ventures with the People's Republic of China. *Organization Science*. Vol 8 No 6. pp648–662.

LUO, Y. (2002) Building trust in cross-cultural collaborations: towards a contingency perspective. *Journal of Management*. Vol 28 No 5. pp669–694.

MAGALA, S. (2005) *Cross-cultural competence*. Abingdon: Routledge.

MARQUARDT, M. and ENGEL, D. W. (1993) *Global human resource development*. Upper Saddle River, NJ: Prentice Hall.

MARTIN, J. (2005) *Organizational behaviour and management*. 3rd ed. London: Thomson.

MARTIN, J. N., FLORES, L. and NAKAYAMA, T. K. (2001) Principles for a meta-ethic. In: MARTIN, J. N. and NAKAYAMA, T. K. (eds) *Experiencing intercultural communication*. Mountain View, CA: Mayfield.

MASLOW, A. H. (1970) *Motivation and personality*. New York: Harper & Row.

MAURICE, M., SORGE, A. and WARNER, M. (1980) Societal differences in organizing manufacturing units: a comparison of France, West Germany and Great Britain. *British Journal of Industrial Relations*. Vol 18, No 3. pp318–333.

MCCLELLAND, D. C. (1961) *The achieving society.* Princeton, NJ: D van Norstrand.

MCCLELLAND, D. C. (1985) *Human motivation.* Cambridge: Cambridge University Press.

MCFARLIN, D. and SWEENEY, P. (2013) *International organizational behaviour.* Abingdon: Routledge.

MCSWEENEY, B. (2002) Hofstede's model of national cultural differences and their consequences: a triumph of faith – a failure of analysis. *Human Relations.* Vol 55 No 1. pp89–118.

MEAD, M. (1953) *Coming of age in Samoa.* New York: Modern Library.

MEAD, R. and ANDREWS, T. J. (2009) *International management: culture and beyond.* 4th ed. Chichester: John Wiley & Sons.

MENDENHALL, M. E. and ODDOU, G. (1985) The dimensions of expatriate acculturation. *Academy of Management Review.* Vol 10. pp39–47.

MERLOT, E. S., FENWICK, M. and DE CIERI, H. (2006) Applying a strategic international human resource management framework to international non-governmental organisations. *International Journal of Human Resources Development and Management.* Vol 6 No 2/3/4. pp313–327.

MERRITT, A. C. (1996) *National culture and work attitudes in commercial aviation: a cross-cultural investigation. Unpublished doctoral dissertation.* Austin, TX: The University of Texas at Austin.

MEZIAS, J. M. and SCANDURA, T. (2005) Approaches to expatriate adjustment and development. *Journal of International Business Studies.* Vol 36 No 5. pp519–538.

MINKOV, M. (2007) *What makes us different and similar: a new interpretation of the World Values Survey and other cross-cultural data.* Sofia, Bulgaria: Klasika I Stil Publishing House.

MINKOV, M. and BLAGOEV, V. (2009) Cultural values predict subsequent economic growth. *International Journal of Cross Cultural Management.* Vol 9 No 1. pp5–24.

MINKOV, M. and HOFSTEDE, G. (2014) A replication of Hofstede's uncertainty avoidance dimension across nationally representative samples from Europe. *International Journal of Cross-Cultural Management.* Vol 14 No 2. pp1–11.

MINTZBERG, H. (1981) What is planning anyway? *Strategic Management Journal.* Vol 2 No 3. pp319–324.

MOHR, A. T. (2003) *The relationship between trust and control in international joint ventures (IJVs): an empirical study of Sino-German equity joint ventures.* Bradford: Bradford University School of Management.

MONTAGU-POLLOCK, M. (1991) All the right connections. *Asian Business.* Vol 27 No 1. pp20–24.

MOORE, M. (2012) Mass suicide protest at Apple manufacturer Foxconn factory. *Daily Mail.* 11 January.

MORAN, R.T., HARRIS, P. R. and MORAN, S.V. (2014) *Managing cultural differences.* 9th ed. Abingdon: Routledge.

MORGAN, G. (1989) *Creative organization theory: a resourcebook*. London: Sage.

MORGAN, G. (2007) Globalization and organizations. In: KNIGHTS, D. and WILLMOTT, H. (eds) *Introducing organizational behaviour and management*. London: Thomson.

MULLINS, L. J. (2013) *Management and organisational behaviour*. 10th ed. Harlow: FT Prentice Hall.

NAPIER, N. K. and TAYLOR, S. (2002) Experiences of women professionals abroad: comparisons across Japan, China and Turkey. *International Journal of Human Resource Management*. Vol 13 No 5. pp837–851.

NEEDLE, D. (2010) *Business in context*. 5th ed. Andover: Cengage.

OBERG, K. (1960) Culture shock: adjustment to a new cultural environment. *Practical Anthropology*. Vol 7. pp177–182.

OUCHI, W. G. (1981) *Theory Z*. Reading MA: Addison-Wesley.

PANAPANAAN, V., LINANEN, L. and KARVONEN, M.-M. (2003) Roadmapping cororate social responsibility in Finnish companies. *Journal of Business Ethics*. Vol 44. pp133–148.

PARKER, S. K., WALL, T. D. and CORDERY, J. L. (2001) Future work design research and practice: towards an elaborated model of work design. *Journal of Occupational and Organizational Psychology*. Vol 74. pp413–440.

PARKINSON, E. and MORLEY, M. J. (2006) Cross-cultural training. In: SCULLION, H. and COLLINGS, D. J. (eds) *Global staffing*. Abingdon: Routledge.

PATEL, T. (2014) *Cross-cultural management: a transactional approach*. Abingdon: Routledge.

PAUL, A. (2006) Ford vs Toyota: and so the wheel comes full circle. *Straits Times*. 27 January.

PERKINS, S. J. and SHORTLAND, S. M. (2006) *Strategic international human resource management*. 2nd ed. London: Kogan Page.

PERLMUTTER, H. V. (1969) The torturous evolution of the multinational corporation. *Columbia Journal of World Business*. Vol 4 No 1. pp9–18.

PETERS, T. and WATERMAN, R. (1982) *In search of excellence*. New York: Harper and Row.

PILBEAM, S. and CORBRIDGE, M. (2010) *People resourcing: HRM in practice*. 4th ed. Harlow: FT Prentice Hall.

PILLAI, R. SCANDURA, T. A. and WILLIAMS, E. A. (2001) Leadership and organizational justice: similarities and differences across cultures. *The Leadership Quarterly*. Vol 12 No 1. pp31–52.

PINDER, C. C. (1998) *Work motivation in organzational behavior*. Upper Saddle River, NJ: Prentice Hall.

PINDER, C. C. (2008) *Work motivation in organizational behavior*. 2nd ed. New York: Psychology Press.

PORTER, L. W. and LAWLER, E. E. (1968) *Managerial attitudes and performance.* Homewood, IL: Irwin.

POWELL, L. A. (2005) Justice judgements as complex psychocultural constructions. *Journal of Cross-Cultural Psychology.* Vol 36 No 1. pp48–73.

POWELL, W. W. (1990) Neither market nor hierarchy: network forms of organization. *Research in Organisational Behaviour.* Vol 12. pp295–336.

PUGH, D. S. and HICKSON, D. J. (1976) *Organizational structure in its context: the Aston Programme 1.* Farnborough: Saxon House.

RALSTON, D., EGRI, C. P. and STEWART, S. (1999) Doing business in the 21st century with the new generation of Chinese managers: a study of generational shifts in work values in China. *Journal of International Business Studies.* Vol 30 No 2. pp415–427.

RALSTON, D. A., GUSTAFSON, D. J. and CHEUNG, F.M. (1993) Differences in managerial values: a study of US, Hong Kong and PRC managers. *Journal of International Busines Studies.* Vol 24 No 2. pp 249–275.

RALSTON, D. A., HOLT, D. H. and TERPSTRA, R. H. (1997) The impact of national culture and economic ideology on managerial work values: a study of the United States, Russia, Japan and China. *Journal of International Business Studies.* Vol 28 No 1. pp177–207.

RALSTON, D. A., NGUYEN, V. T. and NAPIER, N. K. (1999) A comparative study of the work values of north and south Vietnamese managers. *Journal of International Business Studies.* Vol 30 No 4. pp655–672.

RAO, P. and KULKARNI, A.V. (1998) Perceived importance of needs in relation to job level personality make up. *Journal of Indian Academic Applications.* Vol 24. pp37–42.

RAPP, J. K., BERNARDI, R. A. and BOSCO, S. N. (2011) Examining the use of Hofstede's uncertainy avoidance construct in international research. *International Business Research.* Vol 4 No 1. pp3–15.

RATHMYR, R. (2004) Konsept DENGI petersburgskogo naseleiniya v nachale 1990-x godov. Zhant intervyu: Osobennnosti russkoi ustnoi rechi v Finalndii i Sankt-Petersburge. In: LEINONEN, M (ed.) *Slavika Tamperensia VI.* Tampere: Tampere University Press. pp137–150.

RAYNER, C. and CHRISTY, R. (2013) Professionalism and ethics in managing people. In: REES, G. and FRENCH, R. (eds) *Leading, managing and developing people.* 4th ed. London: CIPD.

REDING, V. (2012) Women on boards: commission proposes 40% objective. Available at: http://ec.europa.eu/justice/newsroom/gender-equality/news/121114_en.htm [Accessed 16 October 2014].

ROBBINS, S. (2005) *Organizational behavior.* 11th ed (international edition). Upper Saddle River NJ: Pearson Prentice Hall.

ROBBINS, S. and JUDGE T. (2014) *Organizational behavior.* 16th ed (global edition). Upper Saddle River NJ: Pearson Prentice Hall.

ROE, R. A., ZINOVIEVA, I. L. and DIENES, E (2000) A comparison of work motivation in Bulgaria, Hungary and The Netherlands. *Applied Psychology: An International Review.* Vol 49 No 4. pp658–687.

RONEN, S. (2001) Self-actualisation versus collectivism: implications for motivation theories. In: EREZ, M., KLEINBECK, U. and THIERRY, H. (eds) *Work motivation in the context of a globalising economy.* Mahwah, NJ: Erlbaum.

ROSENER, J. (1990) Ways women lead. *Harvard Business Review.* Vol 68 No 2. pp119–125.

ROUSSEAU, D. M. (2000) *Psychological contract inventory: technical report.* Pittsburgh: PA: Carnegie Mellon University.

ROWTHORN, R. (2014) *Large-scale immigration its economic and demographic consequences for the UK.* London: Civitas.

RUMBLES, S. and FRENCH, R. (2013) Recruitment and selection. In: REES, G. and FRENCH, R. (eds) *Leading, managing and developing people.* 4th ed. London: CIPD.

RYAN, M. and ALEXANDER, S. (2005) The glass cliff: evidence that women are over-represented in precarious leadership positions. *British Journal of Management.* Vol 16 No 2. pp81–90.

SAGIE, A., ELIZUR, D. and YAMAUCHI, H. (1996) The structure and strength of achievement motivation: a cross-cultural comparison. *Journal of Organizational Behavior.* Vol 17 No 5. pp431–444.

SAGIV, L. and SCHWARTZ, S. H. (2000) A new look at national culture: illustrative applications to role stress and managerial behavior conference presentations. In: ASKENASY, N., PETERSON, M. and WILDEROM, C. (eds) *Handbook of organizational culture and climate.* Thousand Oaks, CA: Sage.

SATHE, V. (1985) *Culture and related corporate realities: text, cases and readings on organisational entry, establishment and change.* Homewood, IL: Irwin.

SCASE, R. and GOFFEE, R. (1990) Women in management: towards a research agenda. *International Journal of Human Resource Management.* Vol 1 No 1. pp107–125.

SCHERMERHORN, J. R., HUNT, J. G. and OSBORN, R. N. (2005) *Organizational behavior.* 9th ed (international edition). Hoboken NJ: Wiley.

SCHERMERHORN, J. R., HUNT, J. G. and OSBORN, R. N. (2009) *Organizational Behavior.* 11th ed. Hoboken, NJ: John Wiley & Sons.

SCHNEIDER, S. C. and BARSOUX, J.-L. (2003) *Managing across cultures.* 2nd ed. Harlow: FT Prentice Hall.

SCHOLTZ, U., DONA SUD, S. and SCHWARZER, R. (2002) Is general self-efficacy a universal construct? Psychometric findings from 25 countries. *European Journal of Psychological Assessment.* Vol 18 No 3. pp242–251.

SCHULER, R. S., BUDHWAR, P. S. and FLORKOWSKI, G. W. (2002) International human resource management: review and critique. *International Journal of Management Reviews.* Vol 4 No 1. pp41–70.

SCHWARTZ, S. H. (1992) Universals in the content and structure of values: theoretical advances and empirical tests in 20 countries. In: ZANNA (ed.) *Advances in experimental social psychology.* Vol 25. pp1–66. New York: Academic Press.

SCHWARTZ, S. H. (1999) A theory of cultural values and some implications for work. *Applied Psychology: An International Review.* Vol 48 No 1. pp23–47.

SCULLION, H. (2005) International HRM: an introduction. In: SCULLION, H. and LINEHAN, M. (eds) *International human resource management: a critical text.* Basingstoke: Palgrave Macmillan.

SCULLION, H. and PAUUWE, J. (2005) Strategic HRM in multinational companies. In: SCULLION, H. and LINEHAN, M. (eds) *International human resource management: a critical text.* Basingstoke: Palgrave Macmillan.

SCULLION, H. and STARKEY, K. (2000) In search of the changing role of the corporate human resource function in the international firm. *International Journal of Human Resource Management.* Vol 11 No 6. pp1061–1081.

SEARLE, R. H. (2003) *Selection and recruitment: a critical text.* Basingstoke: Palgrave Macmillan.

SEBENIUS, J. K. (2002) The hidden challenge of cross-border negotiation. *Harvard Business Review.* March. pp76–85.

SELIGMAN, M. E. P. and STEEN, T. A. (2005) Positive psychology progress: empirical validation of interventions. *American Psychologist.* Vol 60 No 5. pp410–421.

SELMER, J. (2001) Antecedents of expatriates/local relationships: pre-knowledge v socialisation tactics. *International Journal of Human Resource Management.* Vol 12 No 6. pp916–925.

SELMER, J. (2005) Western business expatriates in China: adjusting to the most foreign of all foreign places. In: SCULLION, H. and LINEHAN, M. (eds) *International human resource management: a critical text.* Basingstoke: Palgrave Macmillan.

SILVERTHORNE, C. R. (1992) Work motivation in the United States, Russia and the Republic of China (Taiwan). *Journal of Applied Social Psychology.* Vol 22 No 20. pp1631–1639.

SINCLAIR, A. (1998) *Doing leadership differently: gender, power and sexuality in a changing business culture.* Melbourne: Melbourne University Press.

SMITH, H. (2006) From Iraq to Oman, the future is female. *Observer.* 23 April.

SMITH, P. B. (2007) Book review: Minkov, M. (2007). 'What makes us different and similar: a new interpretation of the world values survey and other cross-cultural data'. *International Journal of Cross Cultural Management.* Vol 8 No 1. pp110–112.

SNELL, R. S. (2004) Managing ethically. In: LINSTEAD, S., FULOP, L. and LILLEY, S. (eds) *Management and organisation a critical text.* Basingstoke: Palgrave Macmillan.

SODERBERG, A.-M. and HOLDEN, N. (2002) Rethinking cross cultural management in a globalizing business world. *International Journal of Cross Cultural Management.* Vol 2 No 1. pp103–121.

SORGE, A. (2004) Cross-national differences in human resources and organization. In: HARZING, A.-W. and VAN RUYSSEVELDT, J. (eds) *International human resource management*. London: Sage.

SPROULL, L. and KIESLER, S. (1991) *Connections: new ways of working in the networked organization*. Cambridge MA: MIT Press.

STEERS, R. M. and SANCHEZ-RUNDE, C. J. (2002) Culture, motivation and work behavior. In: GANNON, M. J. and NEWMAN, K. L. (eds) *The Blackwell handbook of cross-cultural management*. Oxford: Blackwell.

STRAUSS, G. (1976) Job satisfaction, motivation and job redesign. In: STRAUSS, G. MILES, R. E. and SNOW, C. C. (eds) *Organizational behaviour, research and issues*. Belmont, CA: Wadsworth.

SUE-CHAN, C. and DASBOROUGH, M. T. (2006) The influence of relation-based and rule-based regulation on hiring decisions in the Australian and Chinese Cultural contexts. *International Journal of Human Resource Management*. Vol 17 No 7. pp1267–1292.

SUE-CHAN, C. and ONG, M. (2002) Goal assignment and performance: assessing the mediating role of goal commitment and self-efficacy and the moderating role of power distance. *Organizational Behavior and Human Decision Processes*. Vol 89 No 2. pp1140–1161.

SUROWIECKI, J. (2004) *The wisdom of crowds*. New York: Doubleday.

TANG, J. and WARD, A. (2003) *The changing face of Chinese Management*. London: Routledge.

TARIQUE, I. and CALIGIURI, P. (2004) Training and development of international staff. In: HARZING, A.W. (ed.) *International human resource management*. Thousand Oaks, CA: Sage.

TATLI, A. (2005) Strategic aspects of international human resource management. In: OZBILGIN, M. (ed.) *International human resource management*. Basingstoke: Palgrave Macmillan.

TAYEB, M. (1987) Contingency theory and culture: a study of matched English and Indian manufacturing firms. *Organization Studies*. Vol 8 No 3. pp241–261.

TAYEB, M. (ed.) (2003) *International management: theories and practice*. Harlow: FT Prentice Hall.

THOMAS, D.C. (1998) The expatriate experience: a critical review and synthesis. In: CHENG, J. L. and PETERSON, R. B. (eds) *Advances in International Comparative Management*. Vol 12. pp 237–273.

THOMPSON, E. R. and PHUA, F. T. (2005) Are national cultural traits applicable to senior firm managers? *British Journal of Management*. Vol 16 No 1. pp59–68.

THOMPSON, P. and MCHUGH, D. (2009) *Work organisations: a critical introduction*. 4th ed. Basingstoke: Palgrave Macmillan.

TINSLEY, C. H. and PILLUTLA, M. M. (1998) Negotiating in the United States and Hong Kong. *Journal of International Business Studies*. Vol 29 No 4. pp711–728.

TODEVA, E. (1999) Models for the comparative analysis of culture: the case of Poland. *International Journal of Human Resource Management*. Vol 10 No 1. pp606–623.

TORRINGTON, D., HALL, L and TAYLOR, S. (2008) *Human resource management*. 7th ed. Harlow: FT Prentice Hall.

TRIANDIS, H. C. (1989) The self and social behavior in differing cultural contexts. *Psychological Review*. Vol 96 No 3. pp506–520.

TROMPENAARS, F. (2002) *Did the pedestrian die?* Capstone: Oxford.

TROMPENAARS, F. and HAMPDEN-TURNER, C. (1997) *Riding the waves of culture*. 2nd ed. London: Nicholas Brealey.

TROMPENAARS, F. and HAMPDEN-TURNER, C. (2004) *Managing people across cultures*. Capstone: Oxford.

TSUI, A. S. (2004) Contributing to global management knowledge: a case for high quality indigenous research. *Asia Pacific Journal of Management*. Vol 21 No 4. pp491–513.

TSUI, A. S., NIFADKAR, S. S. and OU, A. Y. (2007) Cross-national, cross-cultural organizational behavior research: advances, gaps and recommendations. *Journal of Management*. Vol 33 No 3. pp426–478.

TUCKMAN, B. W. (1965) Developmental sequence in small groups. *Psychological Bulletin*. Vol 63 No 6. pp384–399.

TUNG, R. L. (1981) Selection and training of personnel for overseas assignments. *Columbia Journal of World Business*. Vol 16. pp68–78.

TUNG, R. L. (2008) The cross-cultural research imperative: the need to balance cross-national and intra-national diversity. *Journal of International Business Studies*. Vol 39. pp41–46.

TURNER, Y. (2006) Chinese students in a UK business school: hearing the student voice in reflective teaching and learning practice. *Higher Education Quarterly*. Vol 60 No 1. pp27–51.

TWEED, R. G., WHITE, K. and LEHMAN, D. R. (2004) Culture, stress and coping: internally and externally-targeted control strategies of European Canadians, East Asian Canadians and Japanese. *Journal of Cross-Cultural Psychology*. Vol 35 No 6. pp652–668.

USUNIER, J.-C. (2003) Cultural aspects of international business negotiations. In: GHAURI, P. N. and USUNIER, J.-C. (eds) *International business negotiation*. 2nd ed. Oxford: Elsevier.

VAGHEFI, R. M., WOODS, L. and DAPRILE, N. (2001) Creating sustainable advantage: the Toyota philosophy and its effects. *Financial Times*. 7 October.

VAN EMMERIK, I .J., EUWEMA, M. C. and WENDT, H. (2008) Leadership behaviours around the world: the relative importance of gender versus cultural background. *International Journal of Cross Cultural Management*. Vol 8 No 30. pp297–315.

VENAIK, S. and BREWER, P. (2013) Critical isues in the Hofstede and GLOBE national culture models. *International Marketing Review*. Vol 30 No 5. pp469–482.

VERNON, R. G. (1966) International investment and international trade in the product cycle. *Quarterly Journal of Economics*. May. pp190–207.

VROOM, V. H. (1964) *Work and motivation*. New York: Wiley.

WARNER-SODERHOLM, G. (2013) Beyond a literature review of Hall's context dimension: scale development, validation and empirical findings. *International Journal of Business and Management*. Vol 8 No 10. pp27–40.

WARSCHAUER, M. (1996) Comparing face-to-face and electronic discussion in the second language classroom. *Calico Journal*. Vol 13 No 2. pp7–26.

WATSON, T. J. (2006) *Organising and managing work*. 2nd ed. Harlow: FT Prentice Hall.

WATSON, T. J. (2012) *Sociology, work and industry*. 6th ed. London: Routledge.

WAYNE, S. J., SHORE, L. M. and BOMMER, W. H. (2002) The role of fair treatment and rewards in perceptions of organizational support and leader-member exchange. *Journal of Applied Psychology*. Vol 87 No 3. pp590–598.

WEST, M. (2005) Hope springs. *People Management*. 13 October. p38.

WESTWOOD, R. L. (1992) *Organisational behaviour: South East Asian perspective*. Hong Kong: Longman.

WILLIAMS, K., HASLAM, C. and WILLIAMS, J. (1992) Against lean production. *Economy and Society*. Vol 21 No 3. pp321–354.

WILLIAMS, S., HOWE-WALSH, L. and SCOTT, P. (2013) International human resource management. In: GILMORE, S. and WILLIAMS, S. (eds) *Human resource management*. 2nd ed. Oxford: Oxford University Press.

WILSON, F. (2010) *Organizational behaviour and work: a critical introduction*. 3rd ed. Oxford: Oxford University Press.

WITT, M. A. (2008) Crossvergence 10 years on: impact and further potential. *Journal of International Business Studies*. Vol 39 No 1. pp47–52.

WITTE, A. E. (2012) Making the case for post-national cultural analysis of organizations. *Journal of Management Inquiry*. Vol 2 No 2. pp141–159.

WOODWARD, J. (1958) *Management and technology*. London: HMSO.

WURTZ, E. (2005) A cross-cultural analysis of websites from high context cultures and low context cultures. *Journal of Computer-Mediated Communication*. Vol 11 No 1. pp1–28.

YOUMEE, H. (2011) S. Koreans lament decline in respect for elderly folk. *The Straits Times*. 23 July.

ZAKARIA, N. (2000) The effects of cross-cultural training on the acculturation process of the global workforce. *International Journal of Manpower*. Vol 21 No 6. pp492–510.

ZHANG, C. and ILES, P. (2013) Cross-cultural training and international HRD. In: ILES, P. and ZHANG, C. (eds) *International human resource management: a cross-cultural and comparative approach*. London: CIPD.

ZHU, Y. and WARNER, M. (2004) HRM in East Asia. In: HARZING, A. W. and VAN RUYSSEVELDT, J. (eds) *International human resource management*. 2nd ed. London: Sage.

Index